THE FAUVES

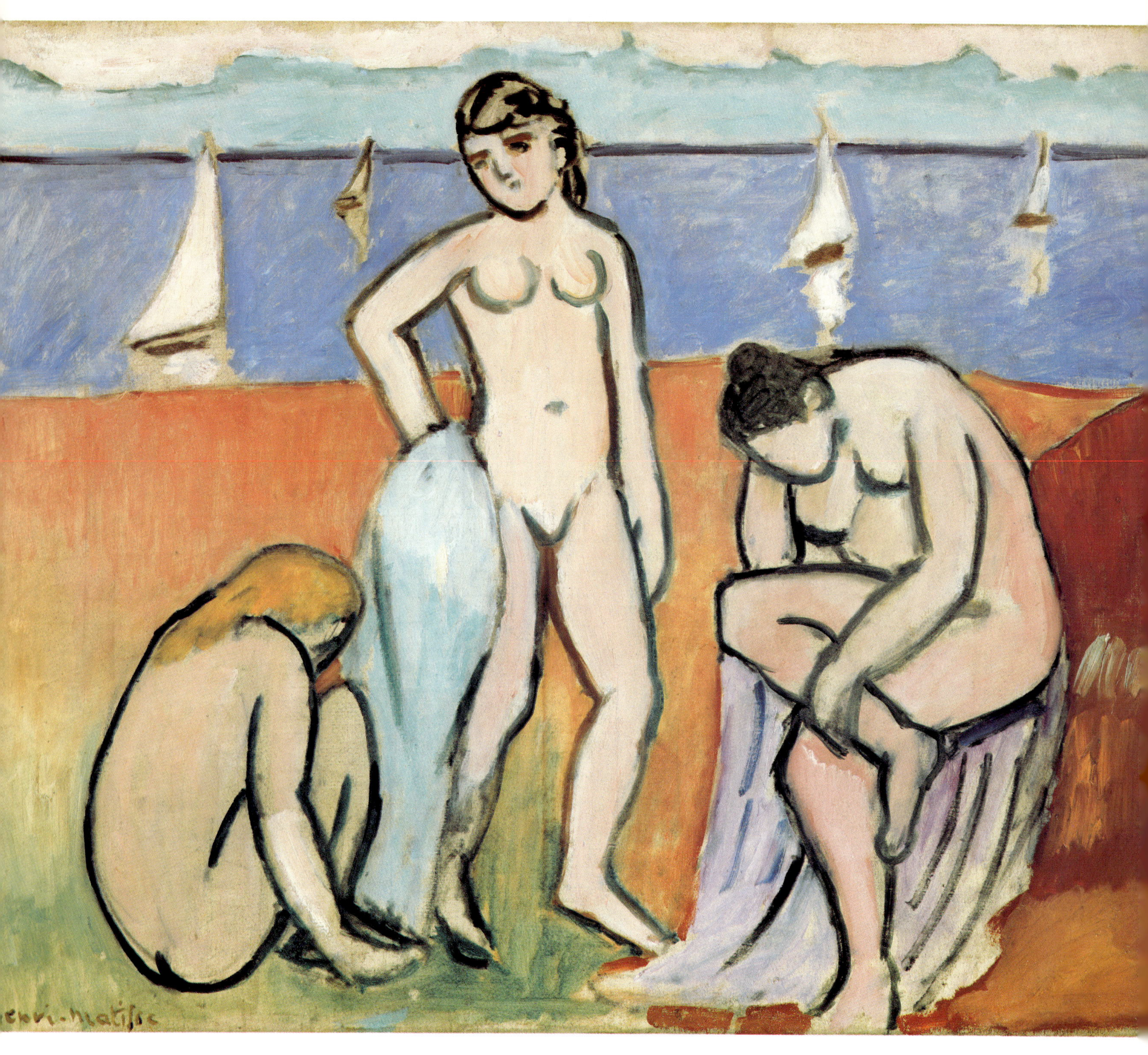

THE

FAUVES

THE REIGN OF COLOUR

MATISSE
DERAIN
VLAMINCK
MARQUET
CAMOIN
MANGUIN
VAN DONGEN
FRIESZ
BRAQUE
DUFY

JEAN-LOUIS FERRIER

TERRAIL

Cover Illustrations

KEES VAN DONGEN
The Gypsy
1910-1911
Oil on canvas, 21¼ x 17¾ in (54 x 45 cm)
Saint-Tropez, musée de l'Annonciade

HENRI MATISSE
Dance (II)
Issy-les-Moulineaux, late 1909 and summer 1910
Oil on canvas, 8 ft 21⅝ x 12 ft 9½ in (260 x 391 cm)
St. Petersburg, Hermitage Museum

HENRI MATISSE
Music
Issy-les-Moulineaux, late 1909 and summer 1910
Oil on canvas, 8 ft 21⅝ x 12 ft 9¼ in (260 x 389 cm)
St. Petersburg, Hermitage Museum

Preceding page:

HENRI MATISSE
Three Bathers
1907
Oil on canvas, 24 x 29 in (61 x 73,7 cm)
Minneapolis, Institute of Modern Art
(Gift of Putman Dana McMillan)

Opposite:

ANDRÉ DERAIN
Sunlight on Water, London
1906
(Detail)
Oil on canvas, 31¾ x 39¼ in
(80.5 x 100 cm)
Saint-Tropez, musée de l'Annonciade

Editors: Jean-Claude Dubost and Jean-François Gonthier
Art director: Bernard Girodroux
English adaptation: Frances Wister Faure
Iconography: Claire Balladur
Biographical Notes: Aude Simon
Composition & Filmsetting: Compo Rive Gauche, Paris
Lithography: Litho Service T. Zamboni, Verona

A subsidiary of the Book Department
of Bayard Presse S.A.

ISBN: 2-87939-013-3
Printed in Italy

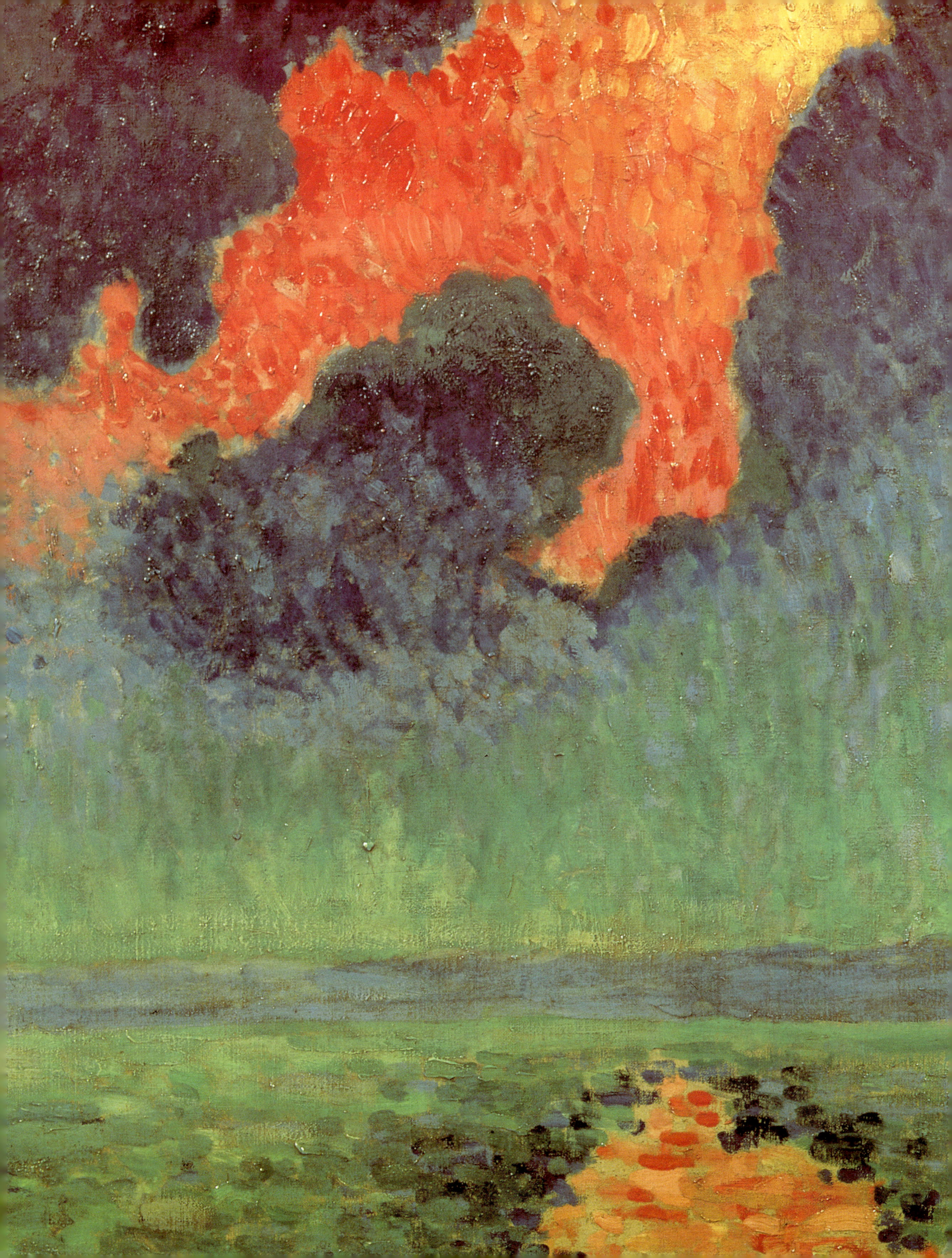

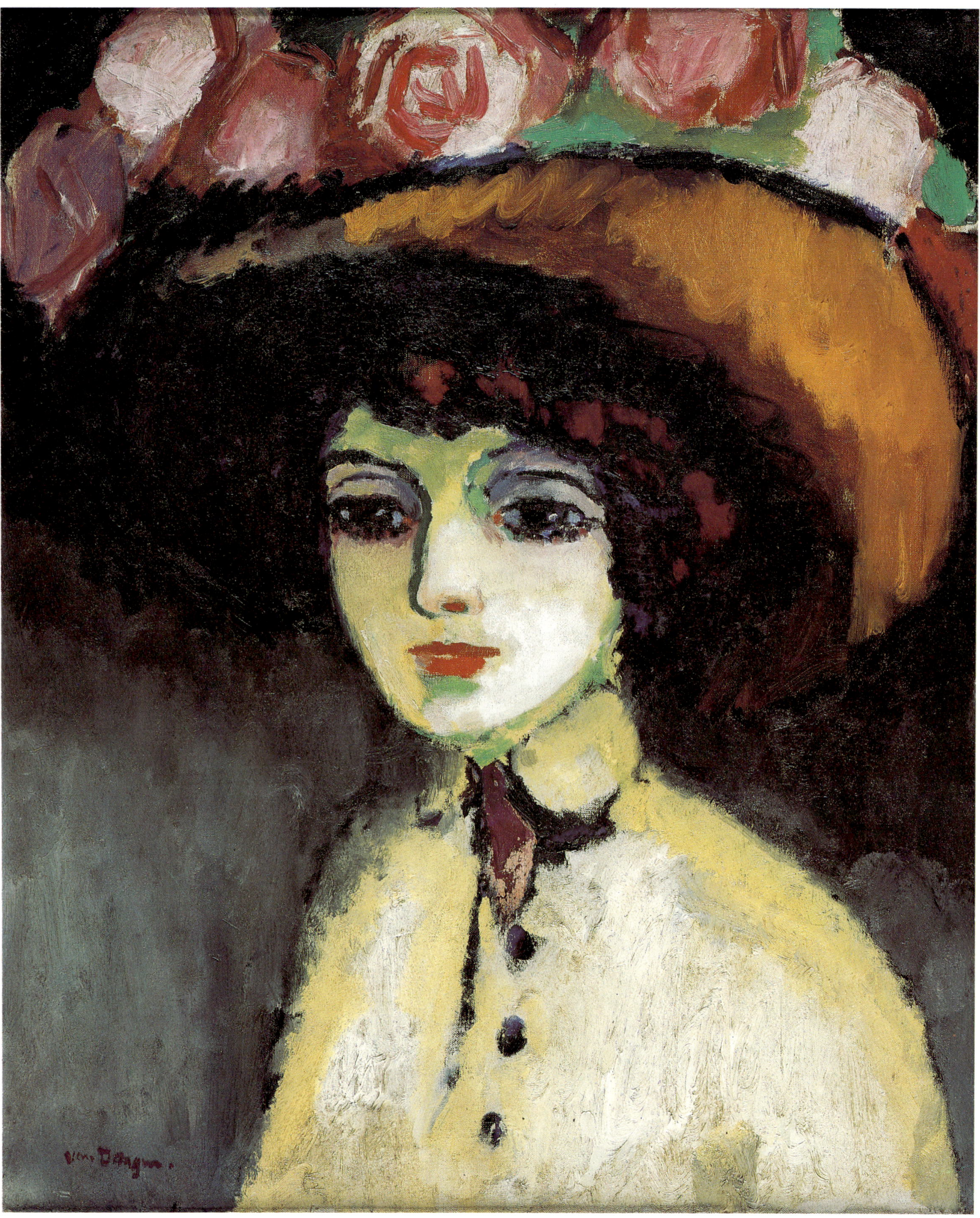

Contents

KEES VAN DONGEN
"La Parisienne" from Montmartre
1911
Oil on canvas, 25½ x 21¼ in
(65 x 54 cm)
Le Havre, musée des Beaux-Arts André Malraux

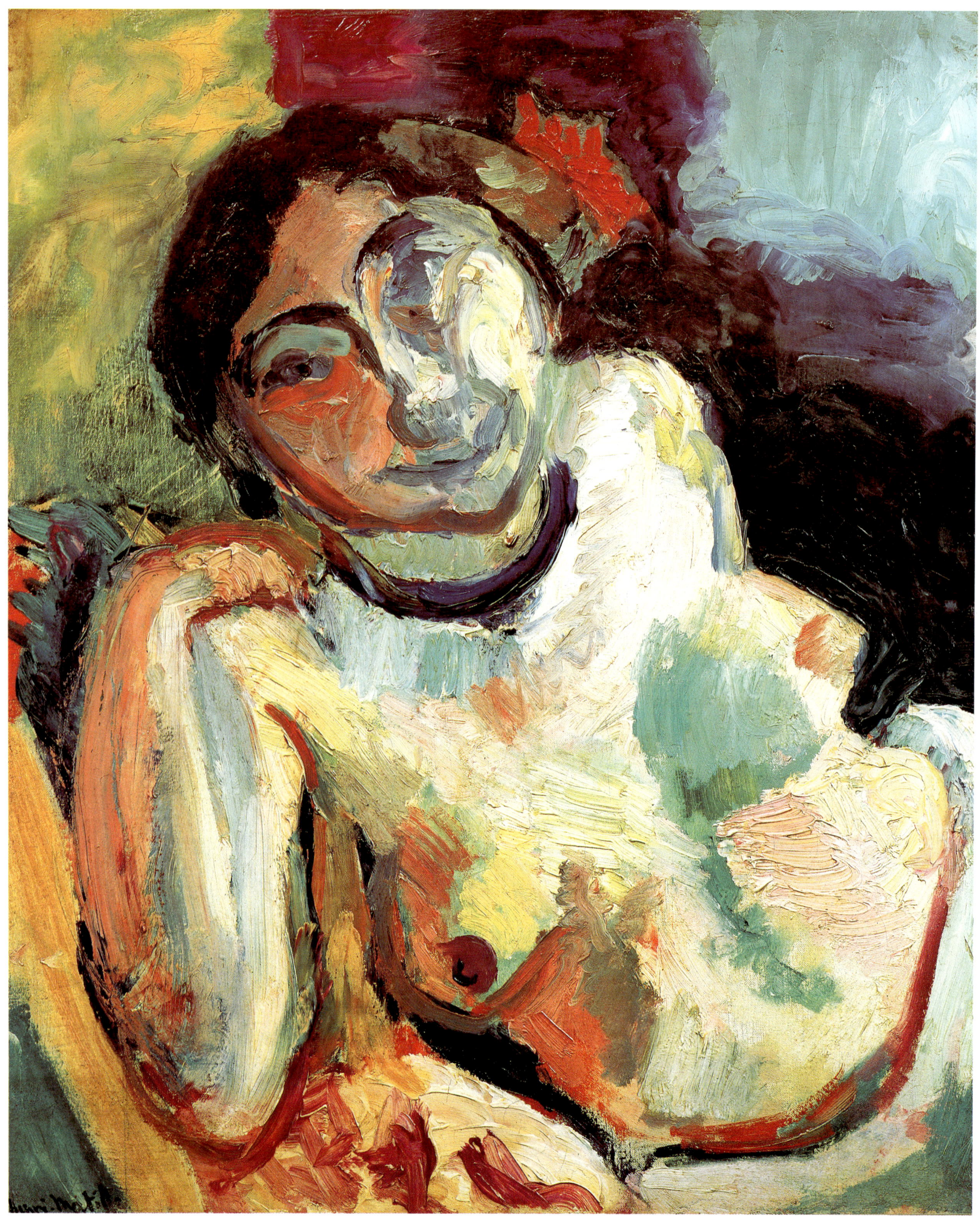

Introduction

The Triumph of Color

For a long time after it ceased to exist, Fauvism was considered as merely a fleeting moment in the history of art. Although it had the effect of a bomb on the public in 1905, it was taken as an epiphenomenon due to a few young talents rather than to a group of artist with a common objective. Fauvism was often compared to a blaze swiftly-lit and swiftly-extinguished, and given less importance than German Expressionism, of which it was supposed to have been an insignificant forerunner. Because it did not present a program or enforce any rules, the movement seemed minor next to Cubism which took over the avant-garde limelight as early as 1908.

Today this judgment must be revised. Expressionism exploded on the scene in 1905, as well, through a group of German avant-gardists from Dresden called *Die Brücke* (The Bridge), which included artists such as Heckel and Kirchner. It cannot be compared, however, to Fauvism in its concept of art and of life. Expressionism was a form of romantic fantasy in which subjective reactions to reality were expressed through exaggeration, distortion, impulses, nightmares, etc. It drew its inspiration from Nordic folklore, which was entirely foreign to the Fauves, who were strongly anchored in Gallic culture. Expressionism grew out of Kierkegaard's *Angst*–a concept central not only to man, but to nature as a whole–Nietzsche's nihilism, and, where painting was concerned, Munch's convulsive forms. The exacerbated Expressionist emotions seem a far cry from Cézanne's slow and patient approach.

As offspring of Newton and Chevreul, the Fauves explored the spectrum; for them, colors were not only mere stimuli on the retina but could also express feelings. To the Expressionists, colors

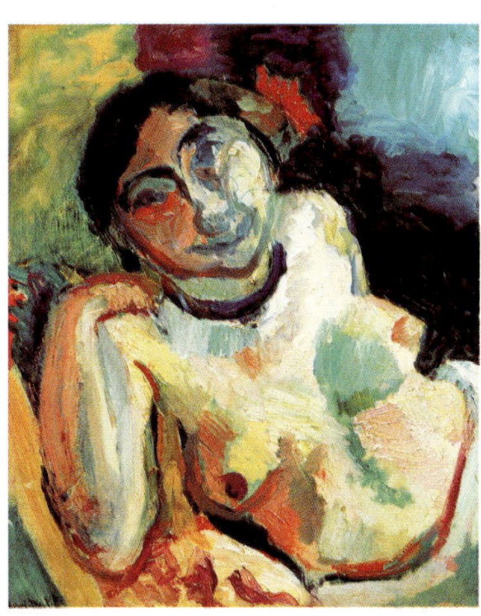

Henri Matisse
Gypsy Woman
1906
Oil on canvas, 21¾ x 18 in (55 x 46 cm)
Saint-Tropez, musée de l'Annonciade

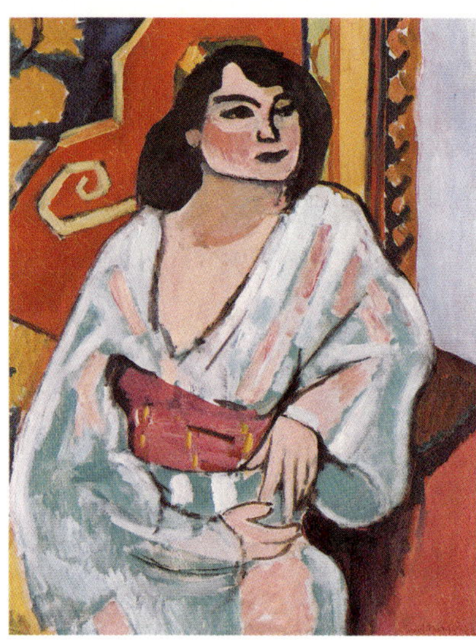

HENRI MATISSE
Algerian Woman
1909
Oil on canvas, 31⅞ x 25½ in (81 x 65 cm),
Paris, musée national d'Art moderne.

were of a symbolic and mythical nature which spoke to the soul, in keeping with the color theories and metaphysics developed by Goethe; they could not look at Van Gogh and Gauguin in the way Matisse, Derain, or Vlaminck did. Many of the Expressionists ideas were tinged with political and social overtones, not to mention the spiritual confusion of the time. In Expressionism, color cries out and lashes out; in Fauvism, it remains under control and gives itself over to joy.

The protagonists of the two movements certainly influenced each other, and a resemblance does exist in their respective works. It is interesting to note, for example, how Matisse's colorful *Gypsy* (1906) inspired so many paintings of contorted faces in Germany and yet how much his *Algerian Woman* (1909) owes–from a graphic as well a chromatic point of view–to Kirchner's *Woman on the Blue Sofa*, painted at a slightly earlier date. Kandinsky lived in Sèvres near Paris for a year starting in the spring of 1906, and although he never met any of the French colorists, he learned about them by seeing their work at the home of his friends Gertrude and Leo Stein's, then went on to elaborate his theory of "the necessary exploration of the inner world," intended to eradicate naturalism in art.

On the other hand, Cubism–whose importance in the evolution of modern painting is not in question–no longer represents "the" moment of rupture with the past. Fauvism had largely paved the way with its disregard for natural forms and its delight in unbridled colors.

It has long been thought that these French painters were decent and patient fellows working under Nature's thumb, occasionally reaping some recognition as a reward for their submission. This idea is no longer appropriate. As we will discover in the following chapters, Fauvism, though truly French in its manner of expressing happiness, was no less free to innovate nor less triumphant.

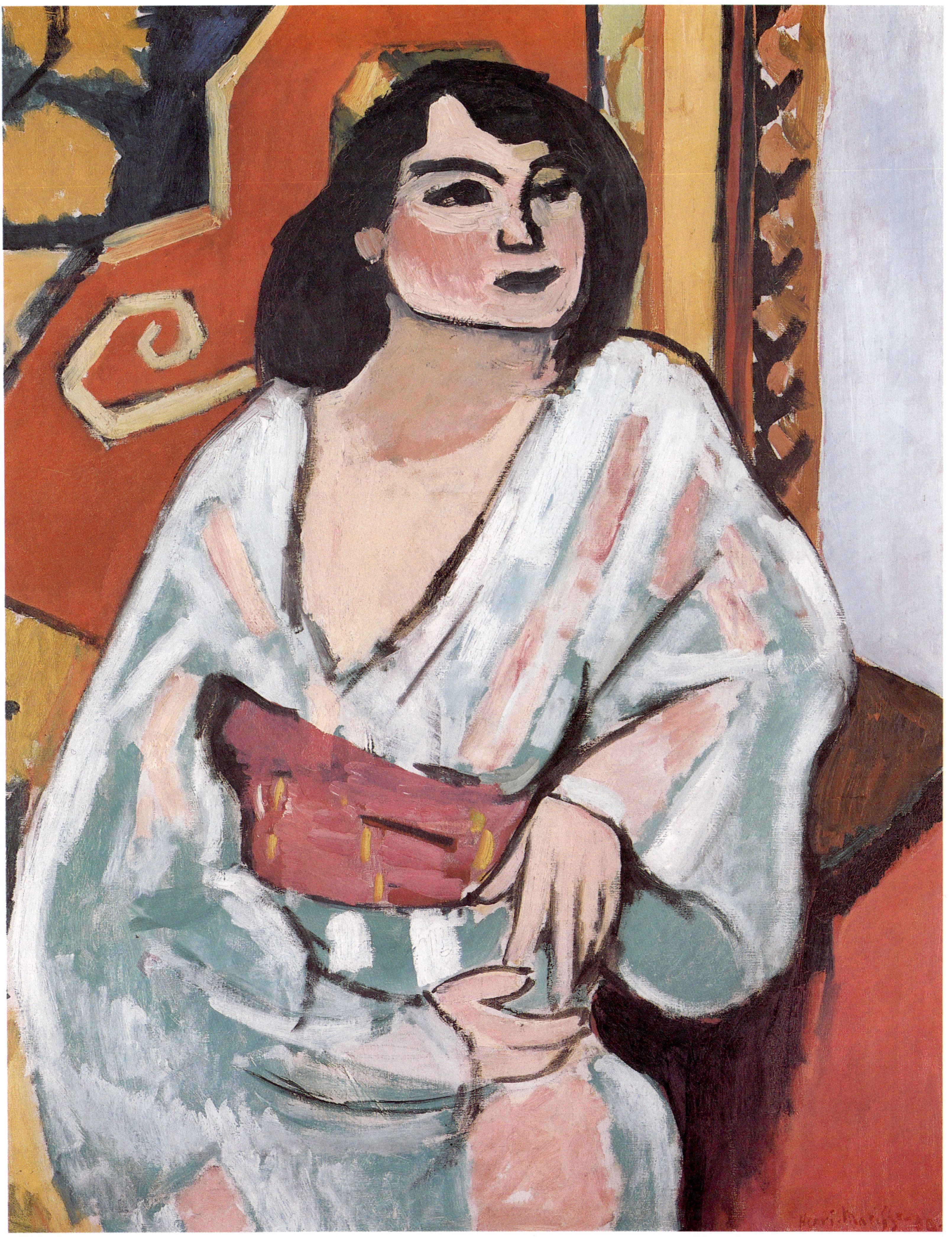

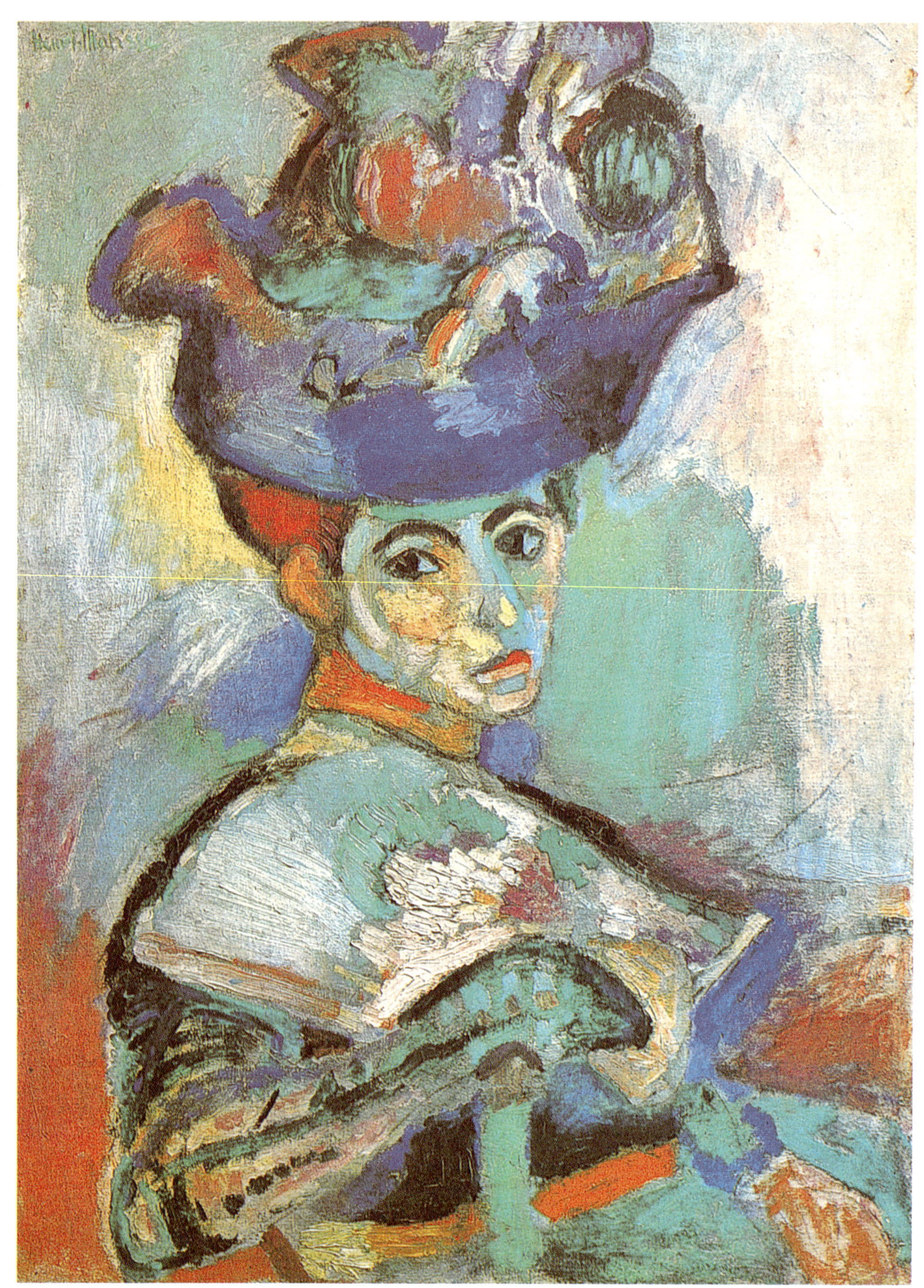

Fauvism 1905-1908

The 1905 Salon d'Automne, Inaugural Exhibition of the Fauve Movement

On October 18, 1905 the third exhibition of the Société du Salon d'Automne opened in Paris at the Grand Palais, off the Champs-Elysées. The Salon was founded and presided by Frantz Jourdain, the architect of the department store La Samaritaine. Under the patronage of such prominent late-19th-century figures as Eugène Carrière and Auguste Renoir–who both served as honorary vice-presidents–the Salon d'Automne was taking precedence over the Salon des Independants. Elie Faure remarked in the preface to the catalogue: "They have successfully brought together the young talents whom the problematic Independent Salon was unable to present in a coherent manner. The standard-bearers of French art themselves have not made so great an effort in the last thirty years." The distinguished art historian added: "We ought to have the freedom and desire to understand an absolutely new language."

Retrospective exhibitions of Ingres and Manet were also being held under the skylight of the Grand Palais, along with 1,636 paintings, drawings and sculptures by contemporary artists from all over the world, including the two Russian colorists Kandinsky and Jawlensky, who had come from Munich for the occasion. Armand Dayot and Léonce Bénédite, commissioners of the Salon, chose to devote Room VII to the works of a group of young painters whose main characteristic was the use of vivid colors scattered over their canvases in spots or spread in flat fields. These paintings were hung in alphabetical order by the author's name and included works by: Charles Camoin, two views of Agay and two of Cassis harbor; André Derain, a portrait and four landscapes from Collioure; Henri Matisse, a portrait, a young woman by

HENRI MATISSE
Woman with a Hat
1904-1905
Oil on canvas, 31¾ x 23½ in
(80.6 x 59.7 cm)
San Francisco, Haas collection

the water in Japanese attire, a still life and two landscapes; Henri Manguin, five paintings; Albert Marquet, five landscapes; canvases by Maurice Vlaminck as well as two nudes by Van Dongen, and others by Friesz, Puy, and Valtat.

The commissioners installed a traditional-style marble bust of a woman and the bronze torso of a child by Albert Marque in the center of the strikingly colorful room, creating a marked contrast and prompting the critic Louis Vauxcelles to comment in an article in *Gil Blas* dated October 17: "*C'est Donatello chez les fauves,*" (It's Donatello amid the wild beasts), a statement that was to become famous. He described Matisse's *Woman with a Hat*–one of the most controversial pieces in the Salon in the following terms: "Hers would be the fate of a Christian virgin offered to the lions in a circus arena." The idea of a circus seemed appropriate for Rouault's *Les Forains, (The Itinerant Troupers)* also shown in the exhibition. The allusion to wild beasts was in response to a very impressive painting by Henri-Julien Rousseau, *Le lion ayant faim se jette sur l'antilope, la dévore; la panthère attend avec anxiété le moment où elle aussi pourra en avoir sa part... Soleil couchant! (The hungry lion leaps on the antelope and devours it; the panther anxiously awaits the moment when she will have her share... sunset!)* From the word *fauve*, of course, was coined the term *fauvisme*–the first revolution in 20th-century art.

Henri-Julien Rousseau, who evidently favored lengthy titles for his works, was dubbed *"le Douanier"* by the writer Alfred Jarry because he earned his living as a toll officer for the City of Paris. Rousseau's imagination was fired by a photograph he had a seen of a lioness and an antelope among a group of animals stuffed by a taxidermist named Quentin and exhibited at the Natural History Museum. The exotic foliage enfolding the wild animals in his paintings owed everything to the tropical greenhouses of the Jardin des Plantes, and nothing to a trip to Mexico which he often pretended to have made. Rousseau strove vainly but bravely to measure up to the type of academic painters he so admired. His inspiration and technique were very different from the Fauves, who painted directly from life and were fascinated by the changing light of Mediterranean landscapes. Nonetheless, like the young artists of Room VII, Rousseau was detested by the public and the critics.

Emile Loubet, the President of the Republic, taking great care not to displease his conservative constituency, refused to inaugurate such an avant-garde event. The critics were practically unanimous in condemning it. In addition to Vauxcelles who meant to be derogatory with his use of the word "fauves," a *Figaro* critic, Camille Mauclair was appalled by the paintings and quoted Ruskin: "A pot of paint has been thrown at the public's head." In the *Journal de Rouen*, a certain Nicolle wrote: "What is present here, besides the materials used, has nothing to do with art; blue, red, yellow, green spots of pure raw color are set side by side, at random– the barbaric and naive games of children trying out a paint box given to them for Christmas."

Maurice Denis gained notoriety in the history of modern art by making the following remark at the age of 20 in 1890: "Remember that a painting before becoming a favorite theme, a nude or a specific anecdote, is just a flat surface covered with colors assembled in a certain order." Although puzzled by the Fauves, Denis had a rather favorable opinion of them. André Gide, who reacted in the same way to Room VII, immediately calling it "a wild-beast cage," wrote this

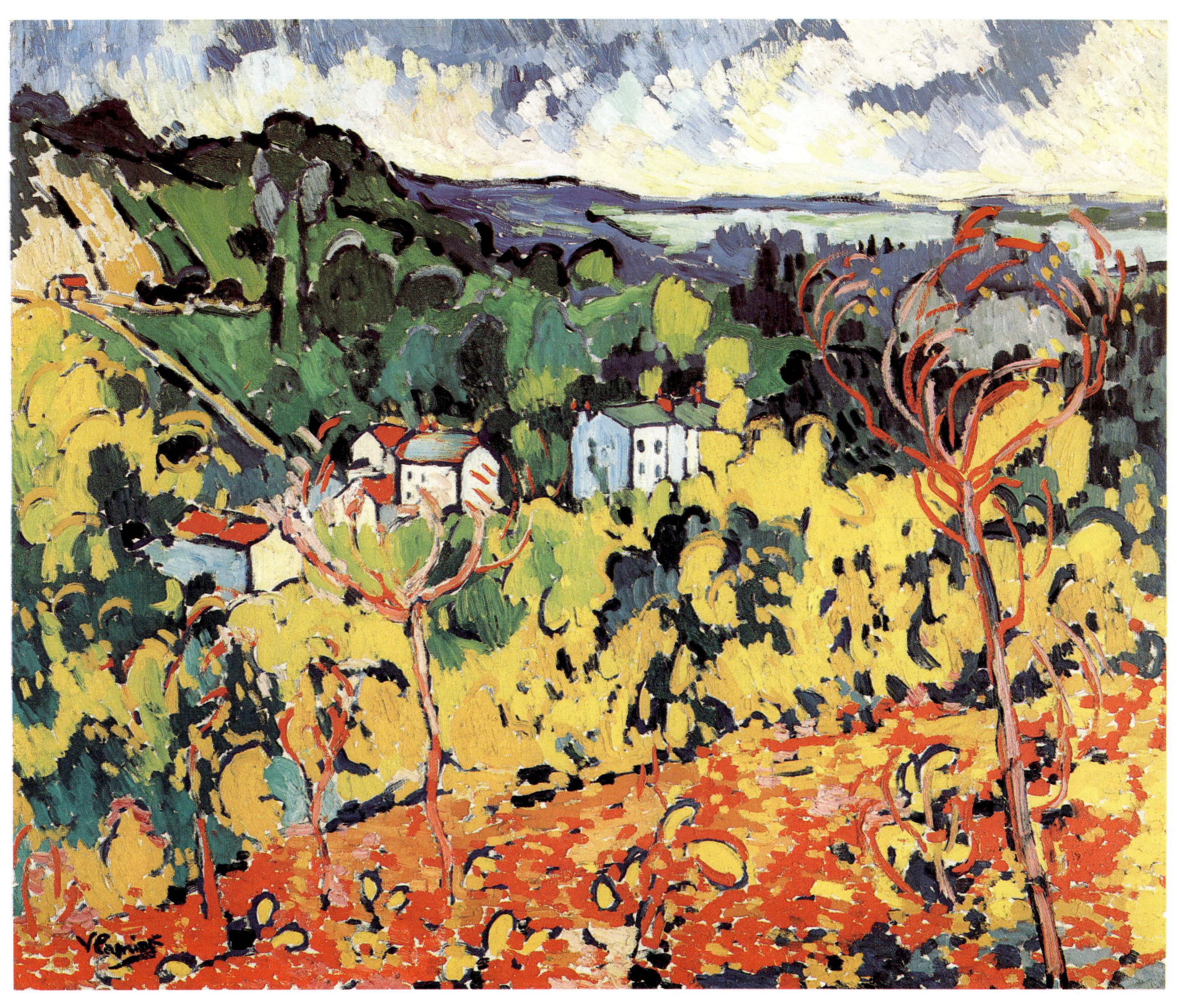

MAURICE DE VLAMINCK
Bougival
1905
Oil on canvas, 31½ x 39 in (80 x 99 cm)
Dallas, Museum of Art
(Wendy and Emery Reves collection)

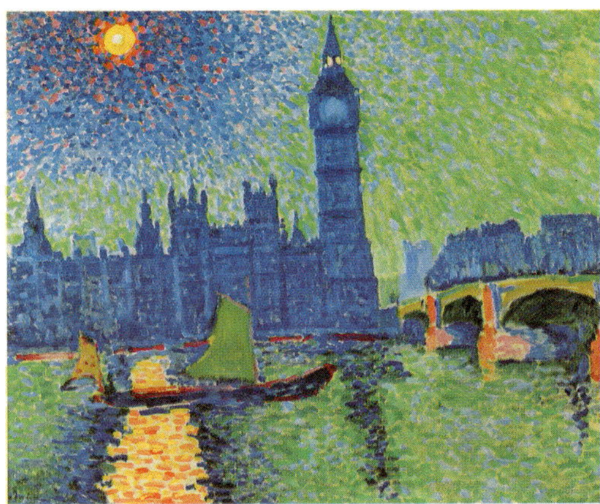

Below and opposite:

André Derain
Big Ben
1905
Oil on canvas, 31 x 38½ in (79 x 98 cm)
Troyes, musée d'Art moderne

commentary in *La Gazette des Beaux-Arts*: "I spent a long time in the room. I listened to people as they passed through, and when I heard some of them cry out in front of Matisse: 'It's madness!' I had the urge to reply: 'Not at all, on the contrary, it's a by-product of theories!'" Those who adopted this opinion, however, were few and far between.

The public's response was more than reserved. Many visitors were infuriated by the blotched green and yellow face of Matisse's *Woman with a Hat*, and some who were not content to merely jeer at it, tried to lacerate the canvas. While the public seemed quite able to stomach the landscapes composed of a patchwork of color, they could not accept the disfigurement of the human body. Two years later, Michel Puy, brother of the Fauve painter Jean Puy, wrote about the Movement: "We never really looked at what they brought us; we crushed them under the weight of the art of the past and the ideology of the times, and the best writers spared no warnings." Except for Gide who made the right judgment when he recognized a theoretical method behind the apparent madness of colors.

Theoretical Sources of Fauvism

The "ugly daubings" perceived by the majority of visitors and critics in the fall of 1905 were not mere products of a slapdash approach. Even though Fauvism was not developed from a deliberate theorization, it evolved from the first and most novel pictorial movement of the last half of the 19th century: Impressionism, which had barely begun to be accepted at that time. Disparaging comments about "palette scrapings" had been made in front of paintings by Monet, Pissarro, Sisley, or Cézanne.

From April 15 to May 15, 1874, an exhibition of the Société Anonyme des Peintres, Sculpteurs et Graveurs took place in the former reception rooms of the photographer Nadar, at 36, boulevard des Capucines. Owing to the presence of a work by Monet called *Impression: Sunrise (Impression: Soleil Levant)*, the participants in the show found themselves referred to as "Impressionists."

This new style, in contrast to the academic art triumphantly exhibited at the official Salon, was characterized by the absence of chiaroscuro and by the use of light colors. It also turned away from mythological scenes replete with sensuous nymphs and large-breasted goddesses. Instead of working in a studio, the Impressionists painted in the Fontainebleau Forest and on the banks of the Seine at Argenteuil, where they sought to capture nature and its myriad, fleeting atmospheric changes. They liked to render the "reflections of reflections" on the ever-changing surface of water and to analyze light filtering through foliage. They were among the first to notice that shadows are not just black, but red, blue, violet, etc. They painted by juxtaposing small touches of color to create centers of visual interest, a technique which gave their contemporaries the feeling that the artist had neglected or had been unable to finish his painting. Baudelaire had already commented on Corot's work exhibited in the Salon of 1845: "All of you ignore the fact that there is a big difference between a work that has been 'completed' and a work that is 'finished,' and that in general those that are 'completed' are not 'finished,' and those which are very 'finished' may not be 'completed' at all." The modern *non-finito* which Malraux would call *"style d'esquisse,"* was already in contradiction with the

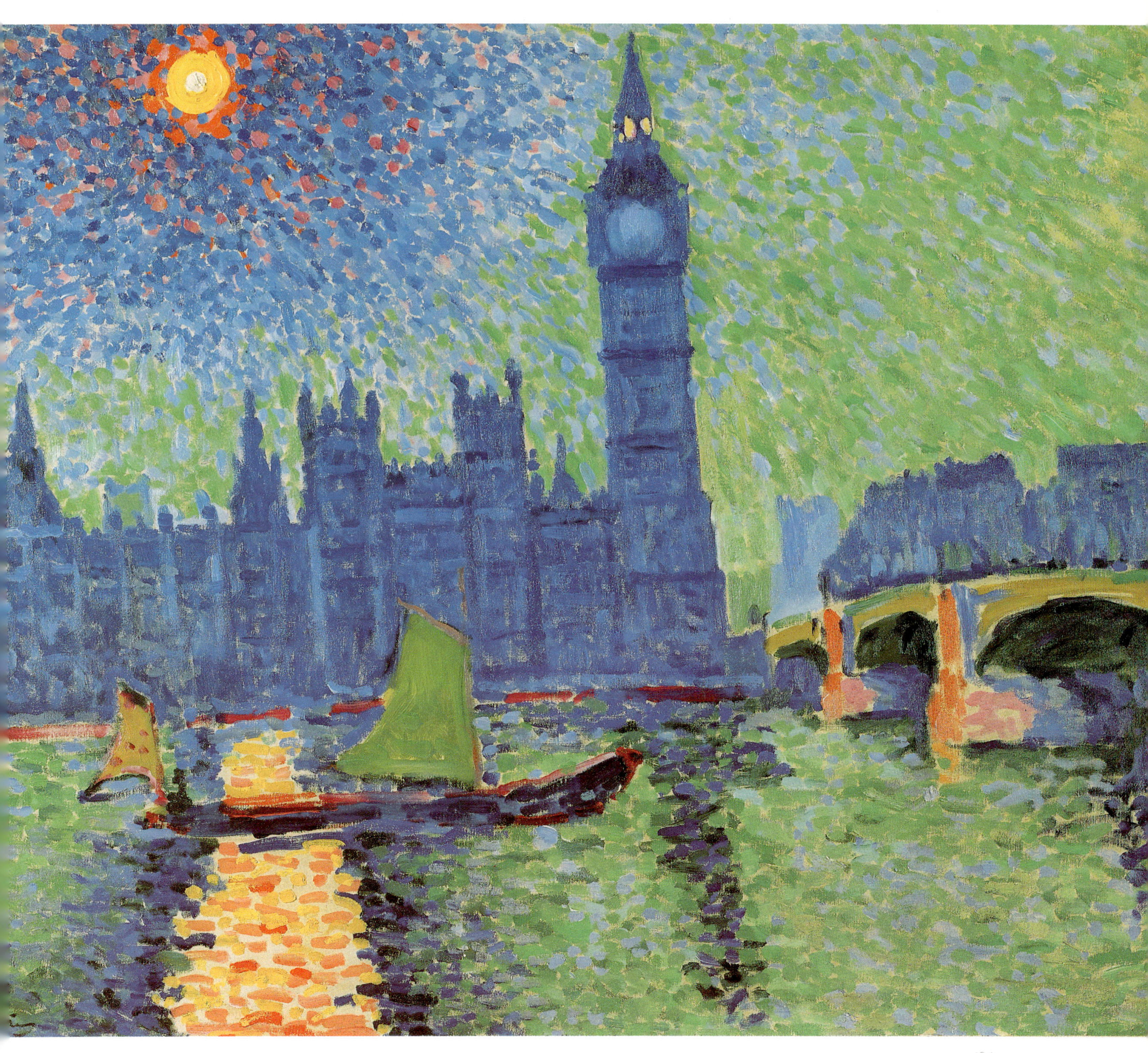

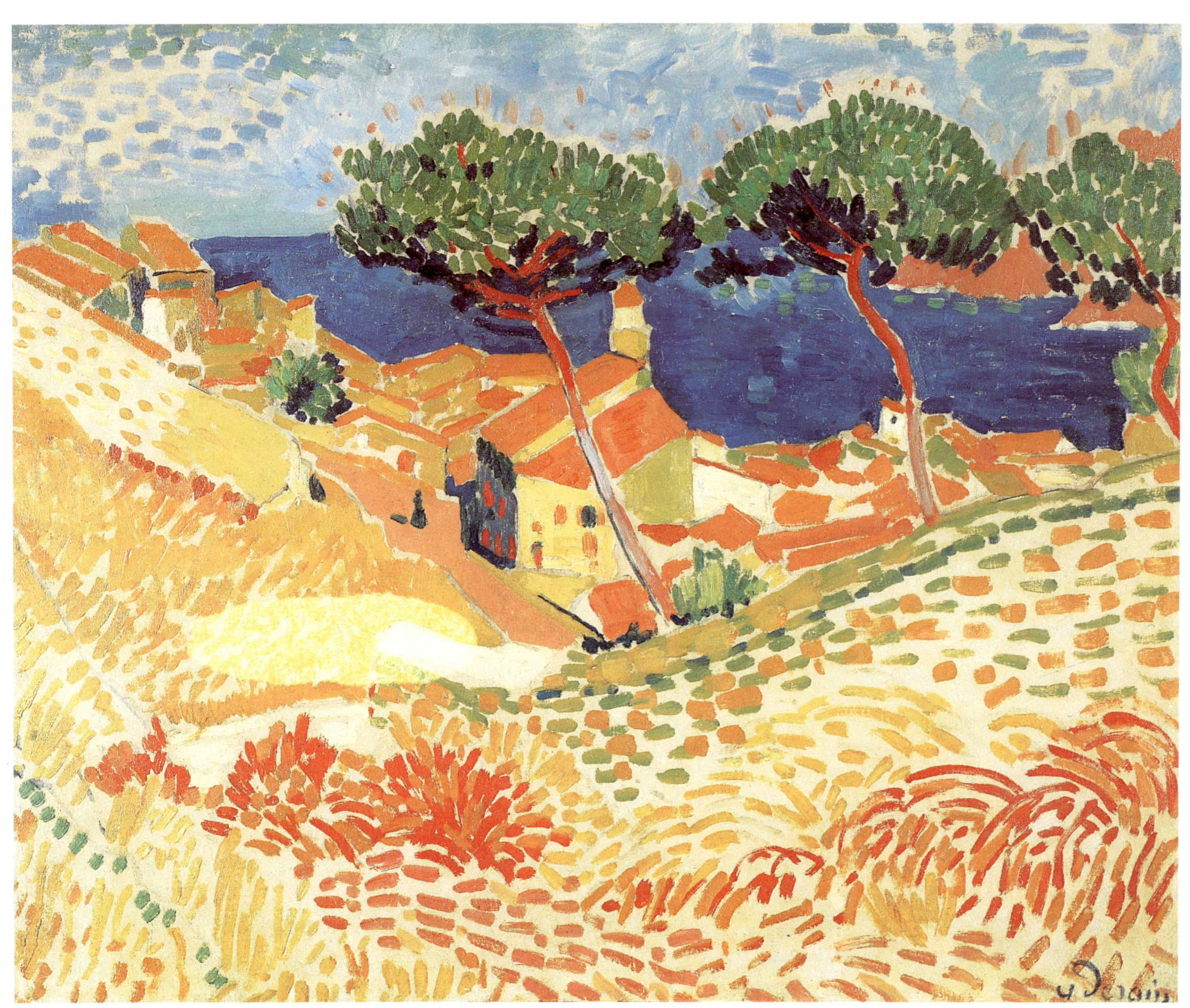

traditional way of making a study or a sketch before executing the final work. Although the public and critics, exasperated by the works in Room VII, were unable to accept the principles governing the art of the Fauves, they were finally beginning to acknowledge the Impressionists.

E. H. Gombrich, the British art historian, rightly pointed out that the Impressionists, although aiming at an imitation of the visual impression, remained prisoners of a tradition that they had pushed into a critical phase. The Fauves, on the other hand, never tried to copy or interpret nature, but sought to exploit it as an autonomous reality within an arbitrary perceptual relationship; they retained from the visible world only what was useful to their purpose. This idea, although perfectly legitimate when viewed with sufficient historical distance was difficult to accept in 1905.

The break came during the decade 1880-1890 with the emergence of the two movements that succeeded Impressionism: Neo-Impressionism (or Divisionism) and Synthetism, represented by the work of three artists, Seurat, Van Gogh and Gauguin.

Seurat developed a kind of mosaic technique in which dots of pure color were juxtaposed in accordance with the law of simultaneous contrast, discovered in 1839 by Michel-Eugène Chevreul, Director of the Department of Dyes at the Manufacture Royale des Gobelins, the famous tapestry works founded in Paris by Louis XIV. The scientist proved the existence of a reciprocal interaction between certain colors placed next to each other. This novel theory explains how colors which fade and disappear when combined, as in traditional academic painting, appear more vivid to the viewers' retina when they are applied in tiny, juxtaposed dots. This is true of red with green, blue with orange, and yellow with violet. In 1867, Charles Blanc demonstrated his familiarity with the laws formulated by Chevreul: in his *Grammar of Painting and Engraving*, he published a "Chromatic Diagram" that opposes, in complementary pairs, the three primary colors–red, yellow and blue–to the three secondary colors–green, orange and violet. It became possible then to execute a painting in a rational scientific manner, using colors in the same way as musical notes to create harmonies or to strike chords.

Most of Seurat's paintings obey the theory of optical mixtures of colors, the best example is the masterpiece on which he worked between 1884 and 1888, *Un dimanche après-midi à l'ile de la Grande-Jatte (Sunday Afternoon at the Grande-Jatte Island).* The final version depicts forty men and women in different postures strolling under the trees with dogs and a monkey on the grassy banks of an island, and shows boaters rowing in the middle of the Seine River. Although based upon sketches made from life, the final work was completed in a studio. Each area of the painting as well as the color of each dot was determined beforehand by the artist, a method which allowed him to work at night without having to worry about distorting the color scheme in gaslight.

On the other hand, the work of Van Gogh, a very successful retrospective exhibition of which was given in 1905 at the Stedelijk Museum in Amsterdam, is not as radical an artist as his reputation as *peintre maudit* would induce us to think. Admittedly, he had a strong personality, but the fervid patches of color he used owed much to Neo-Impressionism. Van Gogh expounded on the subject in a letter to his brother Theo, with a long explanation about the small miracle that allowed him to change the intensity of a tone simply by modifying the colors around it.

André Derain
View of Collioure
1905
Oil on canvas, 26 x 32¼ in (66 x 82,21 cm)
Essen, Folwang Museum

Opposite and following page:

Kees Van Dogen
Torso
1905
Oil on canvas, 36¼ x 32 in (92 x 81 cm)
Private collection
(courtesy of Ellen Melas Kyriazi)

Perhaps even more significant was the Synthetism Movement established around 1888, by the Pont-Aven group of painters, when the future Fauves, in particular Henri Matisse, began to use flat colors. The followers of Synthetism, whose most illustrious exponent was Gauguin, painted the various elements of a composition by distributing the colors in large, flat areas on the two-dimensional space of the canvas. This idea originated from two of his friends, Emile Bernard the creator of Cloisonnism–a technique which encloses colors inside black outlines somewhat like stained-glass–and Louis Anquetin. While watching the play of light through certain colored windows in his parents' house at Etrépagny, the latter noticed that "yellow gives an impression of sun, green evokes dawn, that dark blue produces night, and red announces twilight." Emile Bernard felt that one should paint from memory in order to eliminate the useless complexity of forms and tones. Thus the arrangement of lines and colors and the geometric construction themselves constituted the basis of pictorial art, an approach which permitted a perfect synthesis in the manner of Japanese prints. This was a complete break from the analytic vision of Impressionism and resulted in a total visual disintegration of form.

According to an oft-repeated anecdote, Gauguin counseled the young Paul Sérusier, who was living in Pont-Aven during the summer of 1888: "How do you see these trees? Paint them with pure ultramarine. For the red leaves, use vermilion." With this in mind and under Gauguin's dictation, Sérusier painted a small panel representing the Bois d'Amour–a grove of trees near the banks of the Aven River–by using simple patterns of colored surfaces. This landscape–now considered one of the sources of Fauvism–seemed so remarkable to the group that when Sérusier returned to Paris it was dubbed "Le Talisman" by his friends Bonnard, Vuillard, and Maurice Denis.

Nature and Fauvism

Most of the Fauves were not as systematic as Seurat and Gauguin had been; they leaned more in the direction of Van Gogh (although without going off the deep end). Unlike Neo-Impressionism and Synthetism, Fauvism did not in itself constitute a school of painting with definite precepts and taboos. It was a momentary encounter of several artists animated by the same goals and desires, yet enriched by individual expression. It provided the right blend of elements to motivate a prolific movement, as had been the case in art in the past. Vlaminck and Derain for example, aware of their similarities, used color as "sticks of dynamite." Yet, this does not mean that their immoderate taste for wild colors was purely instinctive.

Matisse–the most talented and the oldest member of the group (he was 36 in 1905, while the others were in their twenties) had gone through a Neo-Impressionistic phase a year earlier when he painted *Luxe, calme et volupté (Luxury, Calm and Sensual Delight).* Although different from his past and future work this aspect was an intrinsic part of his art.

A native of northern climes, Matisse was enthralled by the Mediterranean environment, and in early July 1904 he left for Saint-Tropez to stay in Signac's "delicious and inviting" house, La Hune. Signac, while conforming to the strict division of colors so dear to Seurat, had nevertheless arrived at a less rigid concept of Neo-

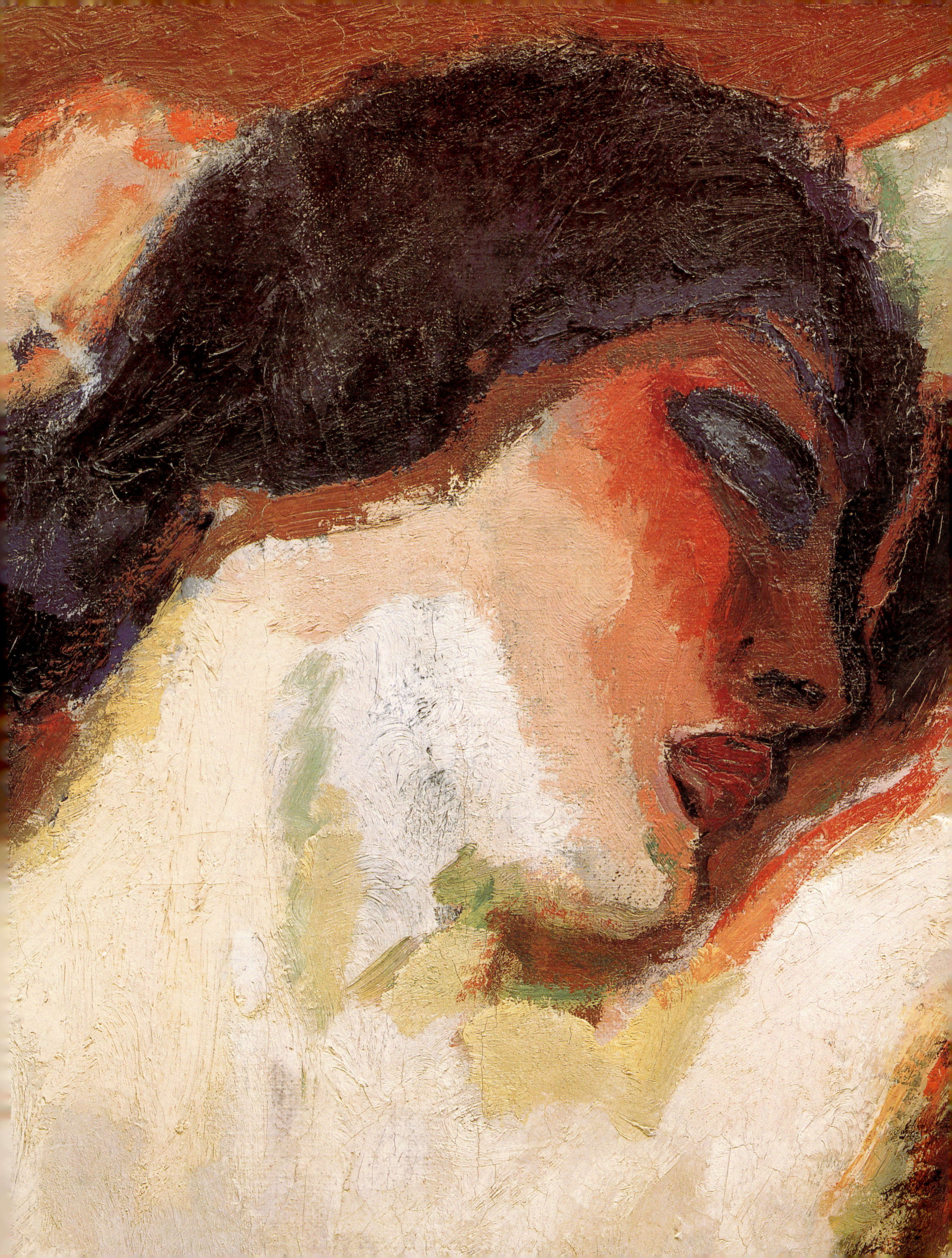

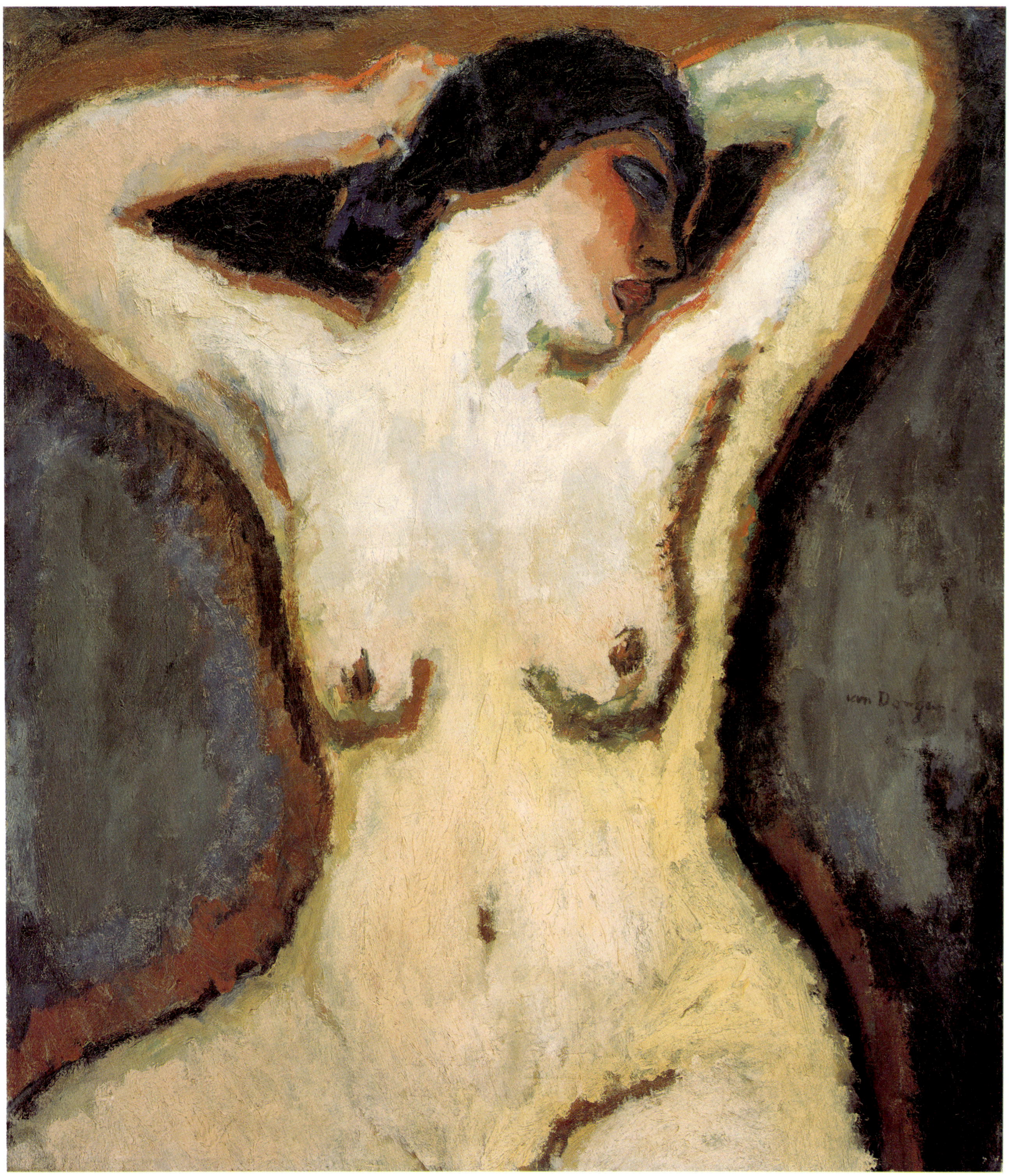
van Dongen

Impressionism. He was attracted to the lush vegetation of southern France and influenced by the work of Delacroix, whom he considered the precursor of optical color mixture and whose technique he described in his book *De Delacroix au Néo-Impressionnisme* (1899). Matisse's *Luxe, calme et volupté*–finished in September upon his return to Paris–appears, even before the subject of bathers on a beach is identified, as an explosion of light undimmed by the passage of time, with regular patches of color methodically placed side by side in radiant and infinite gradations.

In an article considered today as a manifesto, printed on December 25, 1908 by the *Grande Revue*, Matisse wrote: "What I dream of is an art of expression" and went on to specify that, "expression, for me, is not the passion that bursts forth on a face or demonstrates itself in a violent movement. It exists throughout my whole painting." Then further on: "What I dream of is an art of balance, purity and serenity, devoid of troubling or depressing subject-matter. I want my work to be soothing, so that the exhausted, overworked and stressed spectator finds rest and calm in it." This is miles away from the metaphysical torments of Expressionism, with its orgies of discordant colors, so often confused with Fauvism.

The principles of Fauvism may be listed briefly as follows: construction of space with color, purity and simplification of technique, economy of means. Matisse wrote: "When I use a green it doesn't mean grass; when I use a blue, it doesn't mean the sky." This is a statement with two complementary meanings; in a Fauve painting, grass is not necessarily green, nor is the sky blue, but even "if they really are," the green and the blue must be seen first. By putting these observations into practice, Matisse devised ways of bringing a painting to life but avoided all the conventional chromatic daubing of predetermined shapes so often found in the works of his more slavish followers. The extraordinary creative freedom flaunted by the Fauves undoubtedly explains both the visitors' dismay in Room VII at the third Salon d'Automne, and Fauvism's return to the fore of today's pictorial scene.

For the next few years the Fauve group continued to exhibit–and to be taken as a laughing-stock–while new followers like Braque and Dufy joined them. In 1908, however, at the Sixth Salon d'Automne, the winds of favor suddenly changed with the arrival of a younger generation of critics. The public was becoming accustomed to the Fauves, so that even their most rabid detractors, like Jean Mauclair, were forced to recognize the merits and the importance of the movement. A separate section of the show was devoted to Matisse with 11 paintings, 6 drawings and 13 sculptures.

A new scandal broke out; this time among the exhibitors. The jury, which now included Matisse and Marquet rejected six recent paintings by Braque. This one-time Fauve–and now close friend of Picasso–had begun painting in an entirely different style. Matisse, when asked by Vauxcelles which paintings had been refused, answered: "Braque sent canvases covered with little cubes." In order to make his point, Matisse took a piece of paper out of his pocket and drew two interconnected cubes. The rejected paintings were shown in November by Daniel-Henry Kahnweiler in his small gallery at 28, rue Vignon. The avant-garde had changed sides and Cubism was born.

The Fauves, with the exception of Braque, continued to forge ahead and today they are exhibited in great museums all over the world. Some, such as Vlaminck and Van Dongen, did not live up to their

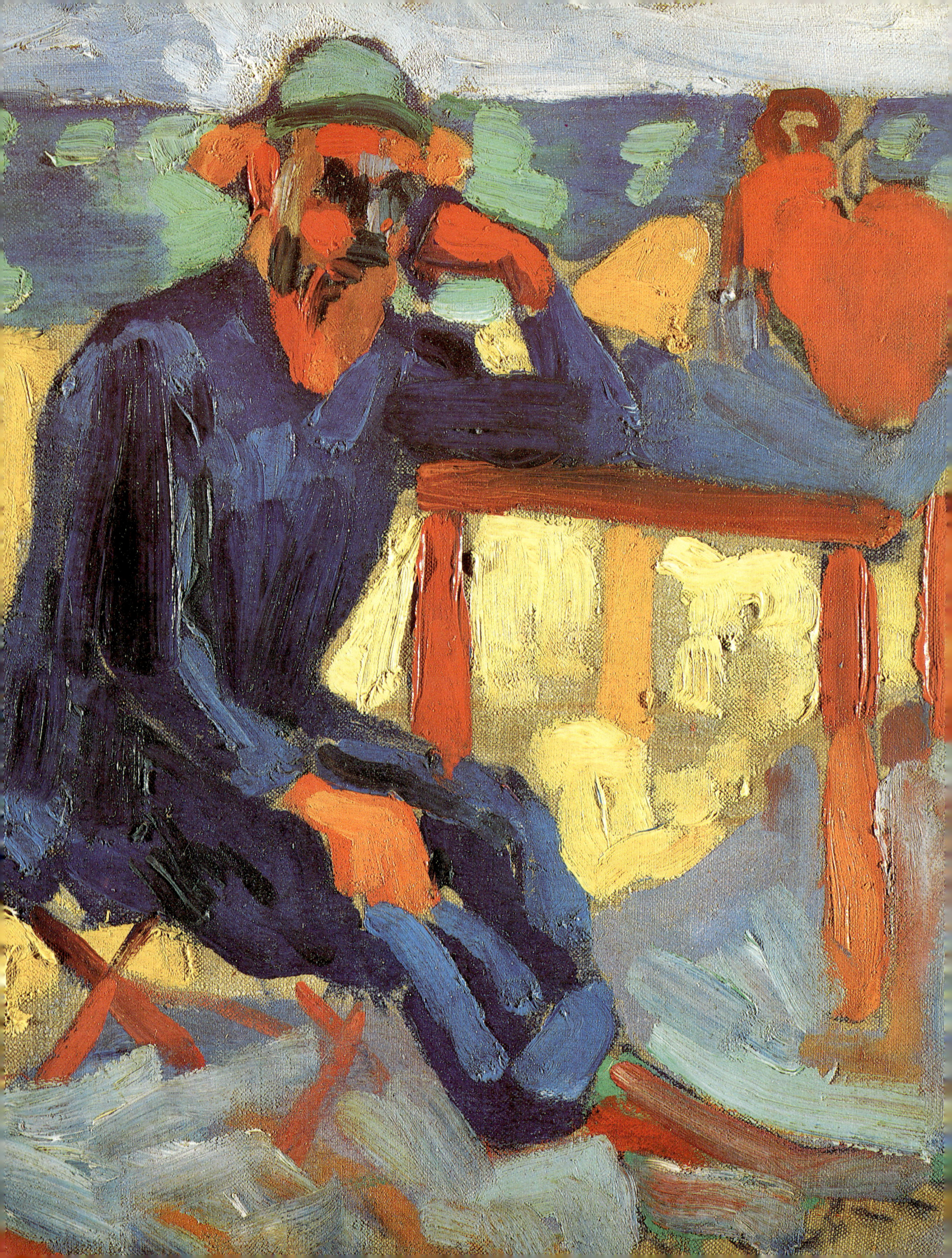

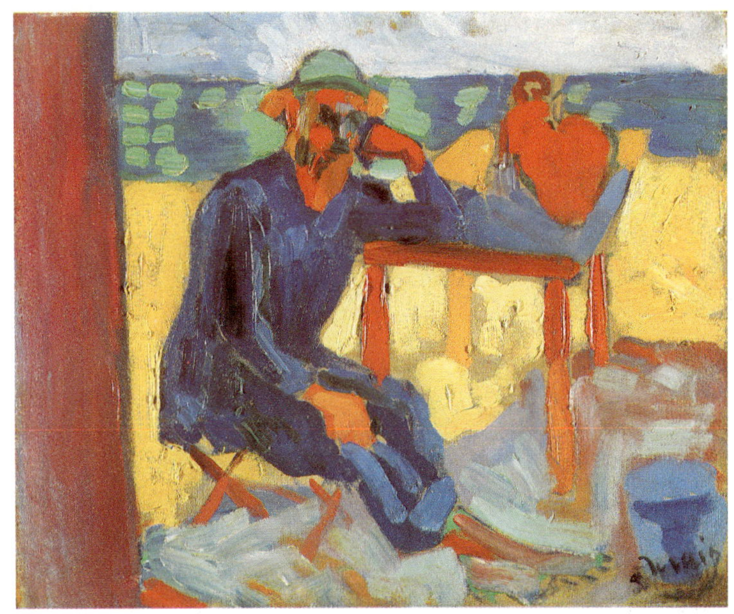

Above and opposite:

André Derain
Portrait of Henri Matisse
1905
Oil on canvas, 9¾ x 12¼ in (25 x 31 cm)
Philadelphia Museum of Art
(E. A. Gallatin collection)

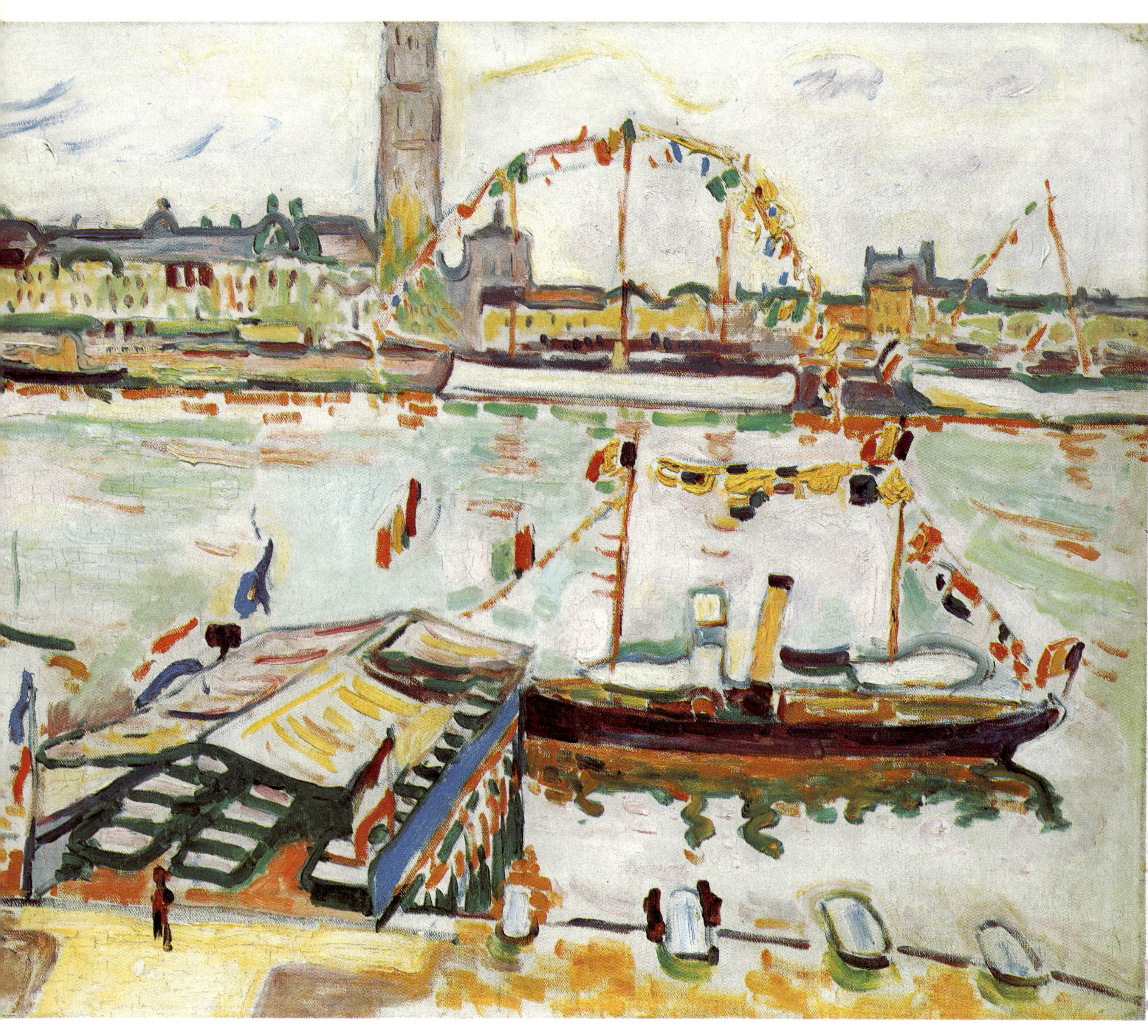

Georges Braque
Antwerp Harbor
1906
Oil on canvas, 20 x 24¼ in (50,5 x 61,5 cm)
Basel, Fine Arts Museum

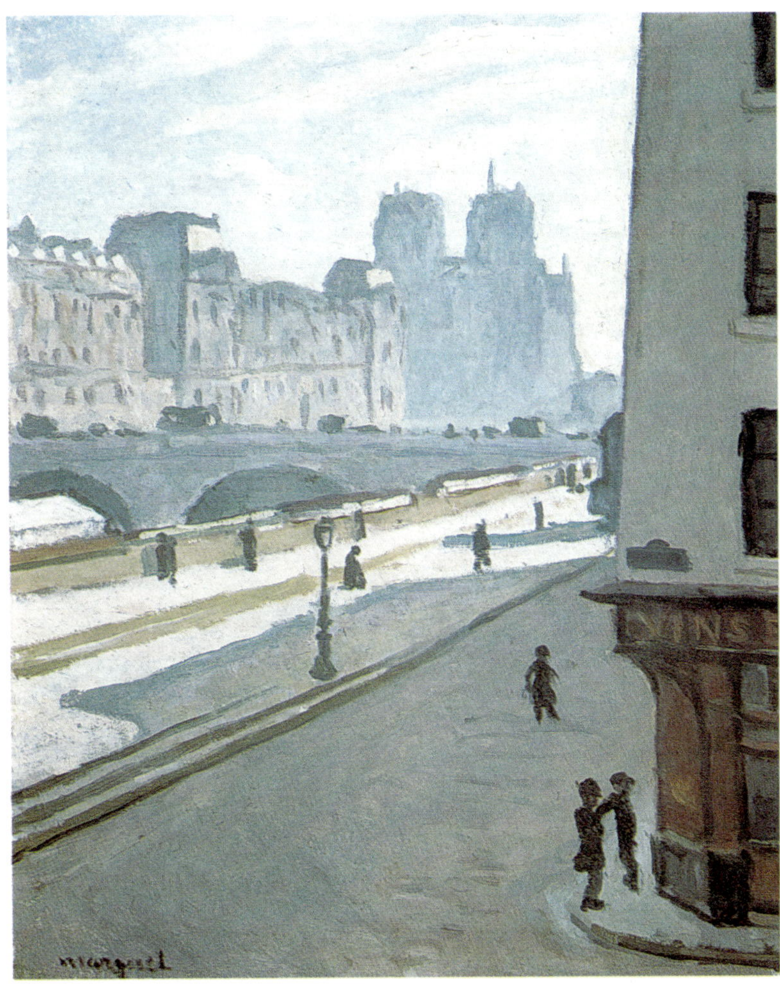

Albert Marquet
Notre-Dame in the Sun
1904
Oil on canvas, 28¾ x 23½ in
(73 x 60 cm)
Pau, musée des Beaux-Arts

promise, and Derain unfortunately returned to a more traditional style; others, such as Camoin, Friesz and Manguin, appear today as minor painters. A group is always composed of more or less daring and more or less assiduous and creative artists. Matisse, called "the doctor" by his friends–as much for his natural authority as for his gold-rimmed glasses–continued to unveil Fauvism's countless treasures until the end of his life. He died in 1954 at the age of 96. Because of Matisse's prominence and longevity, this book begins by retracing his work.

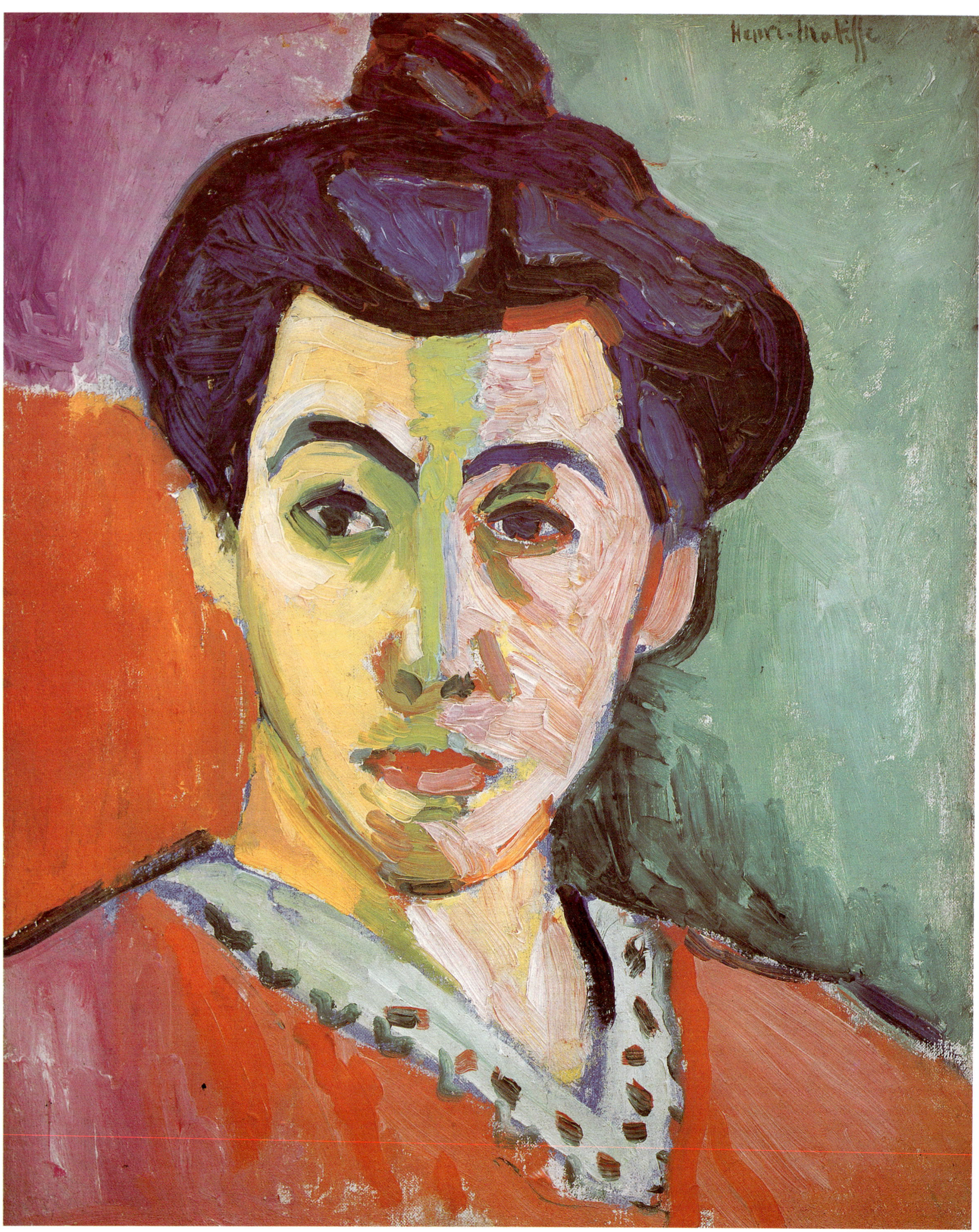
Henri-Matisse

Self-Determination:

Matisse

The Simplification of Painting

The greatest of all the Fauves nearly missed becoming a painter. Matisse's father, who ran a granary-hardware store in Bohain-en-Vermandois in the Département de l'Aisne in the North of France, had planned on a legal career for his second son, Henri-Emile-Benoît, born in the nearby town of Le Cateau on December 31, 1869, and expected his elder son to take over the family business. After Henri finished high school, which he thoroughly enjoyed, he passed his law examinations with excellent grades. He showed such little interest in painting that on a trip to Paris he never even visited the Louvre or any of the city's other museums. Once back at home, he became a legal clerk in an office in Saint-Quentin. His life's course seemed entirely cut and dried until he began to have problems with his health.

Matisse suffered frequent attacks of abdominal pain and finally had to undergo an appendectomy. At that time, the operation was not without risk and, in any case, meant a long period of convalescence. The man with whom he shared his hospital room occupied his days by copying colored etchings of Swiss landscapes. Matisse, attracted by this pastime, asked his mother to bring him a box of colored pencils and tried his hand at making copies, too. He found such great satisfaction in the activity that as soon as he returned to Saint-Quentin, he began taking drawing lessons each morning before going to work and taught himself how to paint by following a small how-to guide entitled *La manière de peindre (How to Paint)*. In 1890 he painted *Still Life with Books* in a Chardin-like style, the first real canvas in which he showed extraordinary promise for a novice. His was a late-blooming vocation as compared to Picasso, for Matisse was 20 years old in 1890. At

Henri Matisse
Portrait of Madame Matisse / The Green Line
Paris, autumn-winter 1905
Oil on canvas, 16 x 12⅞ in
(40.64 x 32.38 cm)
Copenhagen, Statens Museum for Kunst

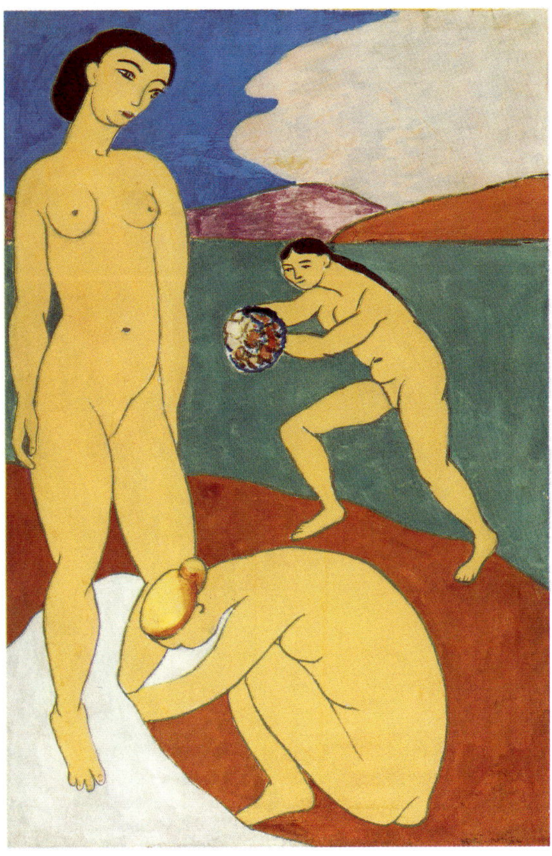

Above and page 33:

Henri Matisse
Le luxe II
Collioure or Paris, 1905
Casein on canvas, 6 ft 10½ x 54⅜ in
(209.5 x 139 cm)
Copenhagen, Statens Museum for Kunst

Opposite:

Henri Matisse
Le luxe I
Collioure, summer 1907
Oil on canvas, 6 ft 10⅝ x 54⅜ in
(210 x 138 cm)
Paris, musée national d'Art moderne

the same age, his future rival–born in 1881–had been painting since his earliest childhood and had already executed nearly a thousand works.

The final decision was near. In October 1892, Matisse's father accepted that his son become an artist. Matisse returned to Paris for good, and enrolled in night school at the Ecole des Arts Décoratifs, where he met and became friends with Albert Marquet.

After "*les Arts déco*," Matisse entered Gustave Moreau's studio at the Ecole des Beaux-Arts which had already attracted Marquet, Rouault and many others. Moreau, whose paintings have been considered as somewhat "kitschy," was, in fact, a great figure in the art world at the end of the century even if his work was more or less unknown. He was intelligent, a remarkable teacher and possessed a broad culture. His classes had little in common with those of his colleagues. Vuillard–a student of Gérôme and Bonnat–recalled that a terrifying atmosphere reigned in the studios of these Beaux-Arts professors. Moreau had the gift of captivating his students. He knew how to instill in them a strength of will and a quest for the absolute, endlessly repeating that the work of an artist is a vocation. Rather than imposing his own point of view, he would help each student develop his own personality. According to Moreau, the purpose of color was not to reproduce reality; on the contrary, it should represent reality, not merely for the eye but also for the mind. He insisted on evoking feeling through line and arabesque. Time would soon show how sensitive Matisse was to these considerations.

But this is not all. "You are going to simplify the art of painting," Moreau would repeat while correcting the work of his students. This was a prophetic remark for Matisse; the apprentice painter was still very far from the conciseness to which he was progressively drawn over the years.

Four Toes Instead of Five

Matisse substantiated his professor's advice in an article that he wrote for the *Grande Revue*: "Everything that is unnecessary in a painting is detrimental to it. A work should contain a harmony of the whole; in the eye of the viewer, superfluous details take the place of essential details." The painter applied these principles from the first to the last of his works, in *Luxe, calme et volupté*, in the many landscapes of Collioure, in the countless nudes, and even in the monumental *Dance* (1932-1933)–one of three variations on this theme–executed for the main hall of the Barnes Foundation in Merion near Philadelphia. There is really nothing in a Matisse that is not totally necessary: the lines, the forms, the colors.... Everything seems to be held in tension throughout the picture plane.

The comparison of two major works, *Luxe I* and *Luxe II*, painted by Matisse in 1907, after several preliminary drawings, demonstrates the process he used to obtain maximal tension. Both paintings depicting three female bathers against a seascape are composed of a frontal standing nude dominating two other bathers, one of whom is stooping down at her feet and the other occupying the middle ground. In the first version Matisse used the same devices–colors that seem to come "straight out of the tube," vibrant modulations and the color streaks–that had shocked the 1905 Salon d'Automne public and were described by the critics as "ugly daubings." Here, in the pure Fauve tradition, he steadfastly

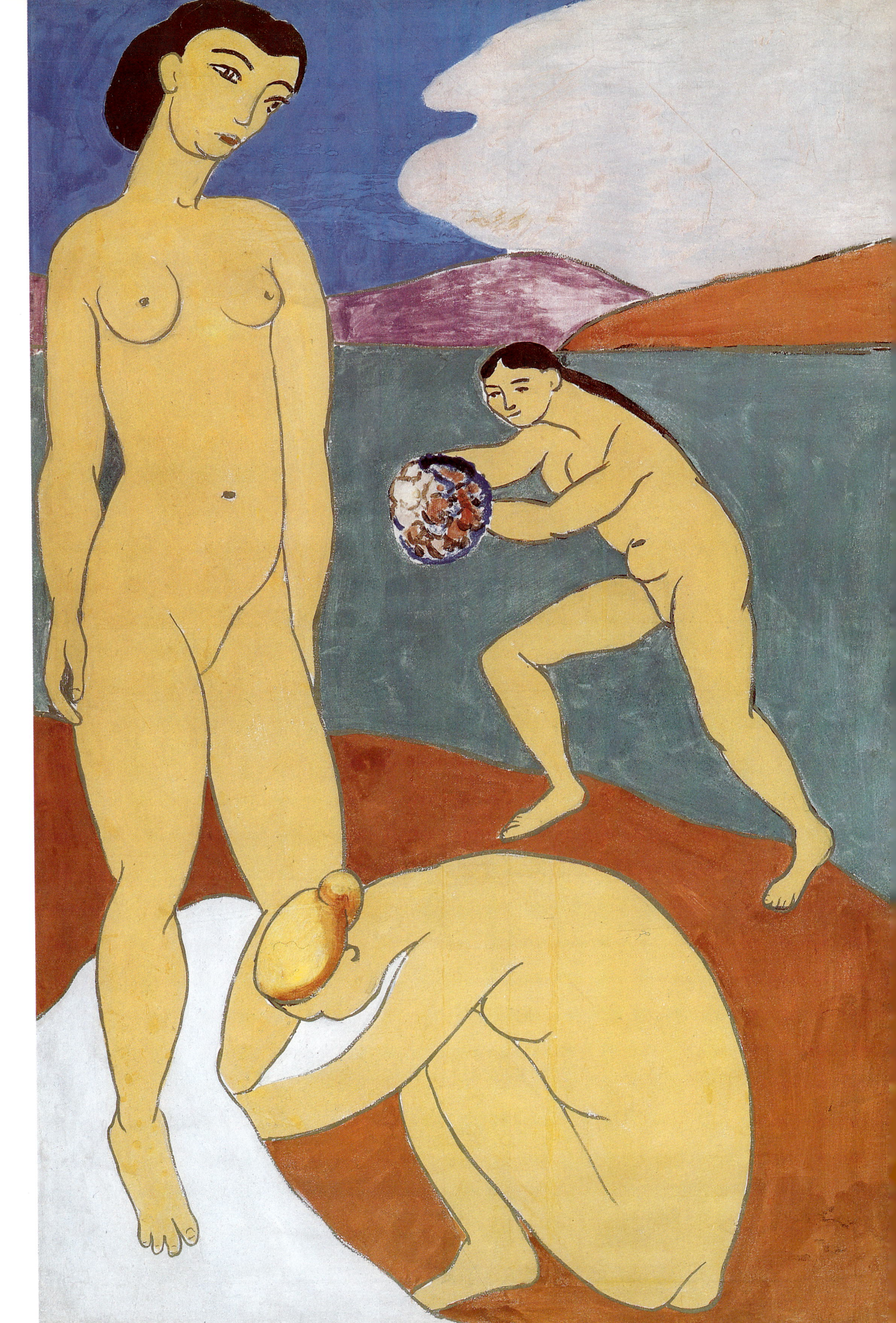

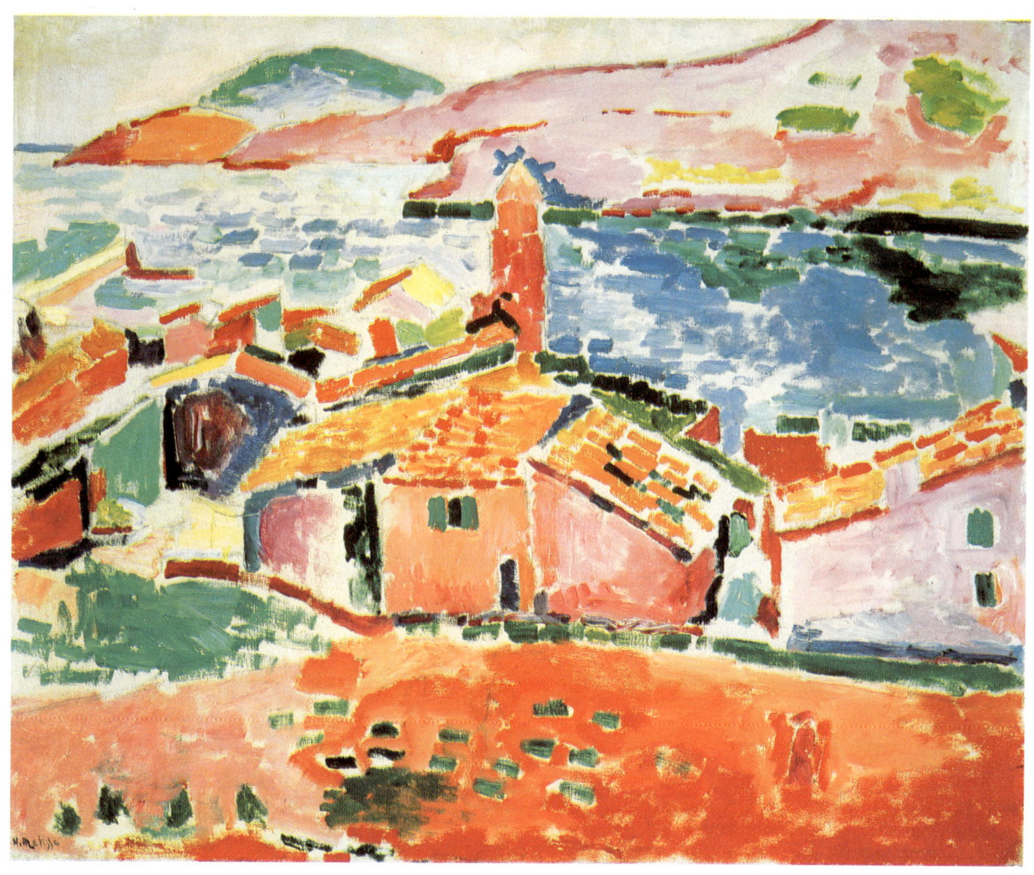

Henri Matisse
The Roofs of Collioure
1905
Oil on canvas, 23⅜ x 28¾ in
(59.5 x 73 cm)
St. Petersburg, Hermitage Museum

Opposite:

Henri Matisse
The Gulf of Saint-Tropez
1904
Oil on canvas, 25½ x 19⅞ in
(65 x 50.5 cm)
Düsseldorf, Kunstsammlung
Nordrhein-Westfalen

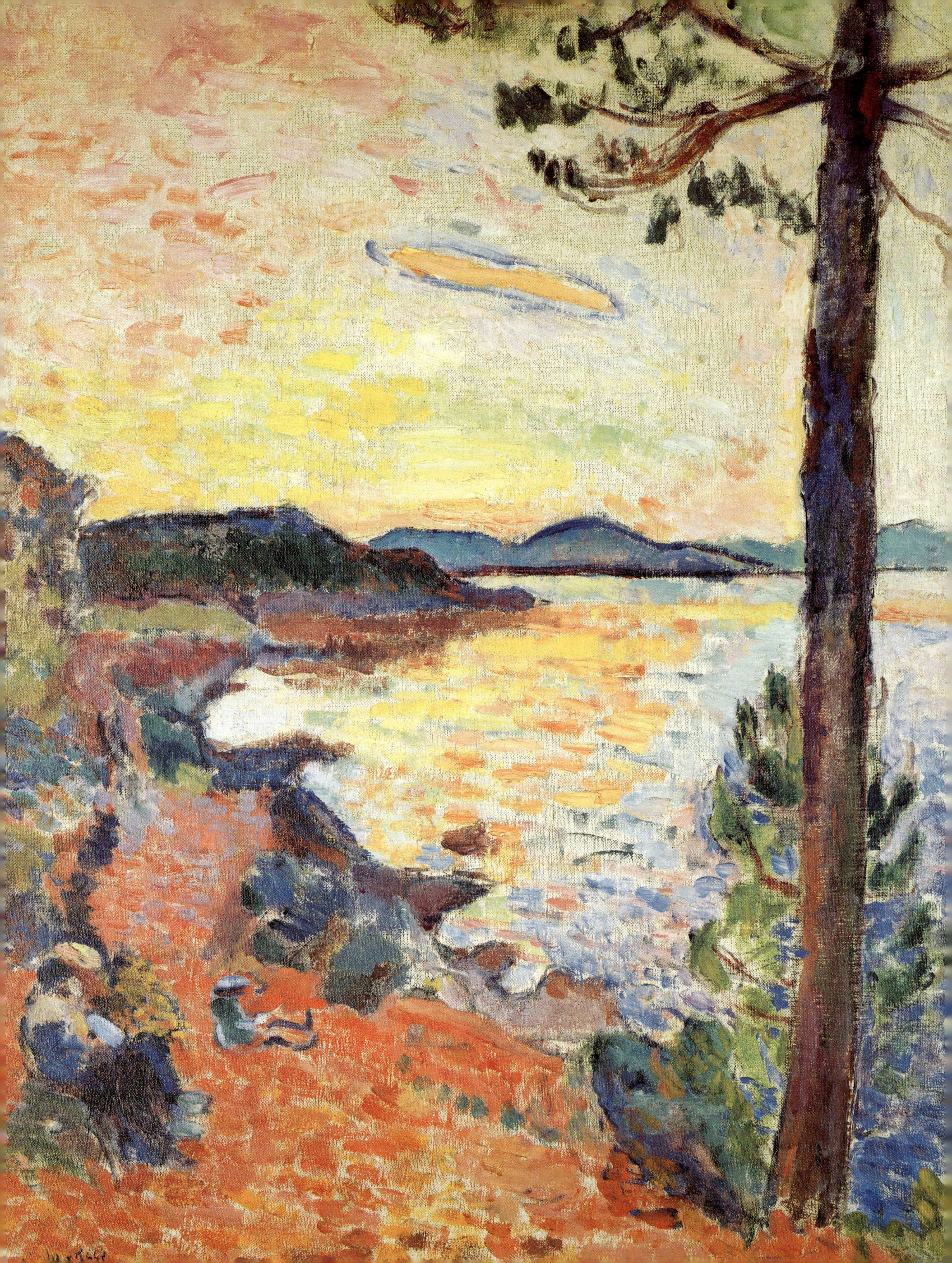

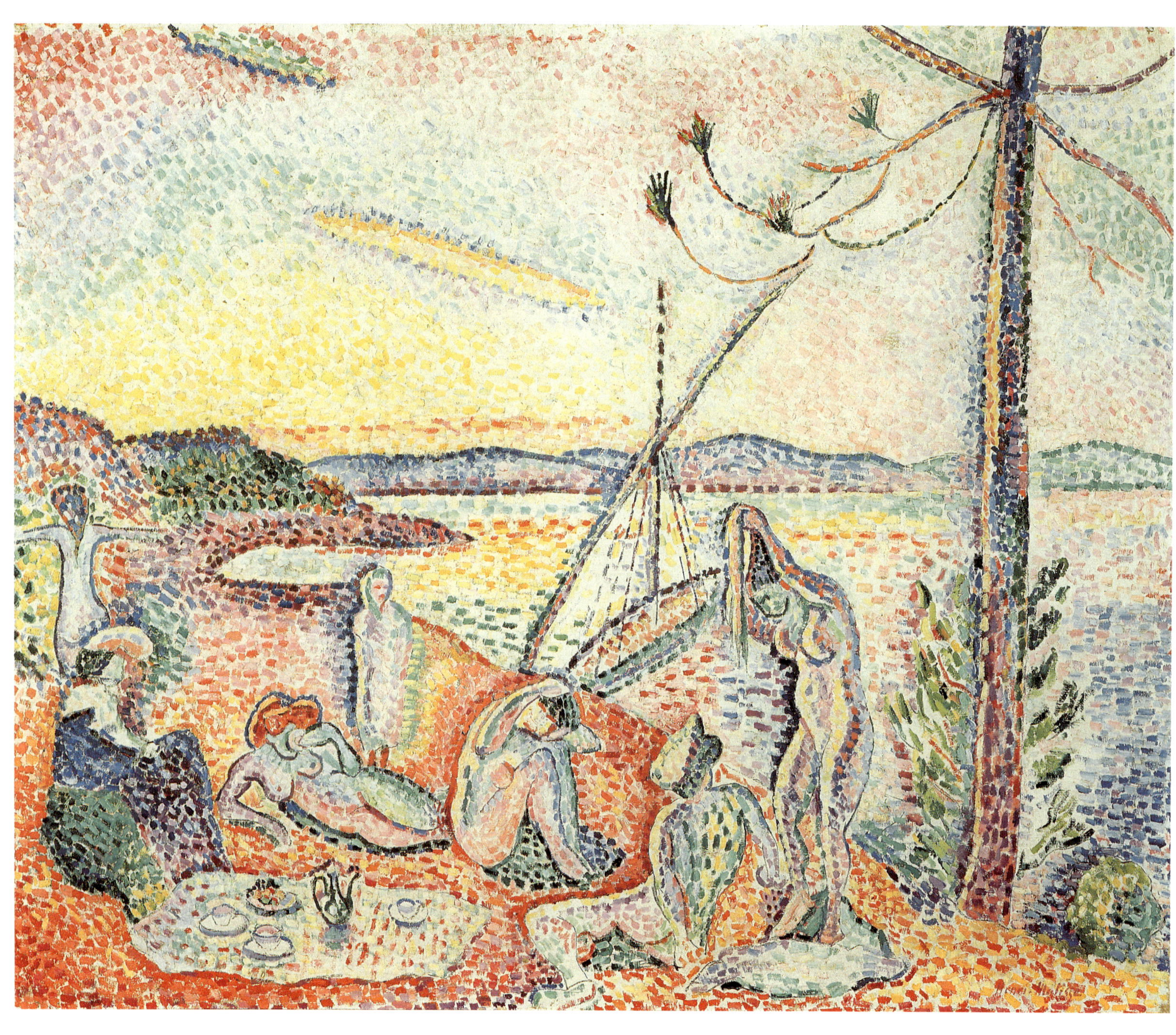

HENRI MATISSE
Luxe, calme et volupté
Paris, autumn-winter 1904-1905
Oil on canvas, 38 x 46½ in (98.5 x 118 cm)
Paris, musée d'Orsay

pinned and pasted on large white canvases hung about the room by an assistant according to his instructions. In this fashion he executed lavish nudes as well as flowers, palm trees and fig leafs.

Matisse's cutout medium, however, should not be confused with the bits of paper that the Cubists pasted on their works during the period 1912-1914. The collage technique allowed them to escape from the confines of Cubism, in which ordinary objects like drinking glasses, guitars, pitchers and mandolins were barely identifiable and had become mere suggestions or fragments. The Cubists had set out to prove that even the most unprepossessing materials such as pieces of newspaper or imitation wood-grain patterns could produce beautiful art. The bits of paper glued to their canvases acted as "painted proverbs," that is, pieces of "raw" reality applied directly to the surface, comparable to the advertising jingles that Cendrars and Apollinaire inserted in their poetry.

The intention behind Matisse's cutouts was very different. His aim was to manipulate color as an independent element by using scissors as a drawing instrument in the same way that a sculptor cuts marble with a chisel and hammer. Like a sculptor guided by the veins in the block of stone, Matisse found that the colored surface was directing his hand: "You cannot imagine the feeling I had during the period I was making cutouts; a sensation of flying overwhelmed me and helped me to better adjust my hand as I wielded the scissors. It's difficult to explain. I would say that I experienced a sort of a linear, graphic equivalence of flying," he declared to André Verdet.

Never mind that his body was abandoning him–Matisse was soaring! He realized from his cutouts that he had reached a perfect creativity, "a sort of hierarchy of all my feelings!" that allowed him to finish his life in a crescendo.

The representation of form and space has been a problem throughout the history of Western painting. The turning-point came around the end of the 15th century, when Leonardo da Vinci made his volumes "turn" in space using pictorial devices such as modeling, *chiaroscuro* and *sfumato* in an illusionist manner, unlike Botticelli, who had represented nature's three-dimensional forms by simply outlining figures and shapes to achieve a rather flat representation of volumes on the pictorial surface.

In *Luxe II*, Matisse found an answer to the contradictory relationship between line and volume, a problem that had been solved, neither by the Neo-Impressionists who dissociated line and color, nor by the Fauves whose volumes were lost in a flux of color. He found a masterly response with his cutouts when he realized that flat solid colors cut into various shapes were enough to suggest volume.

There are many examples of this discovery in his work, but none of them measure up to *The Swimming Pool*, executed in 1952. This immense work composed of two matching panels took its inspiration from a new social phenomenon: people attracted by the outdoor joys of the seaside and sunny beaches. In this work, Matisse's flat blue cutouts portray half-human, half-dolphin creatures intermittently relaxing or contracting their muscles; a flurry of heads and arms swimming the crawl releases an energy that radiates throughout the whole work. What a contrast with Monet or with Renoir, who painted a bathing scene called *La Grenouillière* in 1869. The setting depicts a certain circle of Parisian society enjoying idle pleasures by the waterside with timid bathers wading, light filtering through trees, dandies and their ladies observing each other. Renoir gave a truly remarkable rendition of

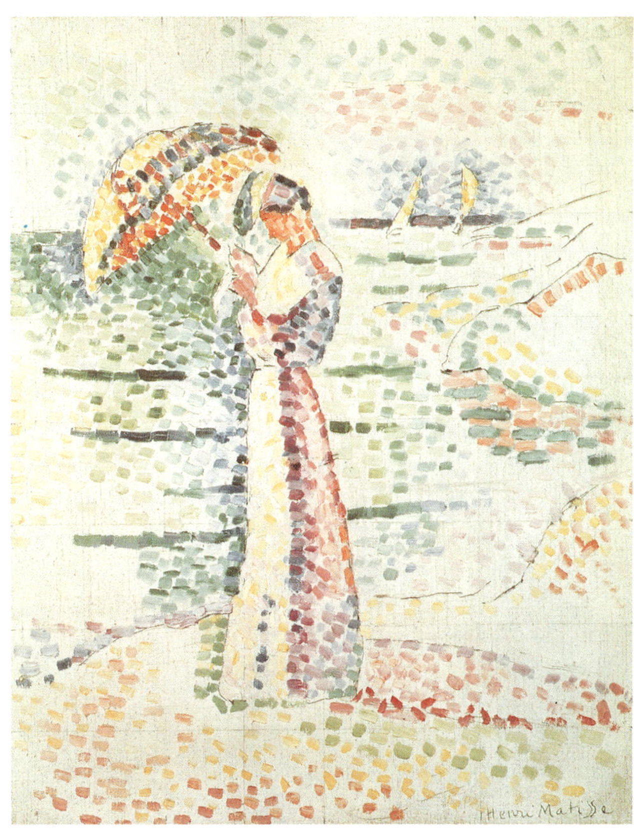

Henri Matisse
Woman with a Parasol
Collioure, 1904-1905
Oil on canvas, 16⅛ x 14⅛ in (42.2 x 37.3 cm)
Nice, musée Matisse

a *guinguette*, a typical river-bank dance hall. Matisse invented a figurative language able to describe the elusive worlds of underwater diving, water skiing, and swimming competitions. Only Fernard Léger achieved a comparative result with *Les Loisirs*.

Light and Space

Collioure, summer 1905
Oil on canvas, 21¾ x 18⅛ in
(55.2 x 46 cm)
New York, Mrs. John Hay Whitney collection

To assert that color plays the major role in Matisse's art would be one-sided and would overlook two other essential elements: light and space. For several centuries, space was identified with perspective, a technique suggesting a third dimension on the flat surface of a painting by drawing the gaze of the viewer into depth. This spatial effect was described as illusionistic. Filippo Brunelleschi, the celebrated architect of the Duomo of Santa Maria del Fiore in Florence, is said to have invented "linear perspective" in 1425. He executed two painted panels (which no longer exist); one was a depiction of the east side of the octagonal Baptistery located in front of the Duomo. In order to keep the entire Baptistery in sight, Brunelleschi had to back up underneath the central portal of the Cathedral and remain motionless with one eye closed because the jambs on either side of the portal hampered his angle of vision.

Brunelleschi produced a small painted panel of about 16 x 16 in (40 x 40 cm) pierced with a peephole at its "central vanishing point." The purpose of the peephole was to allow the viewer to see the picture as a reflected image in a large mirror held in front of it. The building was represented in the painting with such care that the black and white marble slabs matched their model precisely. Even more remarkably, the space above the Baptistery was left unpainted, revealing a burnished silver surface so that the sky–complete with wind-blown clouds–might be reflected in it to further emphasize the illusion of reality. For a long time after Brunelleschi's experiment, linear perspective was considered as a system that recorded nature as it was; in other words, a picture was like a window opening out on the real world.

But a system that depends on the contrived vision of just one eye, that has to select a static position, and must circumscribe space, obviously has little in common with how we actually perceive a beach or a street or any other scene around us. As for Matisse, he opened the window wide–and even broke the pane. This process was repeated throughout his work, starting with a painting from 1905, *The Open Window, Collioure*, in which the sailboats at the marina seem to enter the room and become part of the same space as the objects in the foreground. In *Interior at Collioure/The Siesta*, executed in the same year, there is no distinction between outdoors and indoors. "If I have combined what is outside–the sea for example–and what is indoors, it is because the atmosphere of the landscape and of my room are the same... I do not feel the need to bring the outside and inside closer together. I can associate the armchair by my side in my studio with the rustling palm trees by the edge of the water without making any effort to differentiate between their locations or separate the different elements of the composition in my mind."

Such works, however, could not have been accomplished without totally reinventing the handling of light. The depth effect in a painting is given not only by linear perspective, but also by *chiaroscuro* modeling, another pictorial device that pulls the figures away from the flat surface of the canvas. In this technique, the volumes

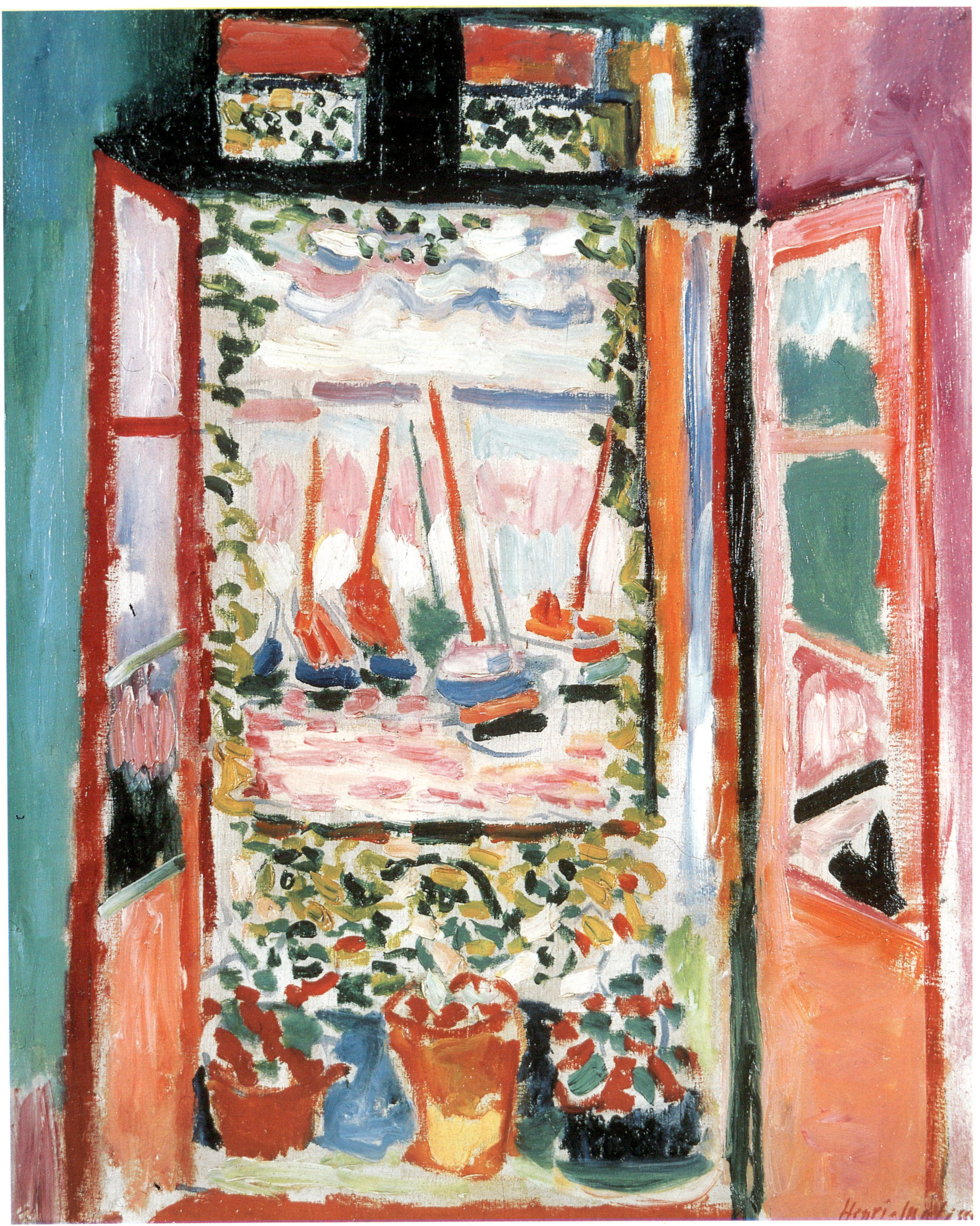

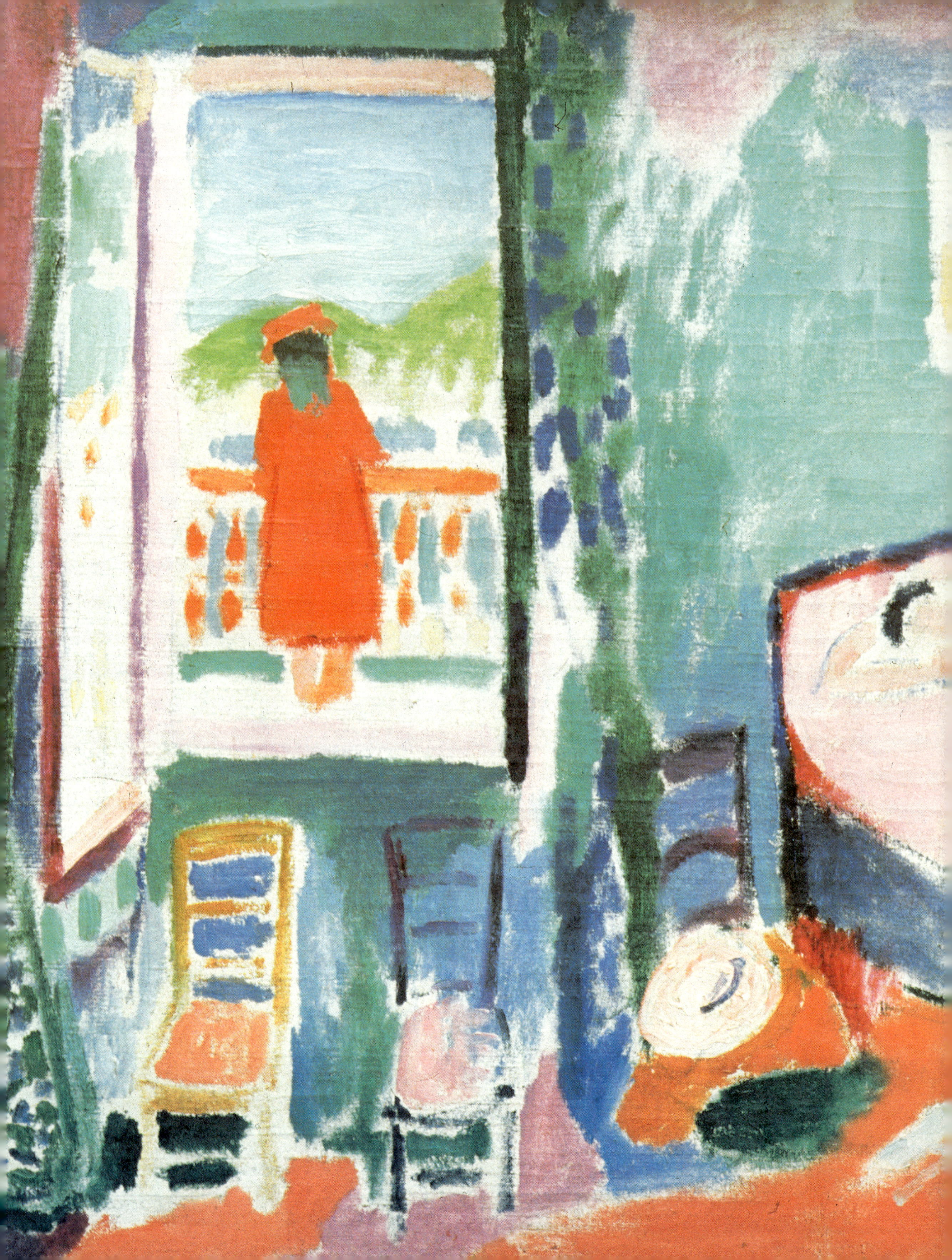

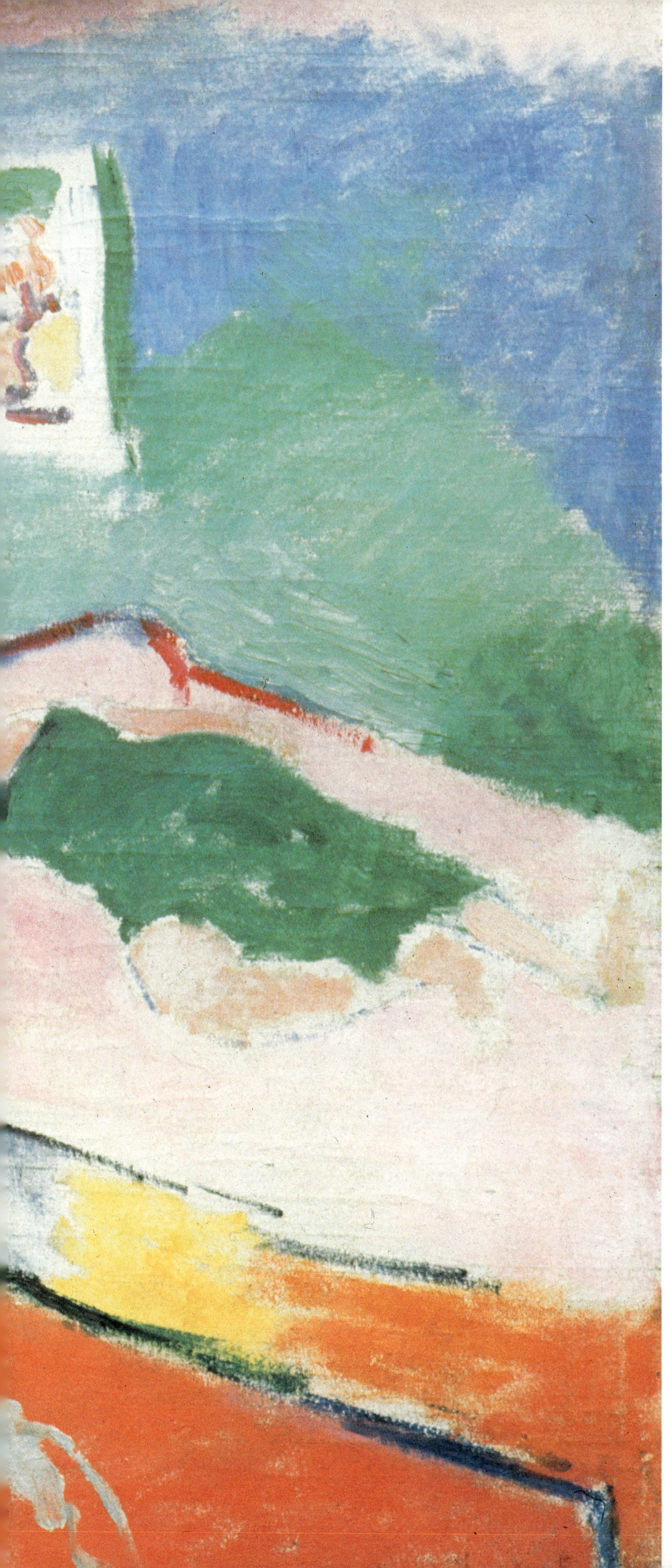

Henri Matisse
Interior at Collioure / The Siesta
Collioure, summer 1905
Oil on canvas, 23¼ x 28⅜ in
(59 x 72 cm)
Zurich, private collection

are separated by almost imperceptible gradations of light and dark, the successive planes bathe in a subdued light, and the background is softened and becomes practically blurred. It is easy to understand that in questioning one of these devices, the Fauves–and especially Matisse–brought about the downfall of the others.

Matisse not only used the flat-color technique, applying color in uniform, unbroken, and unshaded areas, but he often repainted these areas in another hue, not just to change them but, more generally, to change their function and bring about a different mental image, as was the case in *La desserte* (*Harmony in Red*, 1908) that the Russian collector Sergei Shchukin bought from the artist in Paris. Originally a blue composition, the artist later reworked it in red to accentuate the effect of a continuous arabesque. While the Neo-Impressionists–and Matisse himself, with *Luxe, calme et volupté*–had already mastered the optical mixture of colors by carefully juxtaposing primary and complementary colors, the artist was now able to achieve this effect by the use of transparency. The artist was then able to integrate light directly into color, applied as both tone and value. No other Fauve achieved such feats, as his *Dance* and *Music* of 1910. These two masterpieces, executed with such spontaneity that is hard to believe that the artist worked on them relentlessly for a whole year, were commissioned by Shchukin to decorate his town house in Moscow.

HENRI MATISSE
Dance (II)
Issy-les-Moulineaux, late 1909 and summer 1910
Oil on canvas, 8 ft 5⅝ x 12 ft 9½ in (260 x 391 cm)
St. Petersburg, Hermitage Museum

HENRI MATISSE
Music
Issy-les-Moulineaux, late 1909 and summer 1910
Oil on canvas, 8 ft 5⅝ x 12 ft 9¼ in (260 x 389 cm)
St. Petersburg, Hermitage Museum

In spite of Matisse's financial difficulties at the time, he bought Cézanne's *Three Bathers* for 1,500 francs in 1899; he subsequently gave this small painting, whose theme inspired his early work, to the Petit Palais in 1936. This painting represented a sort of absolute goal that he had been determined to reach. "I understand this work fairly well I hope, although not entirely," he wrote in a letter accompanying the donation, "and for 37 years it has kept my spirits up in the critical moments of my artistic career; I draw my faith and perseverance from it." Cézanne wished to paint "the virginity of the world"; in other words, to evoke perceptions that are coming to life beneath an image of reality. This is also what Matisse set out to do but with other methods.

Oranges for Matisse

Above a pedestal table in the hallway of Notre-Dame-de-Vie in Mougins, where he spent his last years, Picasso hung a work executed by Matisse in 1913, *Still Life with Oranges*. Each year, in the month of December, he would place a crate of oranges under the painting, forbidding anyone to touch them, for, as he would repeat: "It's for Matisse's Christmas!" This homage by the artist from Malaga to the greatest of the Fauves takes on even more significance when we recall the harsh words that Matisse used for Picasso. In 1907, after seeing *Les demoiselles d'Avignon* at the Bateau-Lavoir, Matisse vowed that he would find some means to "sink" Picasso; according to the Fauve master, he had brought ridicule to modern painting. Several year later, when he discovered a poster advertising a bouillon cube with the word "Kub" pasted up on the walls of a house he had rented at Collioure for the summer, he threw a fit, claiming it was a provocation by the Cubists.

Not one to hold a grudge, Picasso liked to say: "Basically, you have to be true to yourself. Like the sun in the center of a thousand rays. This is why, for example, Matisse is Matisse. He has a sun in his gut." Picasso, who could dissect any painting at a glance, sensed a

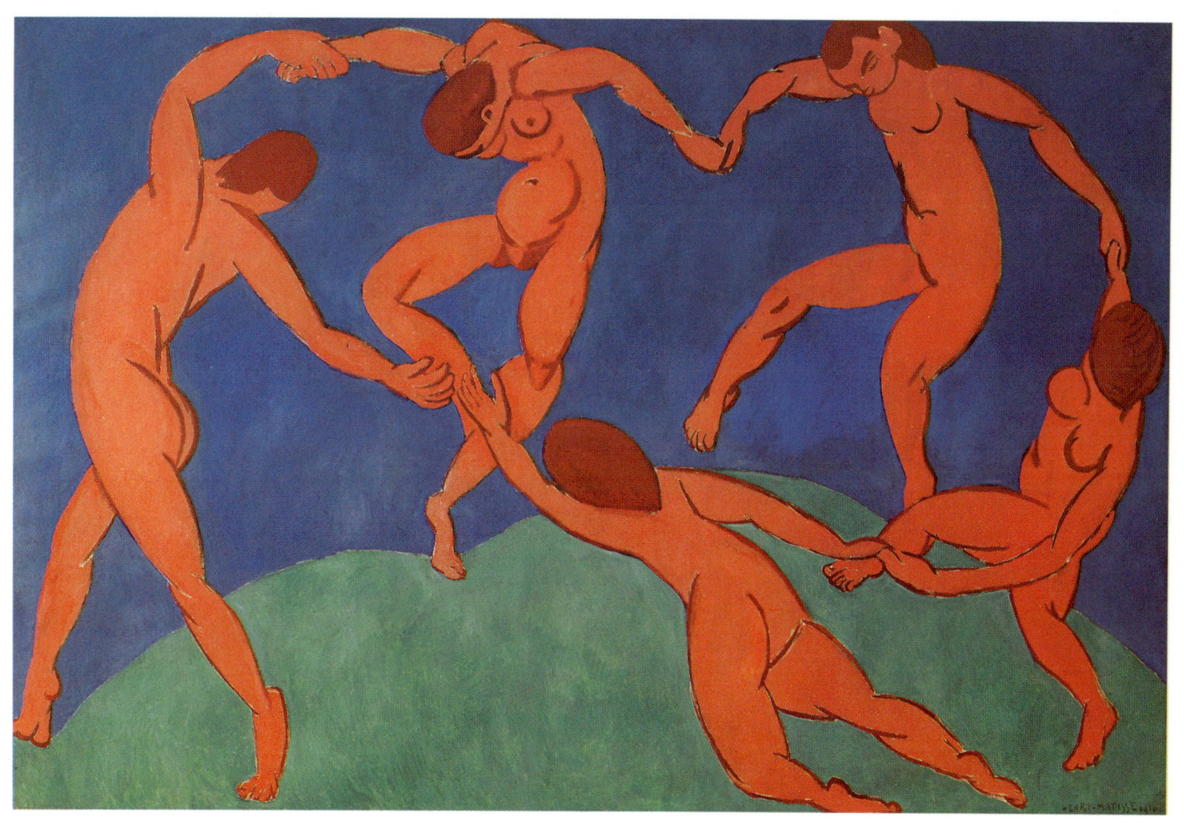

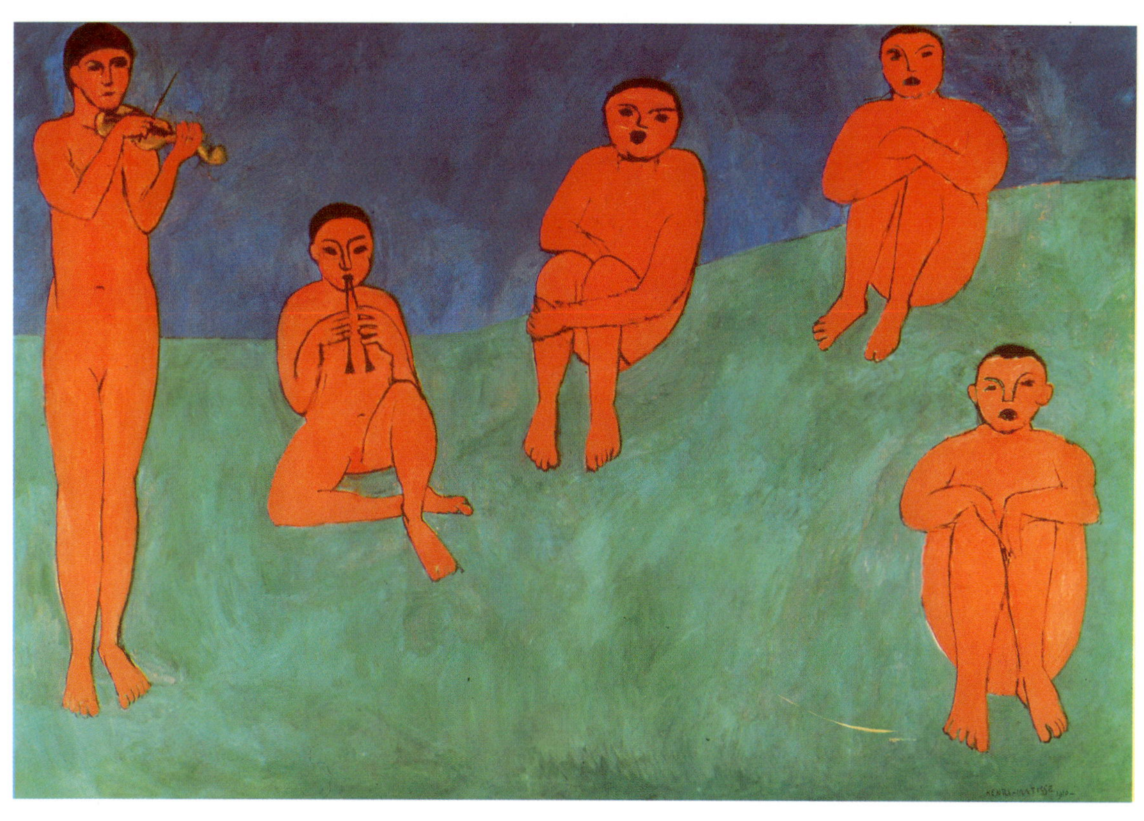

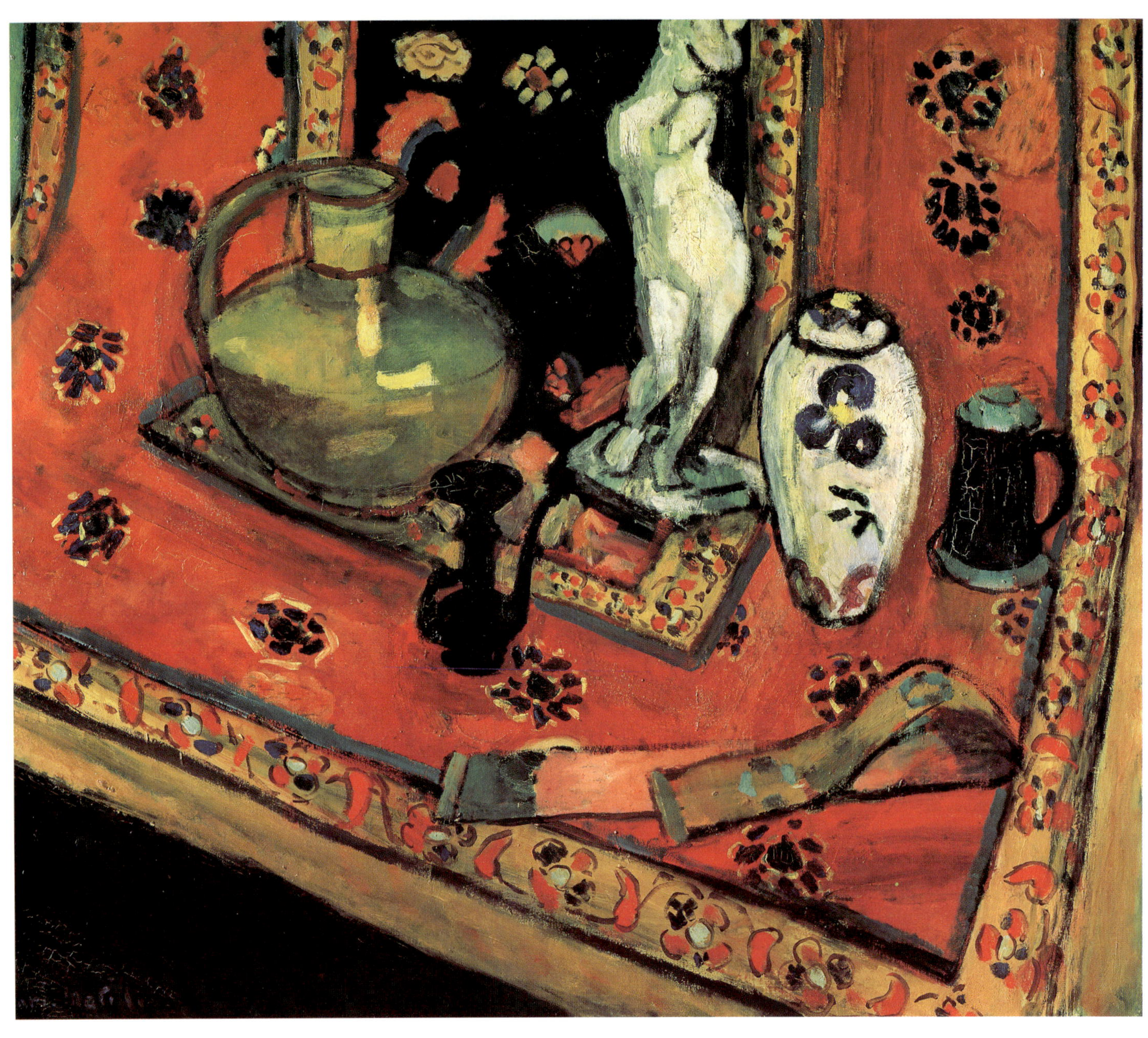

HENRI MATISSE
Still Life in Venitian Red
1908
Oil on canvas, 34⅛ x 40¼ in
(88 x 104 cm)
Moscow, Pushkin Museum of Fine Arts

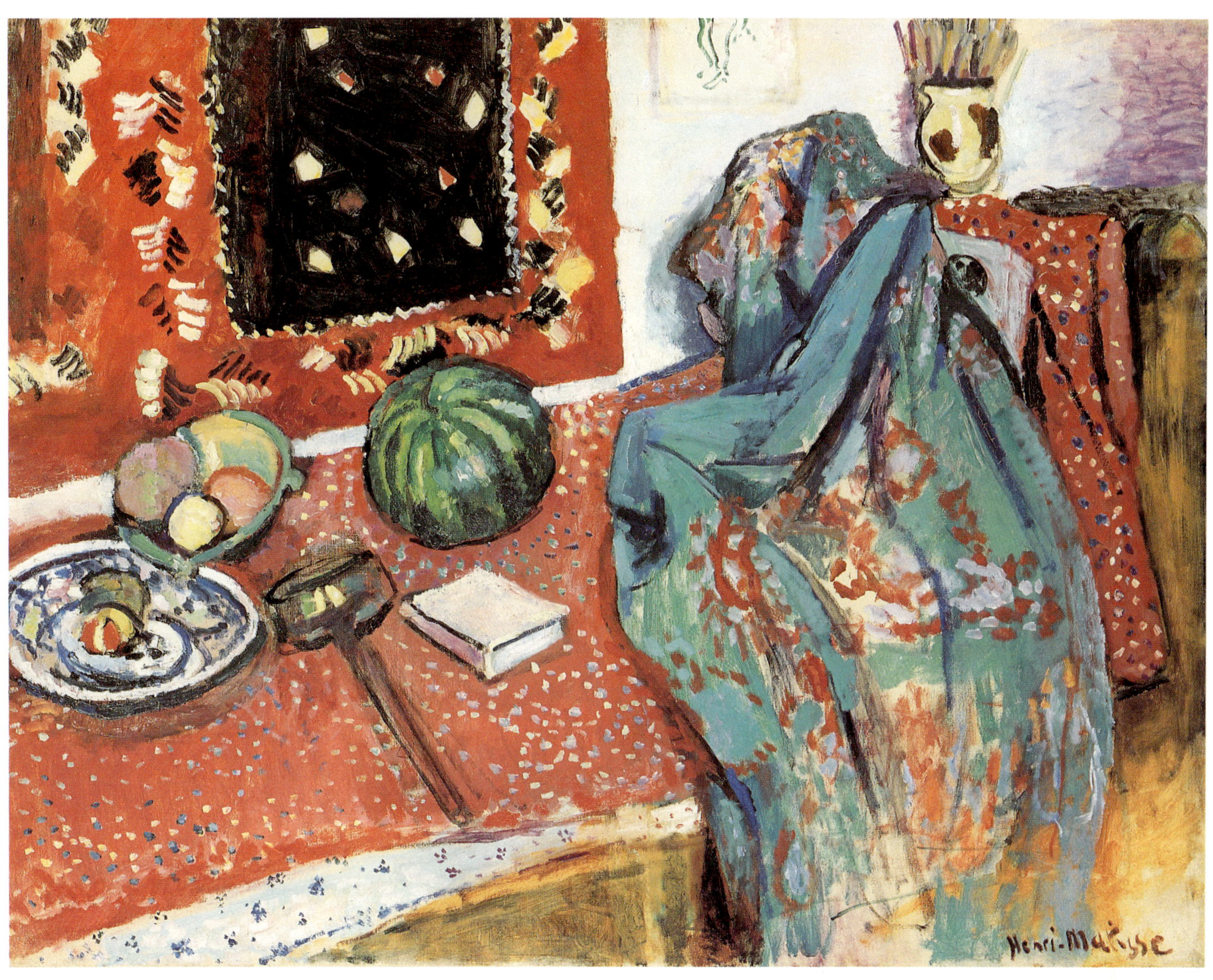

Henri Matisse
Still Life with a Red Rug
1906
Oil on canvas, 35 x 45⅞ in
(89 x 116.2 cm)
Grenoble, musée de Peinture
et de Sculpture (Agutte-Sembat Bequest)

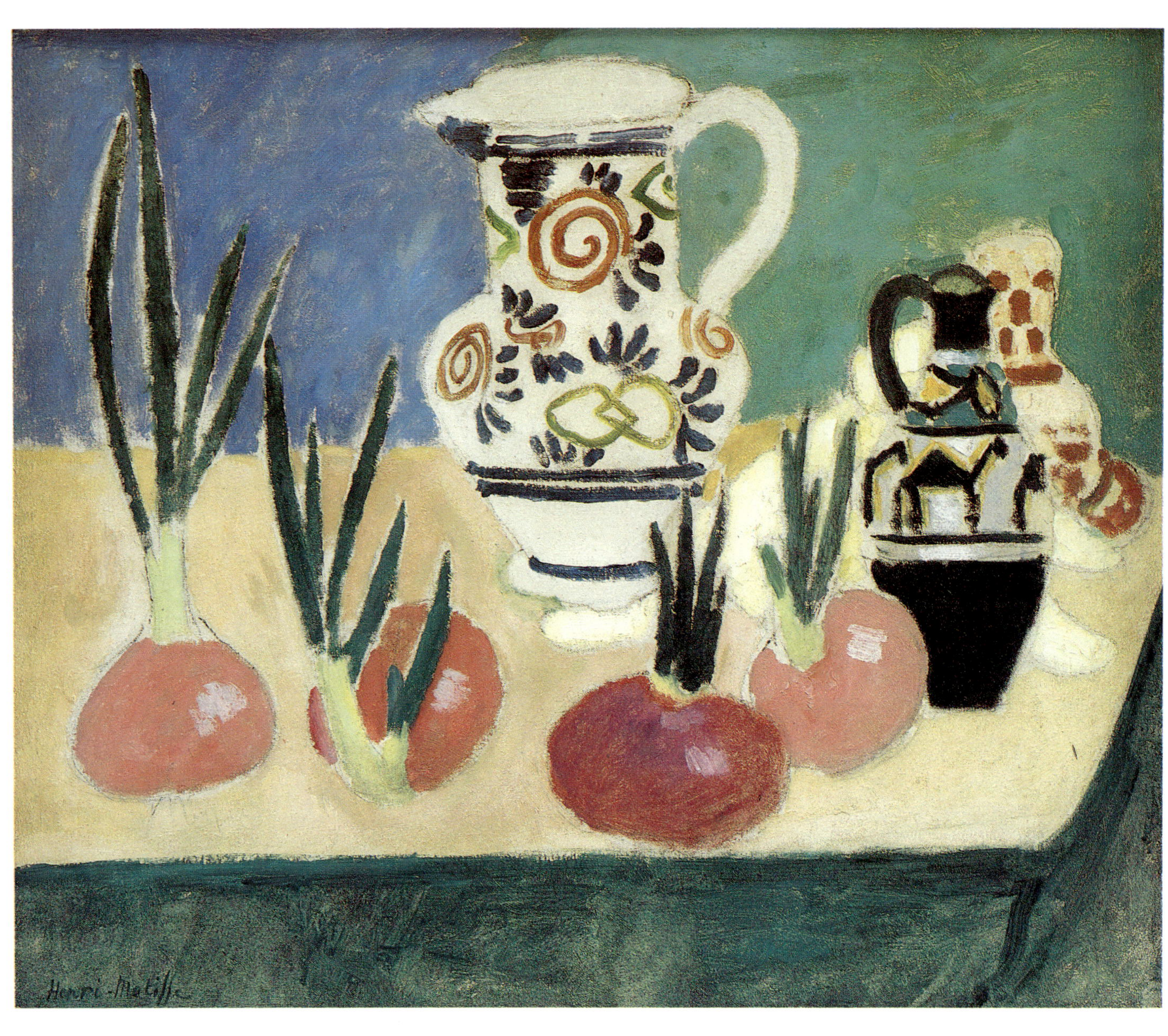

Henri Matisse
Still Life with Red Onions
1906
Oil on canvas, 18½ x 21¾ (46 x 55 cm)
Copenhagen, Statens Museum for Kunst

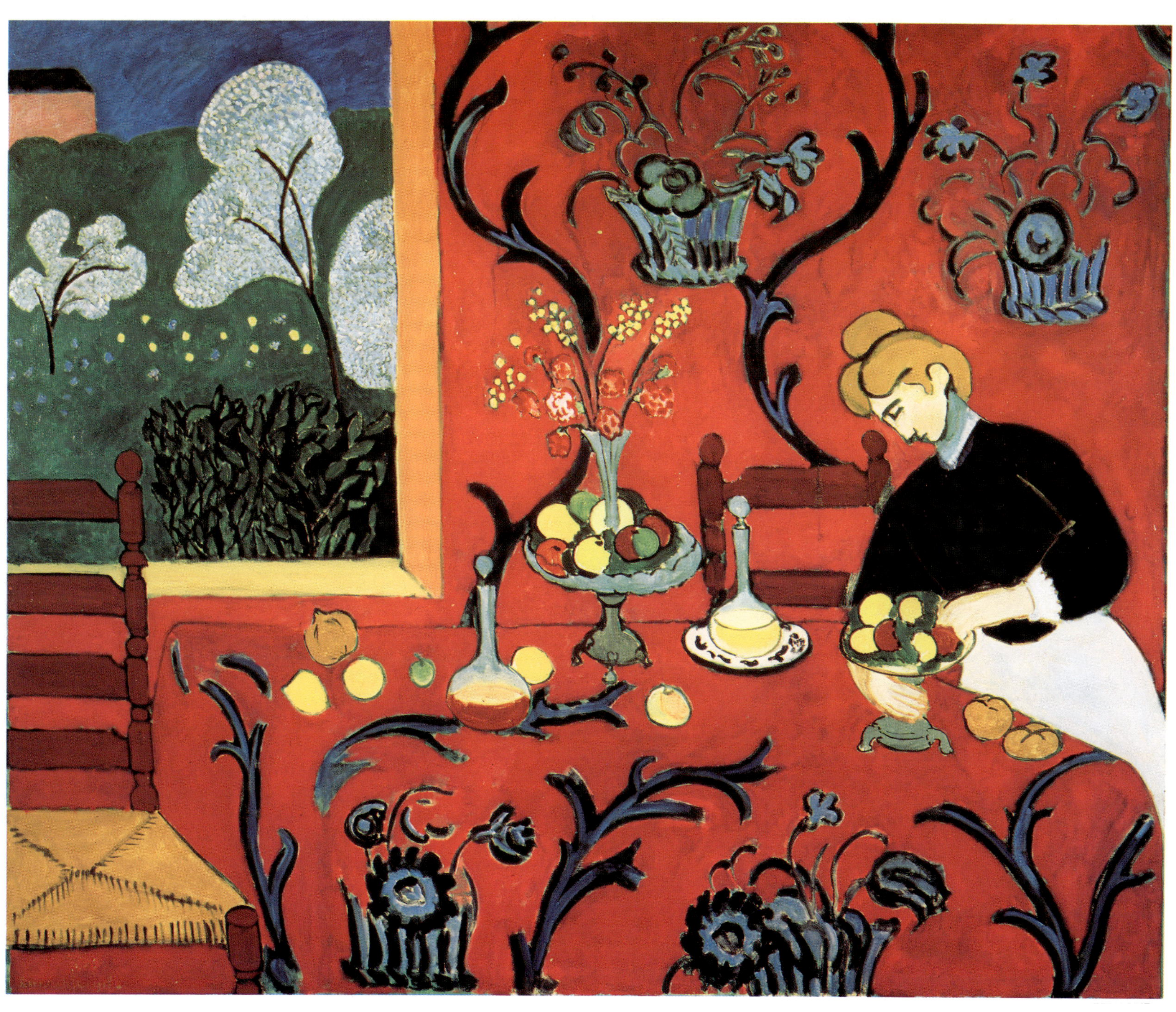

Henri Matisse
Harmony in Red / La desserte rouge
Paris, 1908
Oil on canvas, 70⅞ in x 72⅝ in
(178 x 219 cm)
St. Petersburg, Hermitage Museum

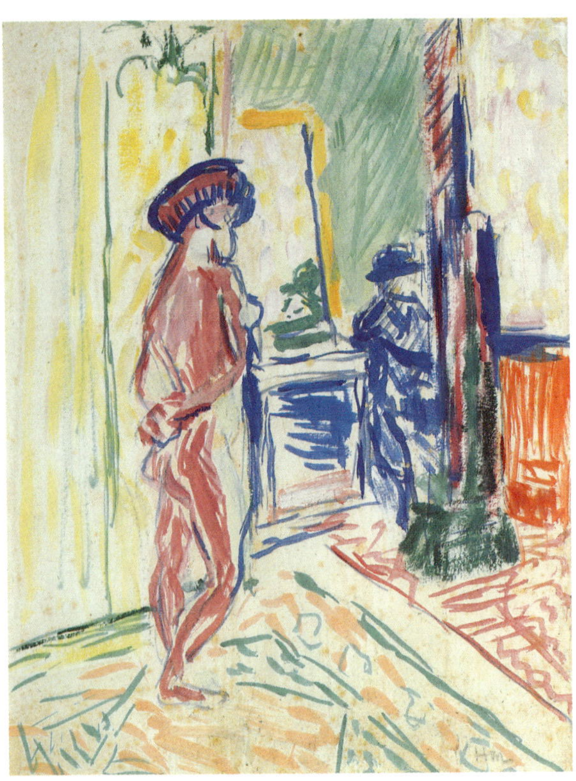

HENRI MATISSE
Study for a Nude in the Studio
Paris, 1904-1905
Oil and watercolor on canvas,
12¼ x 9½ in (31 x 24 cm)
Paris, musée national d'Art moderne

mastery in Matisse's work that he was unable to fathom. Indeed, there is no recipe or theory to explain Matisse's art and he made only a few meager statements to help the public and the critics understand his work. There may be a *Mystère Picasso*, but there is also a Matisse miracle, for Matisse put as much verve into creating beauty as Picasso put into creating savageness. Indeed, Picasso was fascinated by him.

To disregard Matisse's relationship with the Orient–and even to Orientalism–would leave much of the splendor of his work unexplained. For him–following in Delacroix's footsteps–the Orient began in Morocco, where he traveled in 1911 and in 1912 and, as with Gauguin, finished in Tahiti, which he visited in 1930. "I was influenced by Cézanne and the Orientals," he once remarked. His Moroccan landscapes are amazingly lush. The artist described his initial shock at the profusion of acanthus bushes that grew under great trees: "so high, and just as magnificent." He had encountered acanthus leaves only on the reproductions of Corinthian capitals that he had been assigned to copy at the Beaux-Arts. In another of his masterpieces, *Moroccans*, painted in 1916, Matisse curbed his passion for wild colors and integrated black–absent from his palette for some time–into the composition. From then on he treated black as a color. His oriental paintings, although rich with local atmosphere, evoke the purity of Islamic art with their limited range of tones and arabesques. They reach a peak of decorativeness and artificiality, yet at the same time appear more experimental in their handling of external reality. Still, the artist was not always able to avoid an excess of the exotic.

The Orient also inspired a series of Odalisques, his most questionable paintings in the sense that, not only did he go back to using an anecdotal subject-matter, but he also reinstated the techniques which accompany it: a combination of *chiaroscuro* and theatrical space. In these compositions the reclining woman "reposes like a Sultana... covered with sonorous jewels... on delicately scented beds...." These words of Baudelaire demonstrate the damaging influence of literature on painting. Curiously enough, a clear about-face took place in Matisse's reputation because of these paintings, suddenly considered to be the most accessible and praiseworthy of his work, and it was announced that the former Fauve had recanted and could finally be accepted in good society.

Was it to escape this pitfall that Matisse sailed for Tahiti in 1930? He worried more about the perils of success than about the harsh insults that he had been subjected to at the beginning of his career.

Invited to the Pittsburgh Art Festival as member of the Carnegie jury, after having been a laureate in 1927, he took advantage of the trip to continue on to the South Pacific for three months. At first he was disappointed; everything seemed too familiar. Yet, as soon as he turned his attention to the underwater flora that he studied with his nearsighted eyes fixed on the surface of the water, he was enchanted. "The light of the Pacific has an intoxicating quality for the spirit, comparable to looking into a golden cup." Matisse's stay in the Pacific islands was nothing like Gauguin's erotic and tragic pilgrimage, but an awareness of having discovered the innocence of a lost paradise.

Matisse is the only Fauve not to have changed direction. He questioned Fauvism's color, space, and light throughout his whole life, while his fellow artists repeated themselves or took other paths. This explains why his position in the art of our century has not ceased to grow until now, even though he remained unloved among the artists of his own generation for a long time.

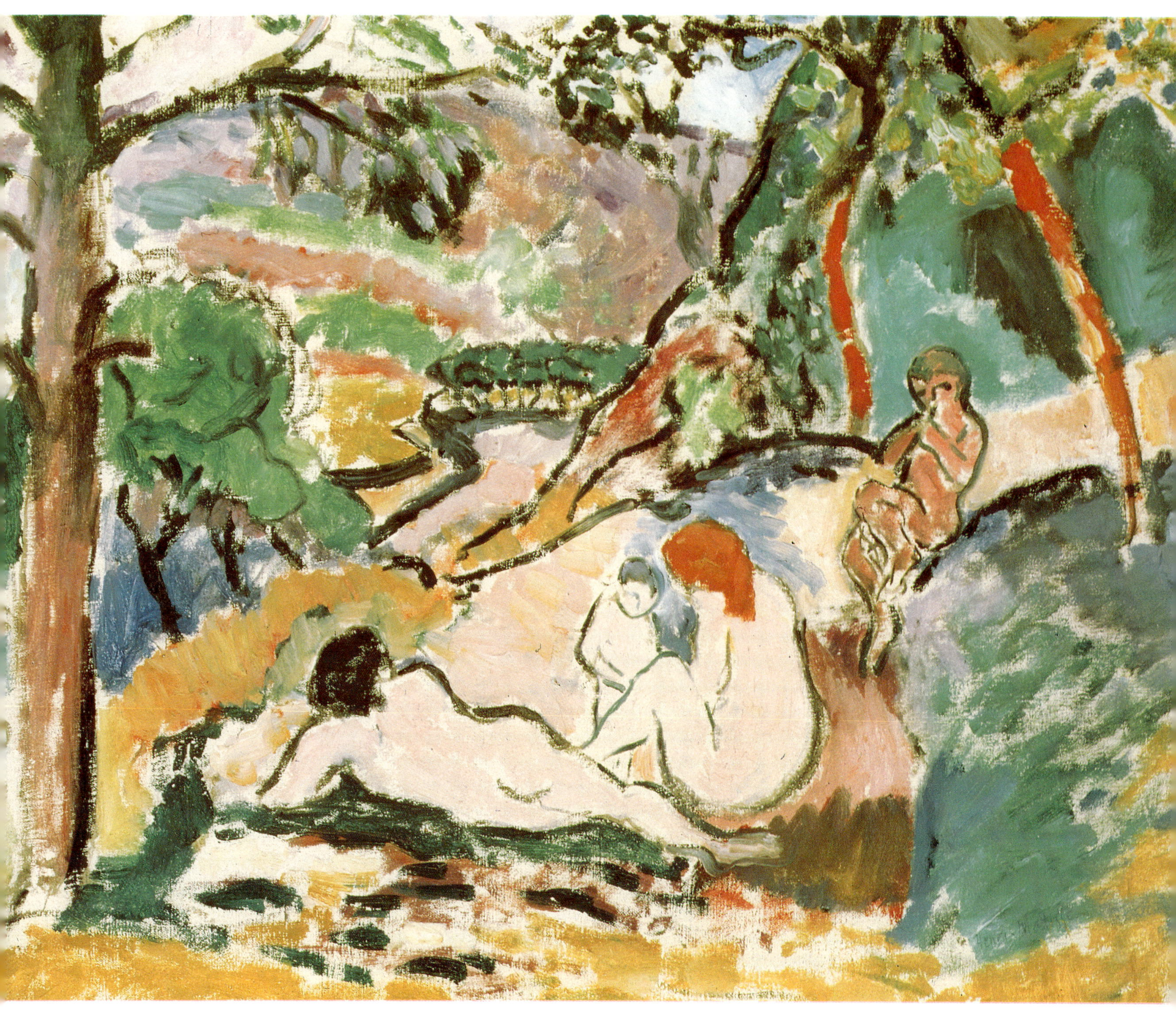

Henri Matisse
Pastoral
Paris, 1906
Oil on canvas, 18⅛ in x 21⅝ in
(46 x 55 cm)
Paris, musée d'Art moderne de la ville de Paris

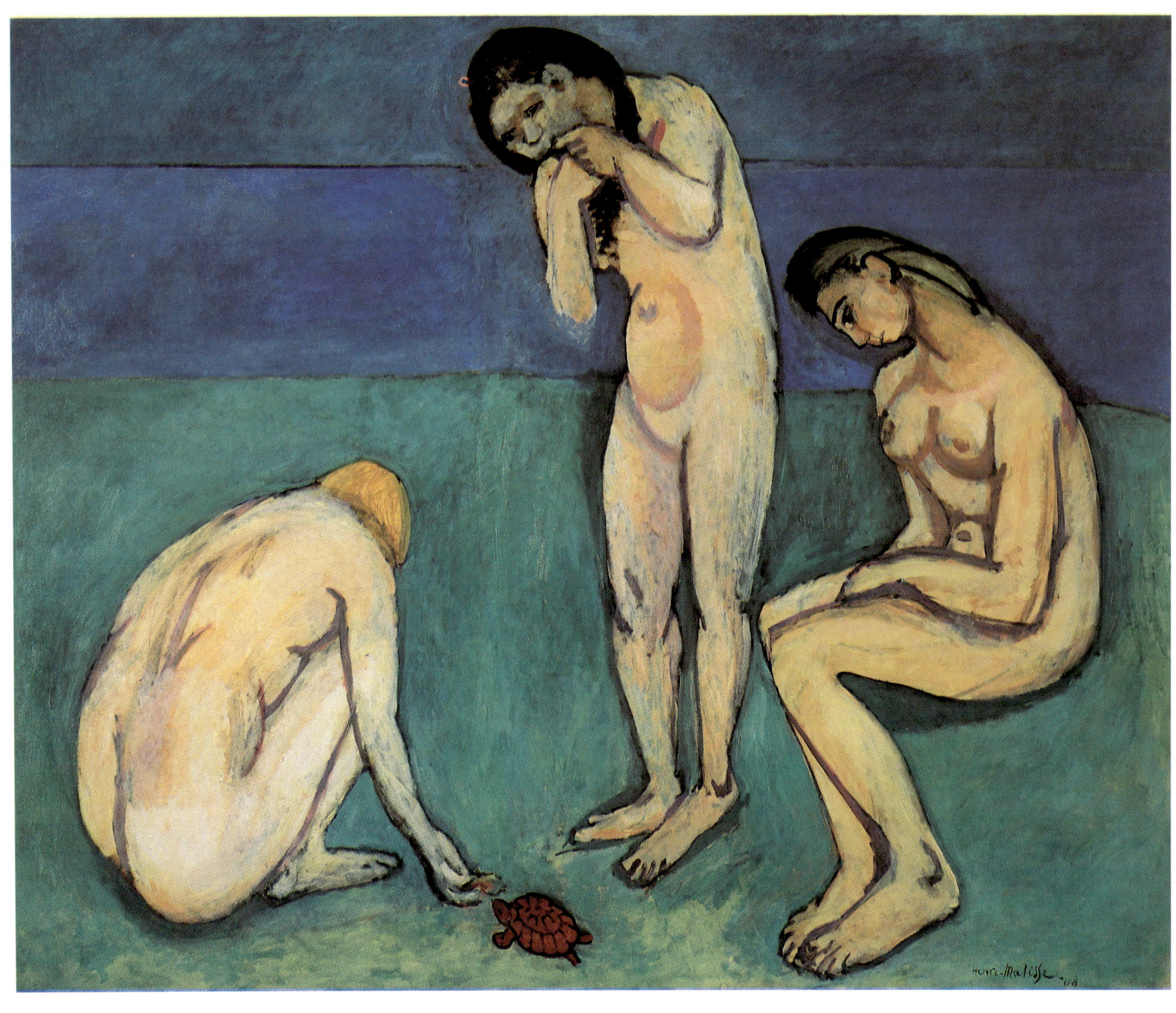

HENRI MATISSE
Bathers with a Turtle
Paris, 1908
Oil on canvas, 70½ in x 73¾
(179 x 220 cm)
St. Louis Art Museum
(Gift of Mr. and Mrs. Joseph Pulitzer, Jr.)

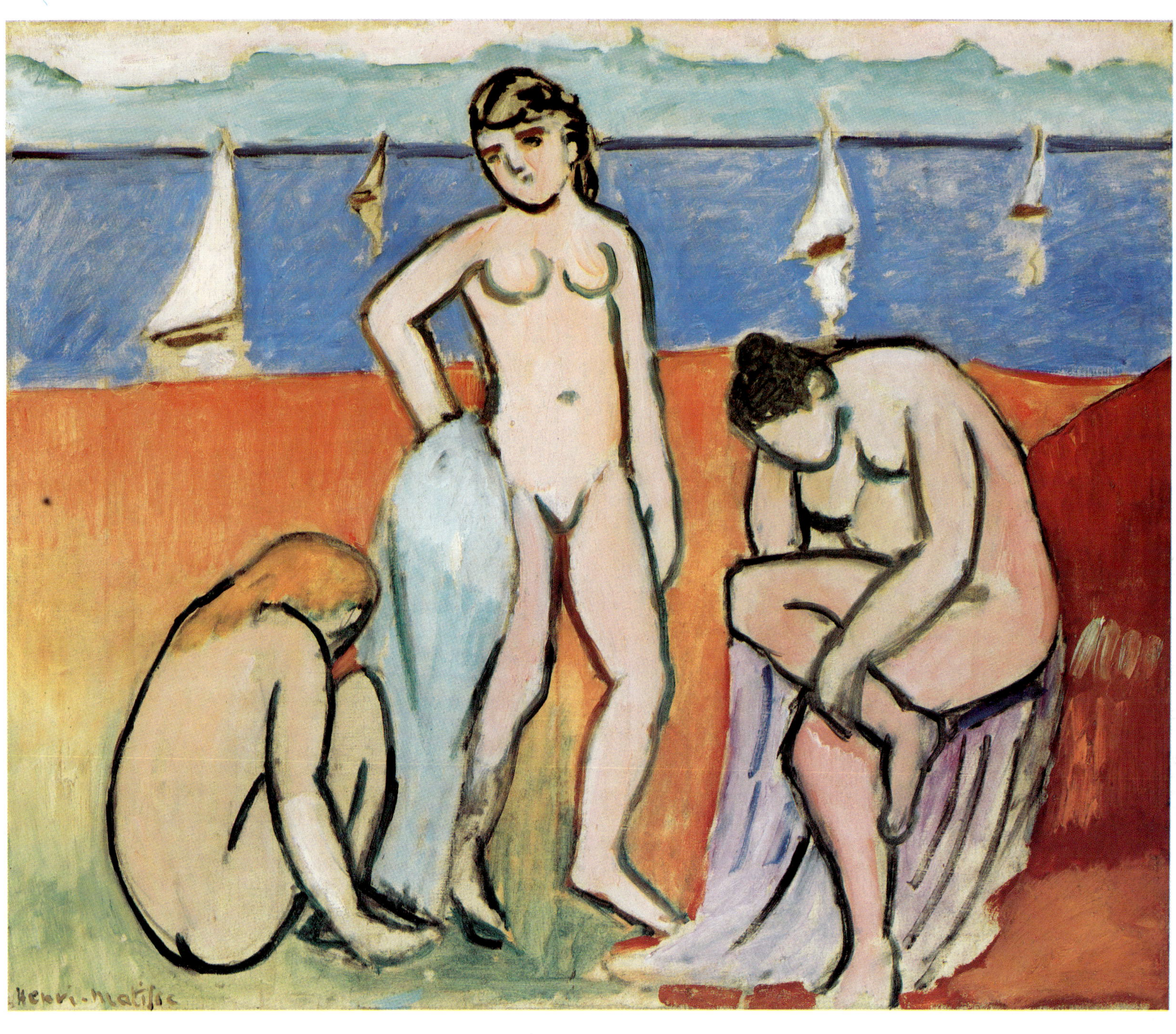

HENRI MATISSE
Three Bathers
Paris, 1907
Oil on canvas, 24 x 29⅞ in (61 x 73.5 cm)
Minneapolis, Institute of Modern Art
(Gift of Putman Dana McMillan)

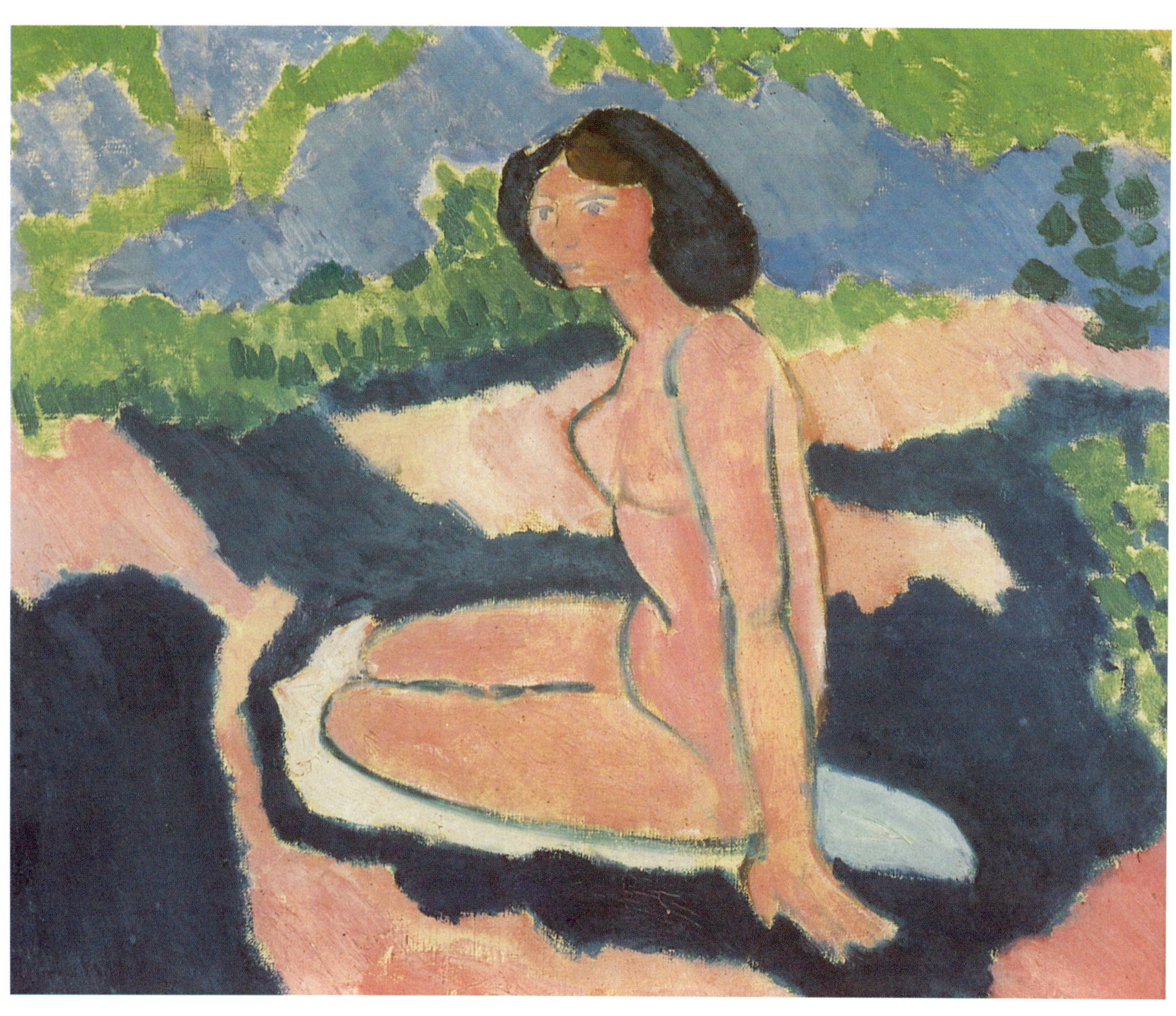

HENRI MATISSE
Small Seated Nude
Paris, 1909
Oil on canvas, 13 x 16⅛ (33 x 41 cm)
Grenoble, musée de Peinture
et de Sculpture (Agutte-Sembat Bequest)

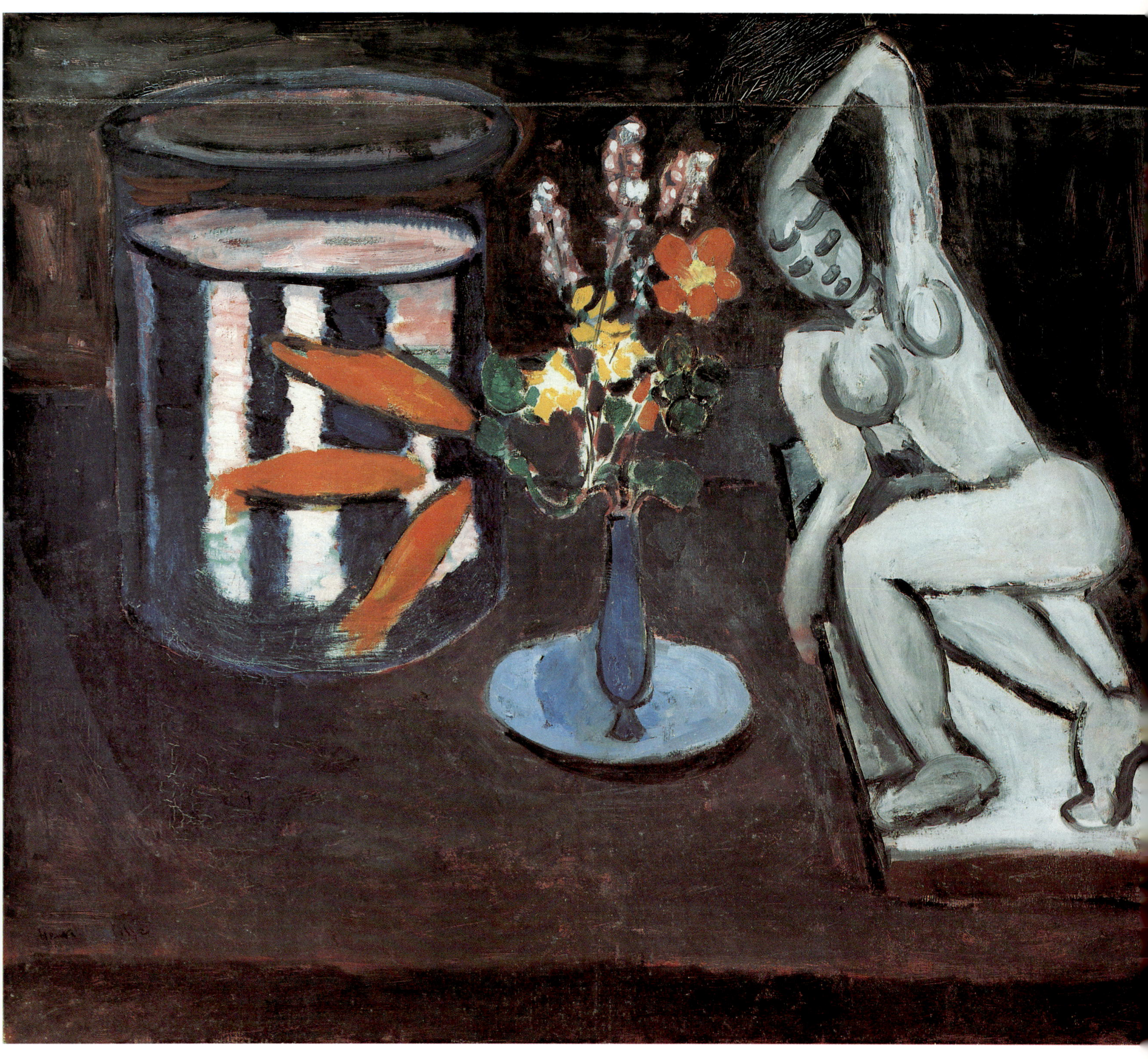

Henri Matisse
Still Life with Goldfish
Paris, 1909-1910
Oil on canvas, 32¼ x 36⅝ (82 x 93 cm)
Copenhagen, Statens Museum for Kunst

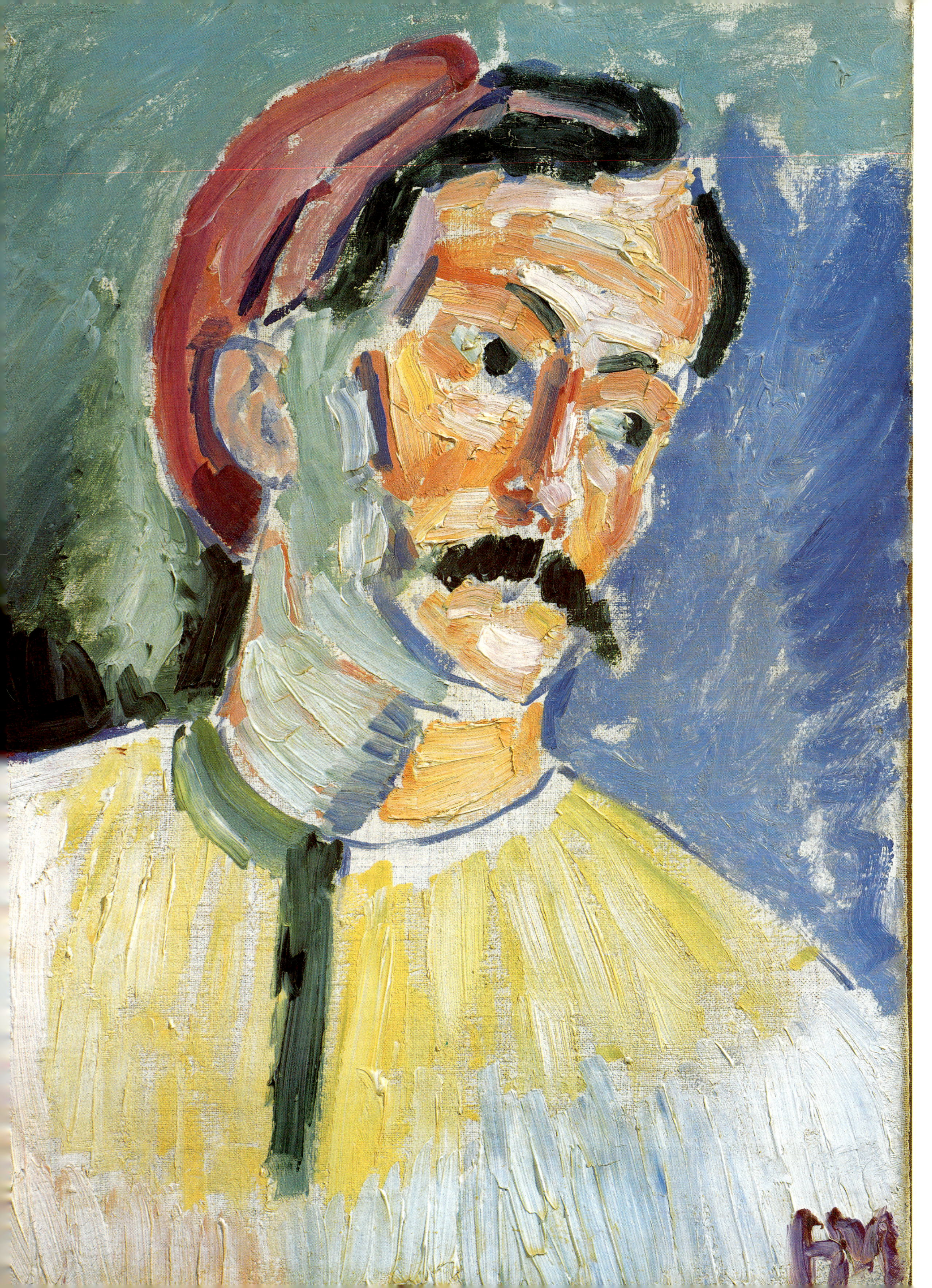

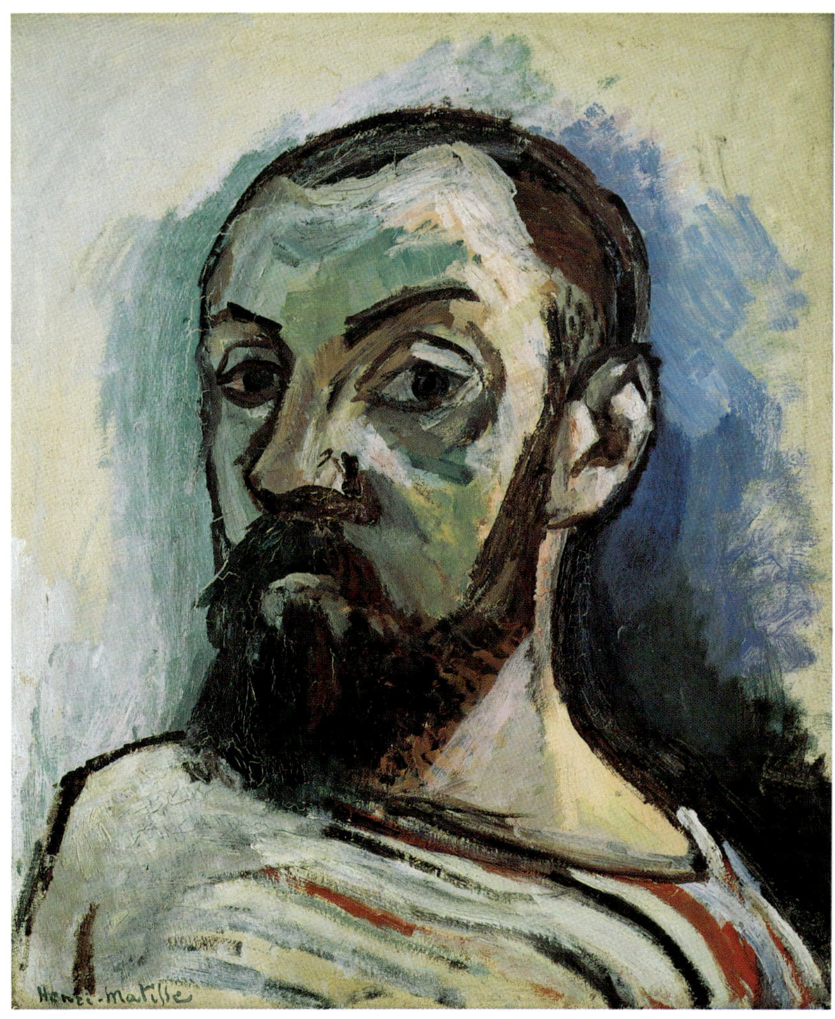

Henri Matisse
Self-Portrait
Paris, 1906
Oil on canvas, 21⅝ in x 18⅛ (55 x 46 cm)
Copenhagen, Statens Museum for Kunst

Opposite:

Henri Matisse
Portrait of Henri Derain
Paris, 1905
Oil on canvas, 15⅜ in x 11⅜ (39 x 29 cm)
London, Tate Gallery

It was at the Armory Show in New York in 1913 that America discovered the modern art which it had so largely ignored until then. The room exhibiting the Cubists was called the "horror chamber" by the public and the critics, but it was Matisse's work that received the worst insults, and these were minor next to the hostile demonstration he encountered when the show moved on to Chicago. The professors and students of the Chicago Art Institute lynched an effigy of the artist and two copies of his paintings were burned in the middle of a riotous crowd that had gathered on Michigan Avenue. But if America has since largely recognized Matisse's genius, France, it would appear, still does not hold this painter of painters in its heart. The French State was unable to keep *The Swimming Pool* inside its borders, and this painting is now the pride of the Museum of Modern Art in New York.

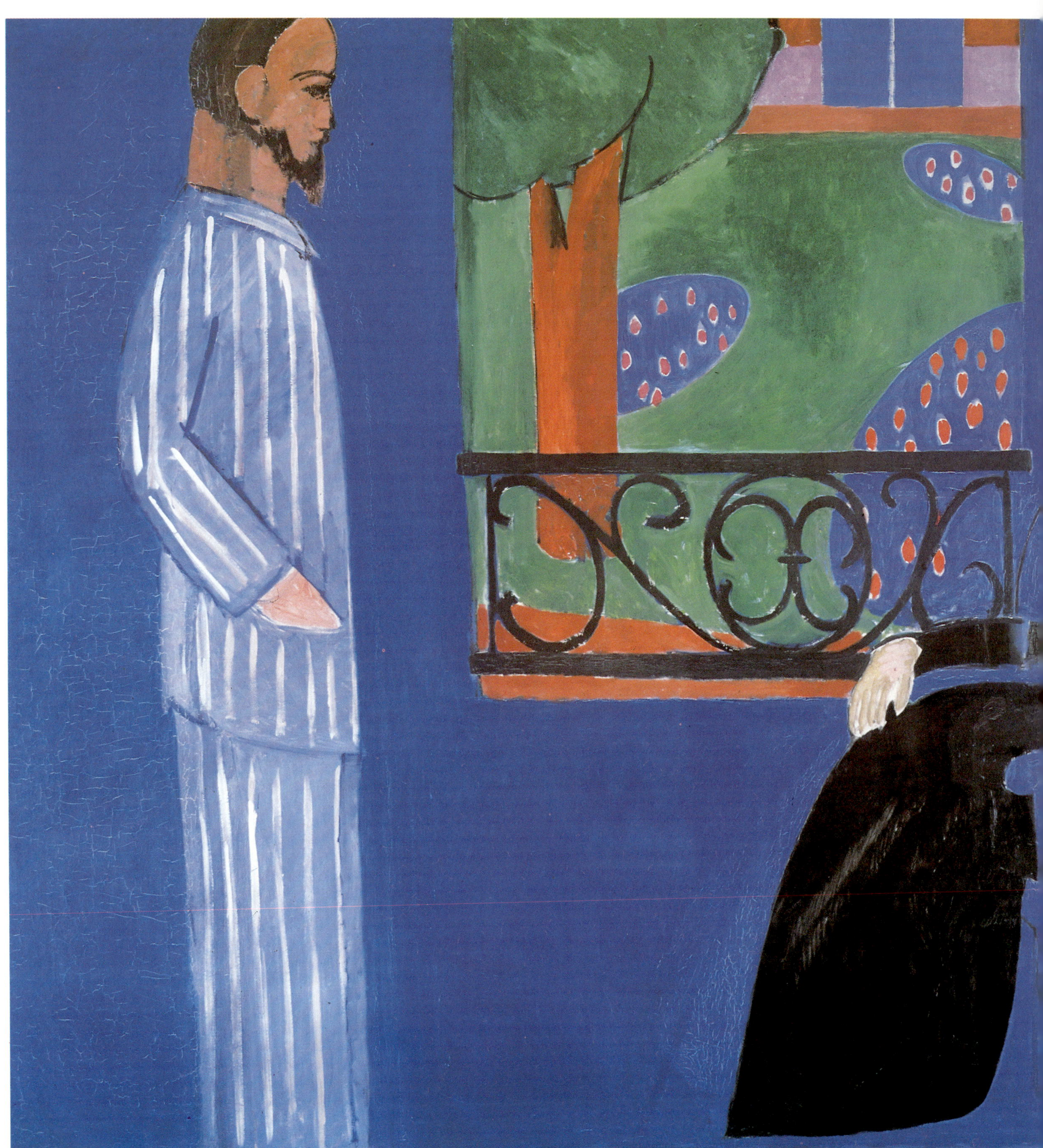

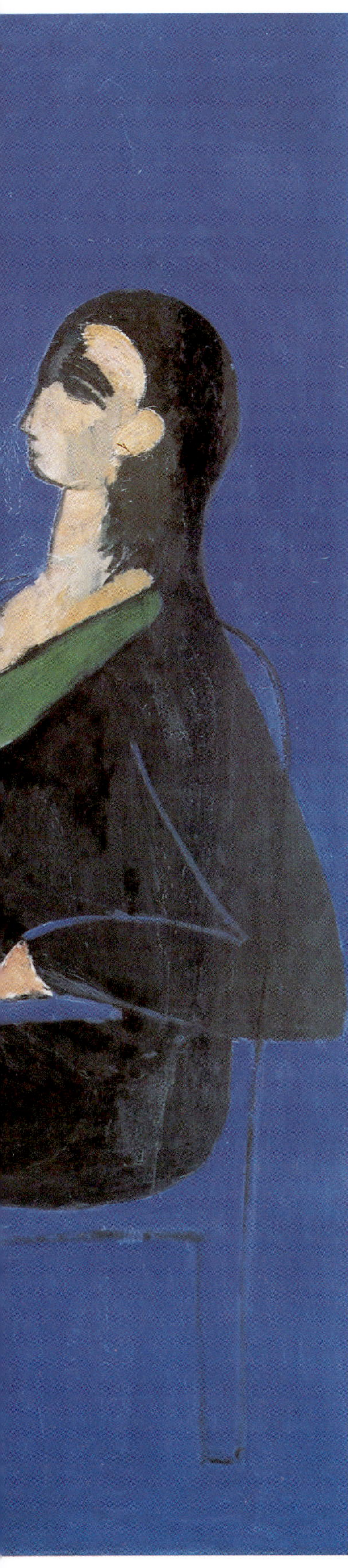

HENRI MATISSE
Conversation
Paris, 1911
Oil on canvas, 69⅝ x 71⅜ in
(177 x 217 cm)
St. Petersburg, Hermitage Museum

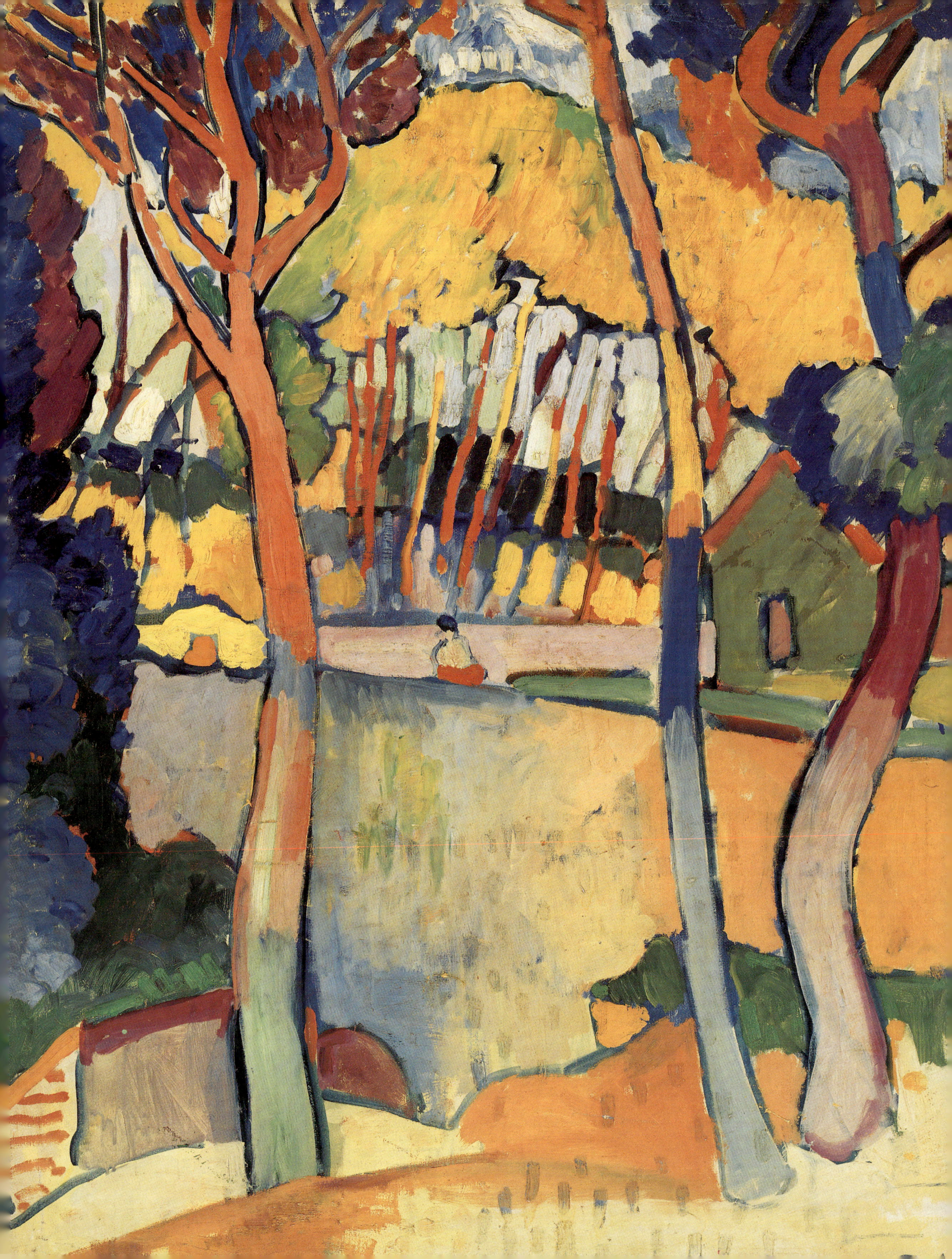

Between Observation and Elation:

Derain

Or a Copy after Ghirlandaio

André Derain, born in Chatou, near Paris, on June 17, 1880, was eleven years younger than Matisse. His father, who ran a catering business at 87, rue de Saint-Germain, was a member of the Municipal Council and expected his son to enter the prestigious Ecole Polytechnique–an aim shared by most well-to-do members of the bourgeoisie. André was sent to the most traditional primary and secondary schools–Sainte-Croix-du-Vésinet and Collège Chaptal in Paris–to be well prepared for the entrance examination to the top engineering school. But the young man's tastes ran to painting, sports and music instead and the family's ambitions for him were rapidly dashed. In his own words: "My mother used to tell me that I was good for nothing, that I would get nowhere, that I never carried anything through and that I was a failure." He left high school at the age of 16 with poor grades in all subjects except ornamental and linear drawing, in which he excelled.

In 1900 in Chatou, Derain met Maurice de Vlaminck, a musician and bicycle-racer who was also destined to become a painter. He entered the Académie Carrière in Paris and met Matisse. The mature artist was able to convince Derain's parents to allow their son to take up an artistic career by making flattering remarks about his great potential. Derain was entirely taken by Matisse's wisdom and by Vlaminck's pictorial vigor. From the very start, his work demonstrated exceptional talent. Showing remarkable ease, a strong and ardent technique, a generous and bold design, he was endowed with a particularly passionate disposition. It was he who compared color to dynamite, saying that color should be projected on canvases by the tubeful. His *Portrait of Matisse*, executed in 1905, for example, is a masterpiece of drive and conviction.

André Derain
Three Trees at L'Estaque
1906
Oil on canvas, 39½ x 31½ in
(100. 33 x 80 cm)
Toronto, Art Gallery of Ontario

André Derain
Portrait of Henry Matisse
1905
Oil on canvas, 18 x 13¾ in (46 x 34.9 cm)
London, Tate Gallery

Always using vibrant tones, he took pains to use softer, duller ones, and to control his exuberance by scrupulously constructing the composition.

Whereas his friend Vlaminck had an aversion for museums, even despising their smell, Derain on the contrary spent long hours at the Louvre where he discovered the Primitives, for whom he felt an "intense passion" in the sense that for him they represented "the true, pure and absolute art." Like many apprentice painters at the time, he held a card allowing him to copy the great masterpieces of the Museum. One day while working in the Louvre galleries, he ran into Linaret, a former classmate from the Collège Chaptal, whom he had not seen for a while and who had also become a painter. Linaret was busy copying Uccello's *The Battle of San Romano*, using nothing but pure tones. Struck by his friend's audacity, Derain undertook the same exercise with *The Bearing of the Cross* by Ghirlandaio (attributed today to Biagio d'Antonio), using such violent colors that he was nearly ejected from the Louvre for "*atteinte à la beauté*" (defiling beauty). His gaudy rendition appears altogether tame today compared with Picasso's version of Velasquez's *Las Meninas* or Manet's *Déjeuner sur l'herbe*.

We may notice here a certain pattern in Derain's behavior; from the start he manifested a marked indecisiveness stemming from two different sources, his instincts and his culture, for he did not possess a Matisse-type analytical mind. Even during Fauvism's wildest moments, Derain never abandoned his pronounced taste for composition. This led him in 1908 to experiment with Cubist-type stylization, as well as to become one of the principal instigators of the "return to order" advocated throughout Europe around 1925, a movement which tried to put a stop to avant-gardism and recommended going back to more traditional techniques.

Chatou was to Fauvism what Argenteuil was to Impressionism

The circumstances that made Derain's and Vlaminck's paths cross remind us of how Bouvard and Pécuchet met each other by chance at the beginning of Flaubert's novel. Indeed, the two artists had already run into each other in Chatou where they both lived, for it was a small town and everyone knew everyone else. But their mutual fondness came about on account of a train accident from which they both escaped unharmed. The accident is said to have taken place at La Garenne-Bezons in June 1900, in the aftermath of which the two young men decided to walk back home along the tracks. It may actually have been just a engine breakdown; Charles Chassé was able to establish from the archives of the western suburban railway line that no derailment took place on the Paris–Saint-Germain line in that year.

Even if the Garenne-Bezons accident was made up, the association of the two artists certainly was not. For ten francs a month, they rented the large dining room of an old inn called "Levanneur" situated between Chatou's two bridges near the Fournaise restaurant where Renoir painted *The Luncheon of a Boating Party* in 1881. They believed that the surrounding elements–the trees and the barges on the Seine–would help them restructure an Ile-de-France landscape which, to their young eyes, had been excessively disintegrated into dots by the Impressionists. To this end, they used choppy brushstrokes

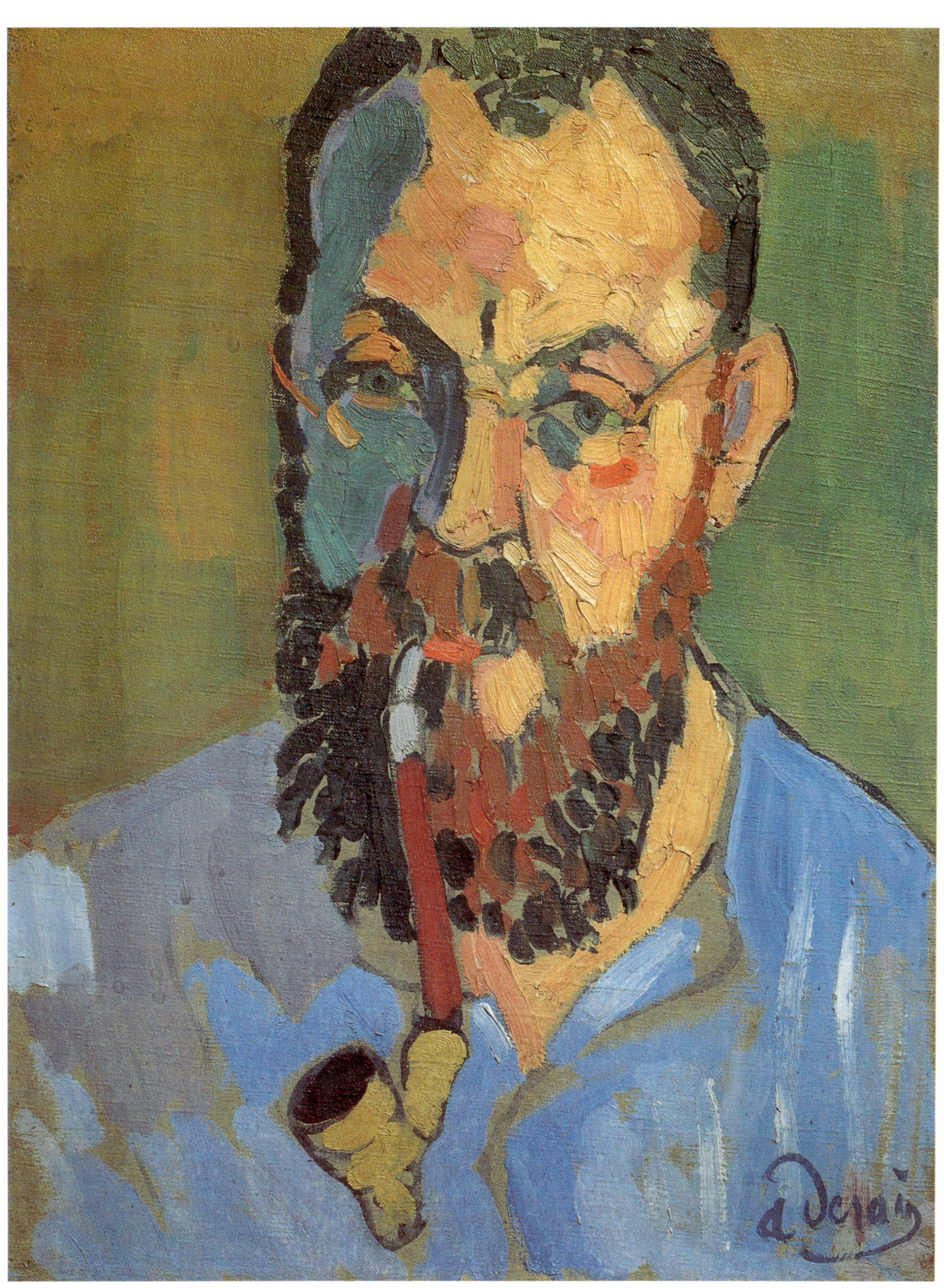
a Derain

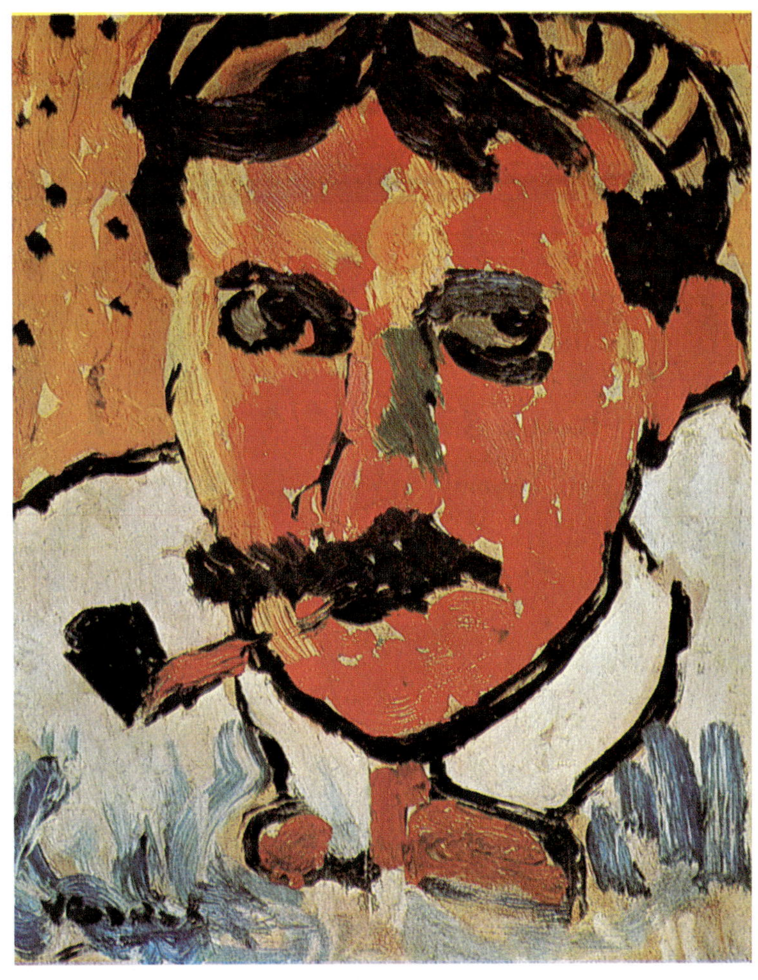

MAURICE DE VLAMINCK
Portrait of Derain
1905
Oil on canvas, $10\frac{3}{4}$ x $8\frac{3}{4}$ in
(27.3 x 22.2 cm)
Mexico, Mr. and Mrs. Jacques Gelman
collection

Opposite:

ANDRÉ DERAIN
Portrait of Maurice de Vlaminck
1905
Oil on canvas, $16\frac{1}{4}$ x 13 in (41.3 x 33 cm)
Chartres, musée des Beaux-Arts

overloaded with paint to produce bright impastoes of highly saturated hues, with the indifference of the color-blind. Their painting technique showed a common sensitivity, but their ideas always diverged. Derain himself felt that nothing was to be gained by a lack of culture, while Vlaminck repeatedly expressed his aversion to museums and his particular dislike for anything vaguely scholarly. He lambasted the "Classics" with the declaration: "Science gives me a toothache."

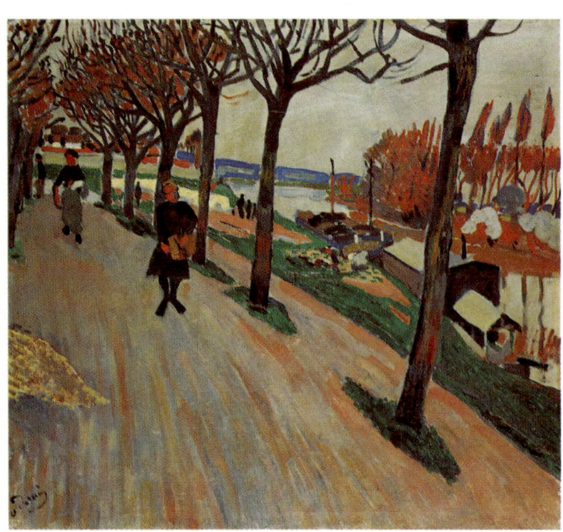

ANDRÉ DERAIN
The Banks of the Seine at Le Pecq
1904-1905
Oil on canvas, 33½ x 37½ in (85 x 95 cm)
Paris, musée national d'Art moderne

Derain's paintings from this exhilarating 15-month period of common experimentation are mostly rough attempts influenced by Van Gogh and by the Neo-Impressionists: *The Seine at Chatou*, which is difficult to date, or *Chatou*, painted toward 1904. It was, however, the period of his first successes. In July 1905, Matisse came to visit the two colleagues and took Derain off to Collioure with him. The paintings that Derain executed during this stay are symphonies of vibrant red, yellow, blue, and green juxtaposed dabs that indicate a certain maturity. Derain, less at ease than Matisse about using this technique, did not fundamentally question perspective devices, for he continued to compose with the kind of perspective that he so fancied, drawn from a elevated point. Nevertheless, the works that he painted during this period are now hung among the masterpieces of Fauvism.

Collioure aside, the usual themes of Derain's paintings were mundane realities: rows of trees in close-up with flowers in the background; low houses in small villages surrounded by fields in the Seine-et-Oise region; river banks with *guinguettes* filled to capacity on Sundays; or less idyllic subjects from the unattractive semi-rural, semi-urban suburbs of the city populated by laborers forced to struggle through life in hostile conditions *(The Bridge of Chatou*, 1904-1905).

Occasionally one hears mention of a Chatou School of painting which seems somewhat inappropriate, for it never consisted of more than two adepts. But in taking into consideration the newness of Derain's and Vlaminck's approach to painting, it is entirely fitting to make an analogy with Argenteuil which, between 1871 and 1874, had been the Mecca of Impressionism.

In his search for self-knowledge, Derain had the very clear feeling that the age of realistic painting was over and that nothing would ever be the same again; but at the same time, he could find no one to show him the way. He distrusted thought and feeling, and believed that to feel and to express oneself were two very different actions. For him, expression was a complex process, while feeling, by itself was insufficient to produce form. He complained moreover: "Form will be the end of me." And in truth it was many years later when he went back to the *beau métier*. For the time being, Derain's brushstrokes were earthy and generous. In spite of the scandal provoked by the daubings exhibited in Room VII at the Salon d'Automne, he sold three paintings to the Russian collector Ivan Morozov.

Two Stays in London

The well-established art dealer Ambroise Vollard, who had just bought a large number of Derain's works, put the young artist under contract. Vollard expected to promote Derain's production, as he had done for Monet during many trips to London between 1870 and 1904. Monet left for London for the first time in the autumn of 1870–followed shortly by his wife and son–to avoid being drafted into the army when the Franco-Prussian war broke out while he was living in

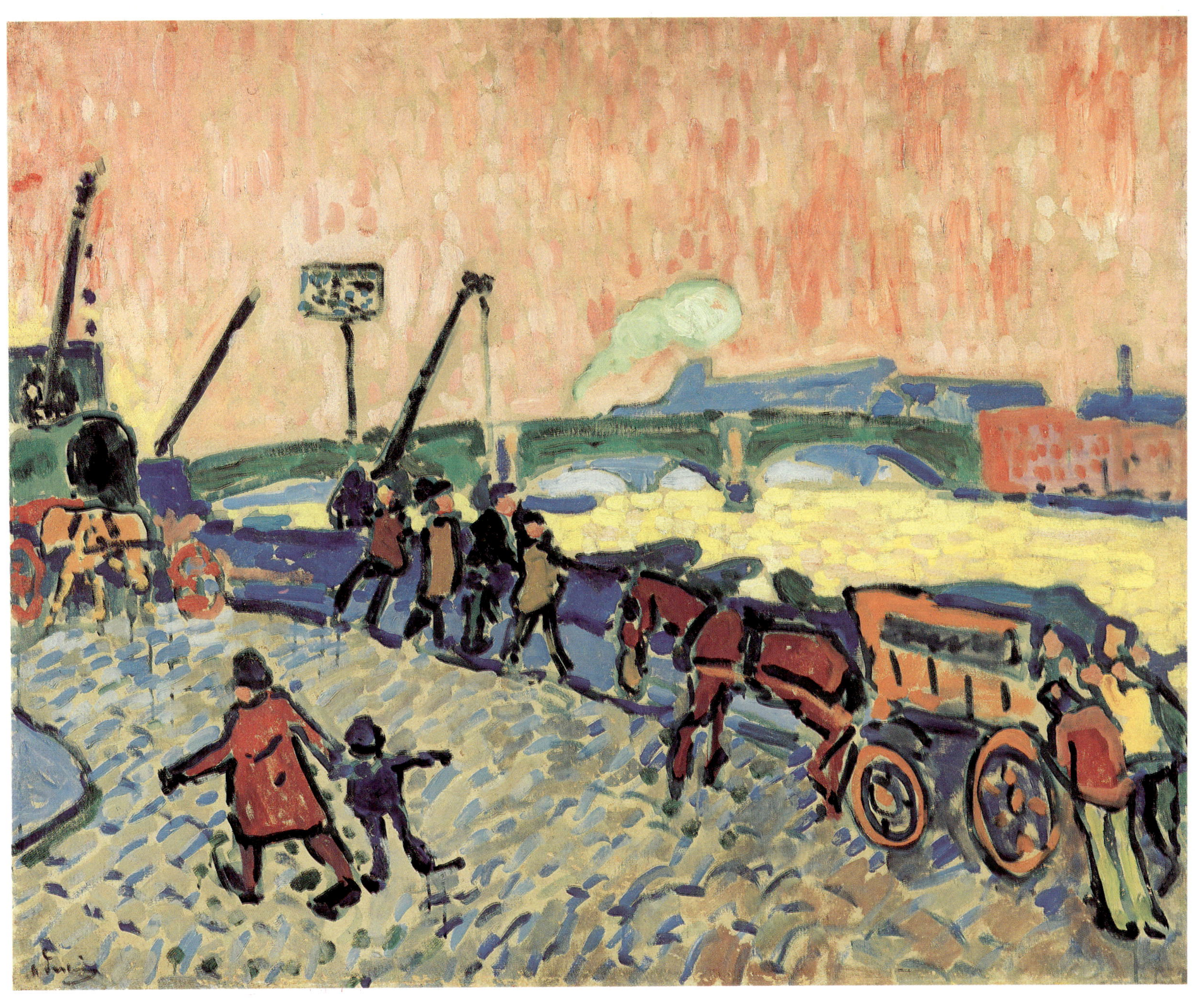

ANDRÉ DERAIN
Le Pecq
1905
Oil on canvas, 32 x 39¼ in (81 x 100 cm)
Paris, musée national d'Art moderne

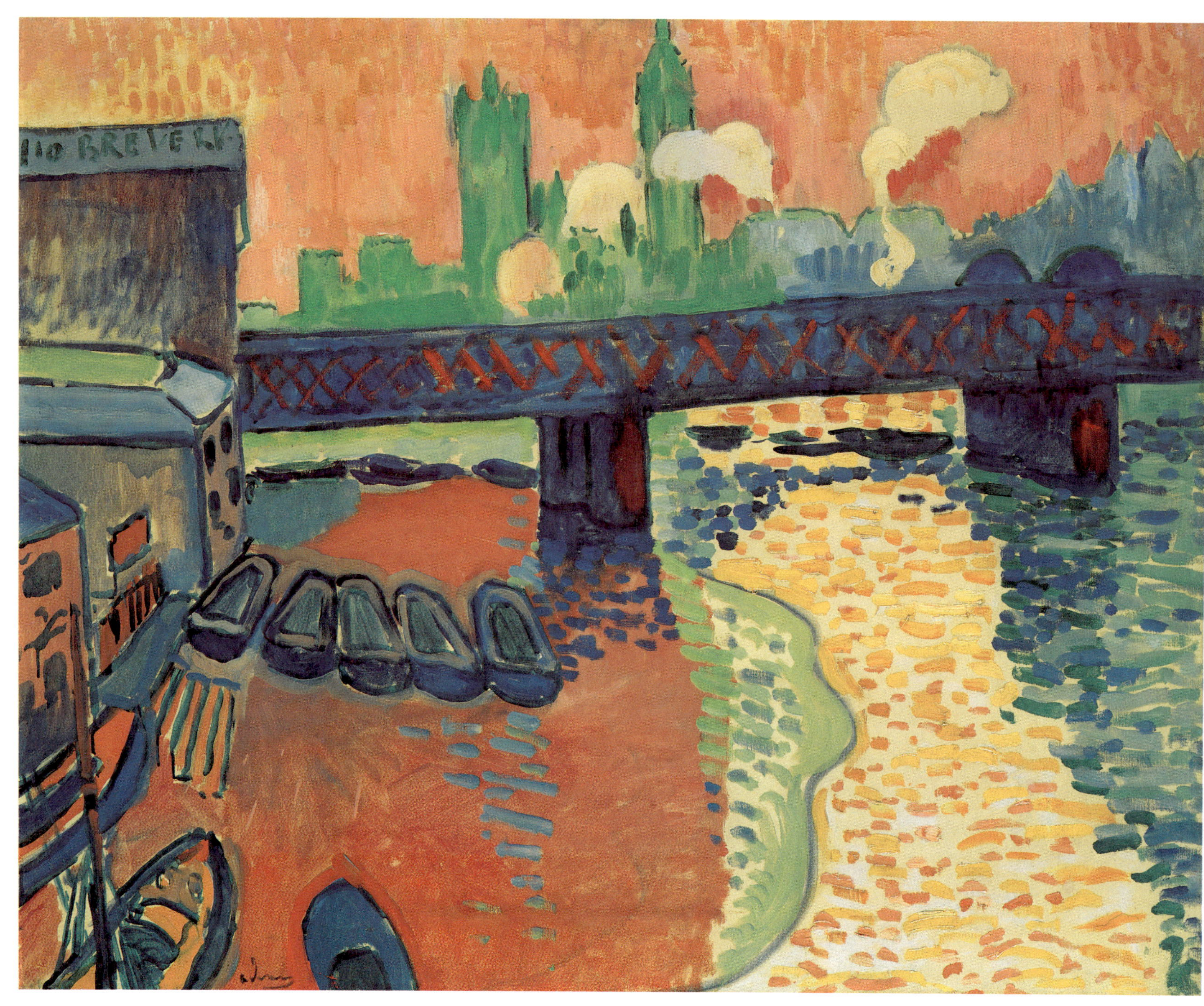

ANDRÉ DERAIN
Charing Cross Bridge, London
1906
Oil on canvas, $31\frac{1}{2}$ x $39\frac{1}{2}$ in
(80.3 x 100.3 cm)
Washington, National Gallery of Art
(John Hay Whitney collection)

Trouville, on the coast of Normandy. In the company of Pissarro, also there in exile, he became acquainted with Constable and Turner in the London museums and thoroughly admired the constant variations of light in the latter's work. Monet did not produce any remarkable paintings on this first trip but the ones he executed during his last stay in England–particularly those of the House of Parliament, painted in 1904 from a window at Saint-Thomas Hospital–display the same acute analysis of retinal impressions as the Haystacks and Rouen Cathedral series. The important point was no longer the subject-matter but the depiction of atmospheric effects produced by minute surface accidents, each acting as sort of a prism and decomposing the rays of light in a different way.

Since Monet's London paintings found a public of art-lovers, Vollard had no difficulty convincing his young protégé to set up his easel on the banks of the Thames. Actually, Derain made two visits to London, in November 1905 and in 1906 from the end of January until mid-March. He disliked the English in general, except for the women whose blond hair, blue eyes and rosy cheeks seemed to him to have been intentionally devised by nature so that they could be seen through the fog. He wrote: "I hate the sad, hypocritical and complaining English temperament; everything is dead here. There is no noise, even in a crowded restaurant. I saw a port with boats coming in and a group of stevedores finishing their work and I thought I was dreaming; there was no noise." On the other hand he was thrilled by the Thames with its piers and bridges such as the Westminster and Charing Cross and the buildings along the river such as the Neo-Gothic Parliament, as well as its portuary activity, so different from the atmosphere of the Seine.

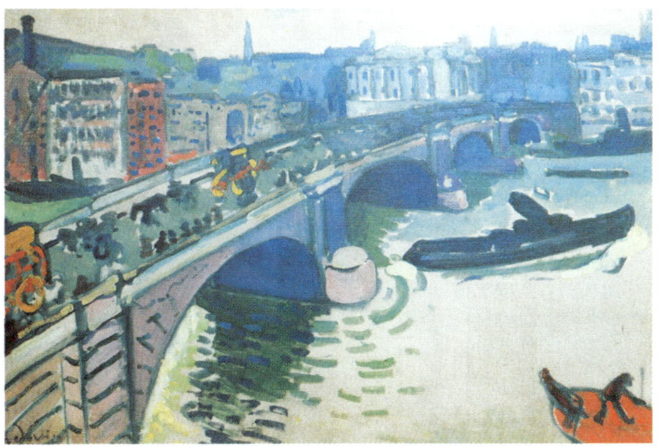

André Derain
London Bridge
1907
Oil on canvas, 24¾ x 37½ in
(63 x 95.5 cm)
Zurich, private collection

Did Derain deliberately detach himself from his illustrious predecessor? While in London, not only did he diversify his themes, but he turned his back on "sensitivity"–a formless feeling in his opinion–in favor of "expression" that, for him, was all encompassing (as we have already pointed out). Derain executed two different styles of painting by using wider brushstrokes–a technique often resorted to by the Fauves–and by working in colored impasto rather than just flat color.

Charing Cross Bridge, with its crisscrossed molten metal girders and the *Big Ben* clocktower aglow, both executed in 1906, demonstrate his first style of painting. From Monet's vaporous atmosphere evolved colorful, imaginative and dynamic works with a clearly arbitrary rendering of light: a fanciful city transformed into a fabulous spectacle, ablaze with fireworks, where the water and sky could become mauve or green or violet; the fiery golds and reds of the *Houses of Parliament and Westminster Bridge* bursting as if from a psychedelic palette. We are reminded of the starry skies of Provence painted outdoors by Van Gogh with a crown of candles around his hat, for even in daytime scenes everything seemed to bathe in twilight.

Derain's second style gave his works a totally different quality. He painted everyday scenes of the great commercial city, depicting strollers with flowing gaits, playful dogs and happy children among the pink paths of *Hyde Park*, bordered by red trees and naturalistic green English-style lawns. He catalogued people as well as sites. For example, in *Regent Street*, clogged by the heavy traffic of carriages with black, white and orange horses pulling in every direction on slippery paving stones, he portrayed the pedestrians in the multicolored crowds shuffling on sidewalks in front of massive gray buildings under a leaden sky. *Pool of London* shows a plunging view of a vessel being unloaded at dockside. "Even with our flat color technique we were attentive to the

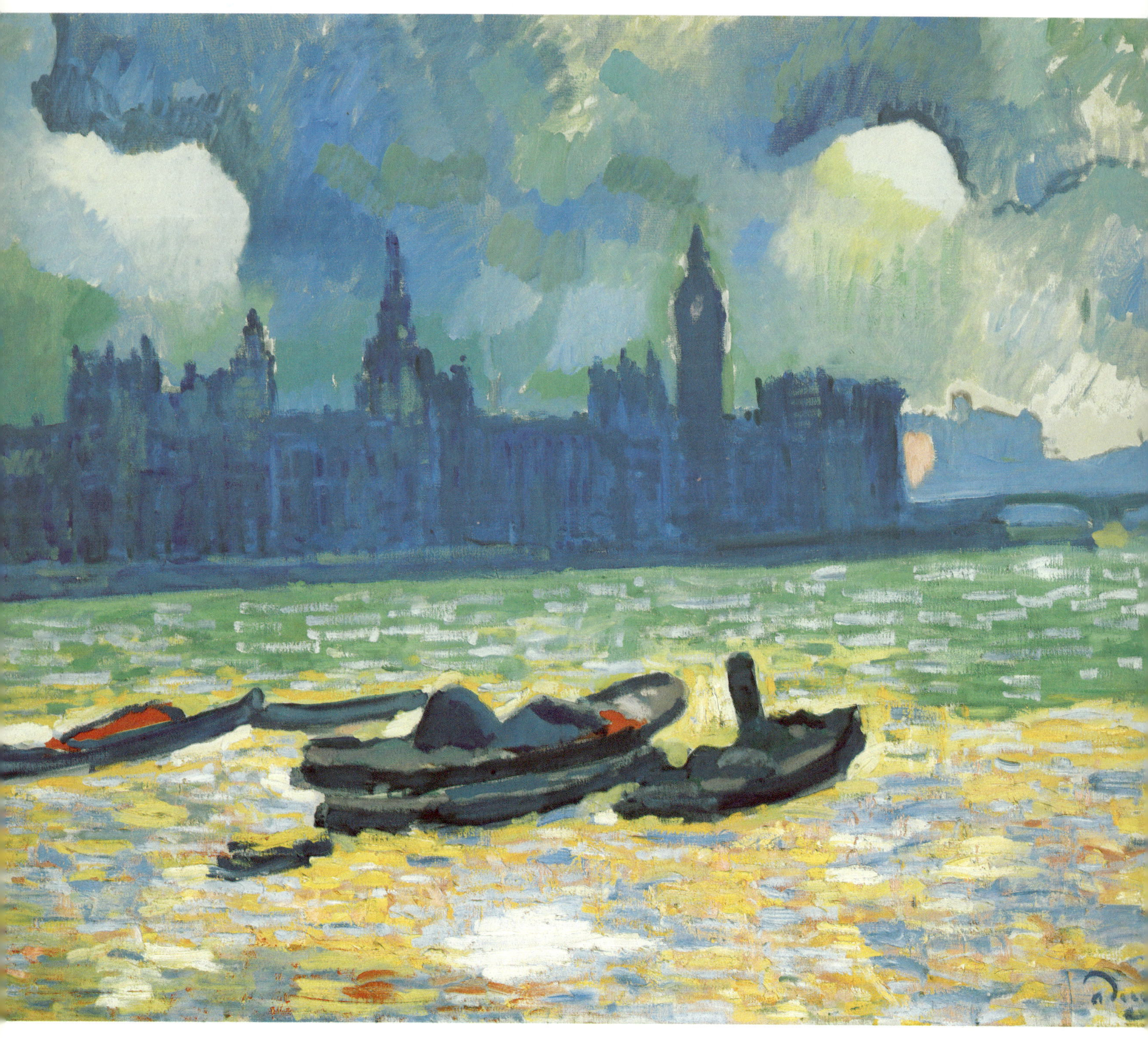

André Derain
The Houses of Parliament at Night
1906
Oil on canvas, 31 x 39 in (78.7 x 99.1 cm)
New York, Metropolitan Museum of Art
(Robert Lehman collection)

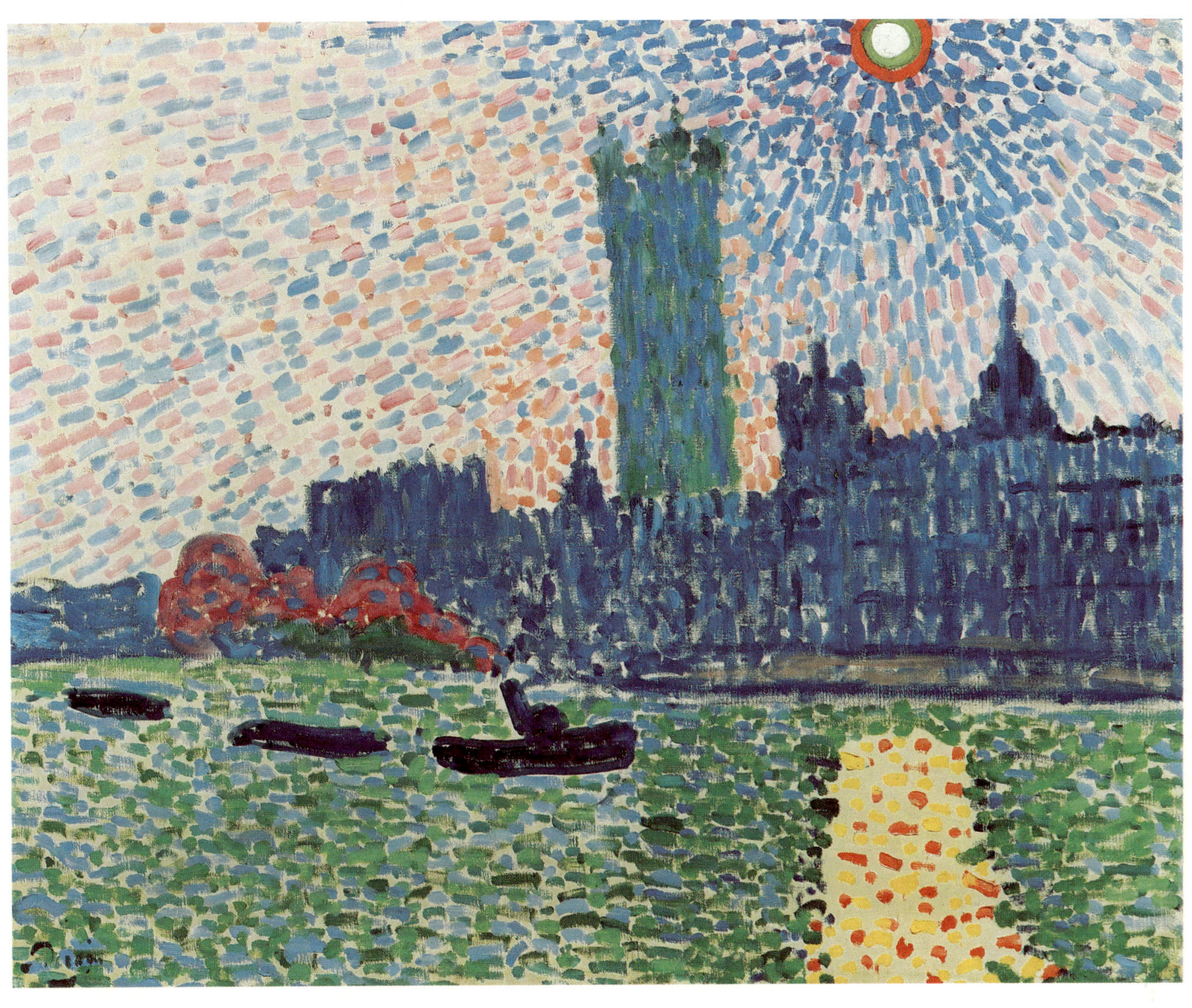

ANDRÉ DERAIN
Westminster
1906
Oil on canvas, 32 x 39¼ in (81,5 x 100 cm)
Saint-Tropez, musée de l'Annonciade

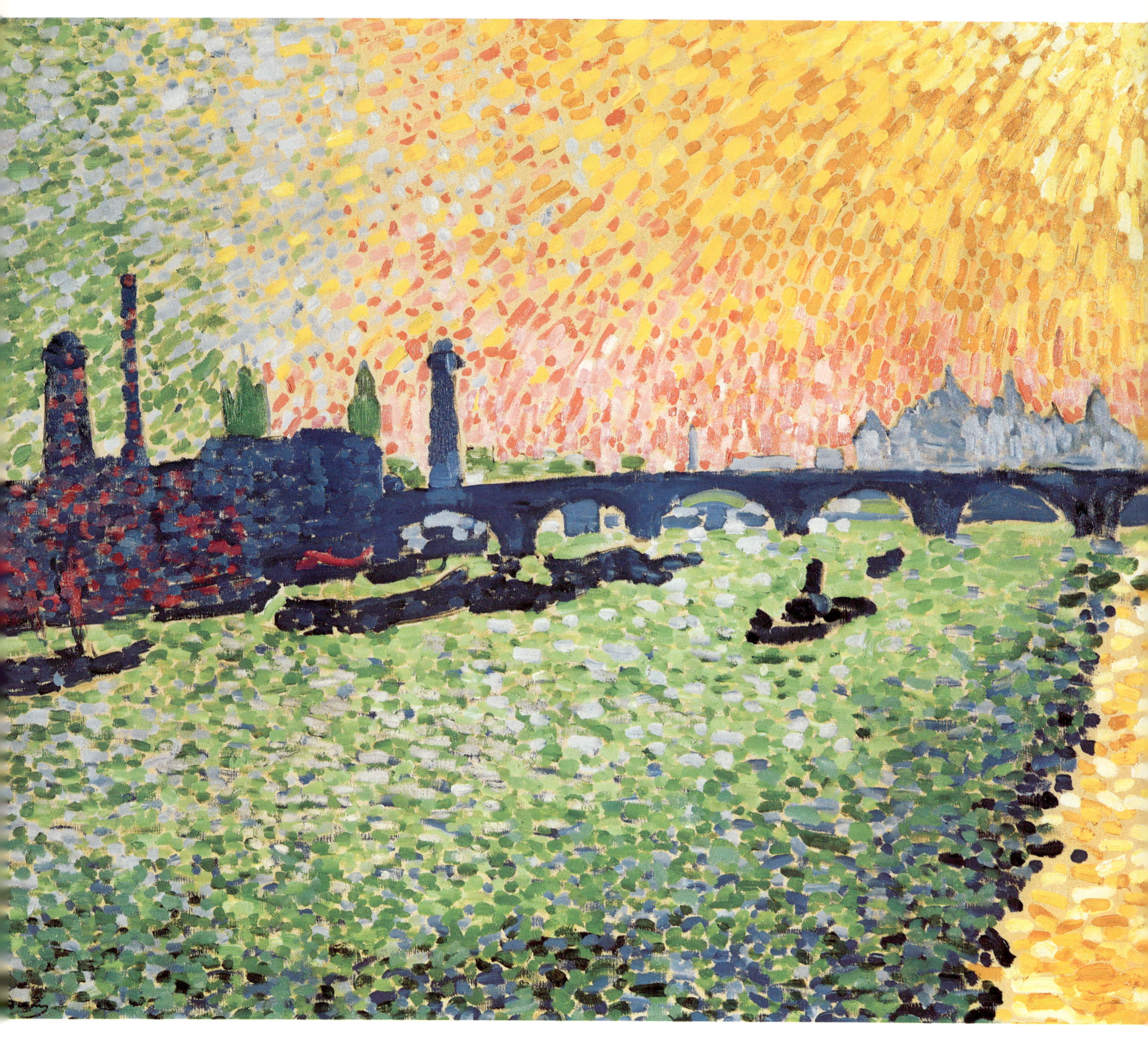

André Derain
Waterloo Bridge
1905
Oil on canvas, 31½ x 39¼ in
(80 x 100 cm)
Lugano, Thyssen-Bornemisza collection

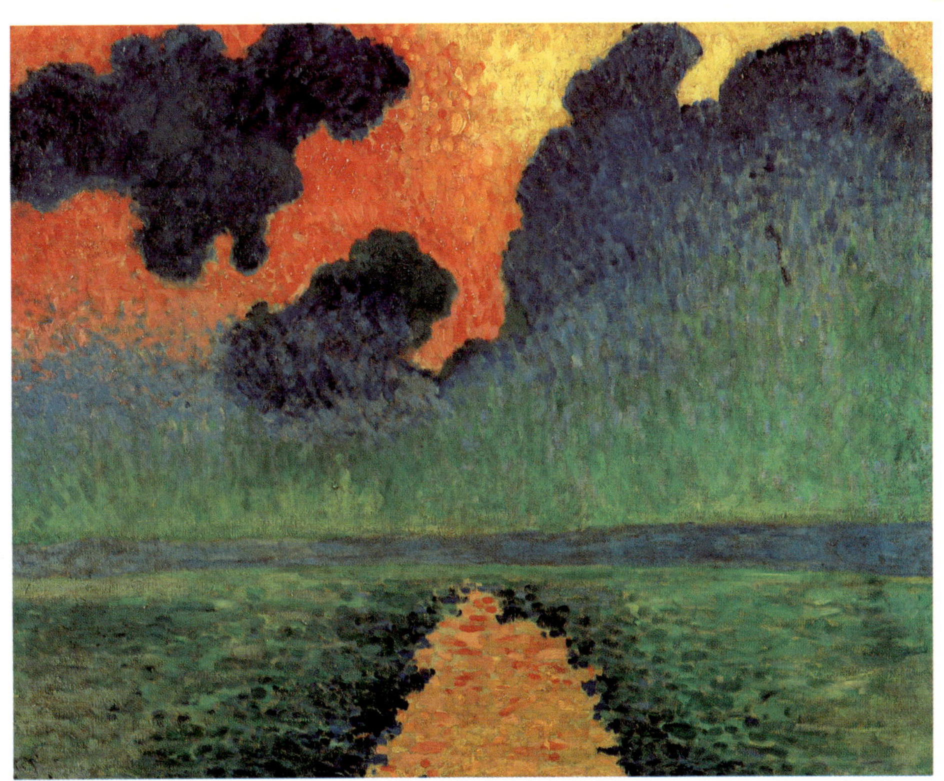

André Derain
Sunlight on Water, London
1906
Oil on canvas, 31¾ x 39¼ in
(80.5 x 100 cm)
Saint-Tropez, musée de l'Annonciade

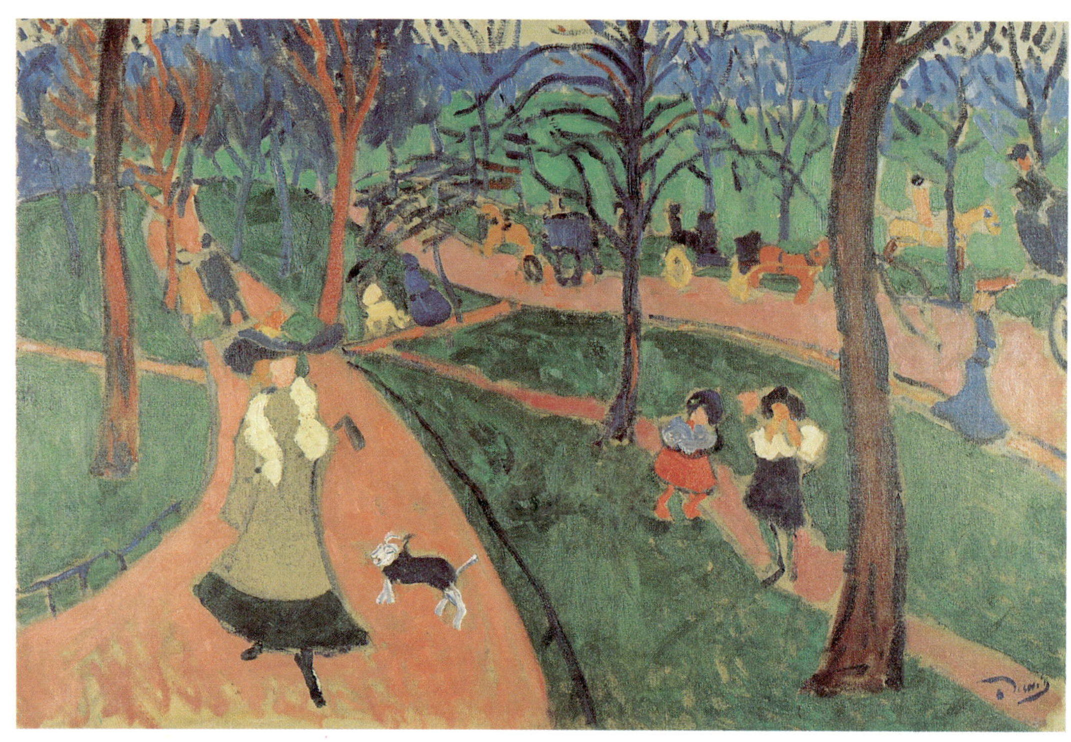

André Derain
Hyde Park
1906
Oil on canvas, 26 x 39 in (66 x 99 cm)
Troyes, musée d'Art moderne

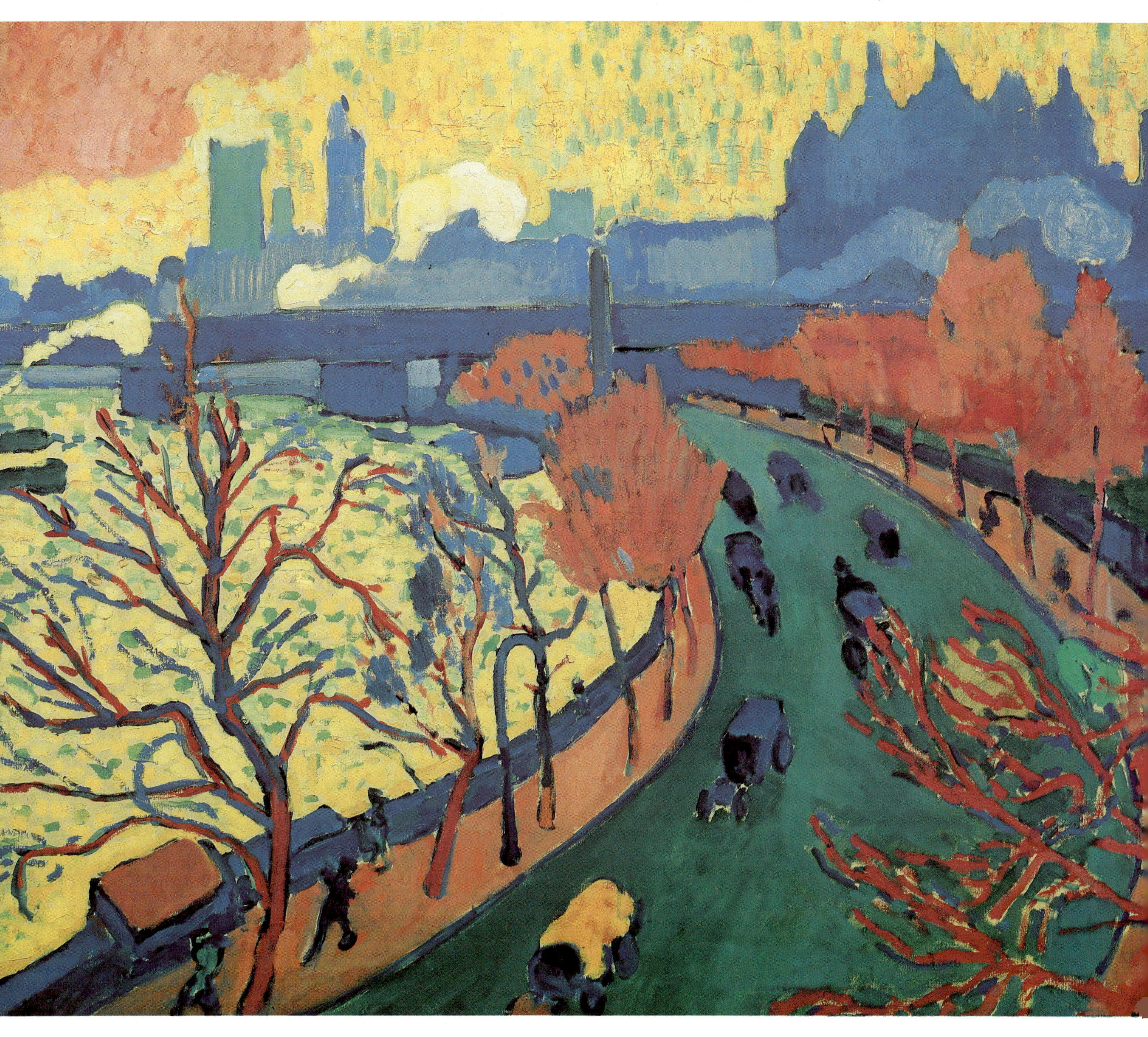

ANDRÉ DERAIN
Charing Cross Bridge
1906
Oil on canvas, 32 x 39¼ in (81 x 100 cm)
Paris, musée d'Orsay

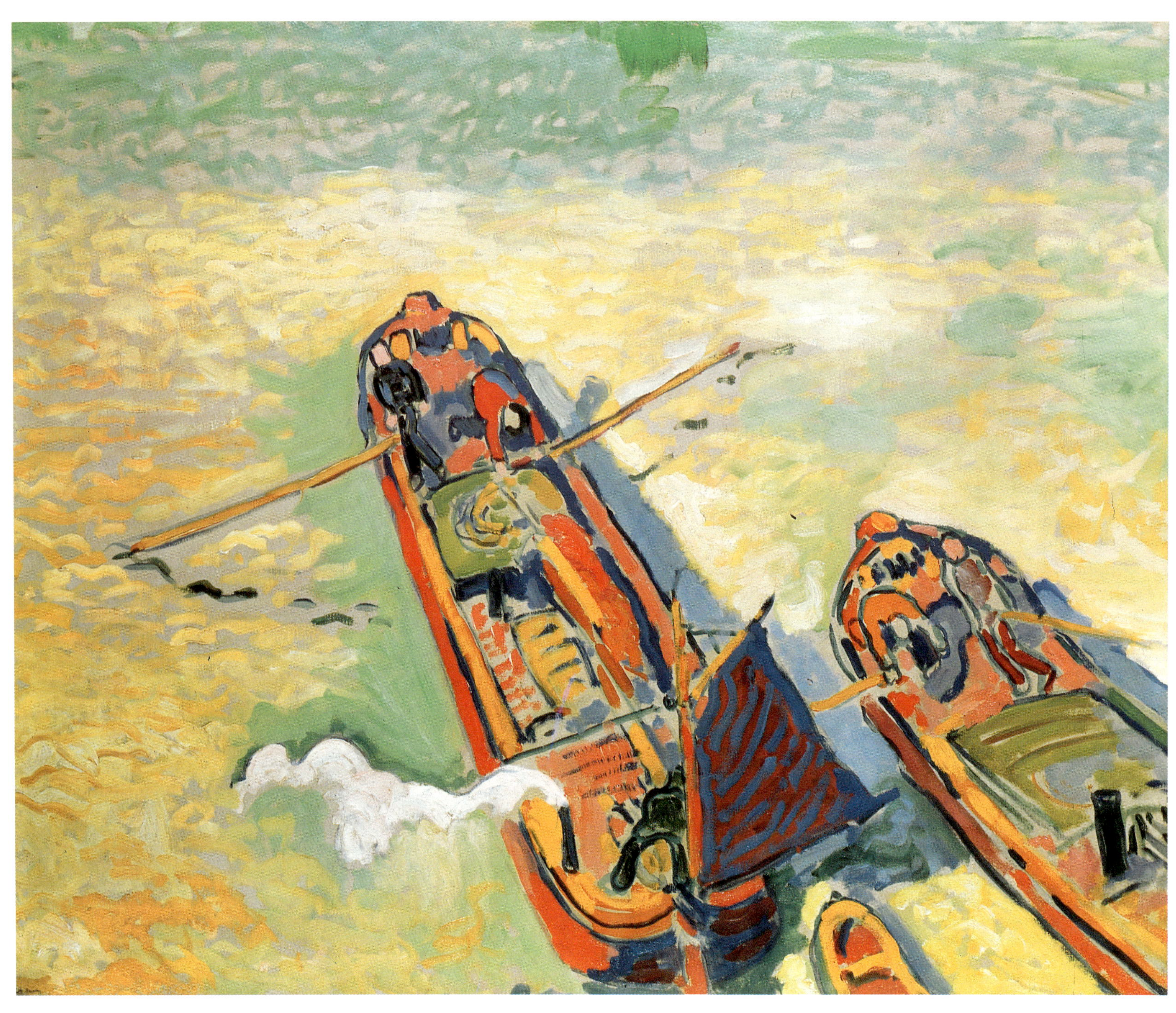

André Derain
Two Barges
1906
Oil on canvas, 31½ x 38¼ in
(80 x 97.5 cm)
Paris, musée national d'Art moderne

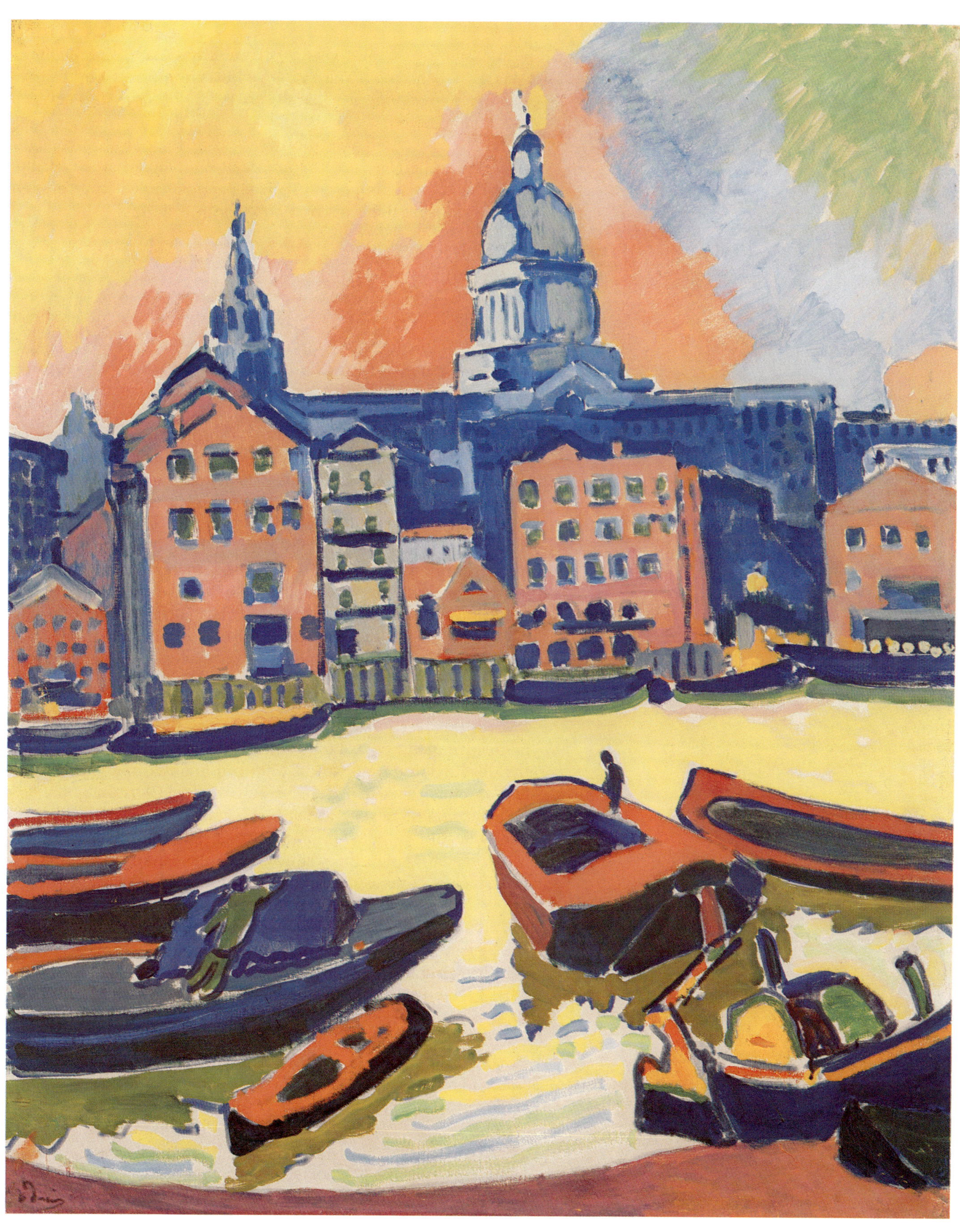

ANDRÉ DERAIN
Saint Paul's Cathedral from the Thames
1906
Oil on canvas, 39¼ x 32¼ in
(99.7 x 81.9 cm)
Minneapolis, Institute of Modern Art
(Putman Dana McMillan bequest)

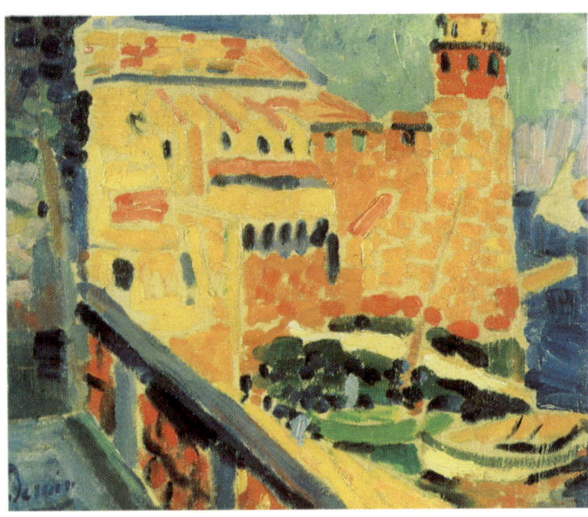

André Derain
Lighthouse at Collioure
1905
Oil on canvas, 12½ x 16 in (32 x 40.5 cm)
Paris, musée d'Art moderne de la ville de Paris

masses in our compositions; for example, by giving more weight to the pile of sand so that the sky would appear airy and the water lighter." This remark, which recalls the heavy yellow ground in several versions of *Collioure Harbor*, indicates that the artist did not forget this device during his London period.

It was another Derain, the one who copied at the Louvre and believed in line and well-contructed composition, who contributed several important stylized paintings to Cubism between 1908 and 1912, thanks to his discovery of African sculpture.

A Return to Order

After 1922–the year that abstract art was forbidden in the Soviet Union following Lenin's declaration: "I do not understand any of it and it gives me no pleasure"–Derain turned back to the past.

At that time in Paris, Montparnasse was the festive center of the arts. Painters led a joyful life and established their studios in the empty stables and hangars abandoned by La Compagnie des Transports Parisiens, whose horses and carriages had just been replaced by the first city buses. New bars, hotels, dance halls and restaurants opened up almost every day, among which Le Dôme and La Coupole, where one went to meet Kiki (Kisling's model), Modigliani, Van Dongen, Derain and many other celebrities. But this merry heyday contrasted curiously with the conventional standards that were returning to favor in painting. Farewell to Fauvism! Farewell to Cubism! The time of innovation and scandalous experiment had come to an end. The new order of the day was: "Return to line, to the true metier, to tradition and embrace nature with fervor." This move was supposed to reconcile modern art with a public that was becoming more and more alienated from it.

Derain took a thoroughly "avant-garde" position towards this reactionary movement. He was almost 50 years old, the age of creative maturity, as he thought. Elie Faure, who in the catalogue of the third Salon d'Automne in 1905 had honored the young painter for his "absolutely new language," now considered Derain as the "greatest French painter," the one whom in this "universal chaos" had been able to put back the "stopper on our pictorial debauch." Derain or Picasso? Many saw in Derain the true genius of the century, an opinion which, when seen with the benefit of hindsight, seems somewhat abusive.

This does not mean that Derain's work from that last period was in any way mediocre. In *Bacchantes*, executed around 1930 the figures gamboling in a mythic forest are painted in white against a dark background; and the *Two Nudes with Still Life* (1935) are imbued with a soft dream-like atmosphere. It seems plausible to think that Balthus and Fautrier were touched by it. But these major efforts were lost among a plethora of mundane portraits such as *Portrait of Madame Paul Guillaume with a Large Hat*, and dancers in tutus like *Sonia the Dancer*, and by bleak landscapes that confirm his earlier fears that form would one day kill the color in his work.

By the time he died in an accident on September 10, 1954, it would be unfair to say that he had been forgotten. Derain, who had overestimated his strength, readily allowed that: "Each time an artist takes up his paintbrush, he must face all the problems of painting." What a contrast to Matisse, who died several weeks later and who ended his life in a crescendo for having dared to continue symplifying his art.

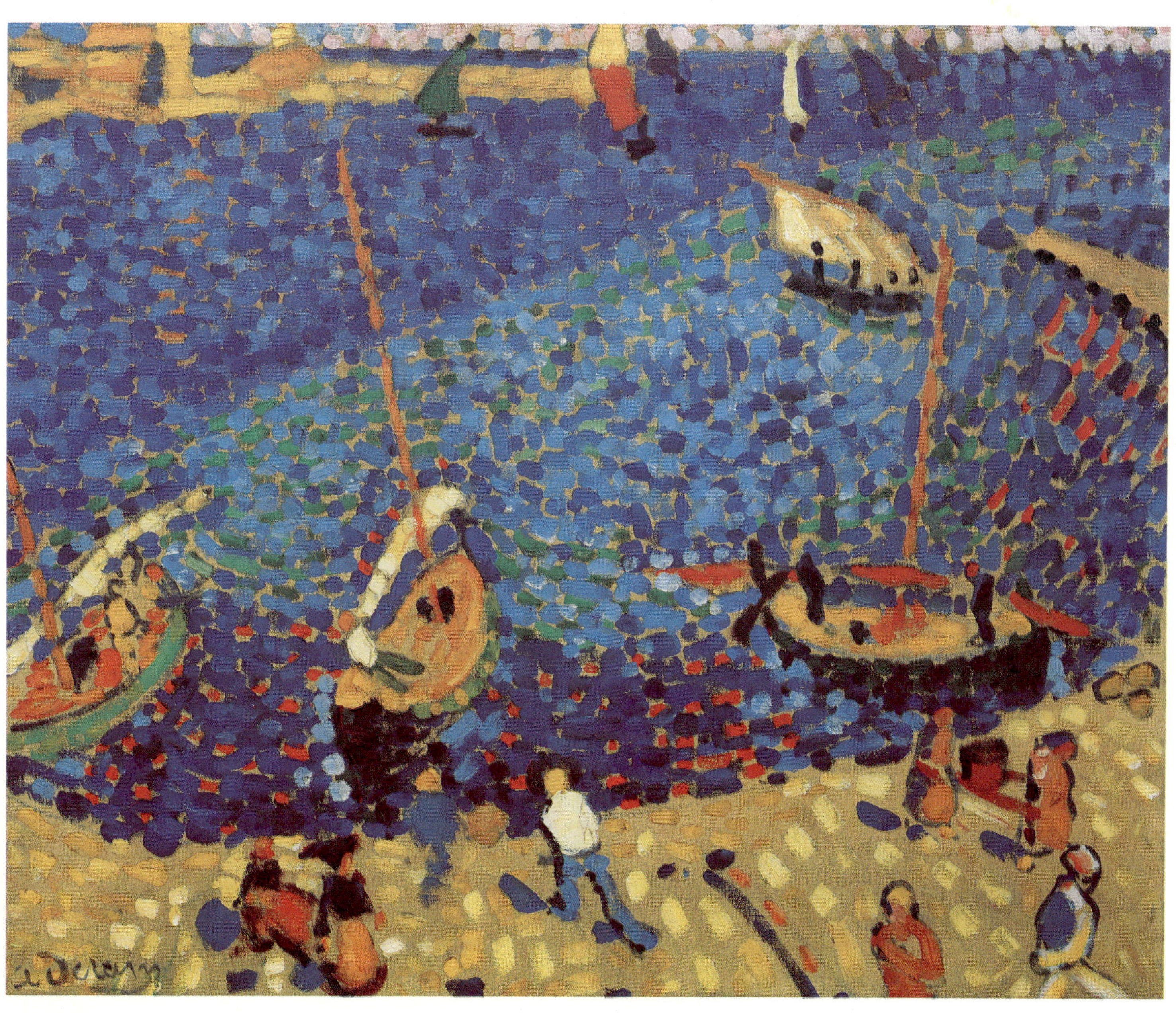

ANDRÉ DERAIN
Boats at Collioure
1905
Oil on canvas, 23½ x 28¾ in (60 x 73 cm)
Düsseldorf, Kunstsammlung Nordrhein-Westfalen

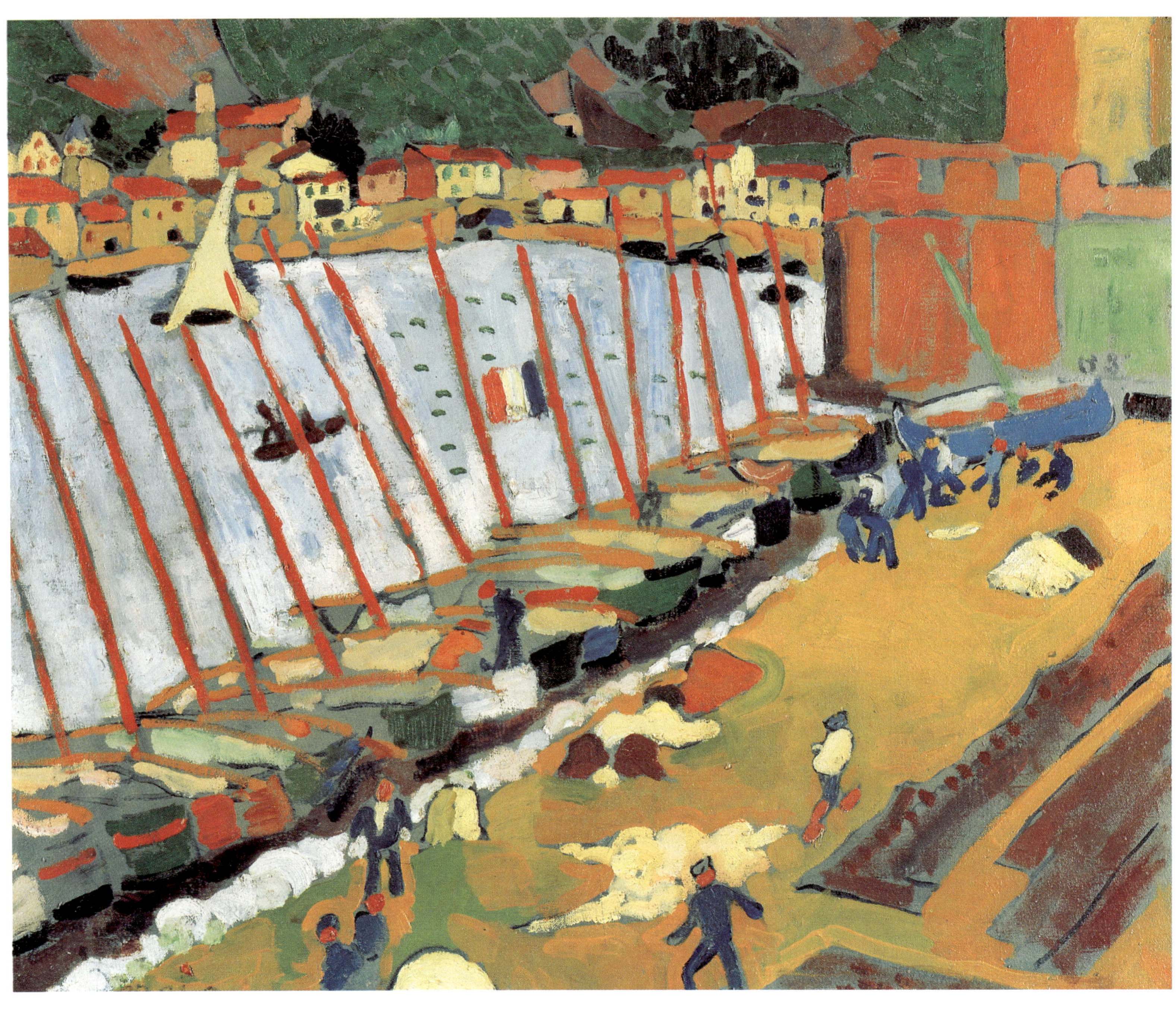

André Derain
Suburb of Collioure
1905
Oil on canvas, 23½ x 28¾ in (60 x 73 cm)
Paris, musée national d'Art moderne

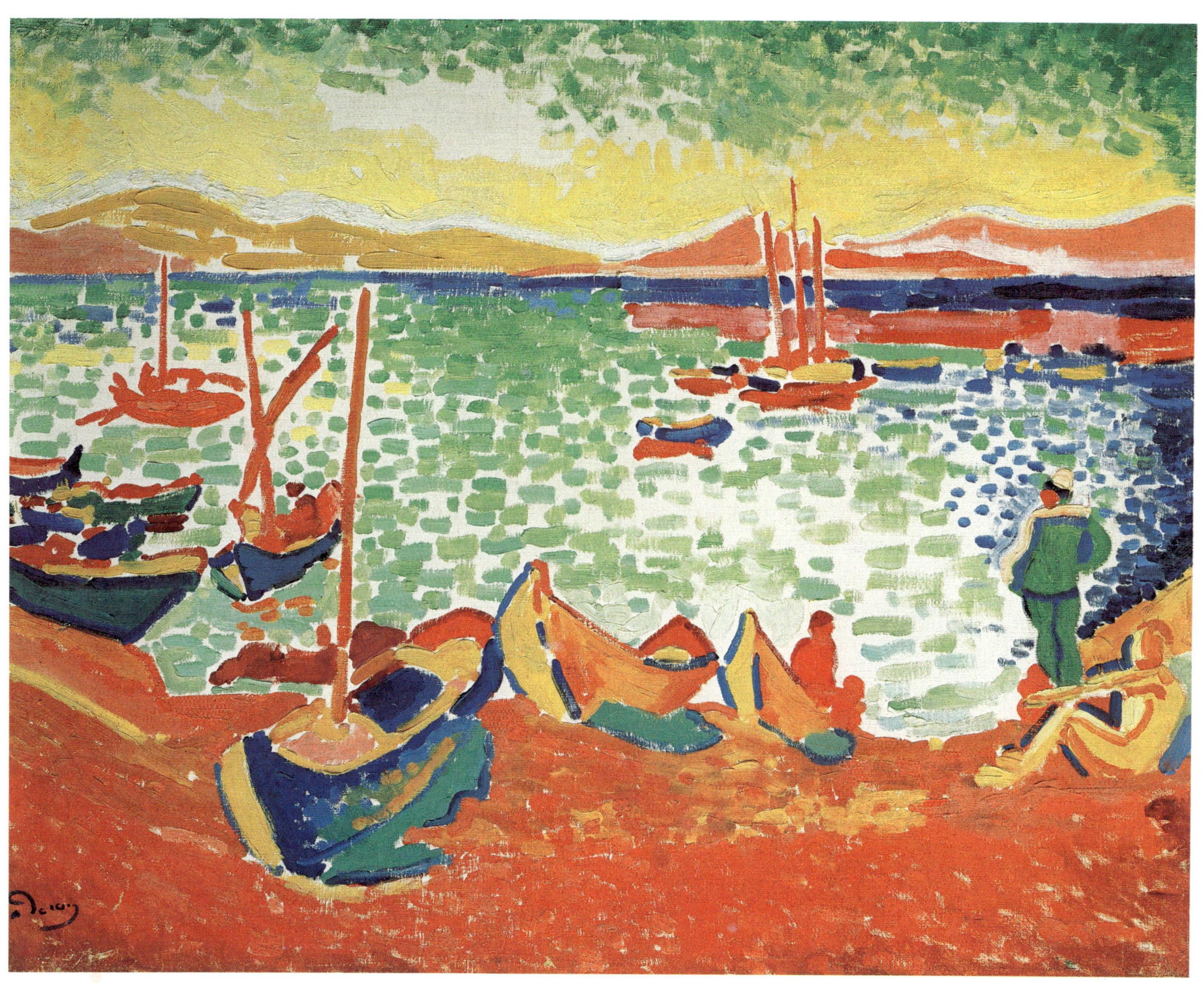

André Derain
Boats in Collioure Harbor
1905
Oil on canvas, 28¼ x 37½ in (72 x 95 cm)
Zurich, private collection

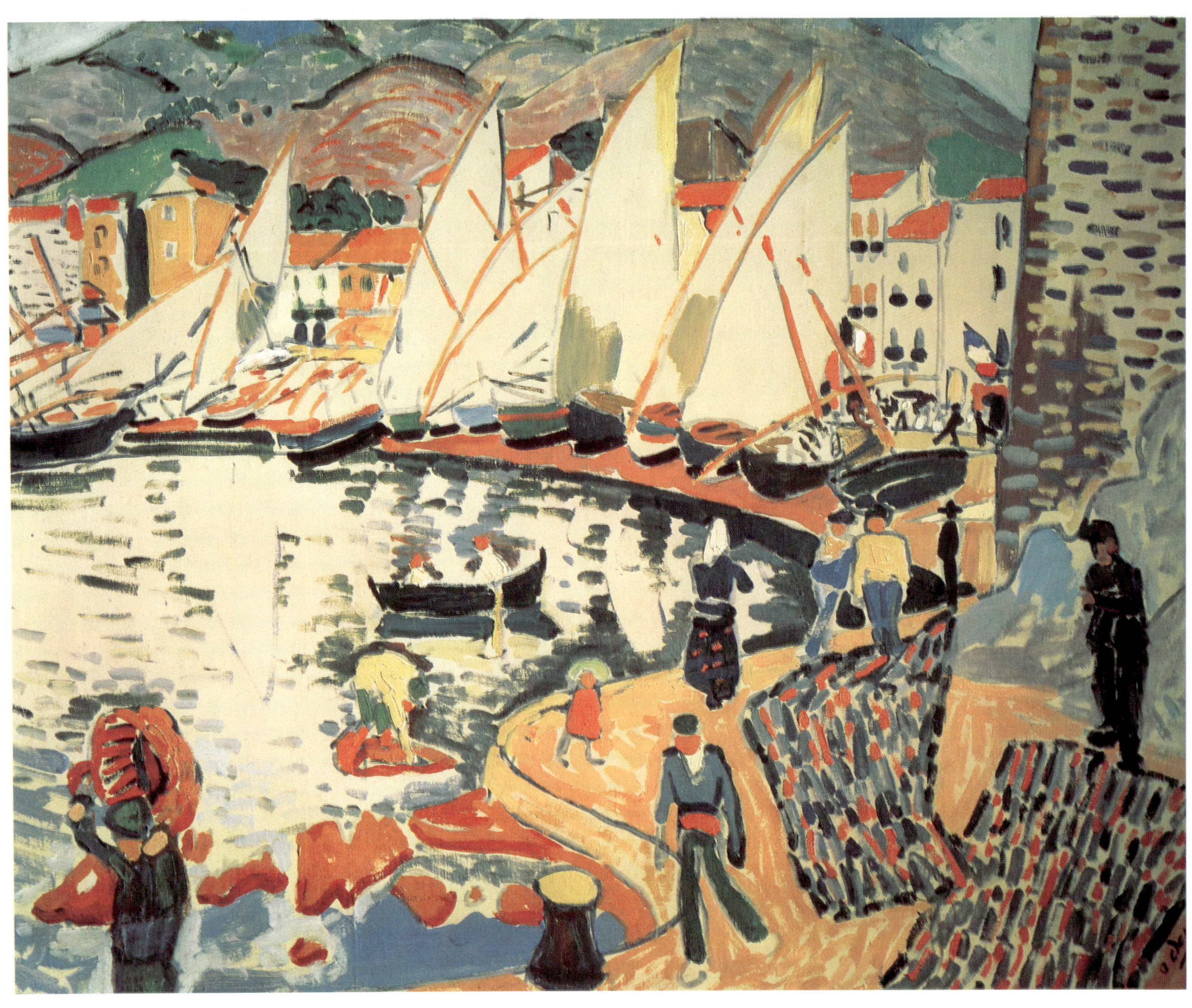

André Derain
Drying the Sails
1905
Oil on canvas, $32\frac{1}{4}$ x $39\frac{3}{4}$ in
(82 x 101 cm)
Moscow, Pushkin Museum

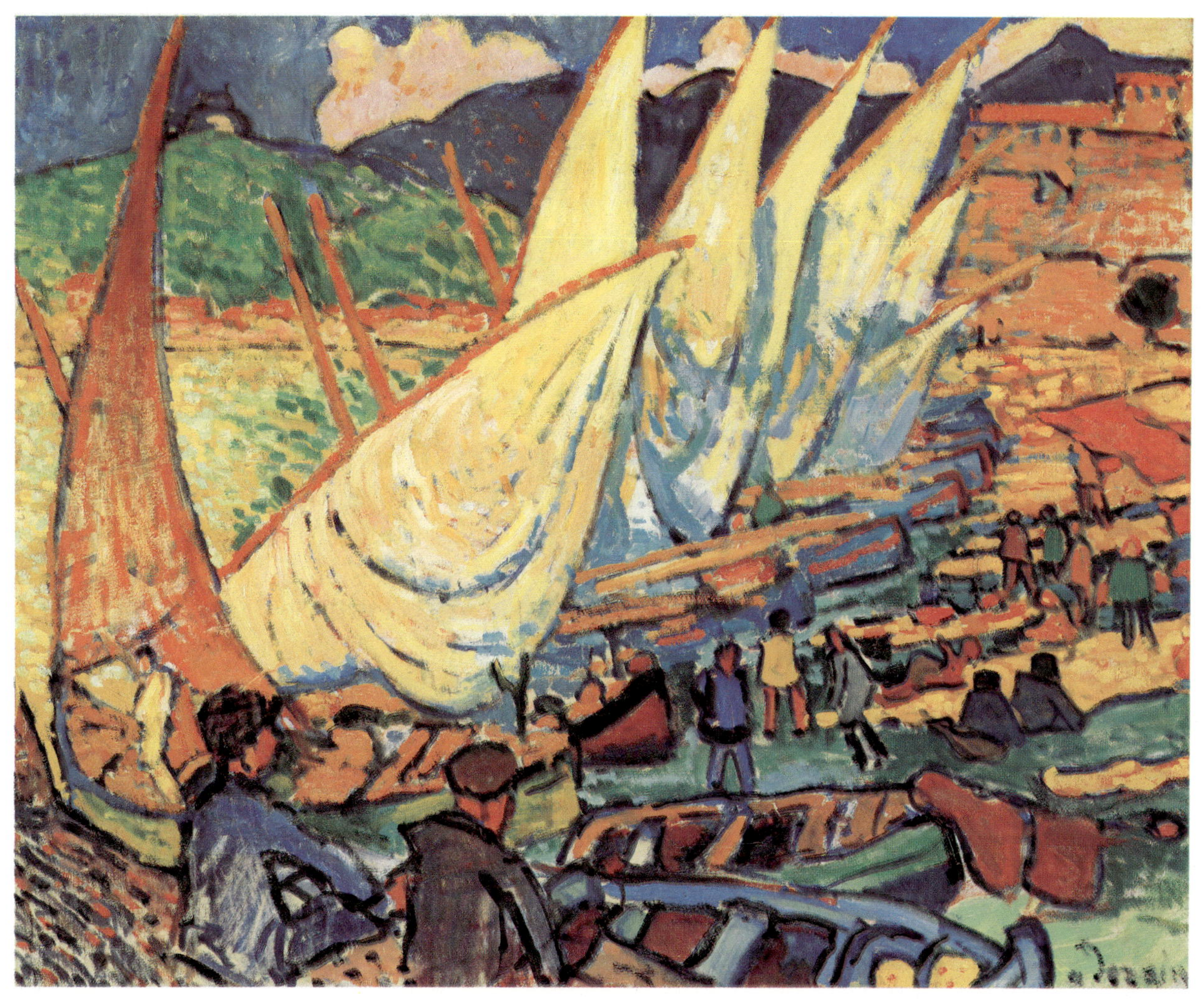

André Derain
Fishing Boats at Collioure
1905
Oil on canvas, 32 x 39½ in
(81 x 100.3 cm)
New York, Metropolitan Museum of Art
(gift of Raymonde Paul)

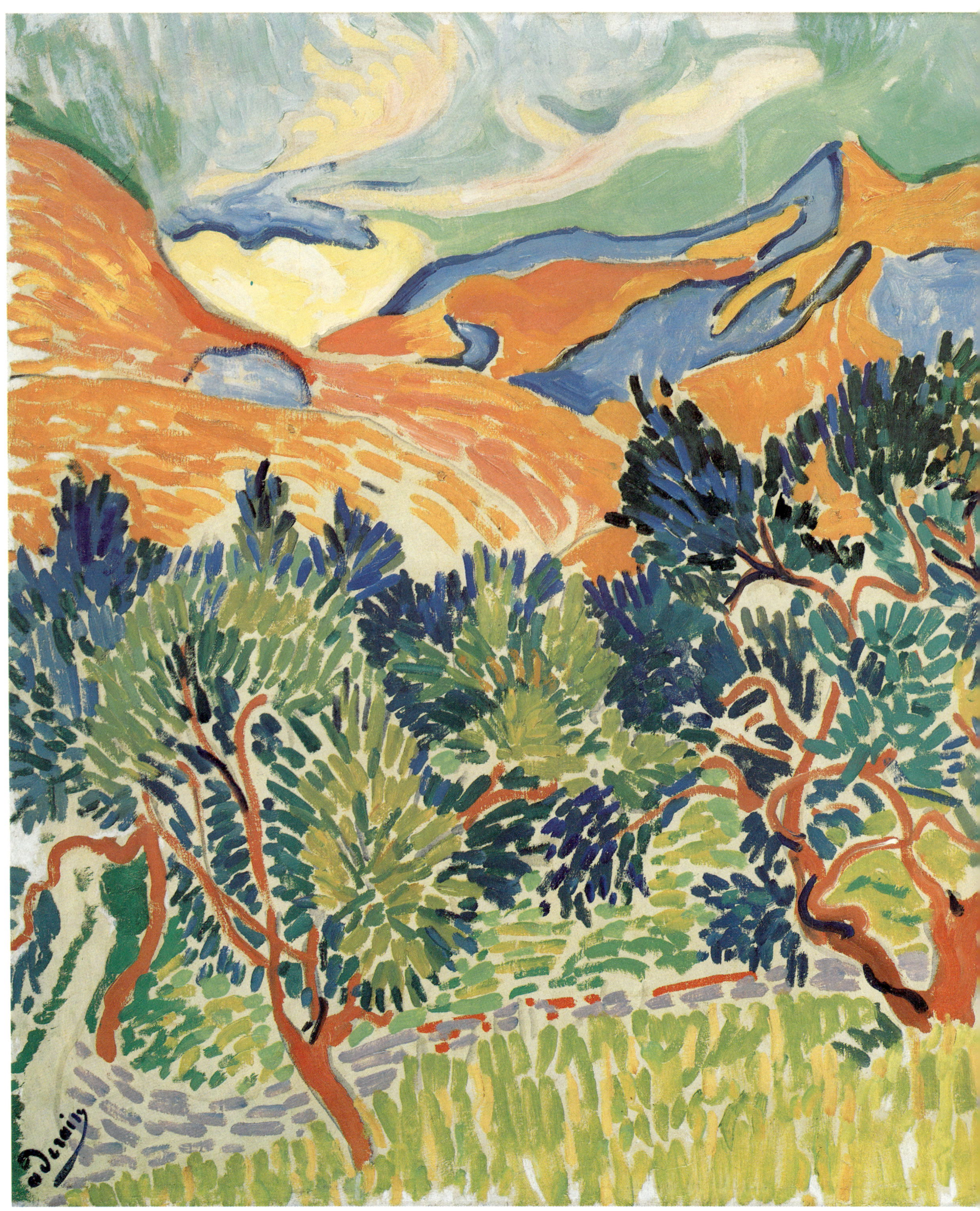
a Derain

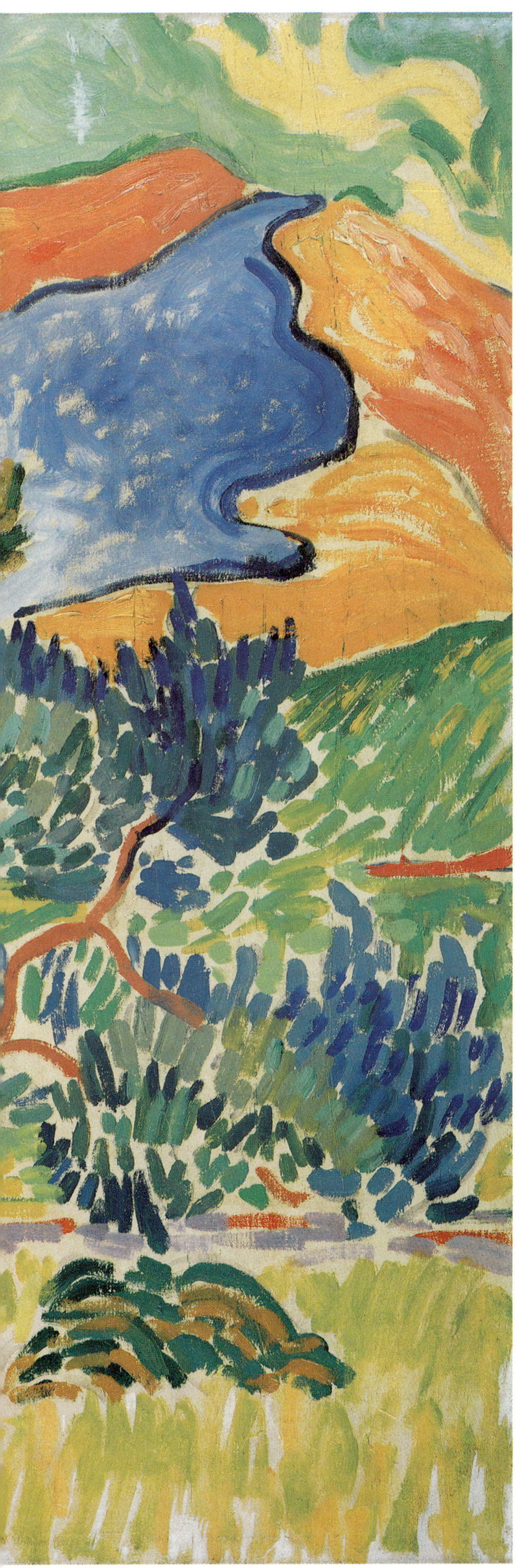

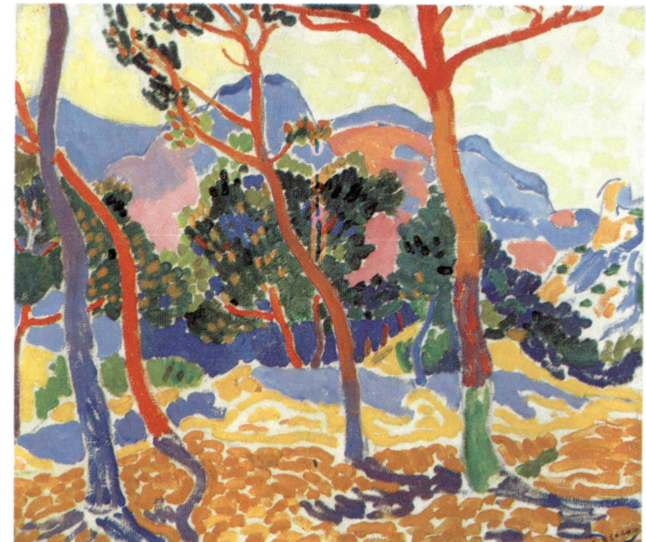

ANDRÉ DERAIN
Trees
1906
Oil on canvas, 23½ x 28½ in
(59.4 x 72.4 cm)
Buffalo, Albright-Knox Art Gallery

Opposite:

ANDRÉ DERAIN
Hills of Collioure
1905
Oil on canvas, 32 x 39½ in
(81.3 x 100.3 cm)
Washington, National Gallery of Art
(John Hay Whitney collection)

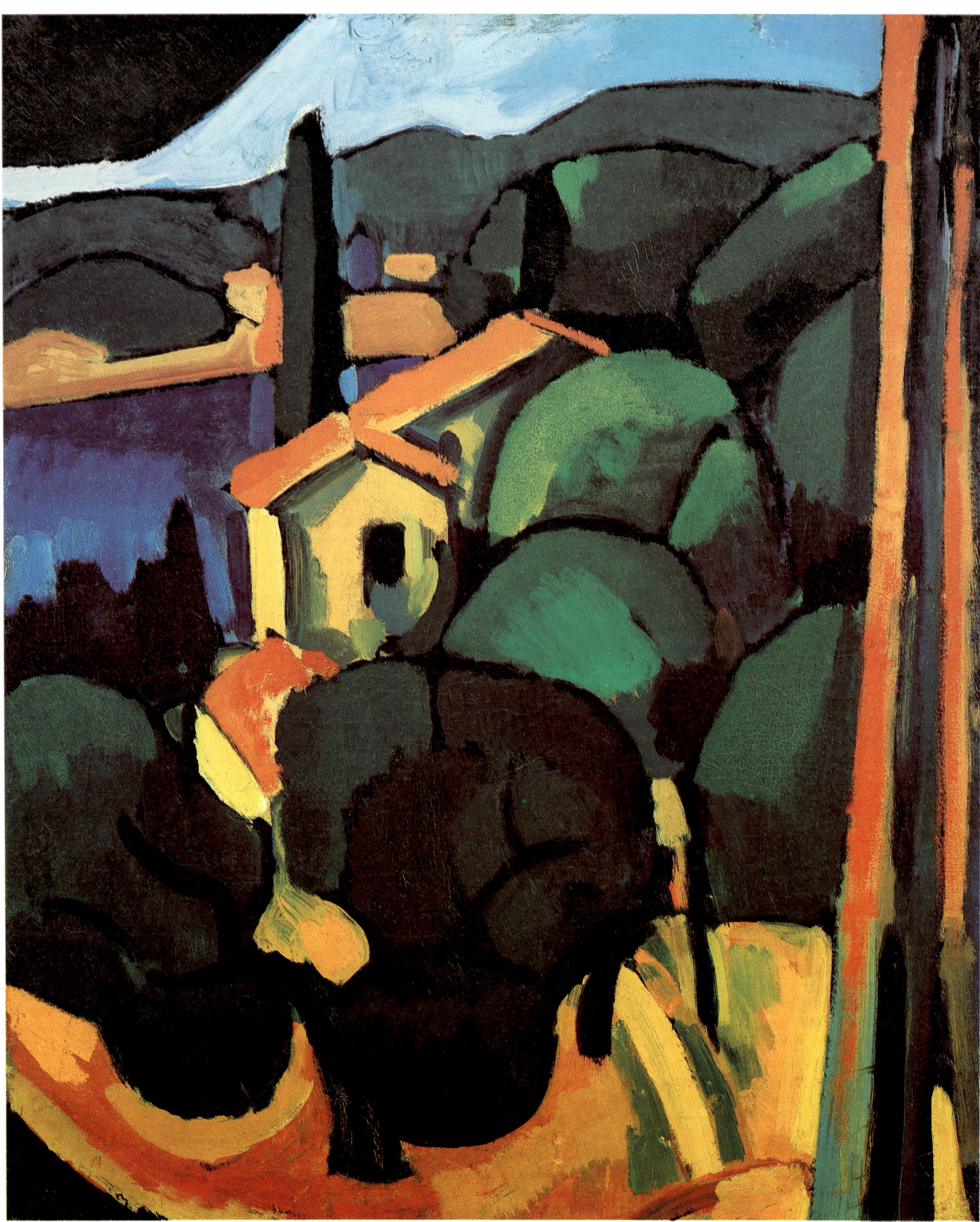

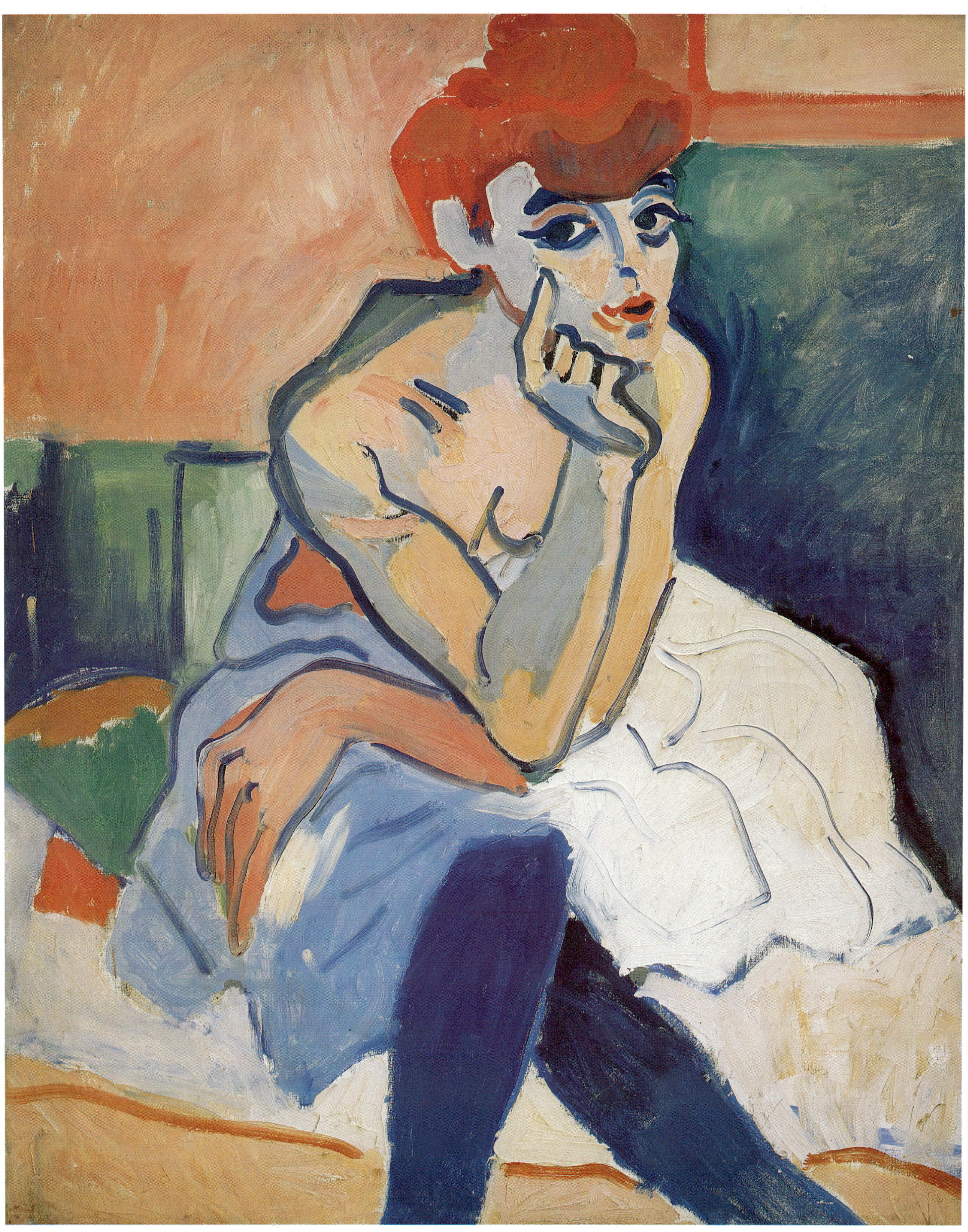

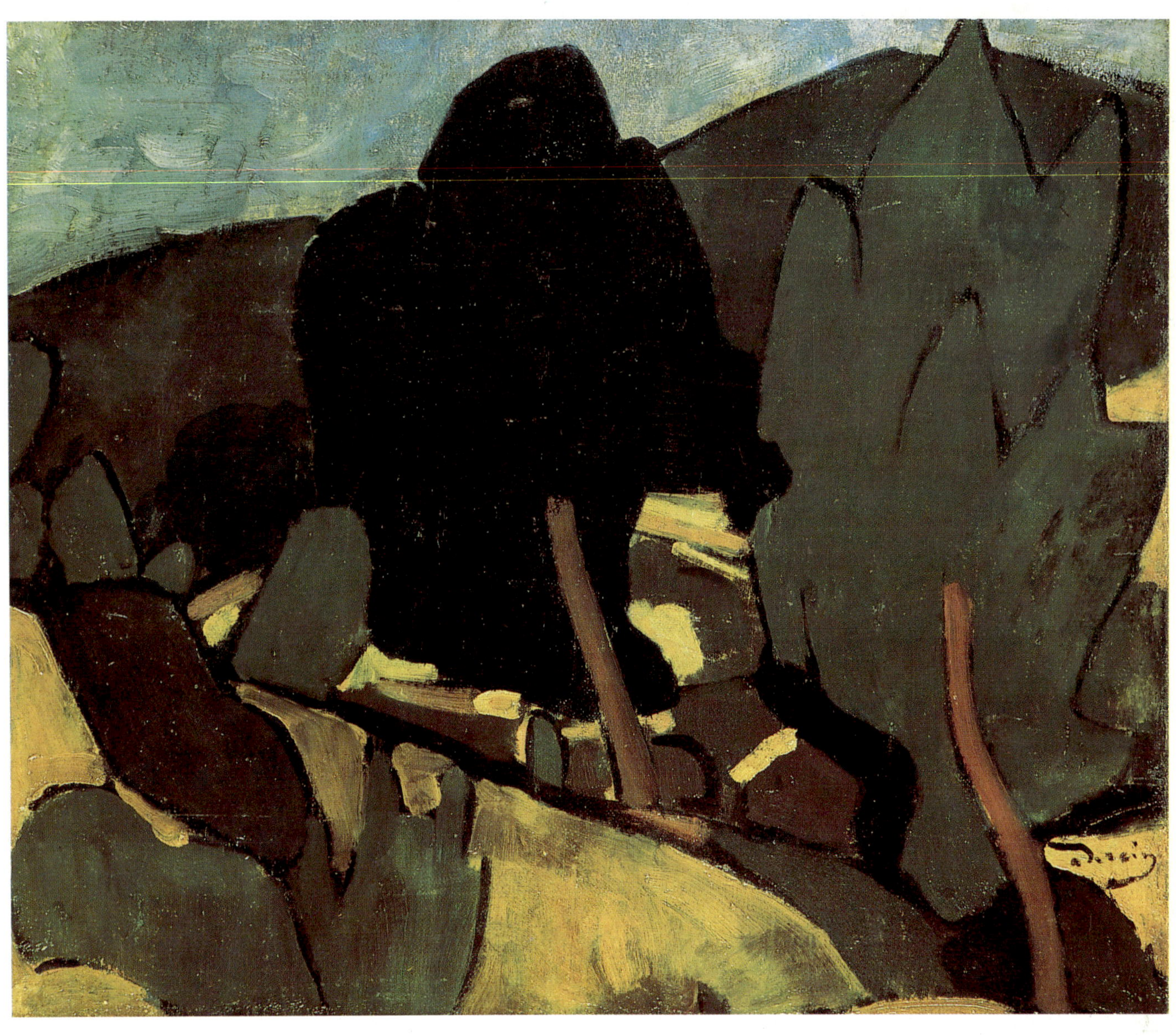

ANDRÉ DERAIN
Landscape at Cassis
1907
Oil on canvas, 21¼ x 25½ in (54 x 65 cm)
Troyes, musée d'Art moderne

Opposite

ANDRÉ DERAIN
Landscape at Cassis
1907
Oil on canvas, 24 x 20 in (61 x 50.8 cm)
New Orleans, Museum of Art
(gift of William F. Campbell)

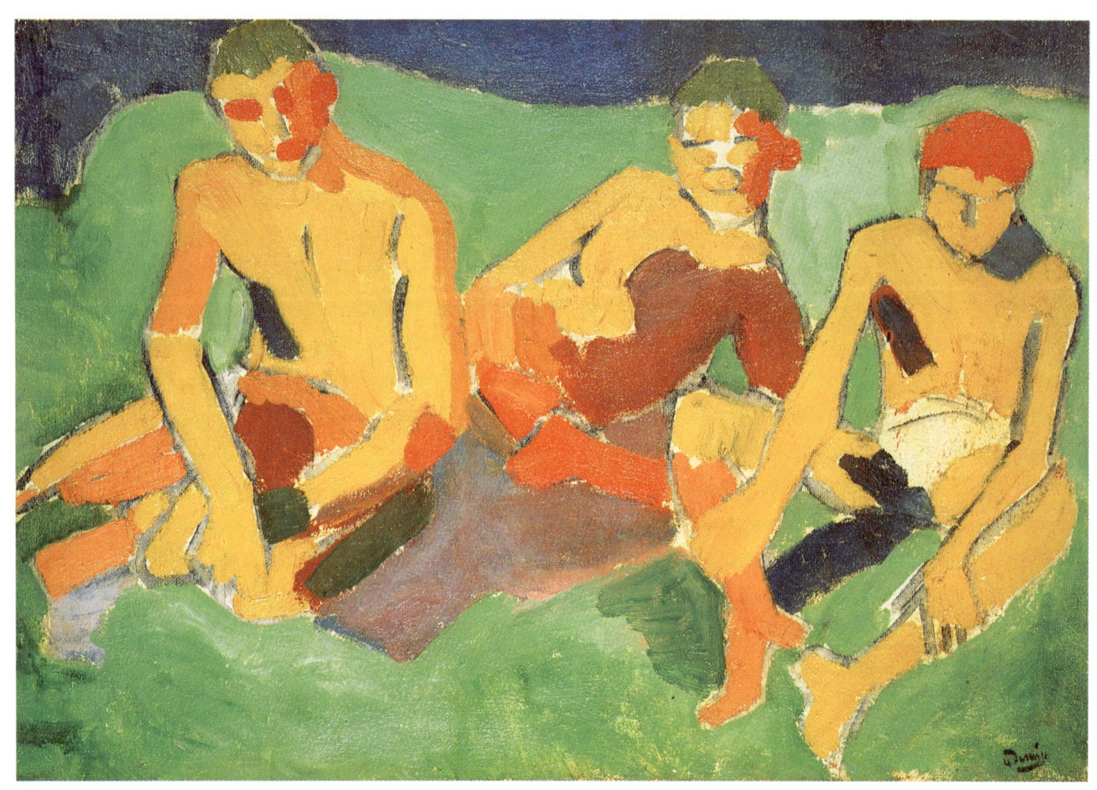

André Derain
Three Figures Seated on the Grass
1906
Oil on canvas, 15 x 21¾ in (38 x 55 cm)
Paris, musée d'Art moderne de la ville de Paris

Opposite:

André Derain
Woman with a Blouse
1906
Oil on canvas, 39¼ x 32 in (100 x 81 cm)
Copenhagen, Statens Museum for Kunst

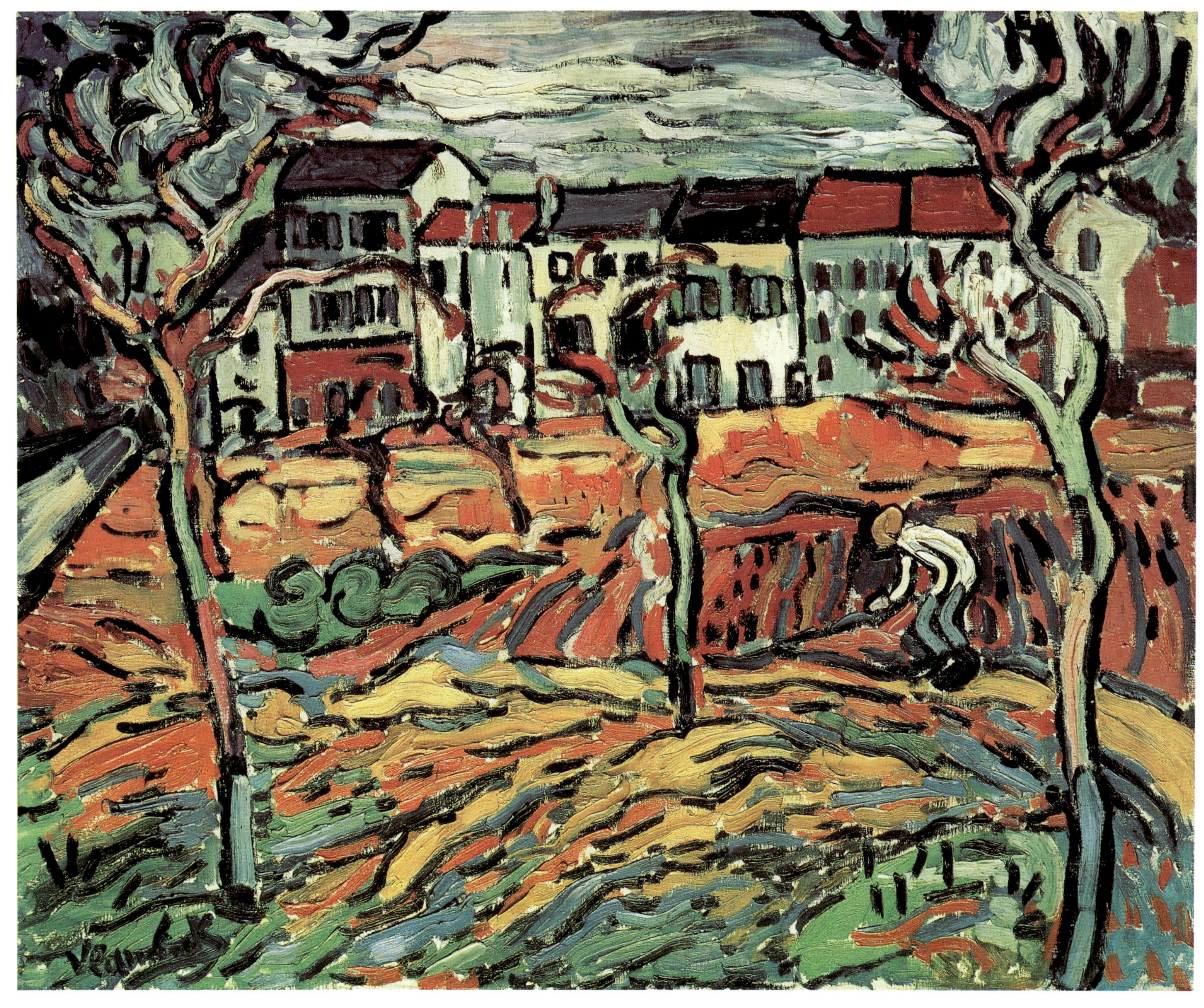

Maurice de Vlaminck
Houses at Chatou
1905-1906
Oil on canvas, 32½ x 39¼ in
(82.5 x 100 cm)
Chicago, The Art Institute

The Celebration of Instinct:

Vlaminck

A Gentle Ruffian

With his passion for Van Gogh as well as bicycles–and eventually motorcycles and cars to satisfy an appetite for speed–Maurice de Vlaminck's personality was like his paintings, quite colorful. Born on April 4, 1876, near Paris' former central market, Les Halles. His Flemish father worked as a tailor before becoming a music teacher (violin and piano). Vlaminck, himself, was entirely self-taught, practicing successively or simultaneously such activities as amateur and professional bicycle-racing (he took part in the Paris-Roubaix and the Bordeaux-Paris races), working in a bicycle factory, rowing in competitions, playing billiards and specializing in slow waltzes and wild czardas on the violin and the bass fiddle. He had also tried his hand at writing before starting to paint. With a very muscular body–he was about 6 ft (1.80 m) tall and weighed 180 lbs (80 kilos)–he practiced weightlifting and greco-roman wrestling on holidays at the fairgrounds in Neuilly. He had to give up most of these activities when he married at the age of 18 and became the father of two little girls. The gentle ruffian who dreamed of exploring the world was now required to earn a living and support his family.

Nevertheless, shortly after meeting Derain in a dreamed-up railroad accident on the Garenne-Bezons line (already mentioned in the previous chapter), the shock that determined his vocation as an artist took place in 1901 at the Bernheim-Jeune gallery in Paris exhibiting fifty works by Van Gogh, whose style represented a total rupture with the taste of the time. What other artist with such a low reputation during his lifetime ended up being placed on art's highest pedestal just a few years later, not just thanks to the critics, but also to

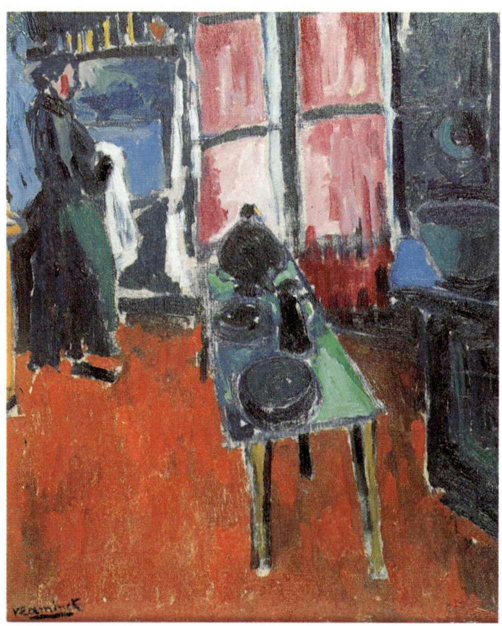

MAURICE DE VLAMINCK
Inside the Kitchen
1904
Oil on canvas, 21¾ x 15¾ in (55 x 40 cm)
Paris, musée national d'Art moderne

the art market? It is common knowledge that he shot himself through the chest in a field at Auvers-sur-Oise on July 27, 1880, and died two days later for lack of medical attention. Van Gogh is the epitome of the *"peintre maudit"*–an alcoholic with epilepsy who sold only one canvas in his entire career. At that time, he was known to only a few Sunday painters and amateurs like Père Tanguy, a second-hand goods merchant who also dealt in art and who tried to sell Van Gogh's works at the very modest price of fifty or a hundred francs.

The exhibition at the Bernheim-Jeune gallery included seascapes, harvest scenes, self-portraits, cypress trees, sunflowers, the famous *Room at Arles* and the fabulous *Starry Night*–the skies in Provence under a shower of fiery comets and shooting stars. Apart from the fact that our eyes have grown accustomed to such pictorial extravagance, the paintings which so excited Vlaminck no longer exactly resemble those that we admire today, for the pigments have lost some of their intensity. Van Gogh used tones of carmine, Prussian blue and Veronese green, colors which darken, evaporate and become drowned by the colors with which they are mixed. We know from a letter that he sent to his brother, Theo, that their optical impact has been blunted by the passage of time. Thus, it is easy to understand why the Dutchman's brutal color-schemes made such a strong impression on Vlaminck, who made this declaration in his *Mémoires*: "On that day, I loved Van Gogh more than my father." When he wrote those words he did not know that he would become a professional artist–and he might never have become one if he had not met Derain.

The act of painting was enough in itself to bring him joy; he felt physical pleasure while applying his colors. He bought canvases when he had enough money, and if he had thought he would be making a living one day by selling his own pictures, he would never have allowed himself paint such "horrors."

At around this time, Vlaminck was among those who discovered African statuettes and carved masks which the Fauves enthusiastically adopted–as well as the Cubists later on–in unusual circumstances that he liked to recall: "One afternoon in 1905, I was in Argenteuil and had just painted a scene of the Seine with barges and the surrounding hillsides. The sun was scorching hot. My colors and my brushes put away, I took my canvas and entered a small restaurant. A group of bargemen and stevedores were at the counter. While I drank a refreshing glass of white wine and soda, I noticed on a shelf–among bottles of Pernod, anisette and curaçao–three African statues, two of them from Dahomey painted over in white and red and yellow ocher. The other from the Ivory Coast was all black."

Vlaminck added: "Was it because I had been out in the sun for two or three hours or the particular mood I was in at that moment? Maybe it coincided with certain ideas that I had been mulling over for some time? The three statuettes impressed me greatly. I instinctively sensed their inherent power. They revealed African art to me... I asked the owner to sell them to me. At first, he refused. I insisted, but after much hesitation, unwillingness, and apologies, he finally gave them to me under the condition that I would pay a round of red wine to everybody there; and I so left with the three statues."

Since Vlaminck did not mimic African art formally, his work does not seem to be as marked by it as that of other early twentieth-century painters. But in fact his *Portrait of Derain* (1905) indicates a definite African influence in its release of instinctive forces.

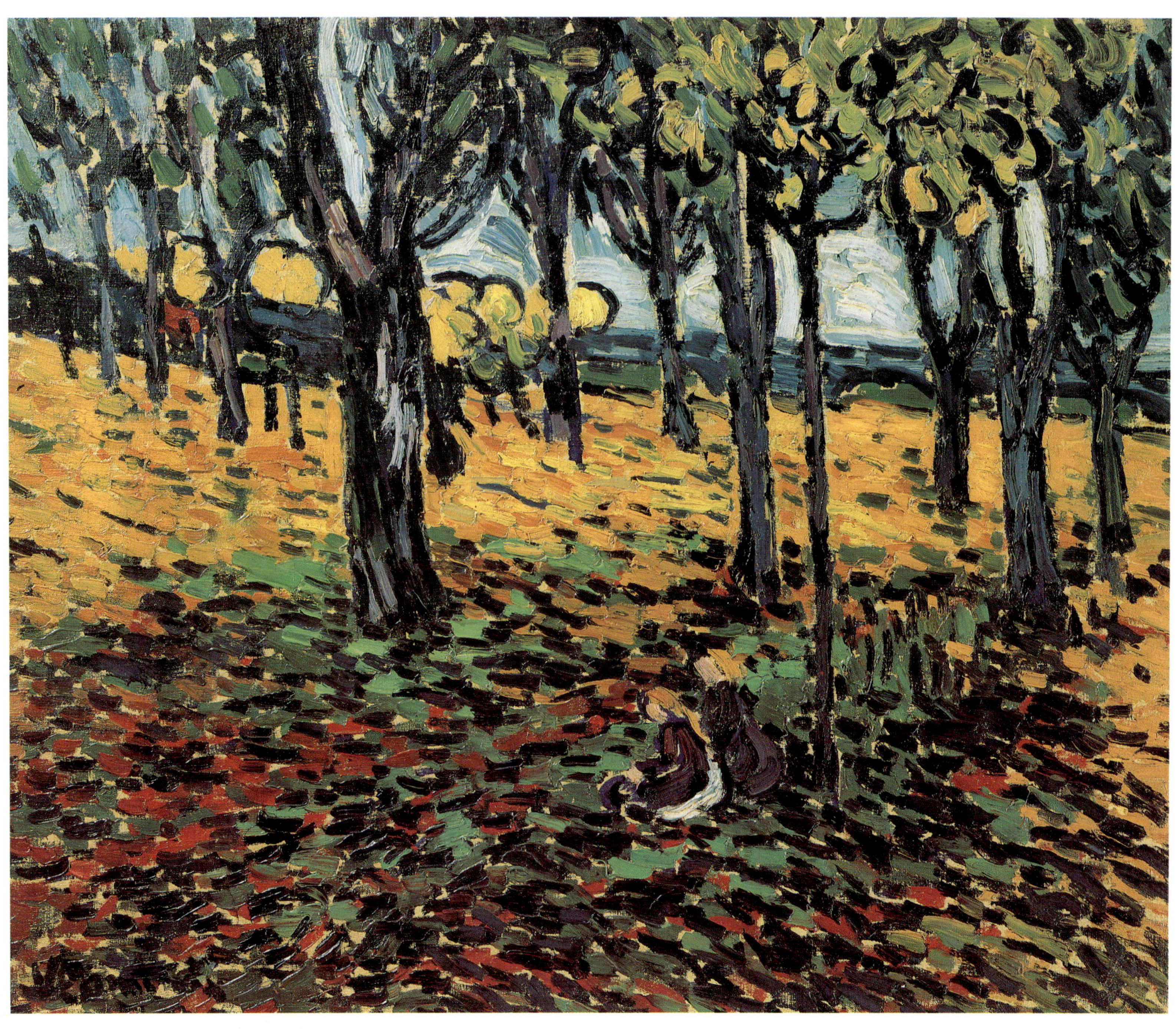

Maurice de Vlaminck
Chestnut Trees at Chatou
1906
Oil on canvas, 23⅝ x 28¾ in (60 x 73 cm)
Troyes, musée d'Art moderne

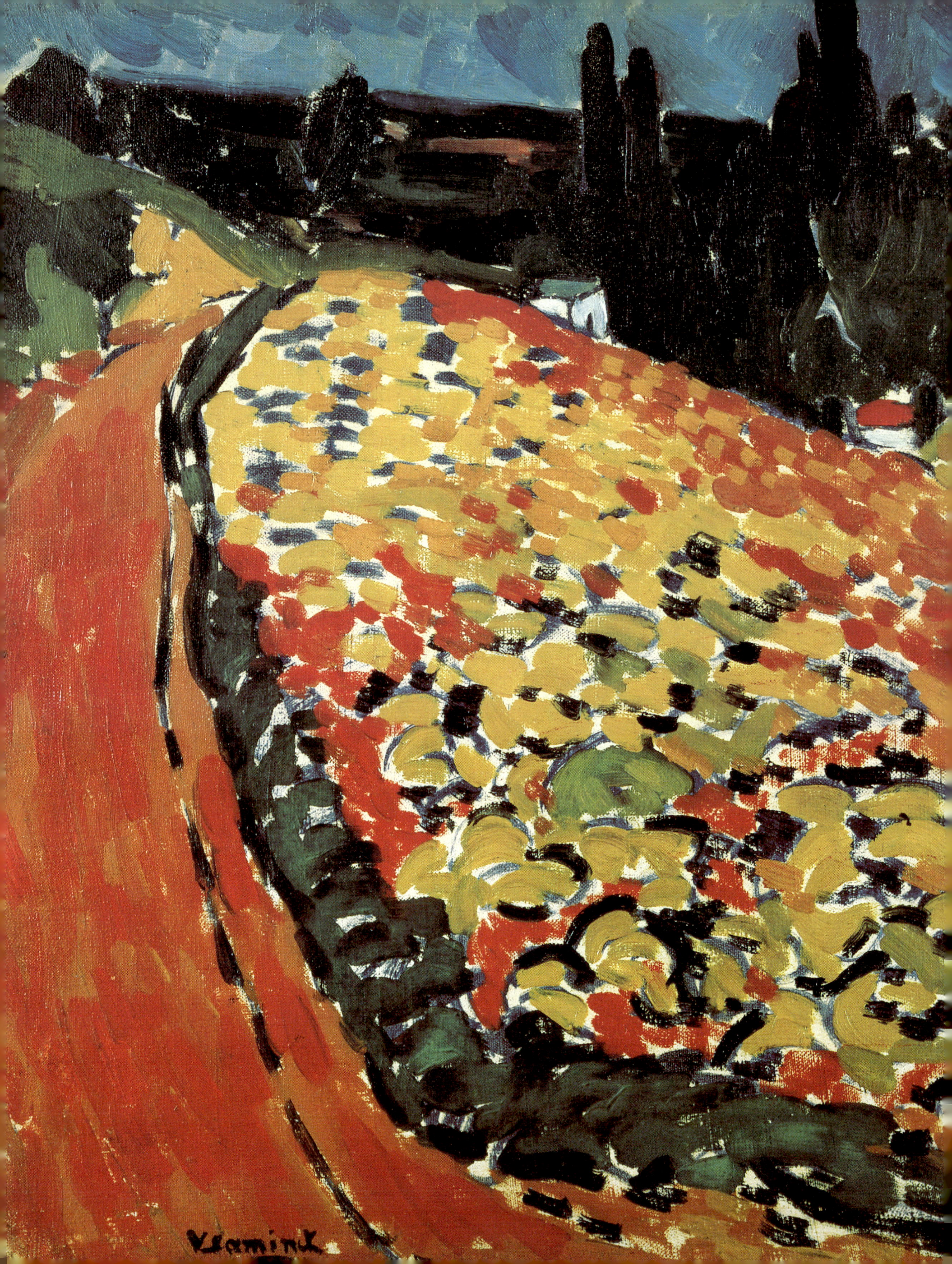

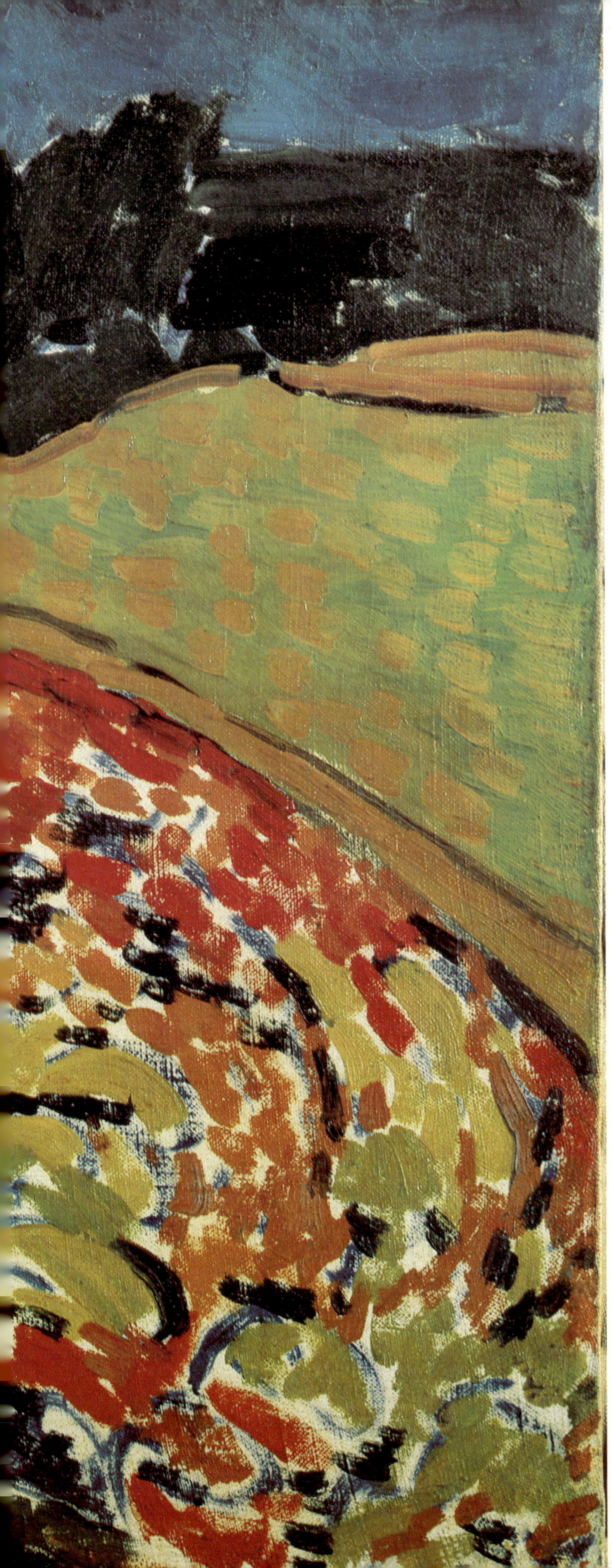

Maurice de Vlaminck
The Hillside of Rueil
1906
Oil on canvas, 18 x 22 in (46 x 56 cm)
Paris, musée d'Orsay

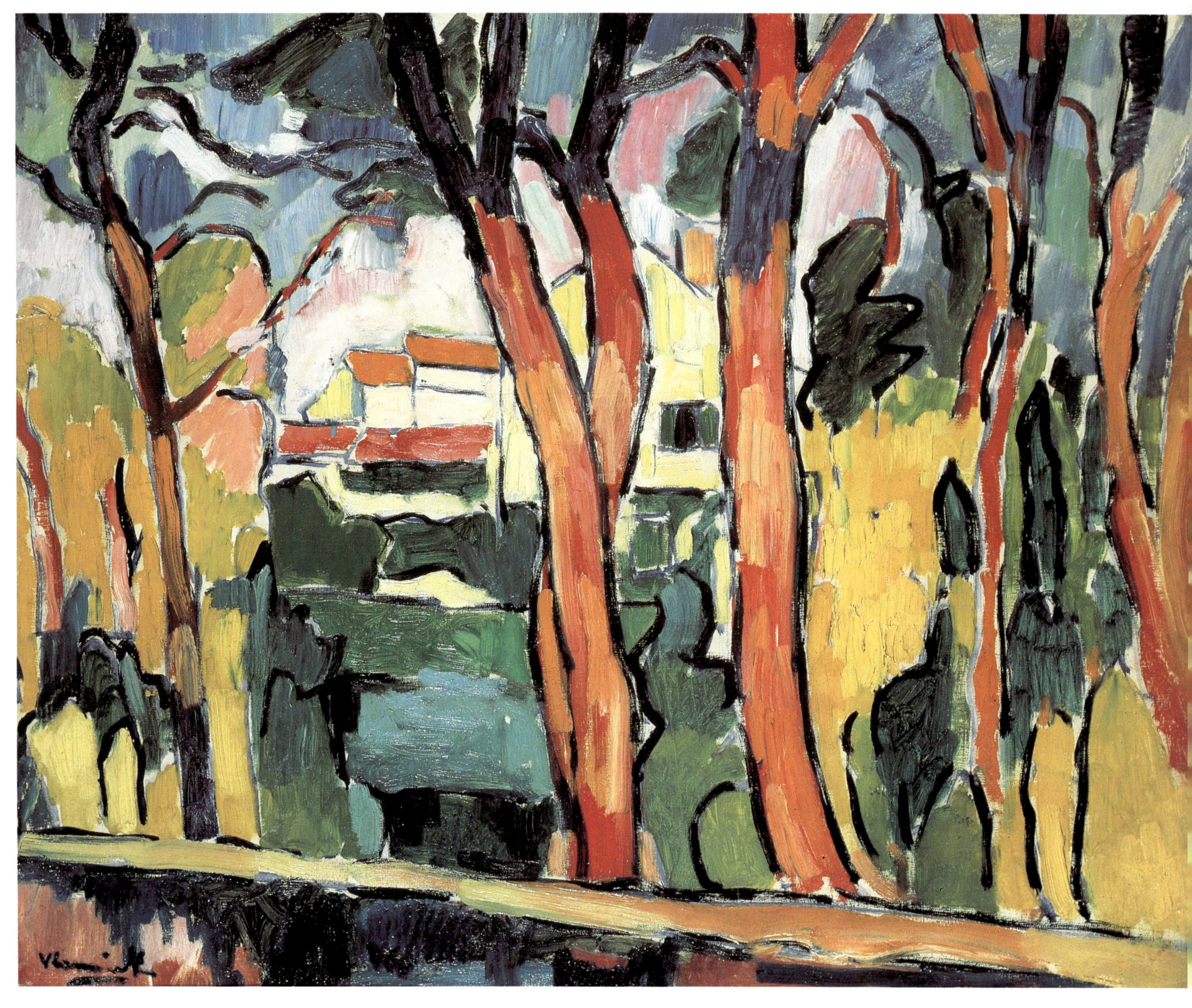

MAURICE DE VLAMINCK
Landscape with Red Trees
1906-1907
Oil on canvas, 25 ½ x 32 in (65 x 81 cm)
Paris, musée national d'Art moderne

Vlaminck, a true colorist above all, displayed a real sense of structure in his impressive *Self-Portrait* (1912), which shows him with a square face, a pipe at the lips, and bowler hat.

The most Painterly Painter of us All

According to his friend and biographer Marcel Sauvage, Fauvism was a reaction against the weak followers of the Impressionists who diluted and numbed their art, an antithesis of Neo-Impressionism which rapidly reached a dead end in fluttering grayness, and a revolt against all the academicism that had grown out of these movements. He described the Fauves as "the brutal flame of a fire-eater." This image referred more to Vlaminck than to any of his colleagues. The poet Apollinaire put it in another way: "M. de Vlaminck has a Flemish sense of joy. For him, painting is like a kermess." Fire and a Flemish carnival! These two elements are metaphorically present in most of his works, and not just in those of his Fauve period.

The island of Chatou was not as yet covered with buildings. It was a place of recreation for the lower classes; the trees grew near the water along the river bank; the low houses and fishermen's shacks hardly made a dent in the woods. Tugboats pulling trains of barges churned up the water as they went by without stopping, for there was no commercial port in Chatou. The only sign of modern times was the Paris–Saint-Germain-en-Laye railway bridge spanning the Seine with its steel arches and heavy stone pilings.

A painting like *Barques* (1905)–actually sailboats floating along the calm water–perfectly expresses the serenity of the suburbs without appearing outrageously garish, for the broad brushstrokes of blues, pinks, whites and greens organized on the pictorial surface make up a harmonious composition. On the other hand, more savage and more "fauve," *The Red Trees* (1906) which shows houses behind a screen of trees in all sorts of shades of red is one of his masterpieces. Gauguin, who gave useful advise to Sérusier as we have seen, also pointed out that the intensity of color will indicate the nature of each color; for example, the blue sea will be a more intense blue than the gray trunk of a tree, being a pure blue, but less intense. Then, as a kilo of green is greener than a half-kilo, you must make up the difference–your canvas being smaller than nature–by putting a greener green than the one in nature. There you have it, the truth behind the falsehood." His comment about a "kilo of green" caused much ink to flow, and Vlaminck's work as a whole seems to have been painted to justify it.

But this artist was not one to be out of touch with the rapidly developing industrial world. He was especially fond of bicycles after his father had given him one of these treasures of technical ingenuity when he was an adolescent. When he became rich and famous he acquired more and more powerful motorcycles and automobiles that gave him a "sensation of space and liberty" and fulfilled his love for speed. Railroad bridges also interested him, and he painted one from a close vantage point–*The Bridge of de Chatou*, 1906–as Caillebotte had once done earlier. Such views were often photographed and used for postcards at the period.

A new era had dawned in which motorcar and airplane meets became fashionable events. Marinetti unhesitatingly took

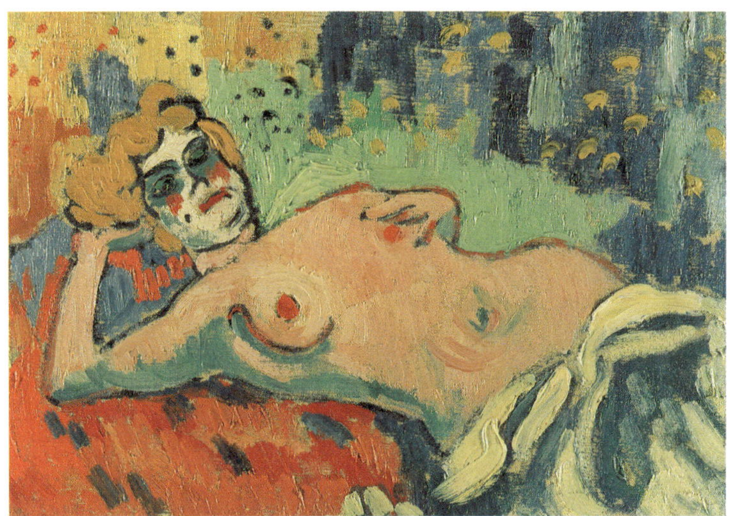

MAURICE DE VLAMINCK
Reclining Nude
1906
Oil on canvas, 10¾ x 16¼ in
(27 x 41 cm)
London, Fridart Foundation

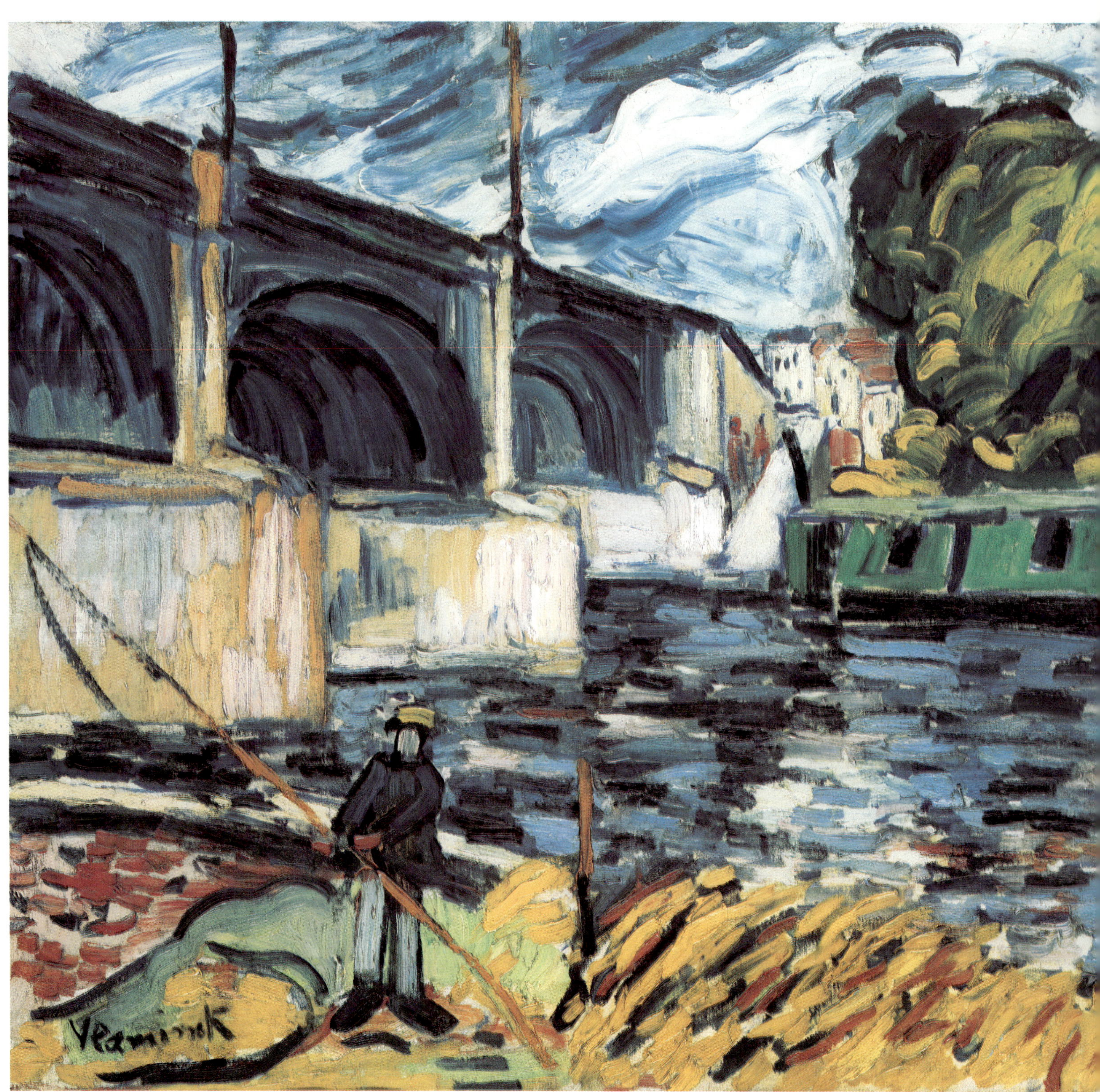
Vlaminck

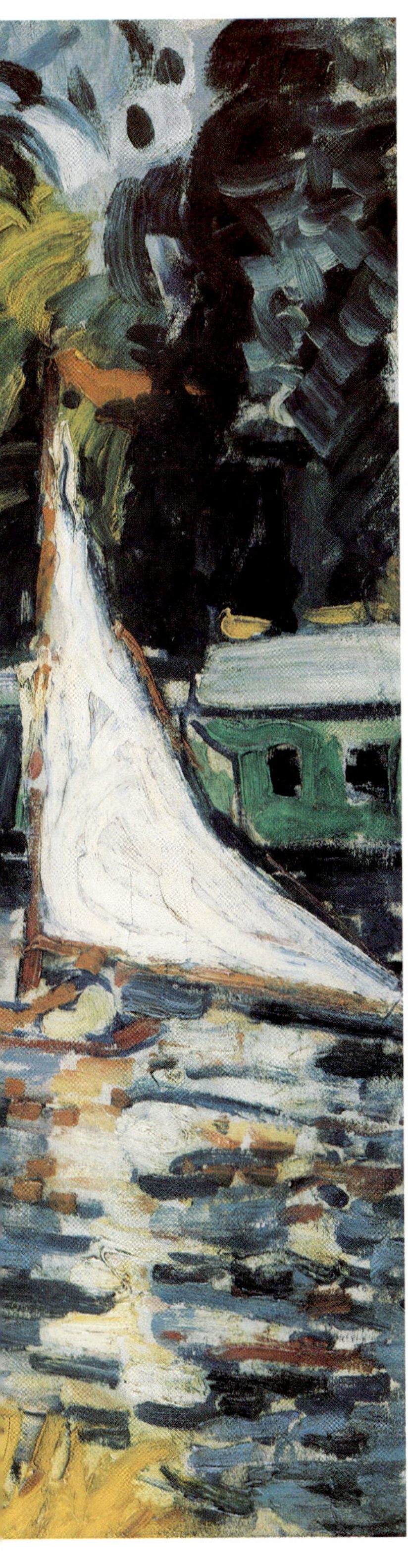

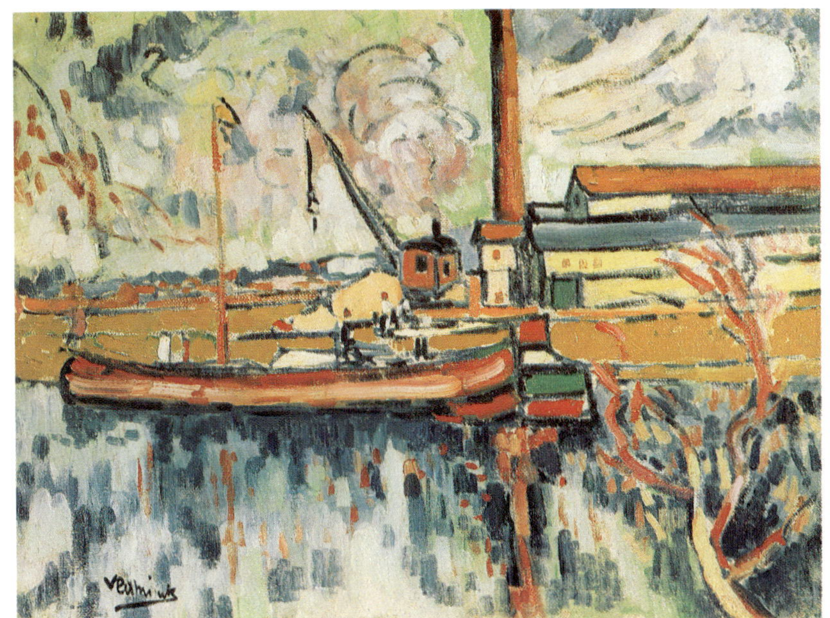

MAURICE DE VLAMINCK
Landscape at Chatou
1906
Oil on canvas, 23½ x 32 in (61 x 81 cm)
Troyes, musée d'Art moderne

Opposite:

MAURICE DE VLAMINCK
The Bridge at Chatou
1907
Oil on canvas, 26¾ x 37¾ in (68 x 96 cm)
Berlin, Staatliche Museen Preussischer
Kulturbesitz Nationalgalerie

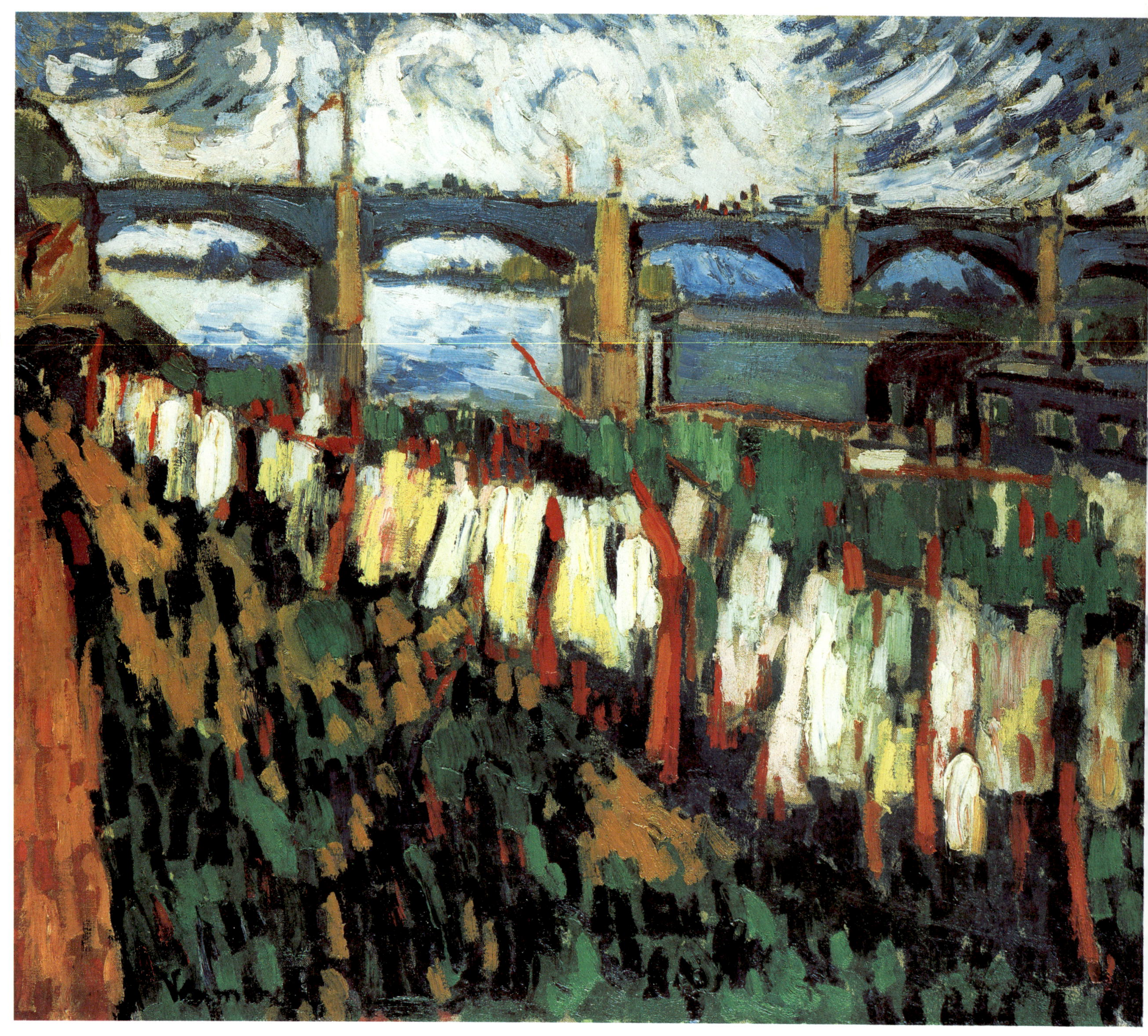

MAURICE DE VLAMINCK
The Bridge at Bezons
1906
Oil on canvas, 26½ x 31 in (67 x 79 cm)
Basel, Beyeler Gallery

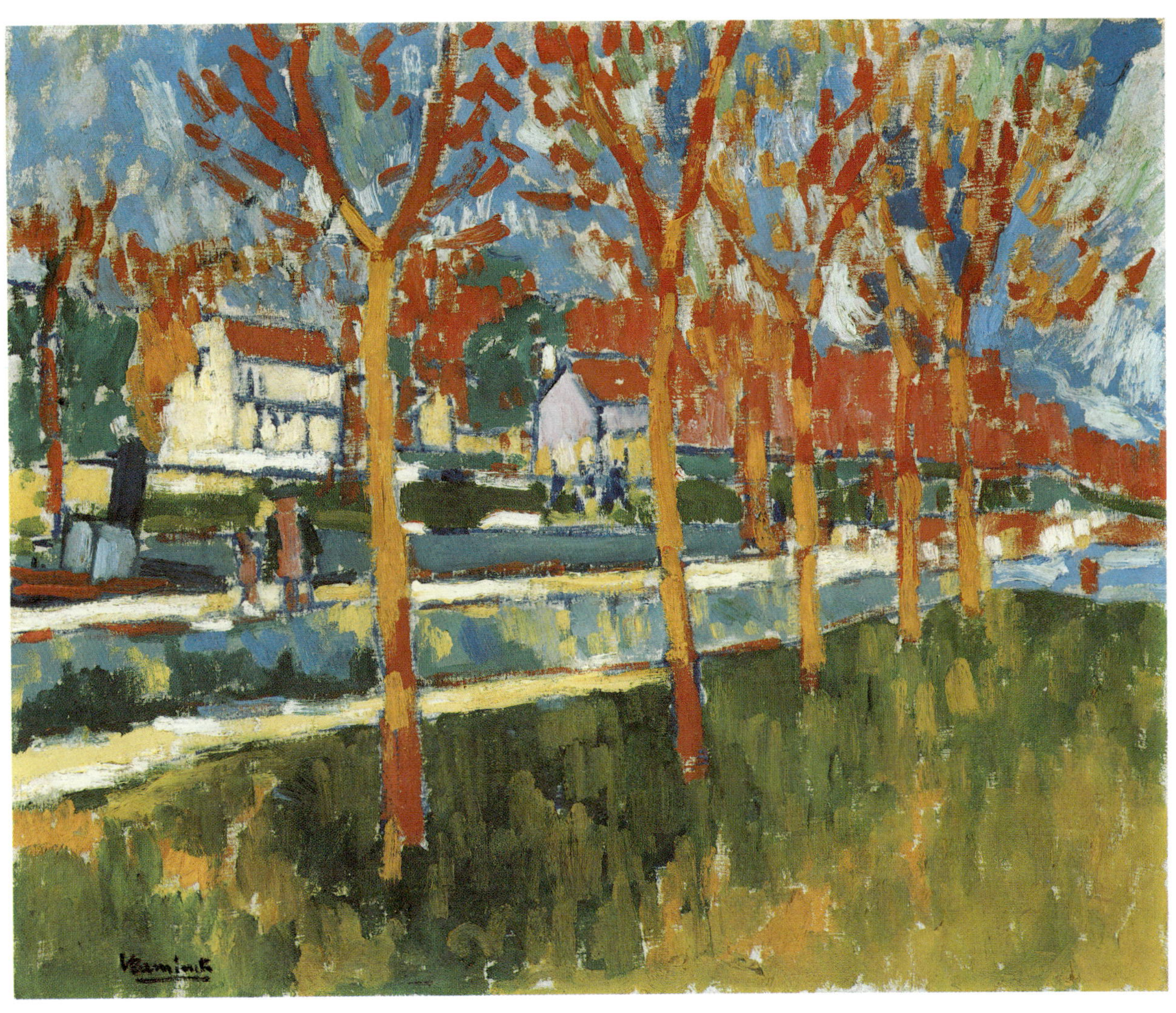

MAURICE DE VLAMINCK
The Locks at Bougival
1906
Oil on canvas, 21¼ x 25¼ in (54 x 64 cm)
Ottawa, National Gallery of Canada

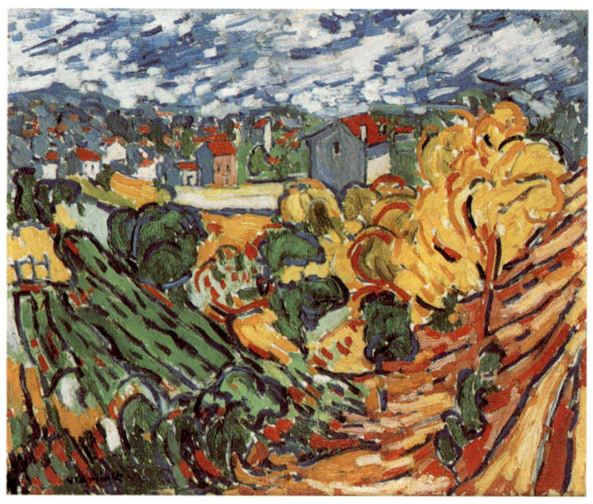

Maurice de Vlaminck
Lanscape near Chatou
1906
Oil on canvas, 23¾ x 29 in (60.5 x 73.5 cm)
Amsterdam, Stedelijk Museum

up three columns on the front page of the *Figaro* of February 20, 1909, for his *Manifeste du Futurisme:* "We would like to announce that the splendor of the world has been enriched with a new beauty: the beauty of speed. Racing cars with bodies adorned with gleaming pipes are like monsters with exploding breath... A roaring automobile that seems to run on a hail of bullets is more beautiful than the *Victory of Samothrace.*" This declaration inspired hundreds of paintings depicting speeding automobiles, not the least of which were by Boccioni and Balla. The Futurists were influenced by Muybridge and by Marey's "chronophotographs," which decomposed the motion of a man running or a horse galloping, frame by frame into long series of pictures. Yet, they never represented motion from more than one fixed point as if they were at the edge of the road watching the cars speed by. They had what could be called a "cinematographic" vision of movement, obtained by successions of still pictures running at a certain speed, like in a movie sequence.

Vlaminck had a different approach; he painted the world from a moving vantage point, as if he were riding a bicycle or driving an automobile. Motion produces fluid patterns of distortion in an either expanding or shrinking space. This explains the feeling of dizziness provoked by the deformed perspective apparent in some of his works with leaning trees, compressed crossroads, and reeling landscapes.

Instead of following the Futurist practice of breaking up shapes to the limit of comprehensiveness, he used the dynamic power of color. This phenomenon is noticeable in many of Vlaminck's compositions with an exaggerated extended foreground and a receding horizon, like in *Marly-le-Roi* or in *Houses at Chatou* (both from 1906). Each of these depicts a site–village, forest or bridge–where one enters, crosses, but does not stop. Ascending and descending terrain and winding roads became the more frequent themes in the artist's later work. His already ample brushstrokes turned into long streaks of earth colors in what has been described as "a violent confrontation with the landscape."

Passionate Brushwork

Vlaminck's espousal of a Cézannian style was doomed to failure. There is nothing transient in Cézanne's landscapes; in his views of L'Estaque or Montagne Sainte-Victoire he emphasized a kind of geological stability with permanent geometric structures: "You must see in nature the cylinder, the sphere, the cone, and put all of them into perspective." A static observer would have no trouble following these recommendations, but what about someone witnessing the disintegration of solid forms through motion? Vlaminck's *The Oise Valley* (1917) is a Cézanne-like compositions in motion that is a contradiction in terms. The artist later commented: "A region that one passes through, a man traveling along a road, the physiognomy of a town, an obscure mass of forest, these all suggest, for some undefinable reason, my expectations and anxieties welling up as they file past, like the vague presentiments that dreams are made of." Sensation having been transformed into sentiment, Vlaminck reached the antipodes of Fauvism.

The heavy brownish, greenish, reddish, or whitish impasto had become part of Vlaminck's pictorial mode of expression. It was a way for him to bring his obsessive fears to the surface. In his

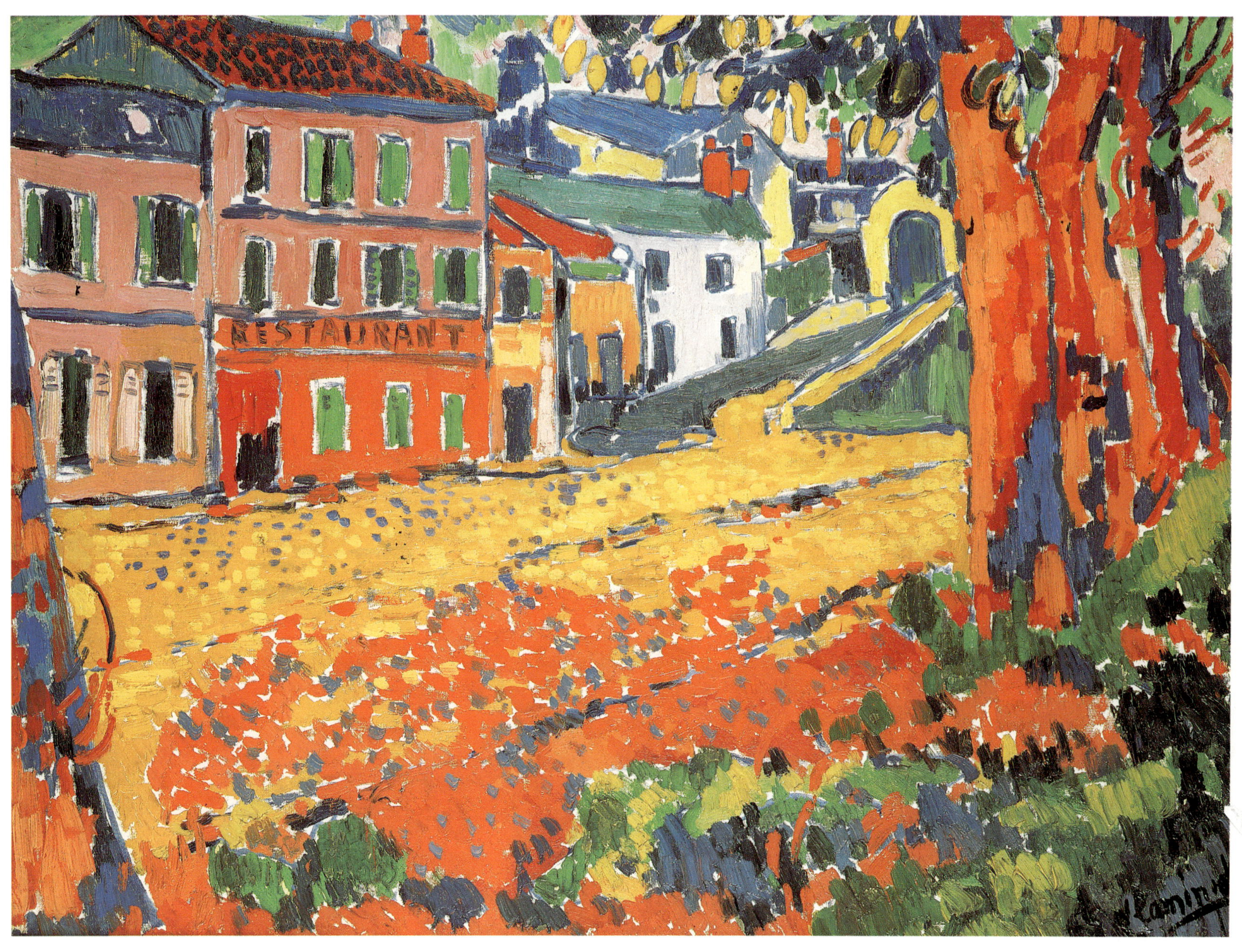

Maurice de Vlaminck
The "Restaurant de la Machine" at Bougival
1905
Oil on canvas, 23½ x 32 in (60 x 81 cm)
Paris, musée d'Orsay

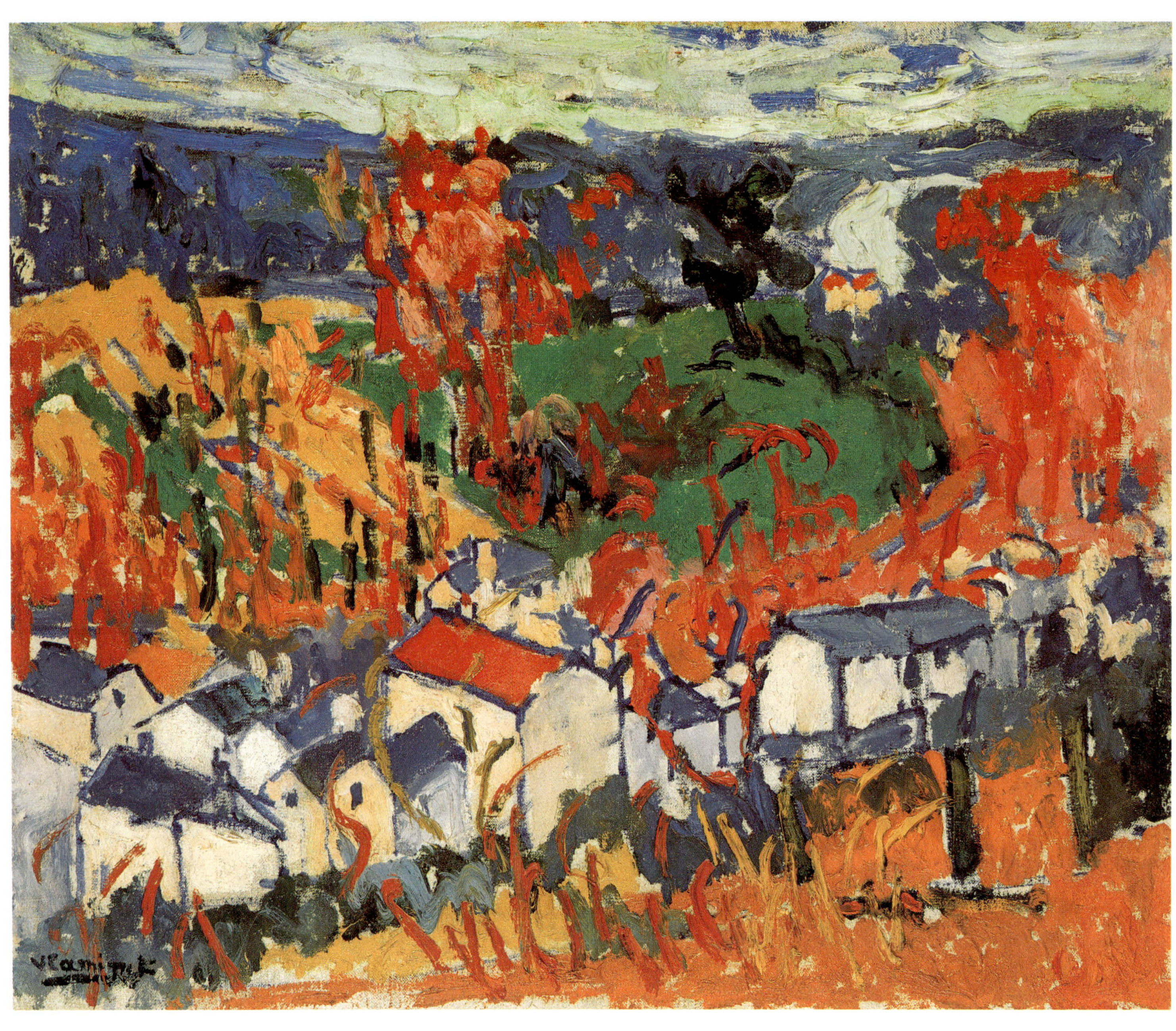

MAURICE DE VLAMINCK
Houses and Trees
1906
Oil on canvas, 23½ x 28¾ in
(54.3 x 64.5 cm)
New York, Metropolitan Museum of Art
(Gift of Raymonde Paul)

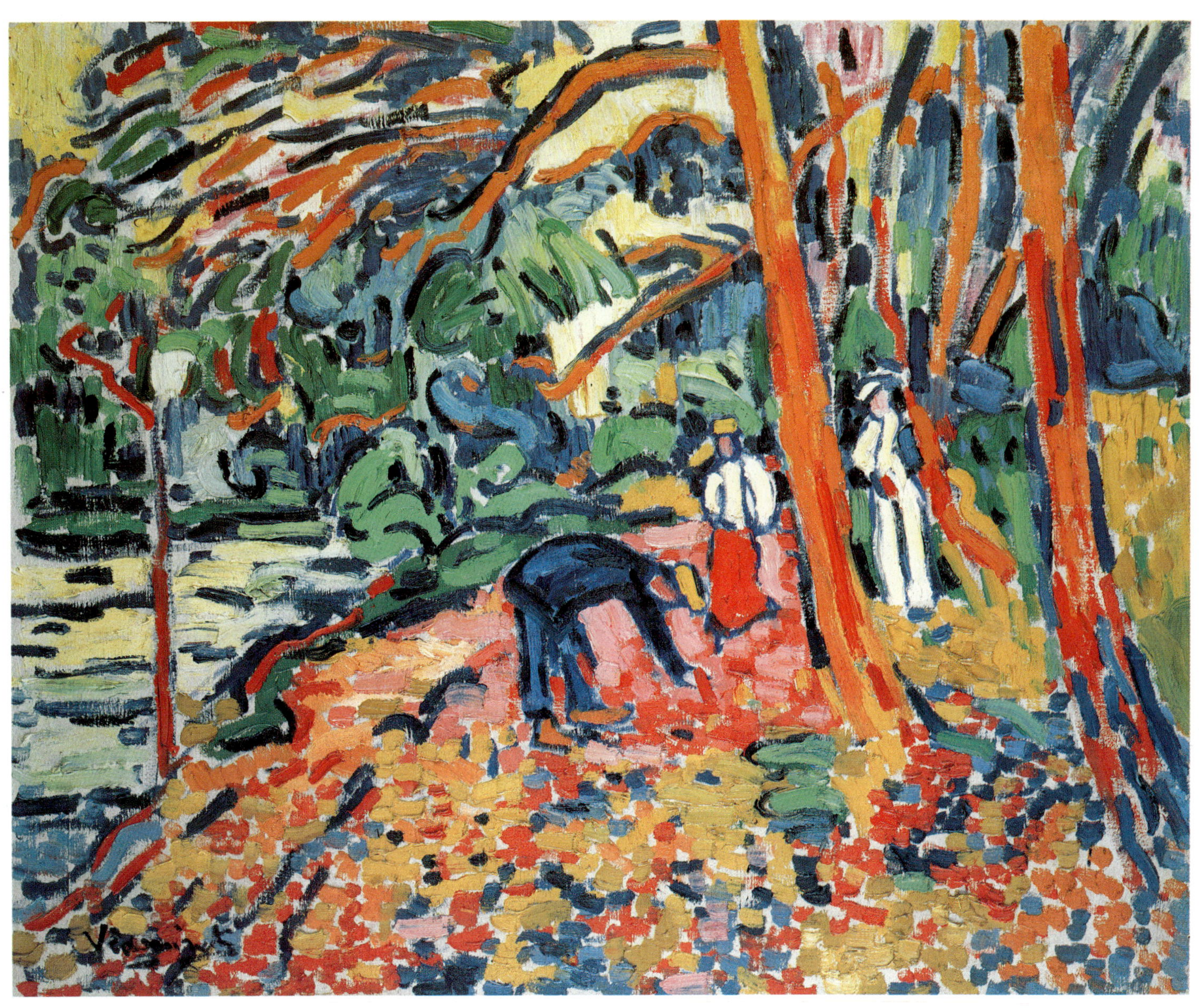

Maurice de Vlaminck
Picking up Deadwood
1906
Oil on canvas, 23½ x 28¼ in (60 x 73 cm)
London, Fridart Foundation

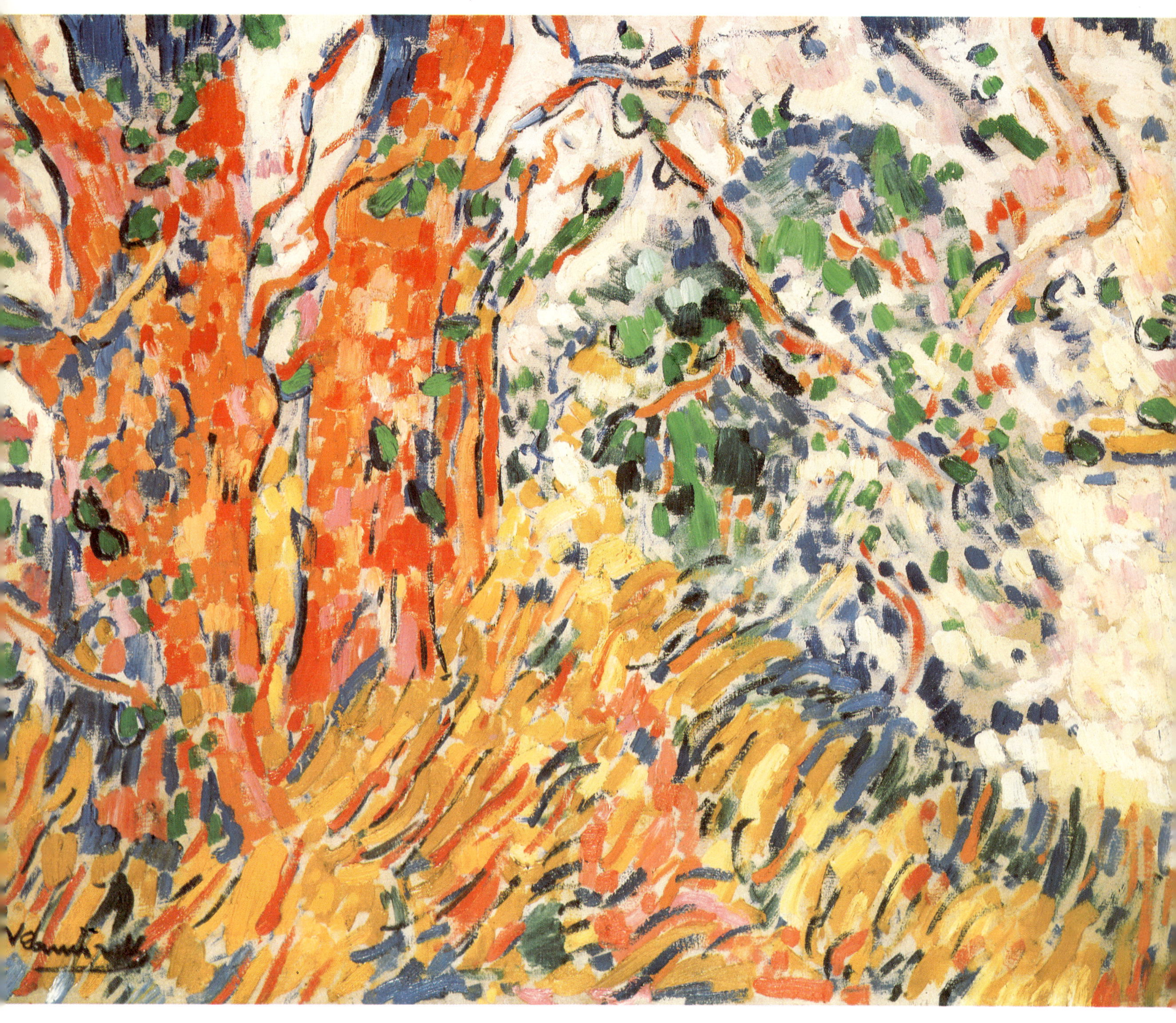

Maurice de Vlaminck
Bank of the Seine at Chatou
1904
Oil on canvas, 23¼ x 31½ in (59 x 80 cm)
Paris, musée d'Art moderne de la ville de Paris

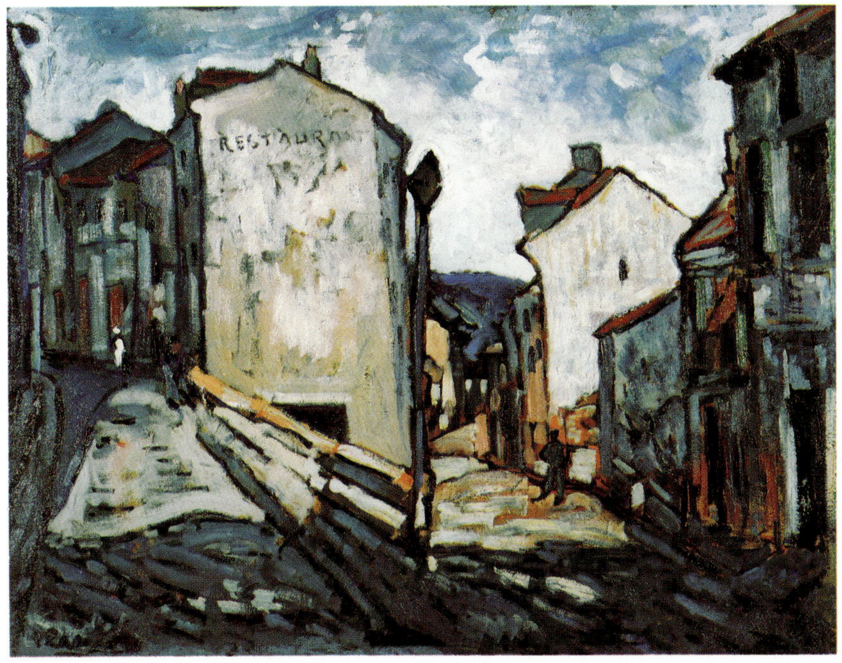

MAURICE DE VLAMINCK
The Village
1904
Oil on canvas, 35 x 45¾ in (89 x 116 cm)
Essen, Folkwang Museum

biography of the painter, Jean Selz noted: "Vlaminck's paintings carry him on a great wind of lyricism that seems to be blowing from a black sky and over everything in his sight: cringing cottages, distorted trees, imbrued suns…."

In 1919, after his successful exhibition at the Druet Gallery, he bought a house in Valmandois to the northwest of Paris. Increasingly taken with the idea of living in close contact with nature, he acquired a property, La Tourillière, lost in the country near Rueil-la-Gadelière in the Eure-et-Loir Department. To his work as painter and writer–he was the author of more than 20 books: novels, poetry and memoires–he added the activities of a gentleman farmer.

It was in this country estate that he died in 1958 at the age of 82, after a lifetime of painting. He asked that his grave be planted with wild grass and that seeds be scattered over it so that birds would come there to feed.

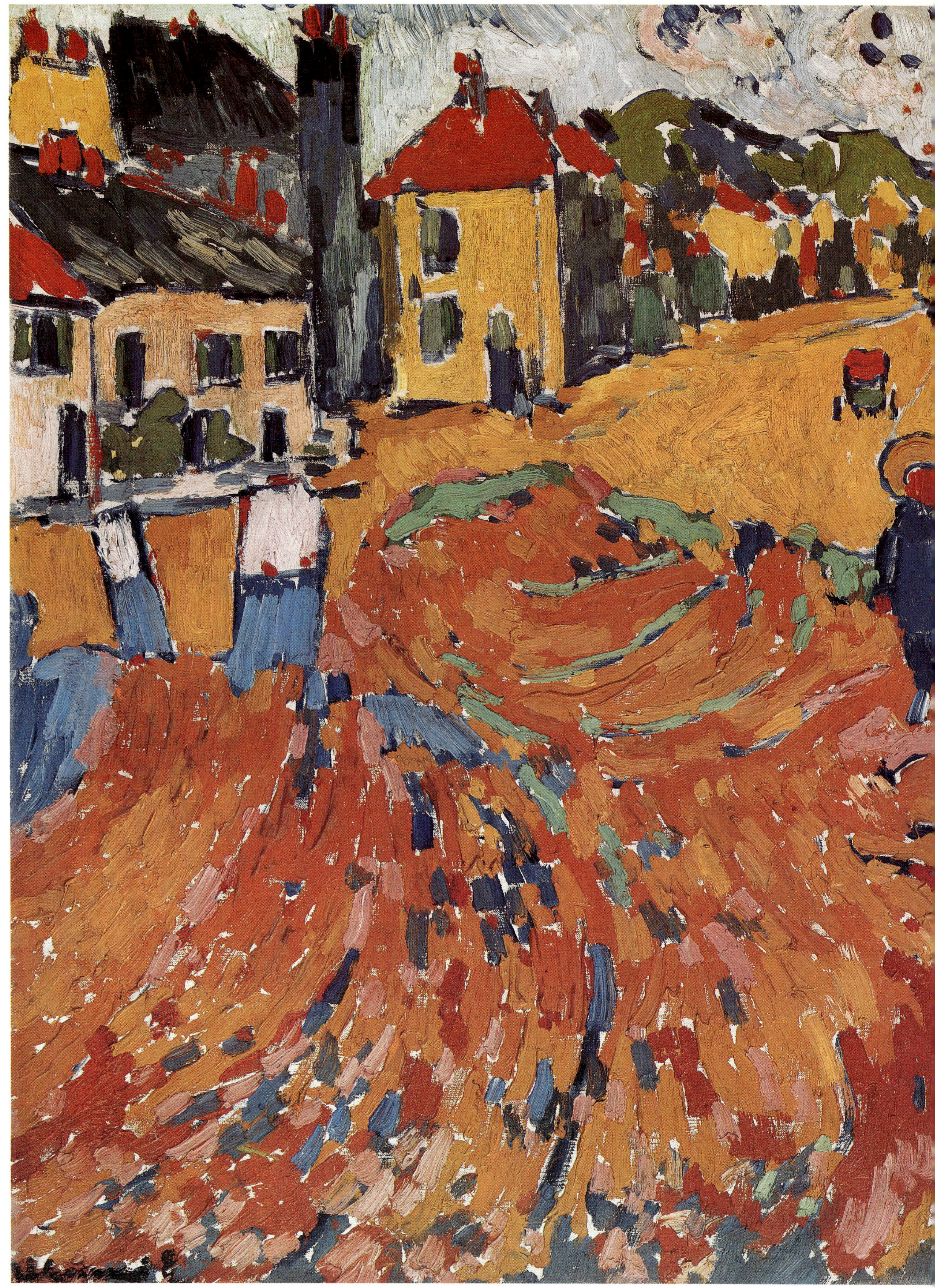

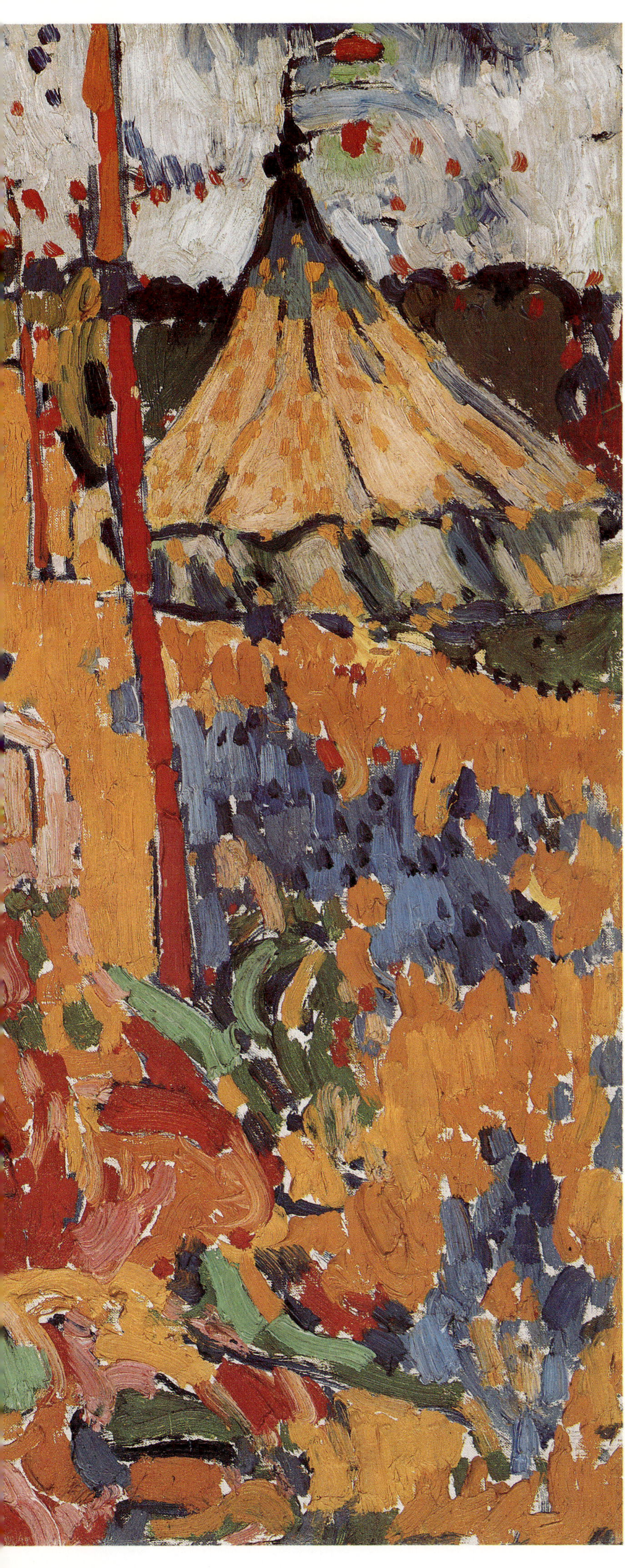

Maurice de Vlaminck
The Circus
1906
Oil on canvas, 23½ x 28¾ in
(60 x 73.3 cm)
Basel, Beyeler Gallery

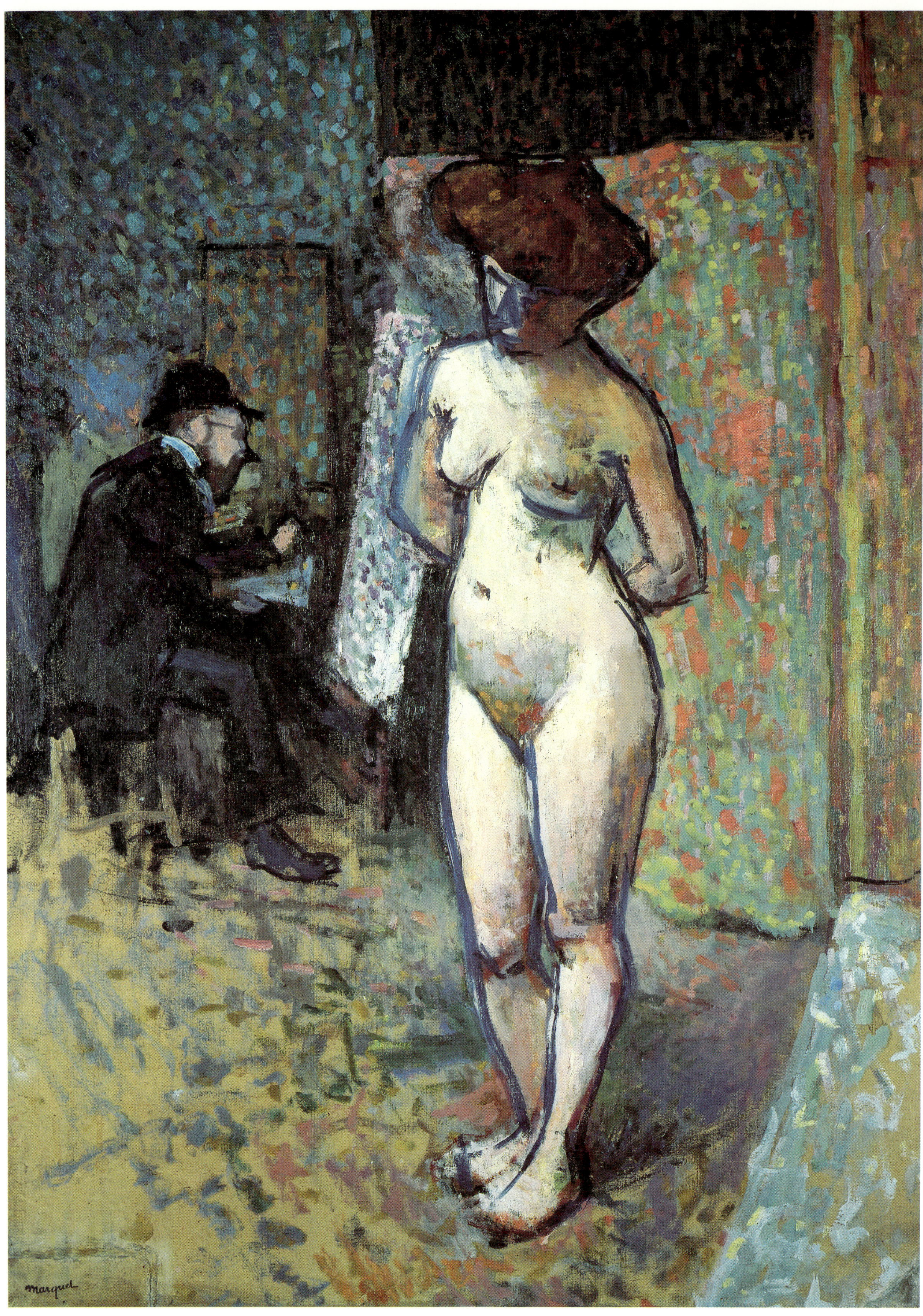
marquet

Integrity in Art:

Marquet

A Slight Limp

Light-hearted in spite of a slight limp, Albert Marquet was undoubtedly the most precocious of the Fauves. As a small child, he began making drawings on the ground with a piece of coal before he had even learned to walk.

Born in Bordeaux on March 26, 1875, he was the son of a very modest railroad employee–a man so easygoing and absent-minded that he almost forgot to declare his son's birth at the town hall. Marquet had a difficult childhood. His school years were fraught with suffering due to the teasing that he had to bear because of his infirmity. His teachers did not understand his ineptness at doing anything with his hands other than drawing. His future would have looked very bleak indeed, had his mother not decided to orient him toward industrial art. Such a course of studies, however, meant four or five years of training at the Ecole des Arts Décoratifs in Paris. Eventually she decided to sell a small cottage and a plot of land in order to open an embroidery store in the nearby rue Monge to pay for Albert's education.

At "*les Arts déco*," which he entered at the age of 15, Marquet made friends with Matisse–a friendship that would last a lifetime. An immediate kinship developed between the two, for Matisse did not allow the other students to bully Marquet about his affliction. Matisse, who had delicate health himself, kept his hat on during class and would counter his professors' remarks with the rejoinder: "I'll remove my hat when there are no more draughts." Marquet felt protected in the company of such a strong personality.

At the Ecole des Beaux-Arts, where he followed Matisse, each class had its specialty. The students who dreamed of taking

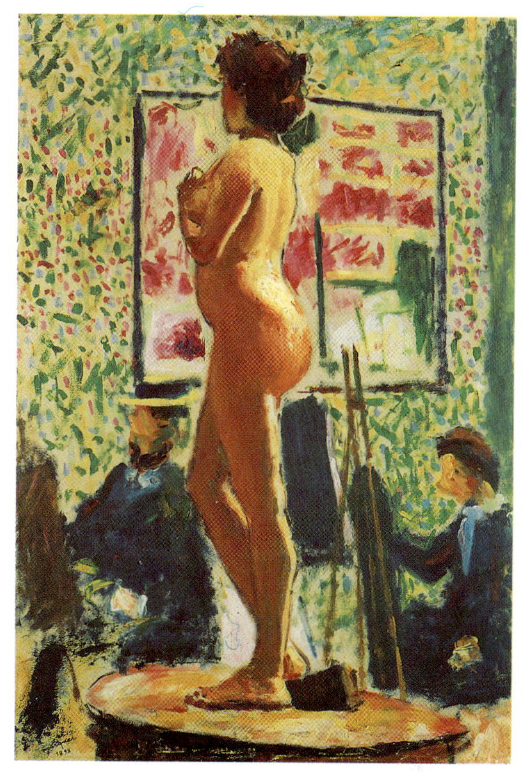

Albert Marquet
The Fauve Nude
1898
Oil on papier collé, 28¾ x 19¾ in
(73 x 50 cm)
Bordeaux, musée des Beaux-Arts

Opposite:

Albert Marquet
Matisse Painting in Manguin's Studio
1904-1905
Oil on canvas, 28¼ x 39¼ in
(71.5 x 100 cm)
Paris, musée national d'Art moderne

up mythological subjects worked under Bouguereau–potentate of the arts and expert in pictures of Anacreontic nymphs and Teutonic goddesses. Those who wished to execute the so-called "grandes *machines*" went to work with Bonnat, where the stress was on physical force and feats; during the model's rest period, the apprentice painters did push-ups and lifted weights. The "intellectuals"–the laughingstock of the student body–or the undecided signed up to work under Gustave Moreau who, although besotted with sphinxes and unicorns, enjoyed the reputation of being liberal-minded and pleasant.

In addition to Matisse, the studio included Manguin, and Rouault–Moreau's favorite student–as well as a young artist by the name of Burdy who was renowned for his extraordinary manual dexterity. Marquet had a strained relationship with Moreau, who took to calling him his *"ennemi intime."* Marquet preferred to portray passers-by, strollers on the sidewalk in a milling crowd, the man in the street, in whom he recognized himself. His biographer, Georges Besson stated the matter very succinctly: "The street saved Marquet from the Ecole."

ALBERT MARQUET
On the 14th of July at Le Havre
1906
Oil on canvas, 32 x 25½ in (81 x 65 cm)
Bagnols-sur-Cèze, musée municipal

Black and White

Although Marquet was a marvelous landscape artist, with an amazing ability to render early-morning light, snowy scenes and misty sunsets, he was the one Fauve who preferred to turn to the city for his subjects. Most of the others in the group agreed with Vlaminck that "cities are fake."

During his stay in Paris in 1887-1888, Van Gogh began a small picture that he never finished, *On the 14th of July*. It shows a street with a lamppost and crowds painted in his early Dutch style with a flood of large red-white-and-blue splashes dashed on the canvas like shooting stars across the sky. Marquet adopted the same theme in his *On the 14th of July at Le Havre* (1906), in which the flags and banners, painted in a flat-color technique, break up and hollow out the entire composition.

The Impressionists had already turned their attention to city decorations during the national holiday and other annual festivities. The motifs fit in with their taste for light, further enhanced by the flags waving in the wind; the decked-out streets were a warm feast for the eye in modern urban life. Marquet followed the Impressionist tradition, but with a wider range of colors set against the gray and brown façades which seemed more appealing to his sensibility.

The posters that began to spread over city walls became another theme for these modern artists in a modern world. It is difficult to imagine how greatly advertising had transformed the urban setting of the period, so accustomed have we become to its effect on the appearance of our cities today. Marquet's *Billboards at Trouville* (1906), which shows two parasols in front of an immense billboard covered with a fabulous polychrome checkerboard pattern of posters, is significant from this point of view. It was, no doubt, influenced by Dufy, who executed a version of his own that same year from the same spot. How preposterous for these painters to turn their backs on the limitless horizon of the ocean–a theme that Marquet had already painted in Fécamp and Saint-Jean-de-Luz–and to choose instead the blocked horizon of a wall glorifying merchandise! At the time, poster art was considered a vulgar medium and altogether inappropriate for artistic treatment. When it came to cavorting Greco-Roman divinities versus

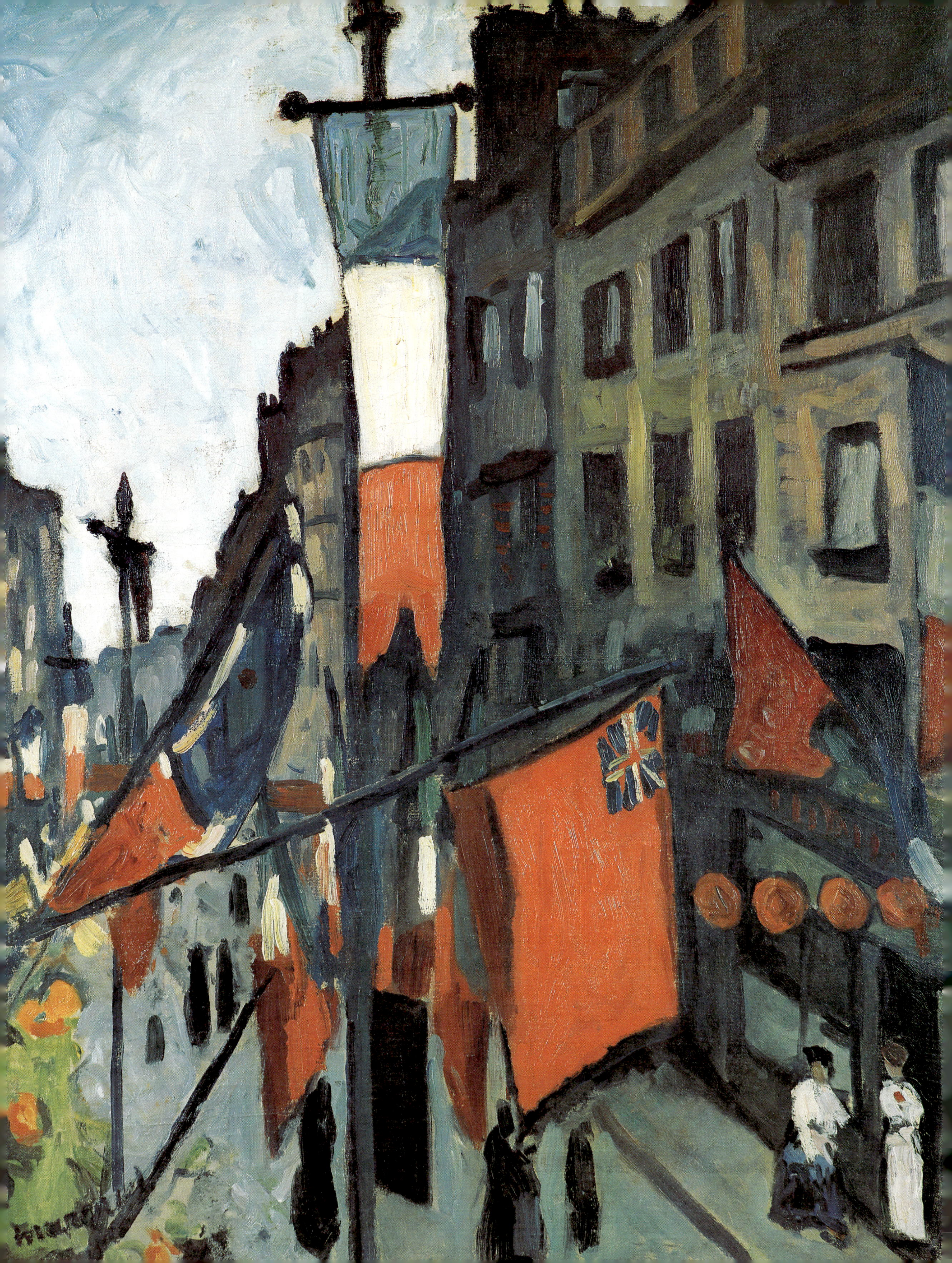

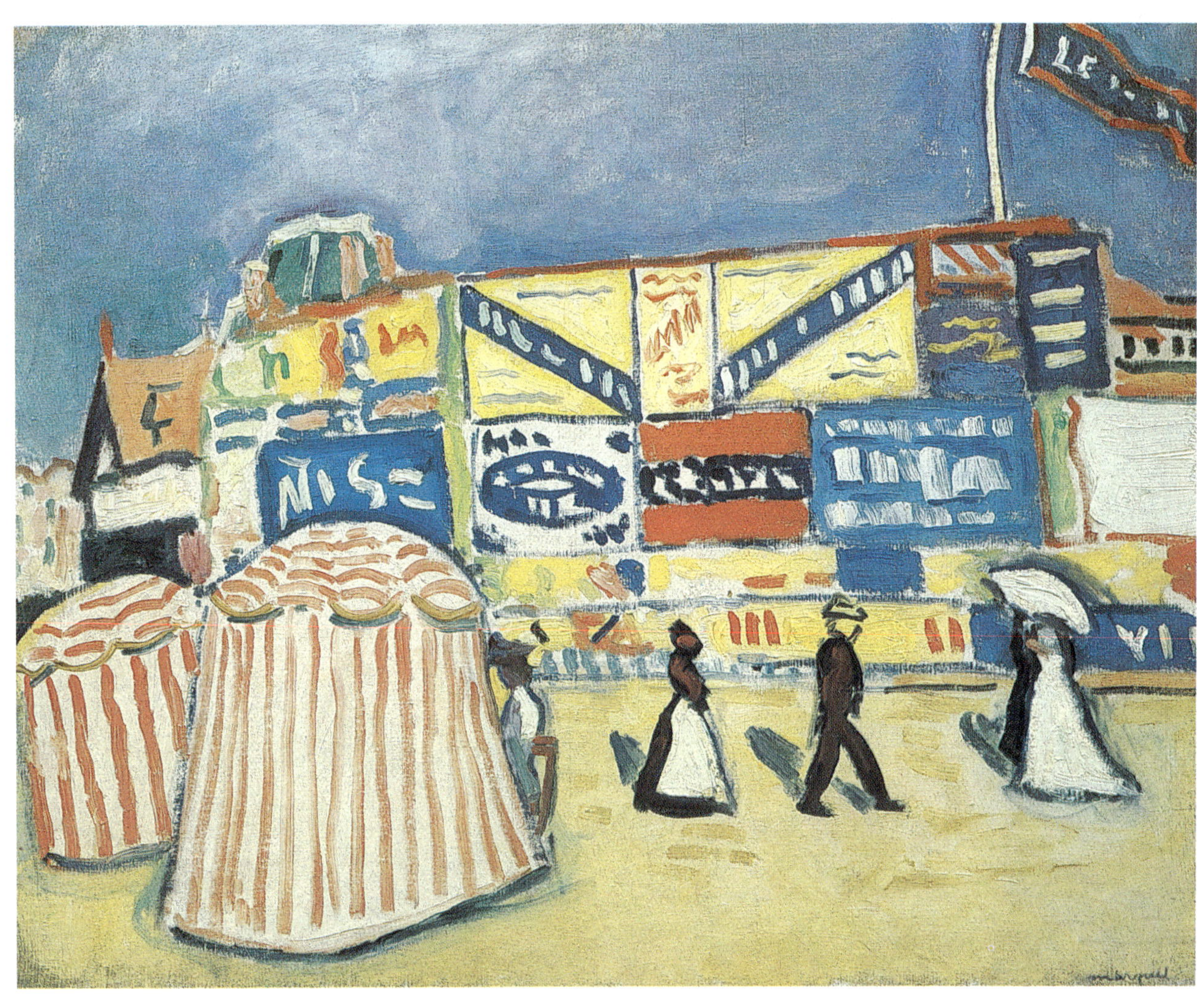

ALBERT MARQUET
Billboards at Trouville
1906
Oil on canvas, 25¼ x 32 in (64 x 81 cm)
New York, Mrs. John Hay Whitney
collection

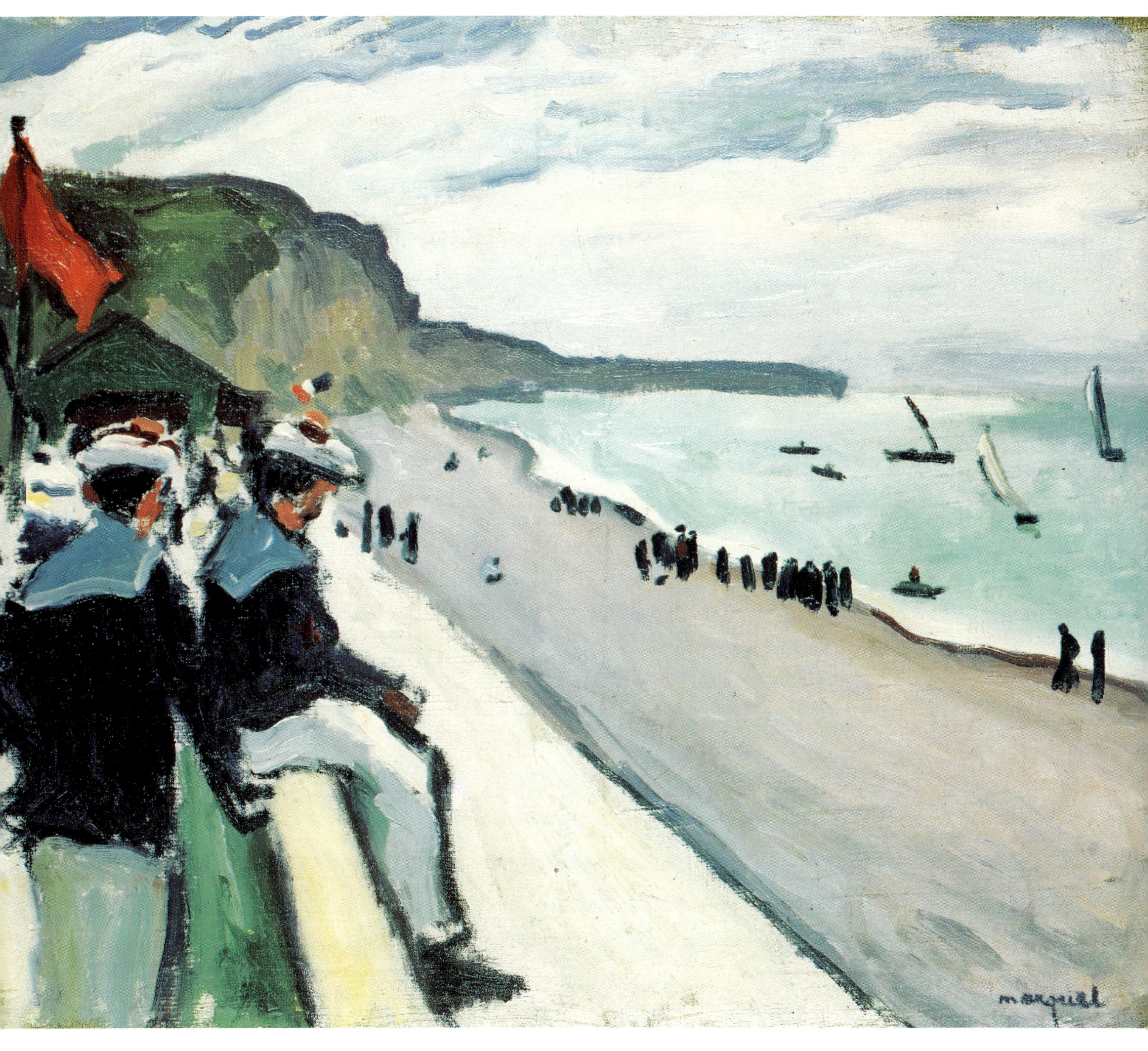

ALBERT MARQUET
The Beach at Fécamp
1906
Oil on canvas, 20 x 24 in (51 x 61 cm)
Paris, musée national d'Art moderne

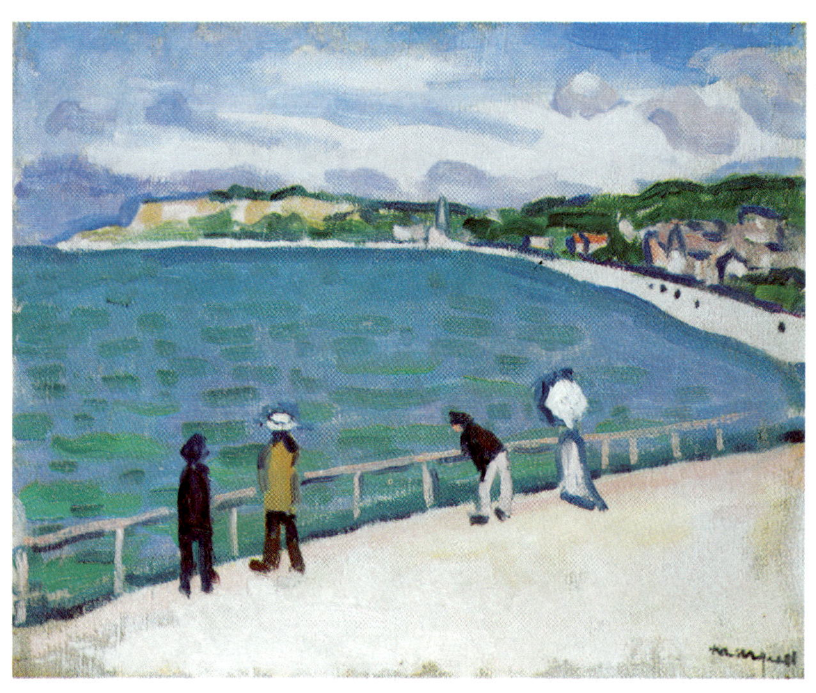

Albert Marquet
On the Jetty at Sainte-Adresse
1905-1906
Oil on canvas, 13 x 16¼ in (33 x 41 cm)
Paris, Daniel Malingue Gallery

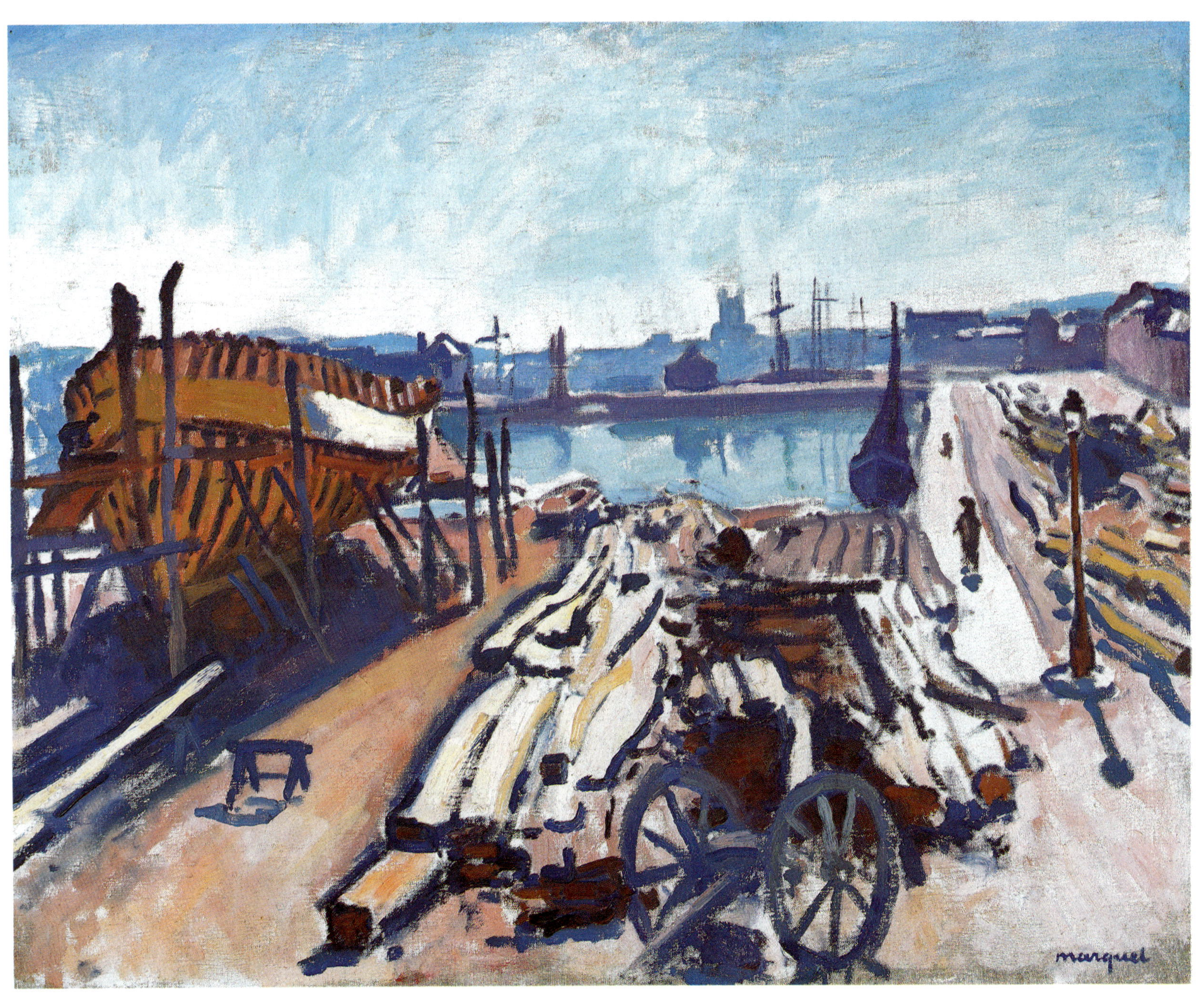

ALBERT MARQUET
Fécamp Harbor
1906
Oil on canvas, 25½ x 31½ in (65 x 80 cm)
Quimper, musée des Beaux-Arts

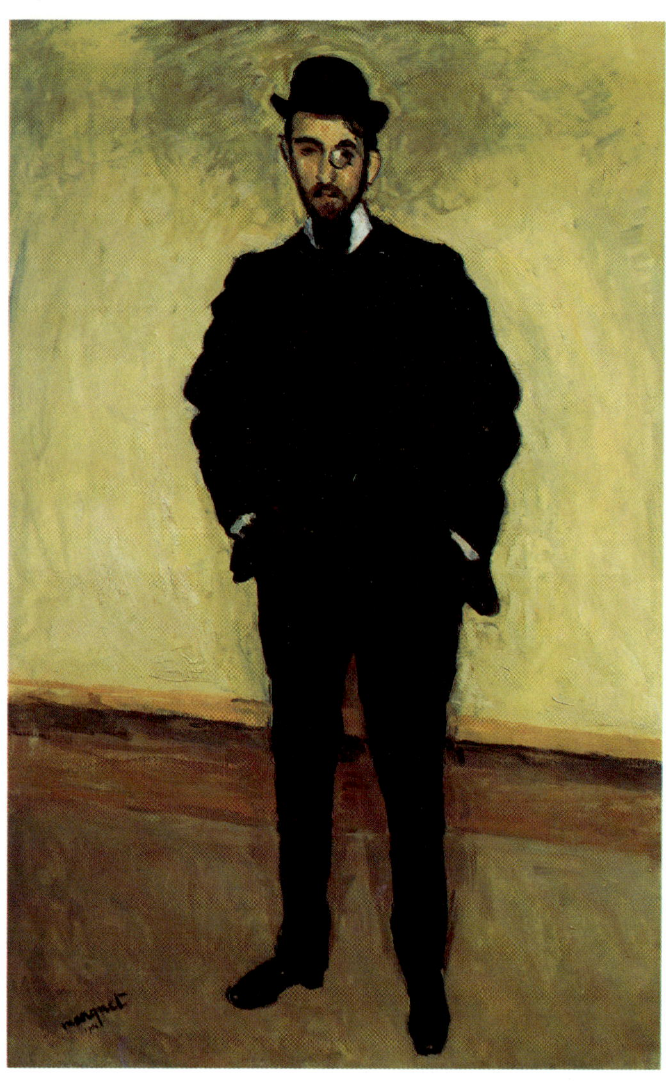

ALBERT MARQUET
Portrait of Rouveyre
1904
Oil on canvas, 36½ x 24 in (92 x 61 cm)
Paris, musée national d'Art moderne

advertisements for *Grains de Vals* laxative, the break with academic painting had become total.

More than Van Gogh and the Impressionists, it was Manet who undoubtedly had the greatest impact on Marquet during his years of apprenticeship. This is demonstrated in *A Sergeant of the Colonial Corps* (1904) which recalls *The Piper*, one of the most enigmatic paintings of the master of the Ecole des Batignolles. The sergeant's uniform, with blue material, brass buttons, red stripes and fluting, and gold epaulettes is not a slavish replica of *The Piper*, whose trousers are black and the tunic white; but there are similarities in the way Marquet loads the colors down in order to create visual weight.

Marquet–the pussyfoot Fauve–confided some years later to his friend Francis Jourdain that his presence in the famous "wild-beast cage" in 1905 was due more to chance than to pictorial considerations; the five pictures that he exhibited in Room VII had been painted under the gray skies of Paris and were "almost entirely in black and white." A black-and-white palette, while far from Gauguin's famous "kilo of green," was closer to the color scheme of the great Spanish masters, such as Ribera and Velasquez who had inspired Manet. When Marquet added dull yellows, harsh pinks and forceful violets to his basically colorless palette he was involved in a mysterious alchemic transmutation. Thanks to this magical process he was able to contain murky water within the stony walls of portuary installations, stretch out piers under the rain, and silhouette trampers and steamers with their funnels in profile sailing across the far-off horizon.

Harbors, piers and boats! Indeed, in 1912, Marquet journeyed from port to port: Le Havre, Rotterdam, Hamburg, Naples, Tangiers. Omnipresent in his work, water is not treated like a mirror to capture ever-changing reflections in Impressionist fashion, nor like an alibi in Vlaminck's manner; it prompted him into "material reveries" in the sense given to these terms by the philosopher Gaston Bachelard. Marquet's water is either quickened by invisible naiads or rendered motionless like a shroud over joy and suffering.

A Lofty Point of View

Though the artist painted the cities of Rabat, Naples and Algiers, his most beautiful urban views are of Paris, particularly the Pont-Neuf, the towers of Notre-Dame and the quai du Louvre observed from the windows of his successive apartments. He lived first at 19, quai Saint-Michel and then on the fifth floor of a building at the angle of rue Dauphine and quai des Grands-Augustins.

The great master Camille Pissarro, who liked plunging views in his compositions, had unwittingly paved the way for Marquet, several years earlier. In 1891, the younger artist underwent an eye operation that left him unable to paint out of doors, for the slightest speck of dust carried by the wind would irritate his eyes. After many painful relapses, he decided to work from rented apartments or hotel rooms, first in Rouen and then in Paris. With his easel set up in front of a window sheltering him from bad weather, he would execute street scenes in complete peace of mind. He moved into a room at the Grand Hôtel de Russie over the boulevard Montmartre and then into an apartment at 204, rue de Rivoli, where he made several paintings of the Tuilerie Gardens.

Marquet's limp may have been another reason compelling him to paint views of Paris from his window. Like many artists,

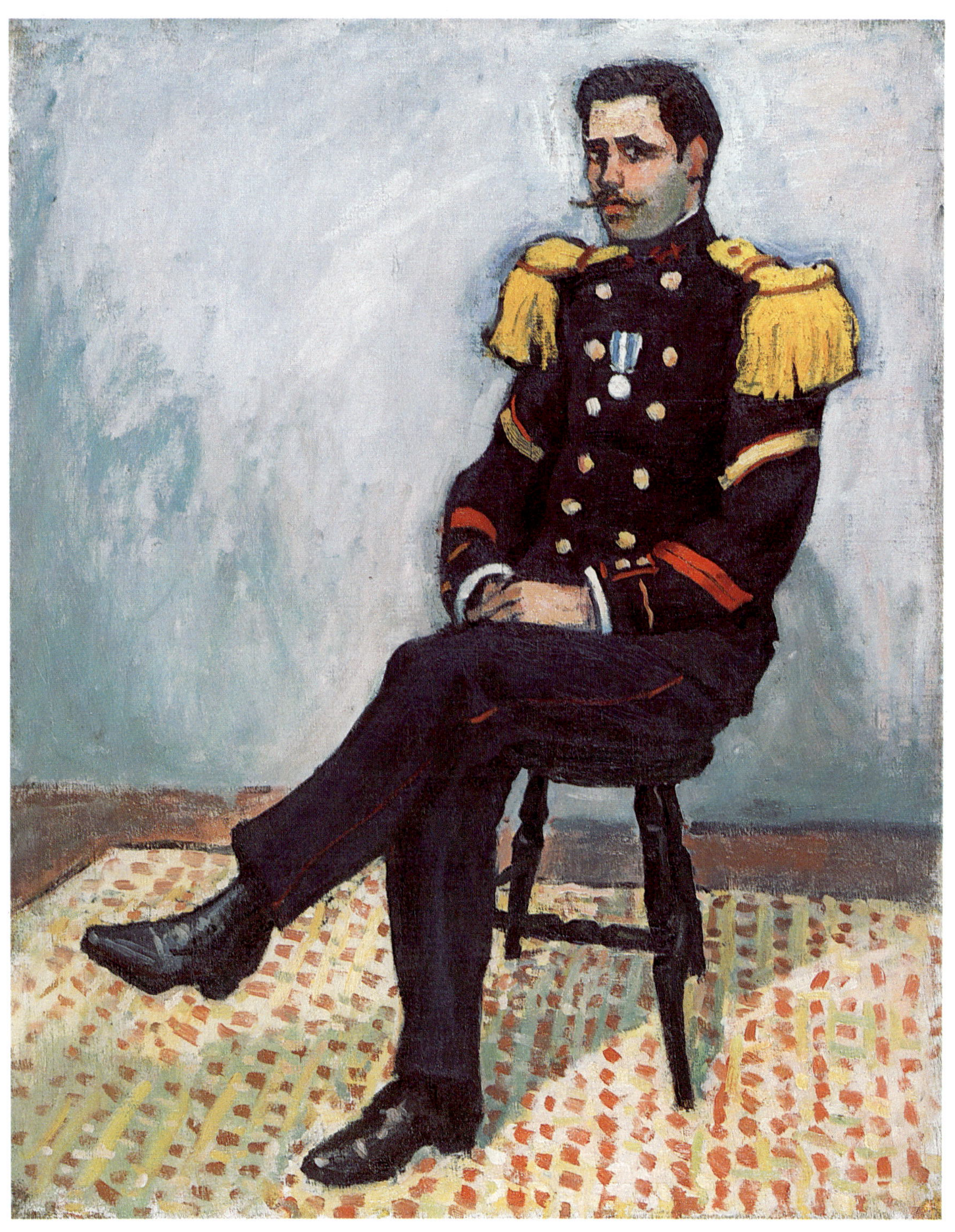

Albert Marquet
A Sergeant of the Colonial Corps
around 1906
Oil on canvas, 32 x 25½ in (81 x 65 cm)
Bordeaux, musée des Beaux-Arts

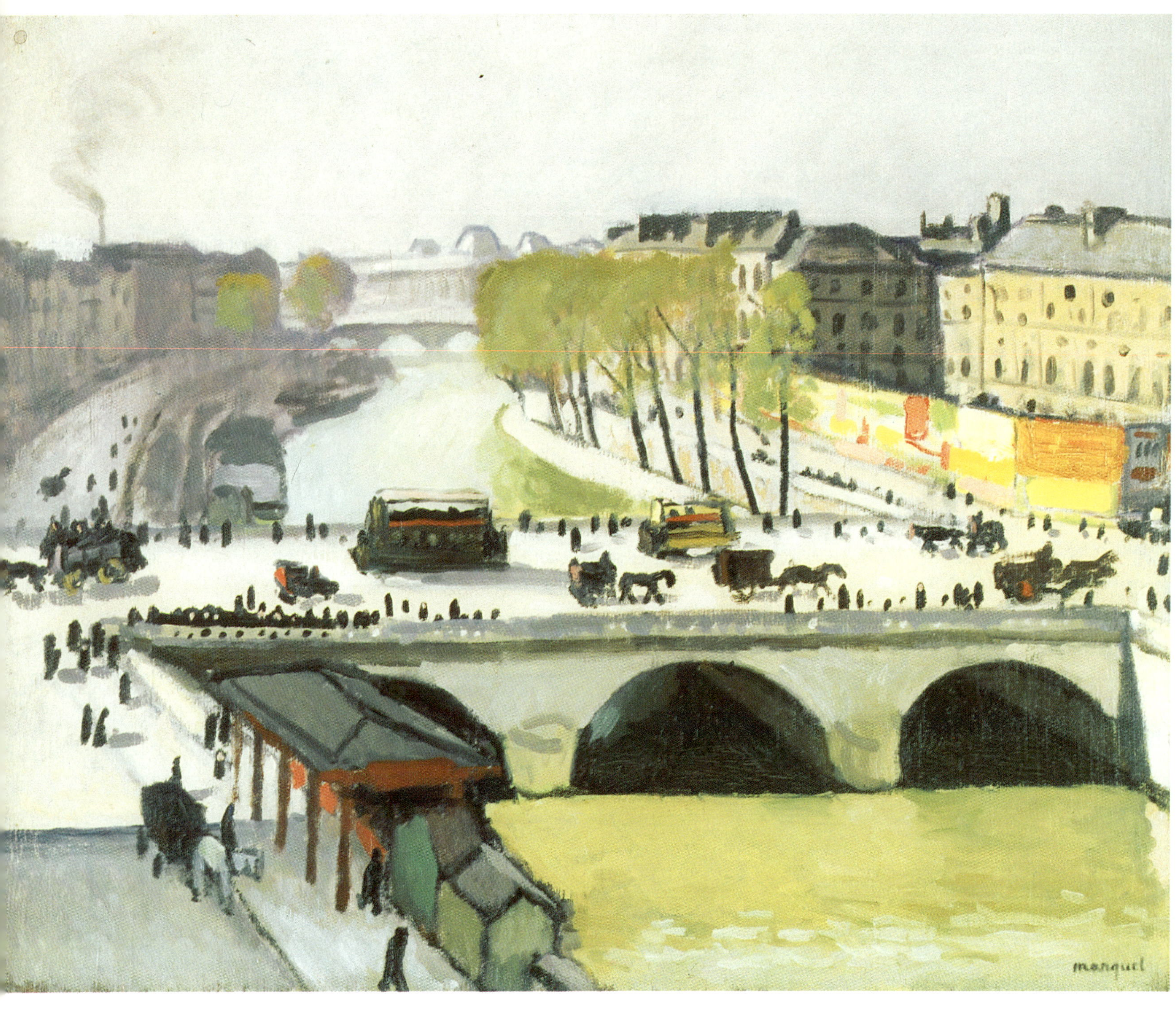

ALBERT MARQUET
Pont Saint-Michel
1908
Oil on canvas, 25½ x 32 in (65 x 81 cm)
Grenoble, musée de Peinture
et de Sculpture (Agutte-Sembat Bequest)

he was fond of painting the city in snow, but dared not venture out on the street under such bad conditions.

No matter how the story went, views of Paris such as Marquet's *Sunset on the Pont-Neuf*, 1906; *Notre-Dame under Snow*, 1908; *The Saint-Michel Bridge*, 1910, to mention just these few, drew Fauvism into a very specific corner. The minuscule pedestrians in the background hardly larger than dots, automobiles and trucks no bigger than toys, remind one of a passage in Shakespeare's *King Lear* (Act IV, scene VI) in which Edgar describes to his blind father, the Duke of Gloucester, what the view is like on top of the Dover cliffs where they are standing:

> Come on sir; here's the place: stand still.
> How fearful
> And dizzy 'tis to cast one's eyes so low!
> The crows and choughs that wing the midway air
> Show scarce so gross as beetles; half way down
> Hangs one that gathers samphire, dreadful trade!
> Methinks he seems no bigger than his head.
> The fishermen that walk upon the beach
> Appear like mice, and yond tall anchoring bark
> Diminish'd to her cock, her cock a buoy
> Almost too small for sight. The murmuring surge,
> That on the unnumber'd idle pebbles chafes,
> Cannot be heard so high. I'll look no more,
> Lest my brain turn, and the deficient sight
> Topple down headlong.

The sociologist Marshall McLuhan (*The Gutenberg Galaxy*, 1962; p. 16) points out that this excerpt is the first verbal expression of anxiety of the third dimension. But anxiety aside, are we not also reminded of Marquet? Matisse, as we saw in an earlier chapter, brought space into a room through a window, even a closed one–*Siesta* (1905), from his Collioure period–in such a way that there is no longer any separation between indoors and outdoors. Marquet treated the scenes that he saw through an open or closed window with illusionistic perspective, but as he perceived them from such a high vantage point they took on an entirely different aspect. Although the effect is the exact opposite of Matisse's, it is comparable in the sense that his plunging views, in a similar way eliminated the traditional frame of space.

Marquet got caught up in the game; he rented a maid's room on the quai du Louvre which allowed him to change his observation points; with the quais of the Right Bank in sight, he was able to see the Left Bank unfold below him at the same time.

Marquet's art was not, of course, limited to his Parisian series–he was a talented painter of nudes and still lifes–but he owed his greatest works to this City. Before his death in 1947 at the age of 72, he took up the theme of the Pont-Neuf once again. Curiously enough, *The Pont-Neuf at Night* (1935), with its lampposts and automobile lights shining through the dark and the red, yellow, and blue neon signs on the roof of the Samaritaine department store in the background, is one of his most purely Fauve paintings although a later work.

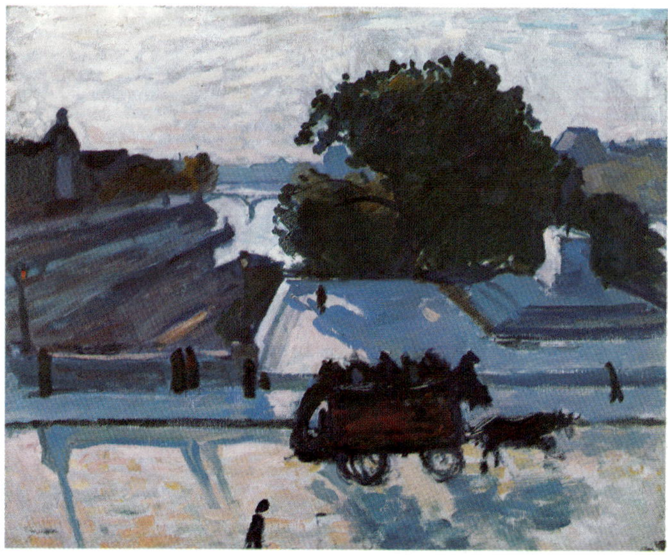

ALBERT MARQUET
The Pont-Neuf in the Sun
1906
Oil on canvas, 28¾ x 36¼ in (73 x 92 cm)
Rotterdam, musée Boymans-van-Beuningen

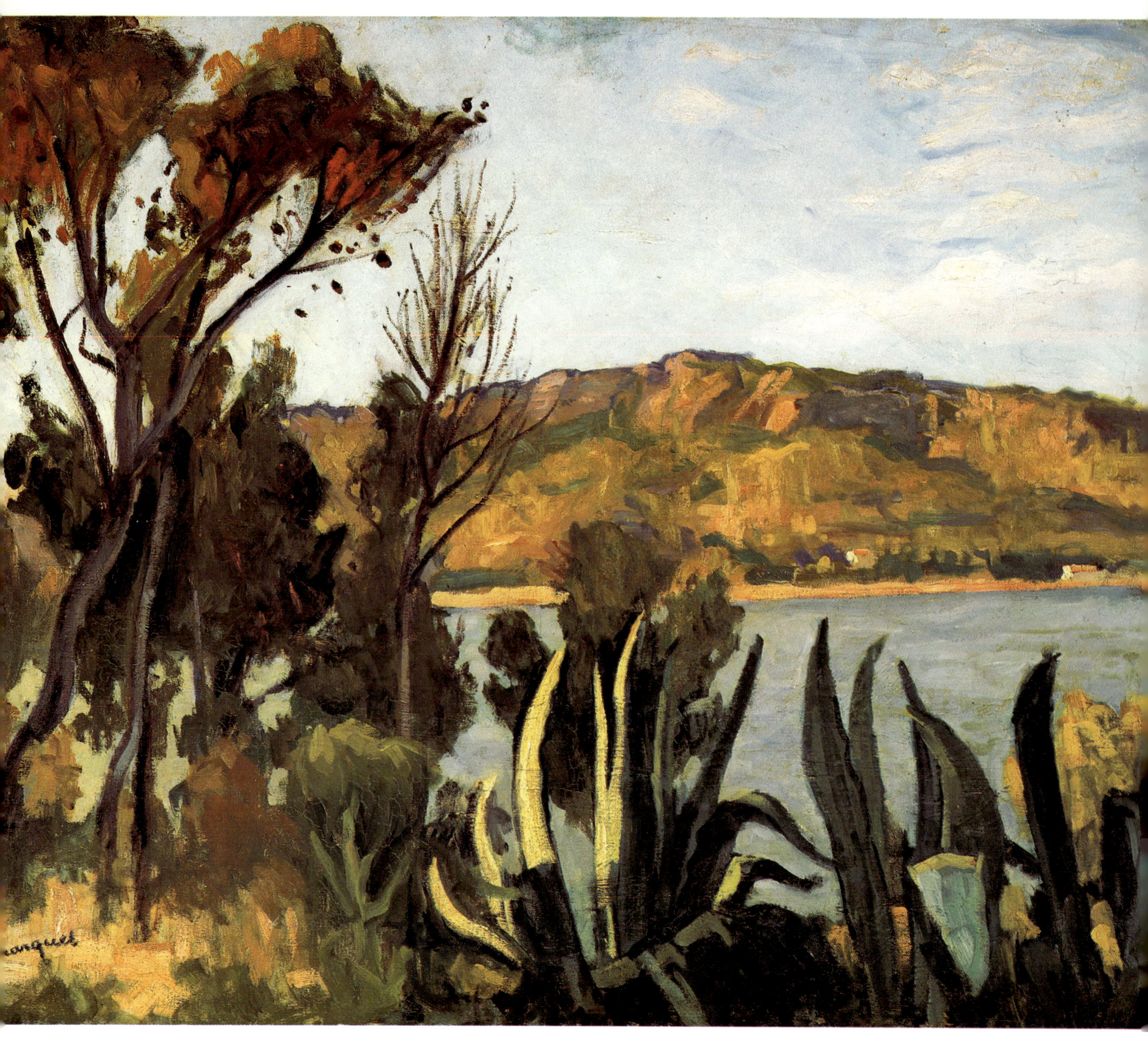

Albert Marquet
View of Agay
1905
Oil on canvas, 25½ x 31½ in
(65 x 80 cm)
Paris, musée national d'Art moderne

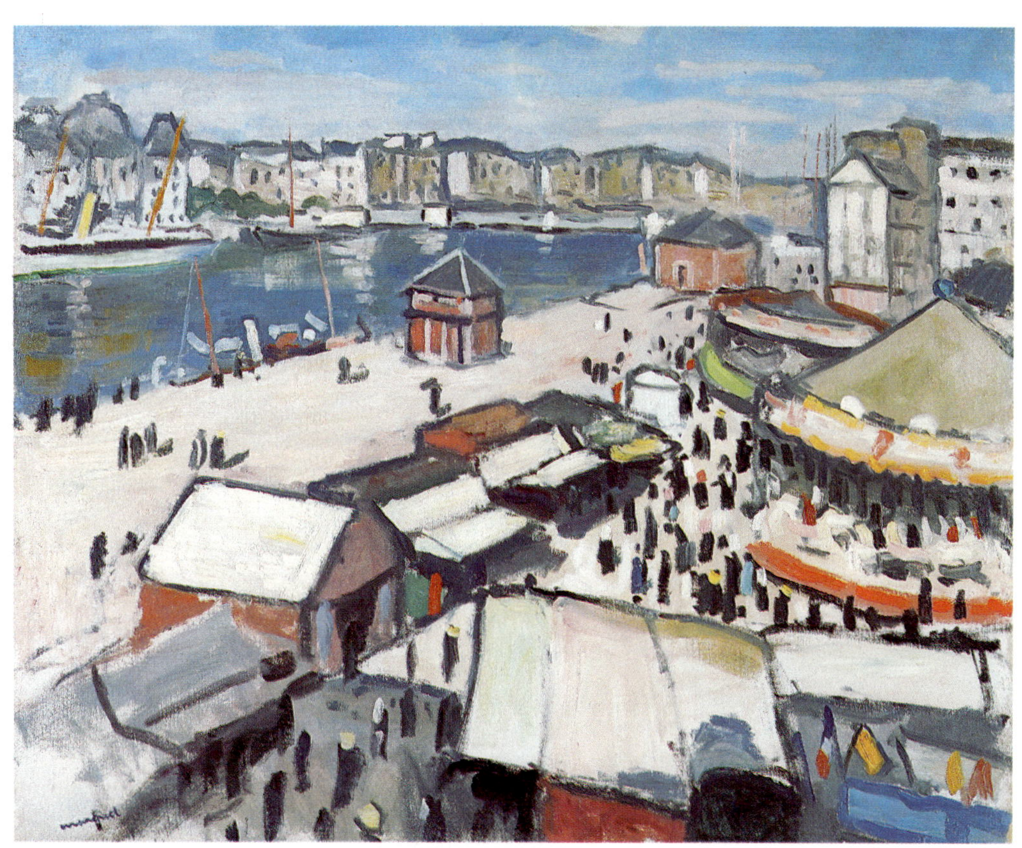

ALBERT MARQUET
The Fair at Le Havre
1906
Oil on canvas, 25½ x 32 in (65 x 81 cm)
Bordeaux, musée des Beaux-Arts

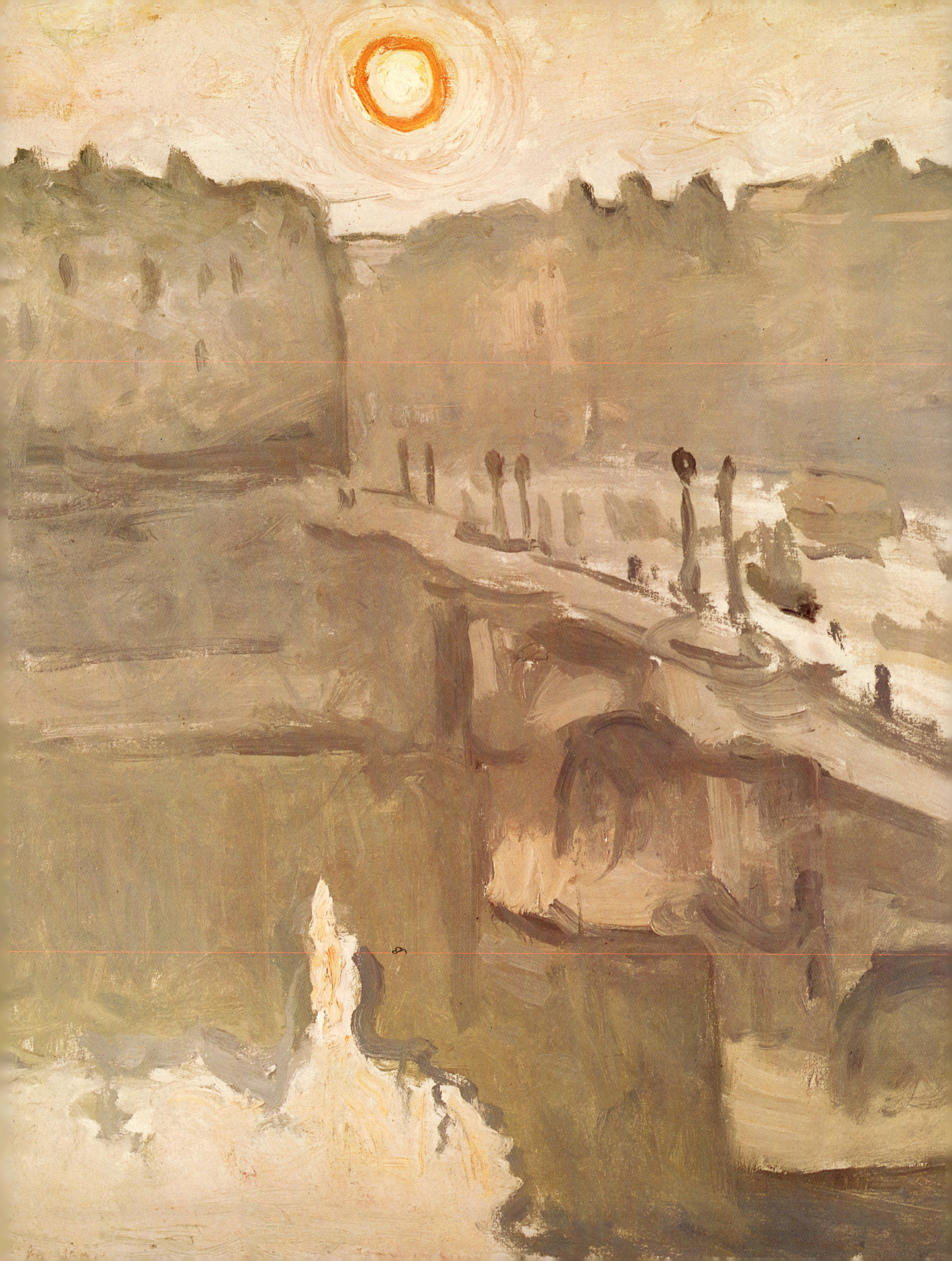

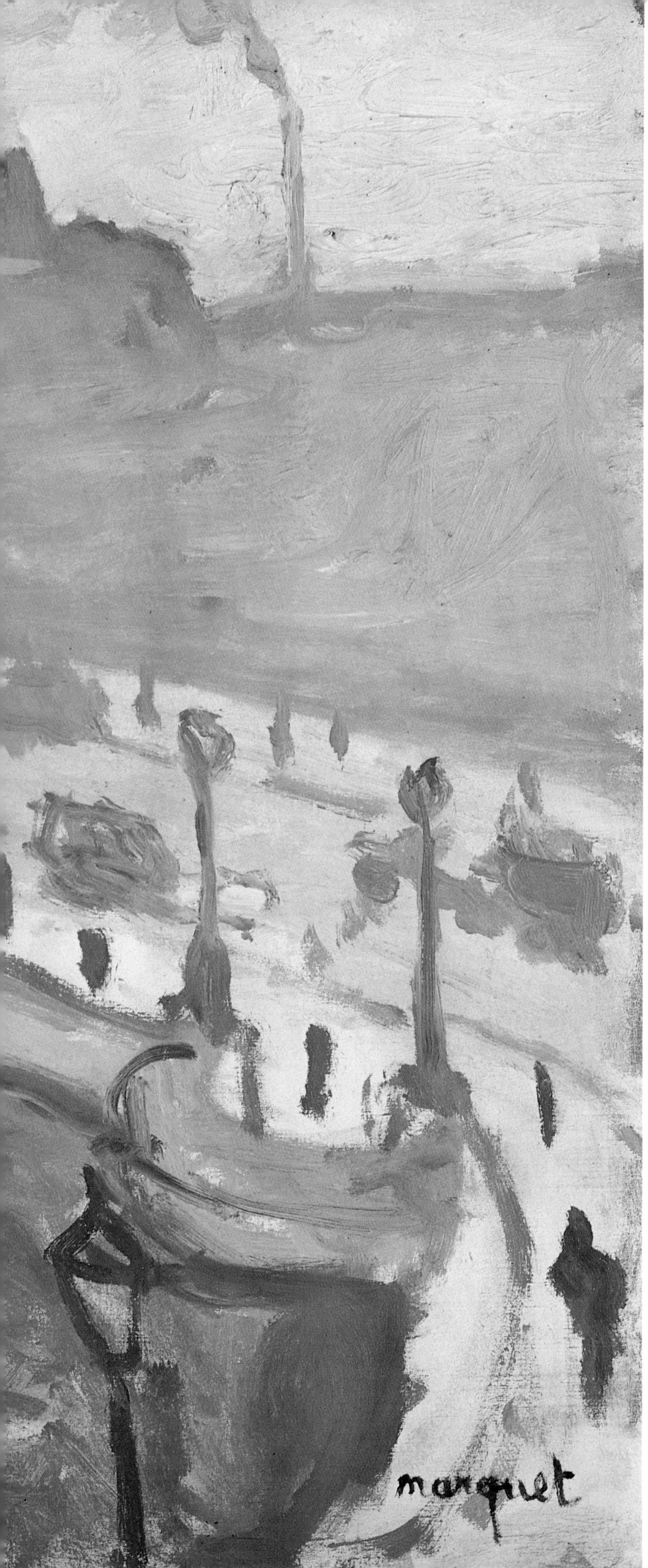

Albert Marquet
The Seine at the Pont-Neuf in Fog
1907
Oil on canvas, 25½ x 32 in (65 x 81 cm)
Nancy, musée des Beaux-Arts
(Bequeathed by Galilée)

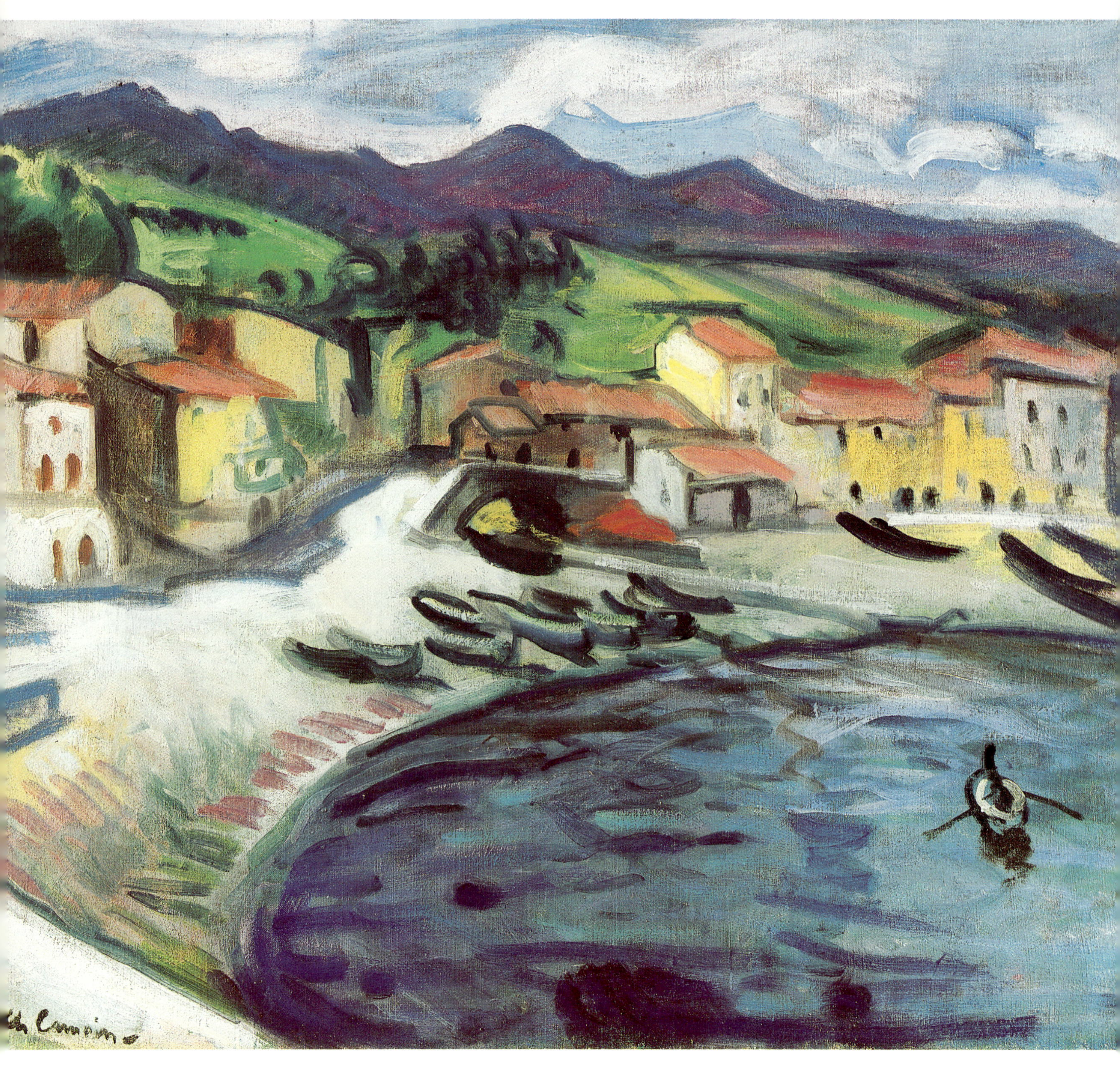

Charles Camoin
Village by the Sea
1905
Oil on canvas, $21^{1}/_{4}$ x $25^{1}/_{2}$ in (54 x 65 cm)
Geneva, musée du Petit Palais

Well-Tempered Chromatics:

Camoin

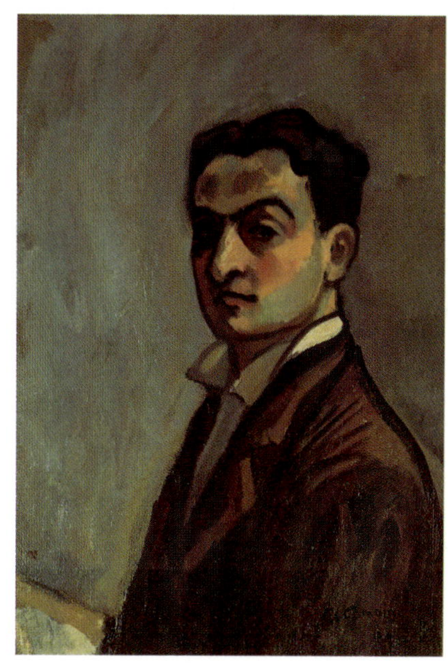

CHARLES CAMOIN
Self-portrait
1905
Oil on canvas, 23½ x 17 in (60 x 43 cm)
Geneva, musée du Petit Palais

When Charles Camoin was born on September 23, 1879 in Marseilles into a family priding themselves on seventeen generations of farmers and craftsmen, his mother, a gifted pastel painter, exclaimed: "This one's going to be an artist." His rather flighty father, who directed the family's house-painting and decorating business, died when the boy was only six years old. Charles was a serious and anxious youngster, troubled by his family's instability. He changed schools thirteen times before ending up at the Lycée Montaigne in Paris, where he was immediately reprimanded for drawing nude women in the margins of his notebooks. Unsuited for a classical education, he returned to Marseilles to study business and at the same time to follow a drawing course at the art academy. Then, in the hope of carrying out his mother's prediction, he went back to Paris and entered Gustave Moreau's famous class at the Beaux-Arts, the cradle of the Fauves. He was, alas, not able to benefit from Moreau's lessons for he arrived only a few weeks before the great master's death in 1898.

Camoin therefore learned to paint on the streets of Paris, in the company of Matisse and Marquet, who had become his friends. They took the bus together to Renoir's favorite haunt, the Moulin de la Galette in Montmartre, spent hours working in the Luxembourg gardens and along the quais of the Seine. In order to master drawing with elliptical lines–a technique very much in vogue at the time–they drew quick sketches of the passers-by, whom they got to turn around by stomping their feet on the ground. At the Louvre, Camoin was attracted by the great colorists like Veronese, Rubens, and Delacroix.

Sent to Arles for his military service, from which he visited Avignon and Aix-en-Provence, Camoin sought a better

Charles Camoin
Portrait of Marquet
1904
Oil on canvas, 36¼ x 28¾ in (92 x 73 cm)
Paris, musée national d'Art moderne

understanding of his own art through direct contact with other artists. In 1902, he painted *Langlois Bridge* in a very free manner during his quest for the last traces of Van Gogh and then made the acquaintance of the physician who had taken care of the ill-fated artist at the end of his life. The portrait that the Dutch artist had done of Doctor Rey was being used as a make-shift door for a chicken coop. Alerted by Camoin, the art dealer Ambroise Vollard bought the canvas and today it hangs in the Hermitage Museum in St. Petersburg. Later on in Aix Camoin sought out Cézanne and showed him his drawings. The latter gave him a letter of introduction to Monet, who was then painting his *Water Lilies* in Giverny.

Camoin's most famous painting, *Portrait of Marquet* (1905), was intended as a double homage: first of all to his friend–shown seated with clasped hands and a round hat on his head–and to the technique of the Master from Aix, creating simple, clear-cut forms by applying fluid blues to the canvas in wide brushstrokes. During the same period, he painted *The Pont des Arts Seen from the Pont-Neuf* (1904) using a play of complementary greens and oranges, and *Cassis Harbor* (1905), whose forms have more well-defined contours. Although both are fine paintings executed with verve, Camoin never indulged in Fauvist exuberance, for this would have been against his nature. His brushwork with its small strokes is light and flowing compared to the heavy impasto of early Fauvism. He was what could be called a painter of well-tempered chromatics.

Following the peak period of his works from 1905 until 1908, Camoin, like the other Fauves except for Matisse chose a palette of increasingly dull colors until he reached a truly blaek period in 1913 when, for sentimental reasons, his spirits were at their lowest ebb.

Since 1906 Camoin had been living with his muse Emilie Charmy, also a painter. He portrayed her in works such as *Emilie in Front of her Easel* and *Emilie at her Dressing Table*, both executed in the year they met. After a time their relationship fell slowly apart and finally she left him without a word of warning. In a fit of despair, Camoin destroyed some sixty to eighty of his own paintings calling them "black and mediocre." He cut them up and threw them into a trash-can on the rue Lepic, where he lived at the time. But a garbage collector took it upon himself to recover the pieces and sell them to a junk dealer at the Saint-Ouen flea market. The canvases were repaired, restored and found their way into various art galleries for sale. In 1927, when the writer Francis Carco, who had bought several of these works, put some of them back on the market, Camoin had them legally destroyed. This was possible since French law grants authors and artists full moral rights which provide that no one but they can decide if their creative work should be presented or not to the public. Accordingly, the author remains the sole judge of the integrity of his artistic production.

Many years later, the artist made the following remark about his work: "My instinct tells me how to find colors that sing. The forms are enfolded by air and light, but color is what creates them. My palette is my music; I have no technique, I have feelings." He added thoughtfully: "One must get to know oneself to discover what one is made of. I know that I am basically a colorist.... It is my desire and love of creating that makes me paint; I try to express myself through painting."

Camoin never fell into the type of stylization so detrimental to Derain or to Friesz. On the contrary he painted increasingly informal works such as *Bathers*, one of his last works from the early 1960s. He died in Paris on May 20, 1965 at the age of eighty-six.

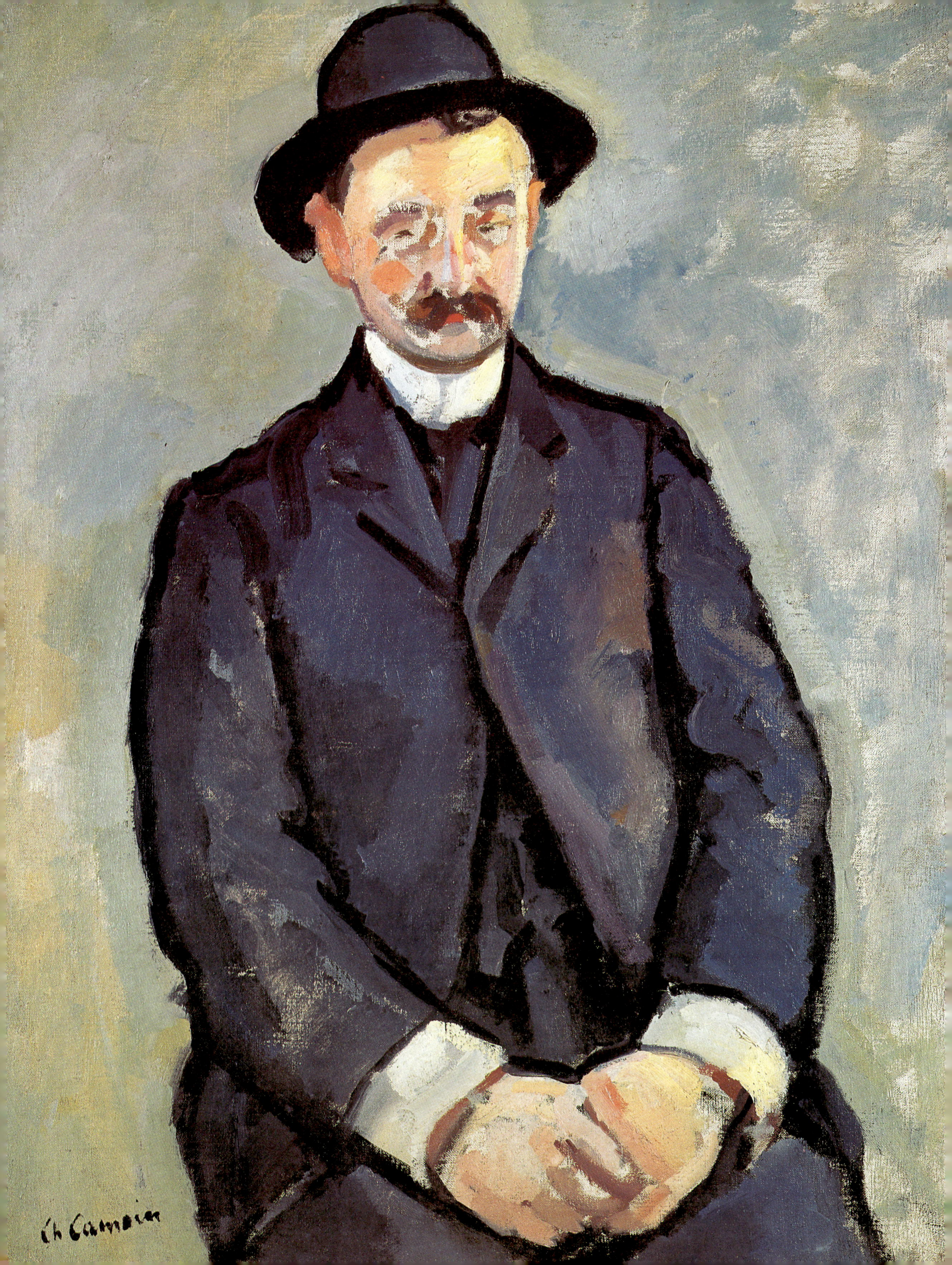
Ch Camoin

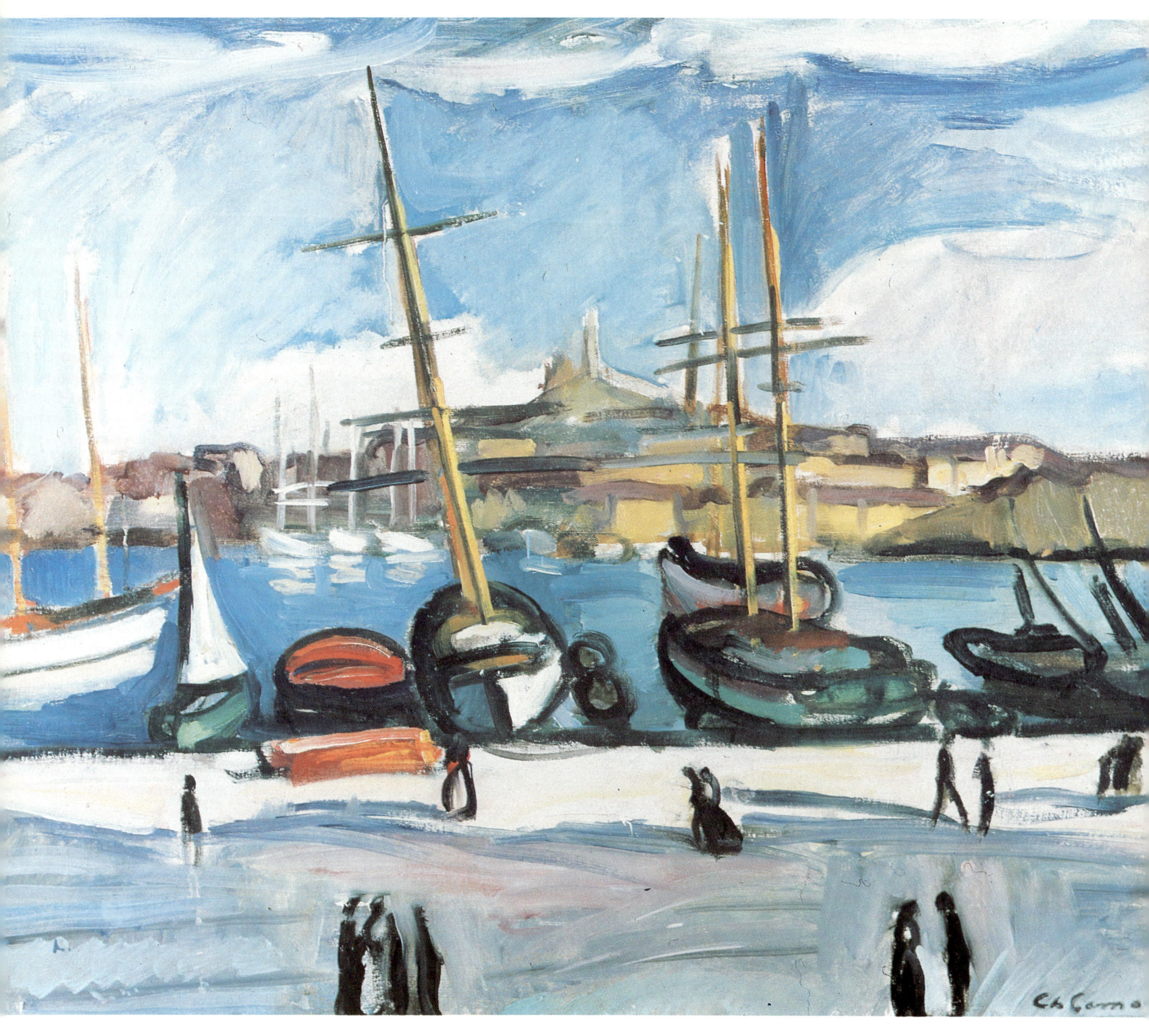

Charles Camoin
The Port of Marseille
1904
Oil on canvas, 25½ x 32 in (65 x 81 cm)
London, Fridart Foundation

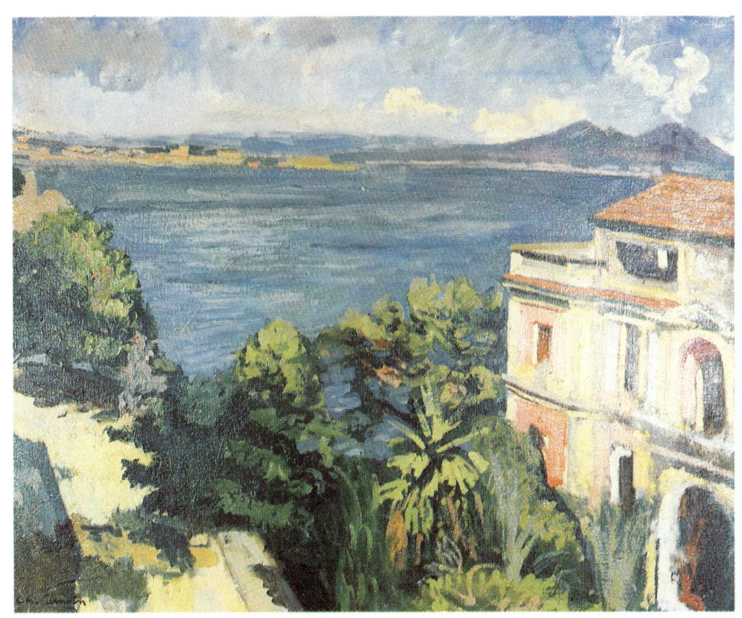

CHARLES CAMOIN
Mount Vesuvius
1904
Oil on canvas, 26¾ x 29½ in (68 x 75 cm)
Draguignan, musée des Beaux-Arts

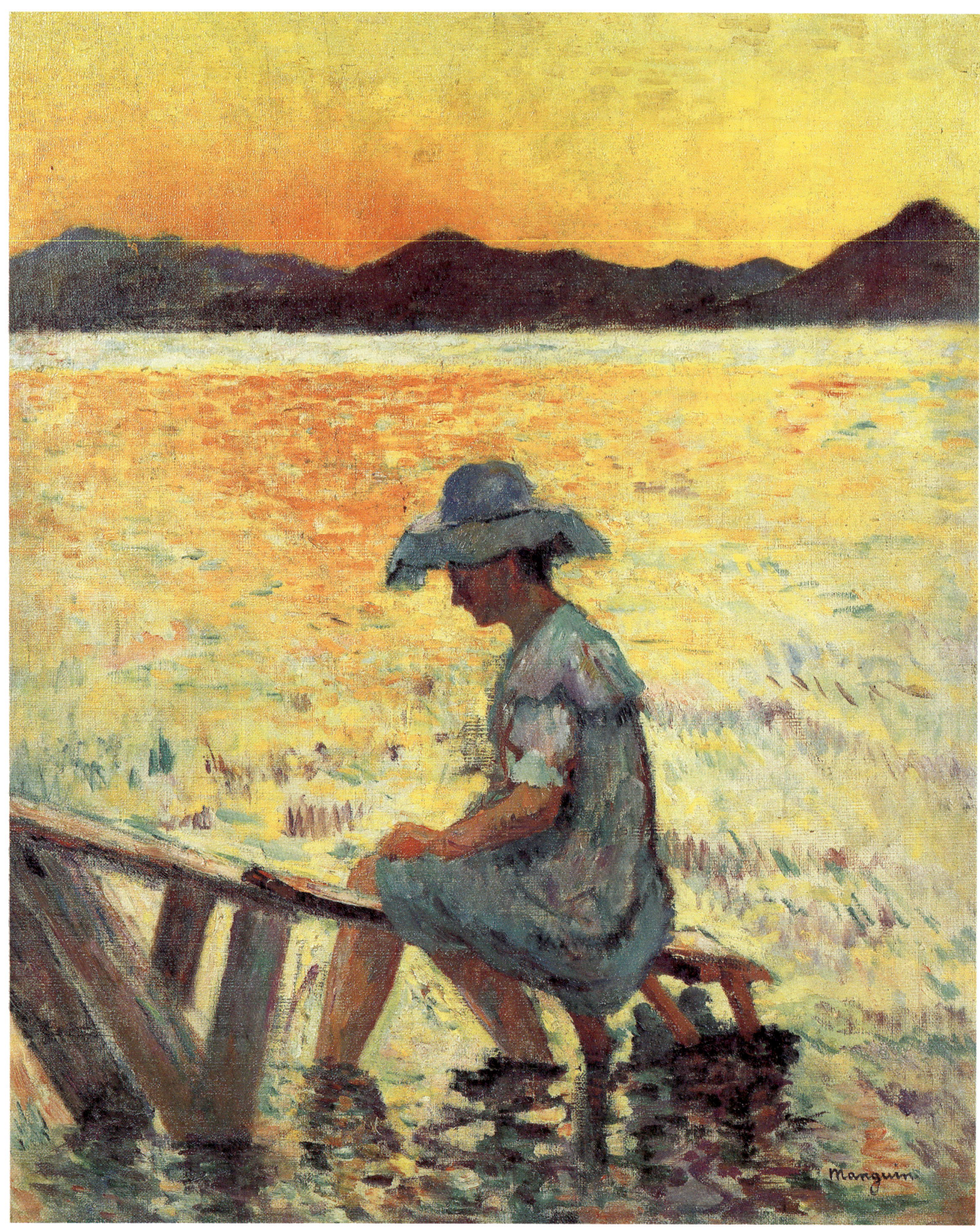
Manguin

Painter of Happiness:

Manguin

A Generous Fauve

With his leonine head, neatly-trimmed beard, high forehead, and a frank countenance on a face that easily broke into a smile, Henri Manguin was the painter of happiness, not only because his paintings rendered a dionysiac vision of life, but because he was the only Fauve to have been well-to-do even at the beginning of his career. Henri was born to middle-aged parent on March 23, 1874, in Paris. Since his father died when he was just six years old, he inherited a respectable income as soon as he came of age. His mother, who brought him and his sister up alone, lavished all her attention on Henri. She had no objections therefore, when he decided to interrupt his studies at the Lycée Condorcet at the age of fifteen and devote all his time to painting.

He left home and moved to rue Bachet in Montmartre. Four years later, in November 1894, he entered Gustave Moreau's class at the Ecole des Beaux-Arts. Little did he know how much Moreau's teaching would influence the Fauve group. Manguin joined Matisse, Marquet, Rouault, Camoin and several others such as Evenepoel and Lehmann, who have since unjustly fallen into oblivion. Besides recommending that his students go to the Louvre to make copies of the Venetians–Titian, Tintoretto, Giorgione, and Veronese–Moreau also imparted a higher sense of art to his students. "You must think out the color in your imagination. If you have no imagination, you will never make beautiful colors. Copy your imagination, that's what makes art." he often said. Judging from Manguin's work, these lessons were not lost on him.

During the summer of 1896 at Percaille, a still natural part of Normandy near Cherbourg, while painting outside Manguin was intrigued by the sound of a piano coming from a nearby

Henri Manguin
Saint-Tropez, Sunset
1904
Oil on canvas, 32 x 19¾ in (81 x 50 cm)
Avignon, private collection

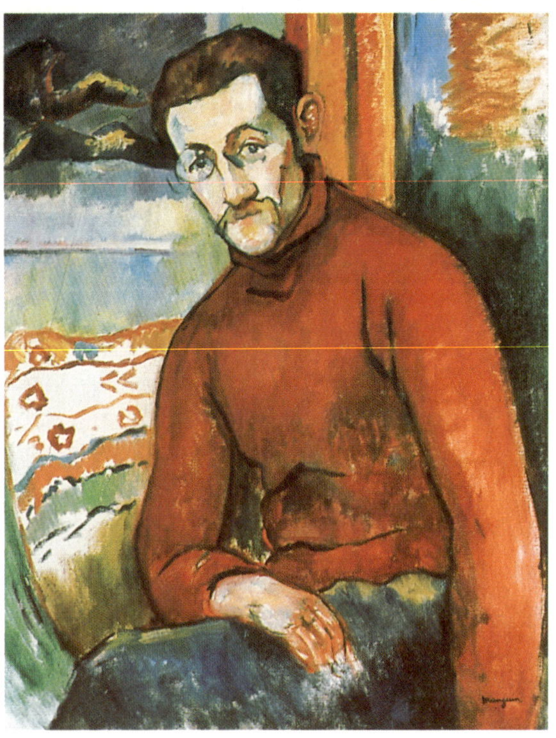

HENRI MANGUIN
Portrait of Jean Puy
1905
Oil on canvas, 32 x 25¼ in (81 x 65 cm)
Private collection

Opposite:

HENRI MANGUIN
Self Portrait
1905
Oil on canvas, 21¾ x 18 in (55 x 46 cm)
Private collection

villa. He stopped to listen to the lovely melody, and when the piece was over he noticed two young women staring at him through the window. He had already met the music teacher and she introduced him in turn to her student, Jeanne Carette. Manguin fell instantly in love with Jeanne, whose ethereal beauty could be compared to the Mona Lisa. They were married in June 1899, in Coulomb near Chartres. The newlyweds moved into a little house with a garden at 61 rue Boursault in the Batignolles neighborhood of Paris. Not having to face the problems of a bohemian life, Manguin was able to give his full attention to his art. He was encouraged by his wife who with few exceptions, became his only model and bore him three children.

Manguin set up a make-shift studio in his garden so that he could find peace and quiet, away from his children's laughter and games. Matisse, Marquet, and Puy were regular visitors and would come to work and talk over problems of form, color, and light together.

The Pleasure of Painting

The broad-rimmed hat and face built up in flat planes in Manguin's *Self-portrait* (1905) reveal Cézanne's influence and are reminiscent of the *Self-portrait* (1879-1882) painted by the reclusive master from Aix-en-Provence. Although Manguin had thoroughly assimilated Moreau's training and he greatly benefited from it like the other Fauves, he cleverly adopted a number of pictorial devices from Cézanne. The art critic Gaston Diehl has pointed out some of these: a strong composition, well-balanced tonal harmony, a predominantly blue color-scheme, and a penchant for atmosphere and setting. Manguin visited Cézanne after being introduced by the writer Joachim Gasquet.

Manguin's most innovative paintings, however, were executed at the Villa Demière near Saint-Tropez, where he spent his summers from 1905 on. In this blissful spot secluded among the pine trees overlooking the sea, Jeanne could pose nude or lightly clad. *Siesta or the Rocking Chair*, *Jeanne*, a picture exhibited in the "wild-beast cage," *The Fauness*, *Villa Demière*, and the lavish *Sleeping Woman* were among the works by Manguin that possessed what Apollinaire called "a pagan frankness."

The masterpiece of that year was *Jeanne Resting at Villa Demière*. We see Jeanne in the foreground her back turned, dressed in a long muslin gown and seated in a chair under a tree with the sea and the hills in the background. The intensity with which the artist rendered the luxuriant Mediterranean foliage is prodigious. Charles Terrasse had this work in mind when he wrote: "A painting by Manguin is a concert of strong colors in which a true red dominates red-oranges, purple violets, deep blues, dark greens and golden yellows. Lines, shapes, everything is strong. Everything is striking. It is an exalted painting that warms the heart and gives joy." The next years saw other major paintings come from his brush such as *Bathers* (1906) and *Still Life with Oysters*, painted in 1908. Even Matisse in his early years had not shown as much talent.

In 1910, the Swiss painter Félix Vallotton introduced Manguin to Dr. Arthur Hahnloser, part of a group from Winterthur, Zurich, and Basel who were among the most perceptive art-lovers in Europe, at a period when the avant-garde movements in France were rejected by the critics. In 1915, free from his military duties, the artist moved to Switzerland, first to Lausanne and then to Colombier–a

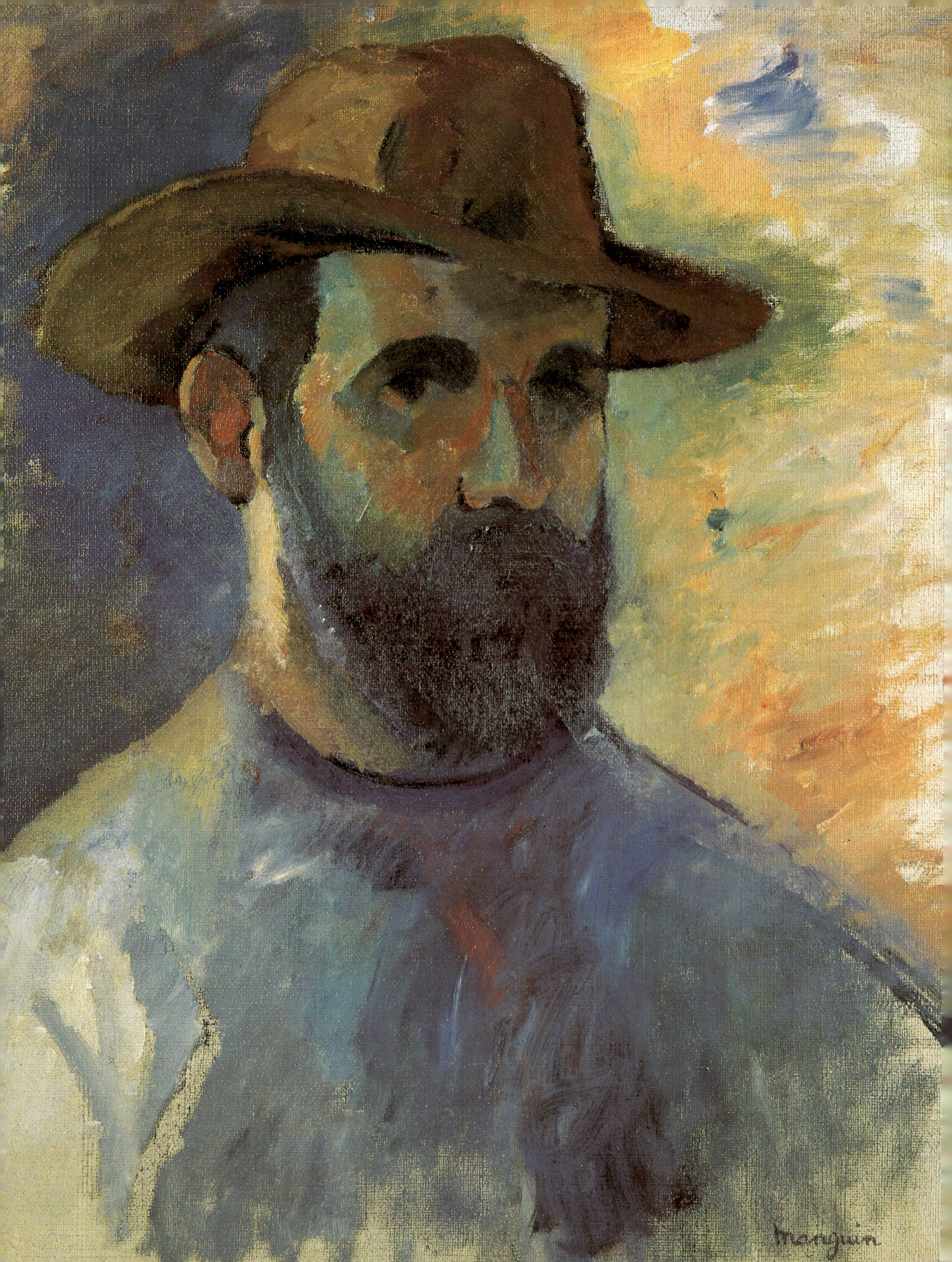
manguin

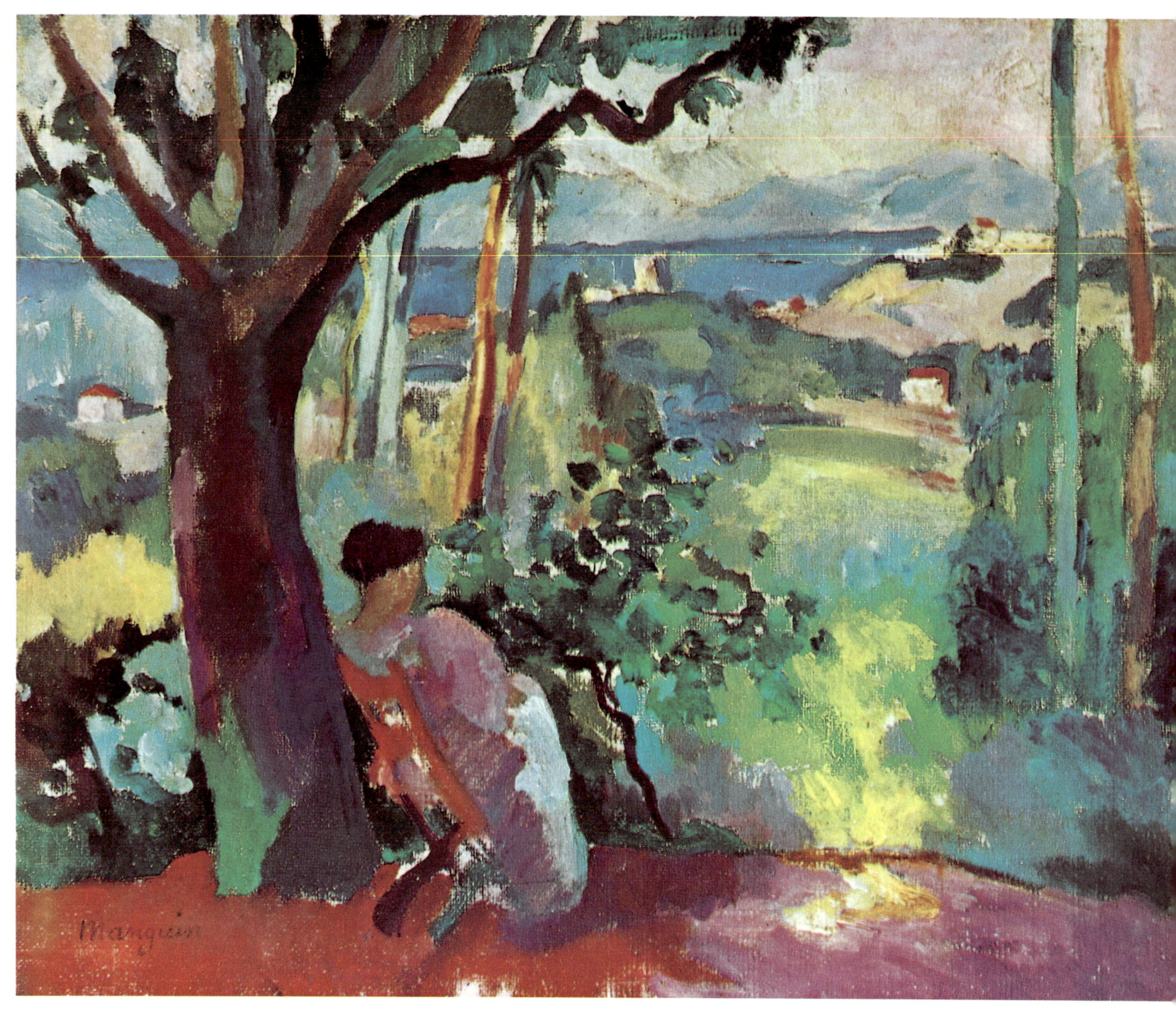

Henri Manguin
Jeanne Resting at Villa Demière
1905
Oil on canvas, 15 x 18 in (38 x 46 cm)
Private collection

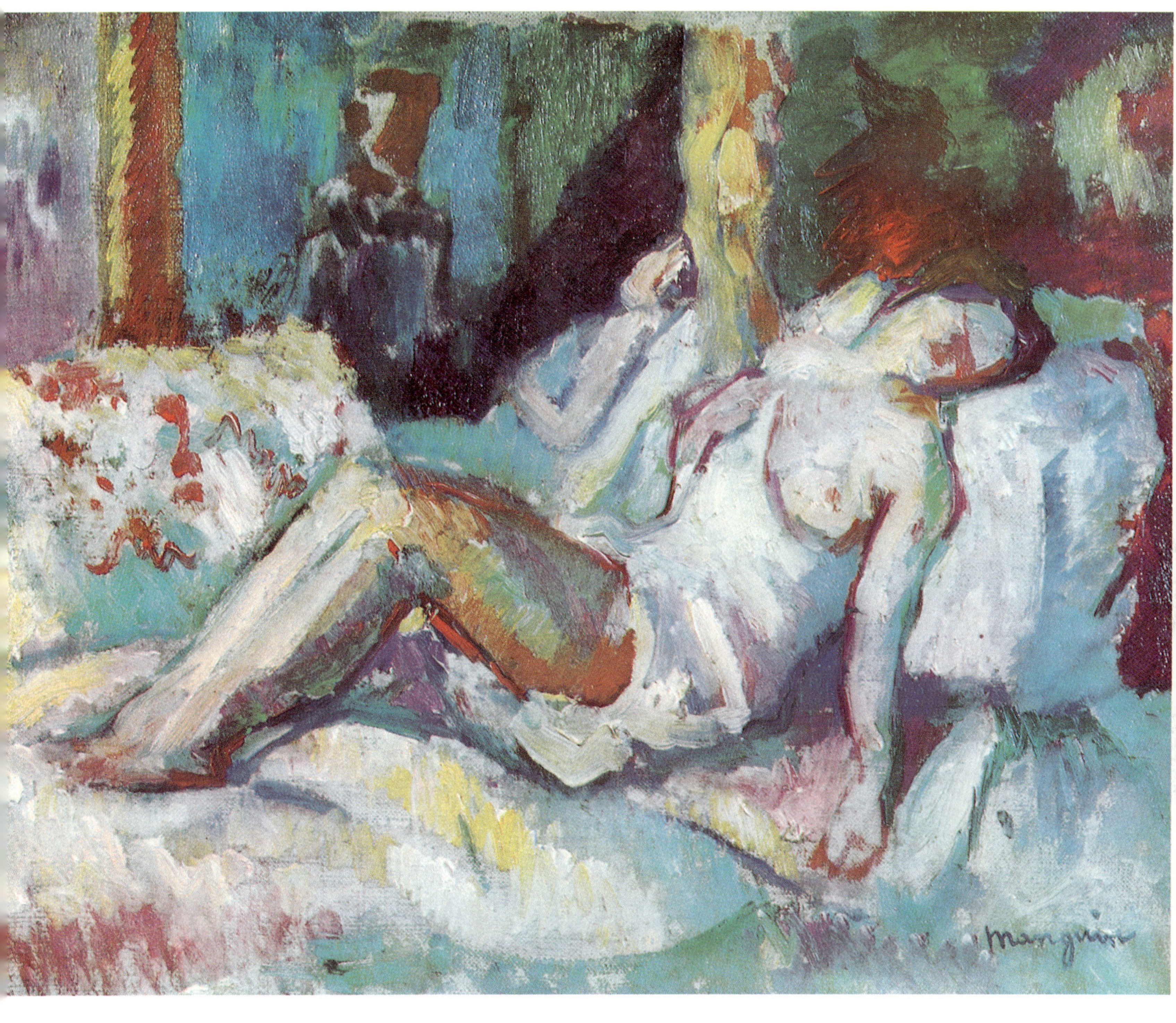

HENRI MANGUIN
Sleeping Woman
1905
Oil on canvas, 13 x 16¼ in (33 x 41 cm)
Private collection

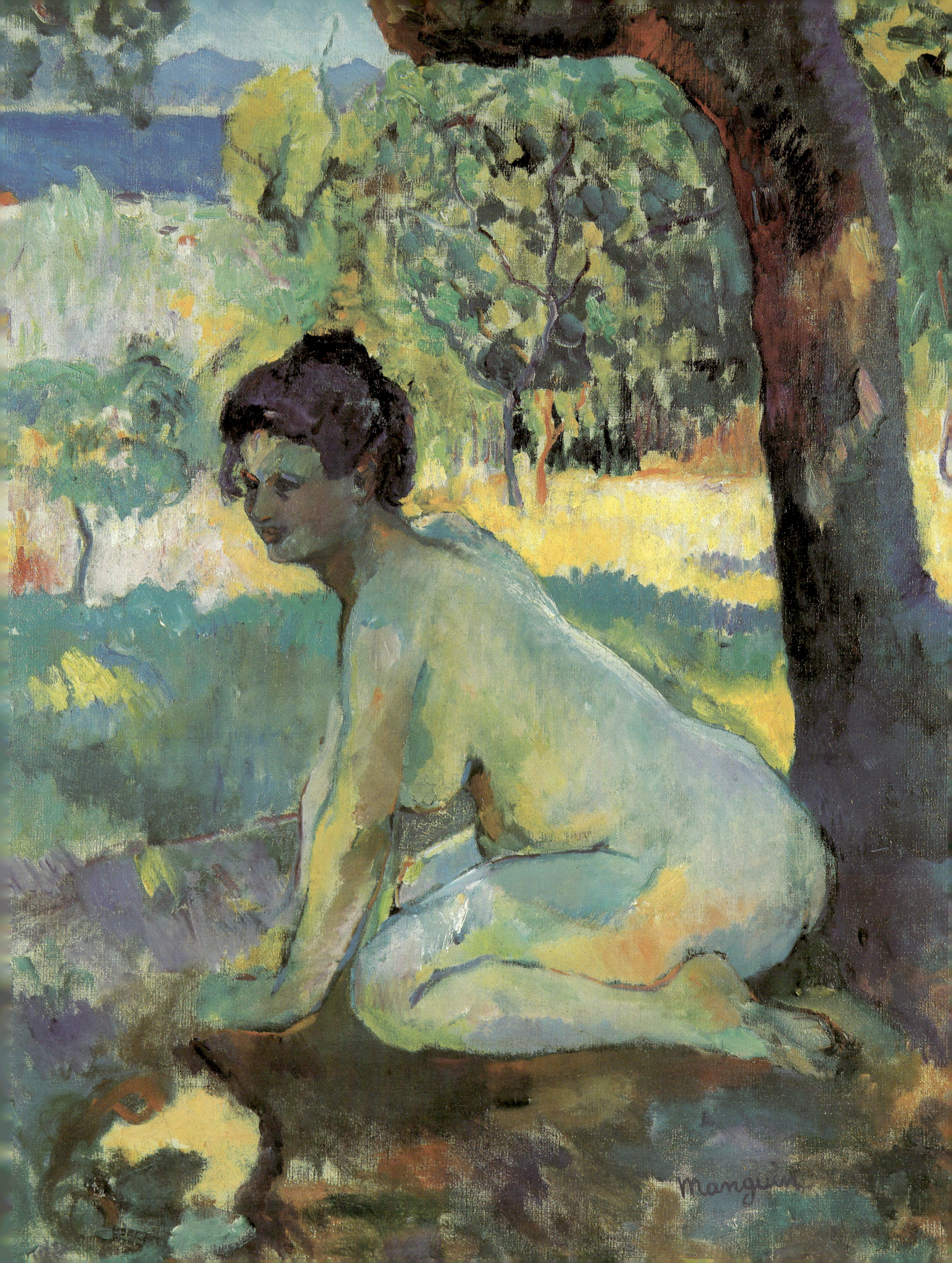
Manguin

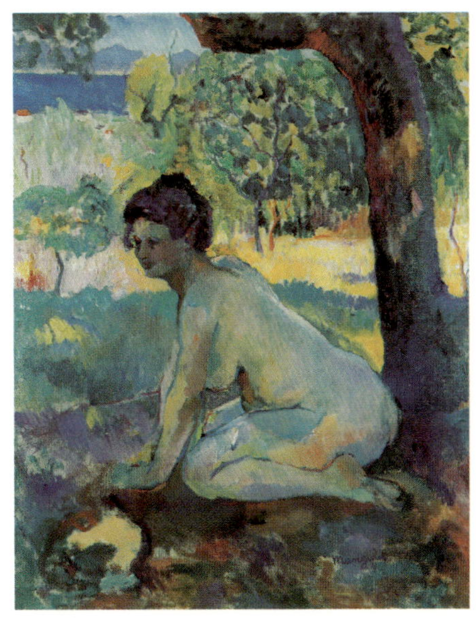

HENRI MANGUIN
The Fauness, Villa Demière
1905
Oil on canvas, 36¼ x 28¾ in (92 x 73 cm)
Private collection

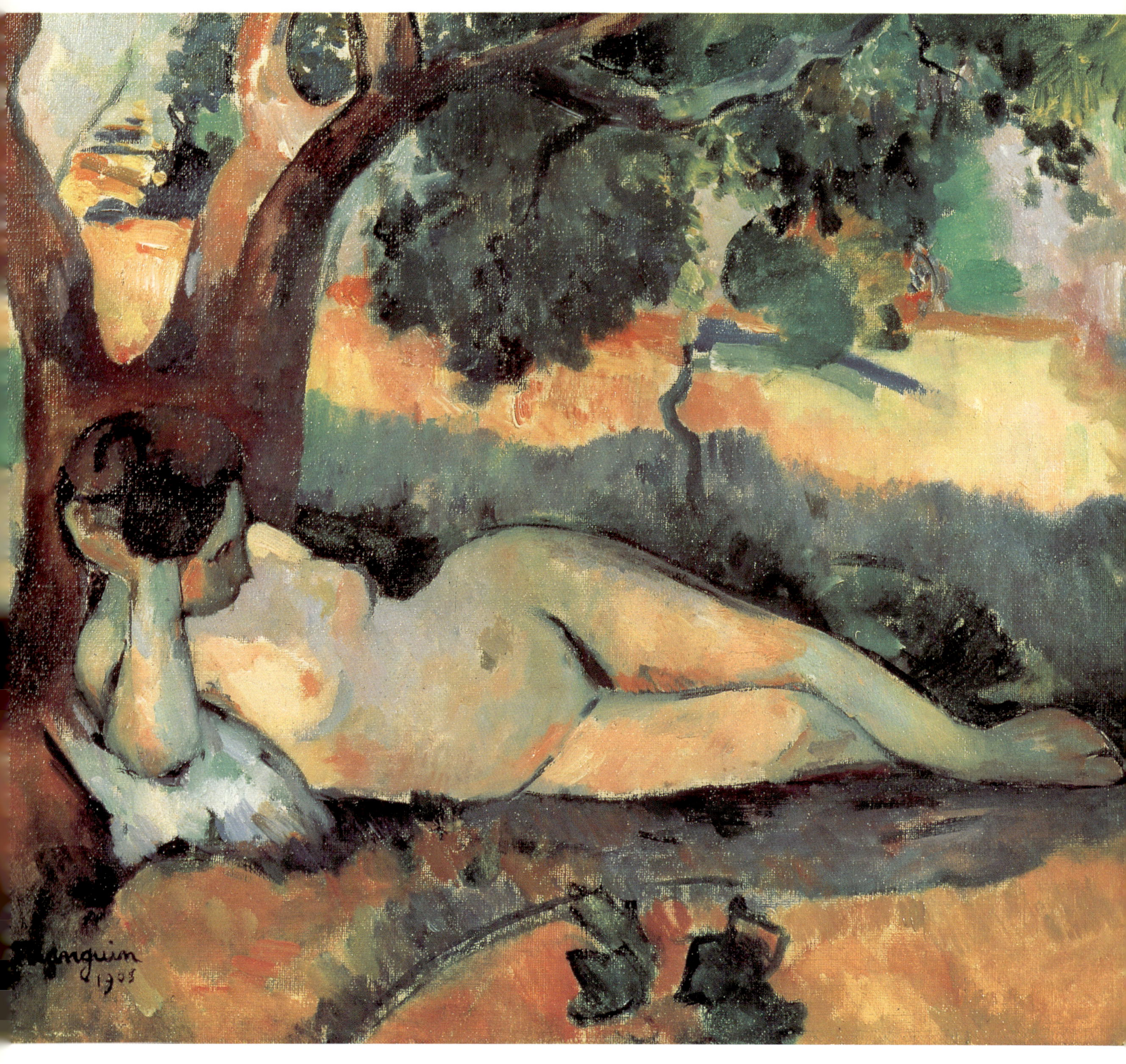

Henri Manguin
Siesta
1905
Oil on canvas, 19¾ x 24 in (50 x 61 cm)
London, Fridart Foundation

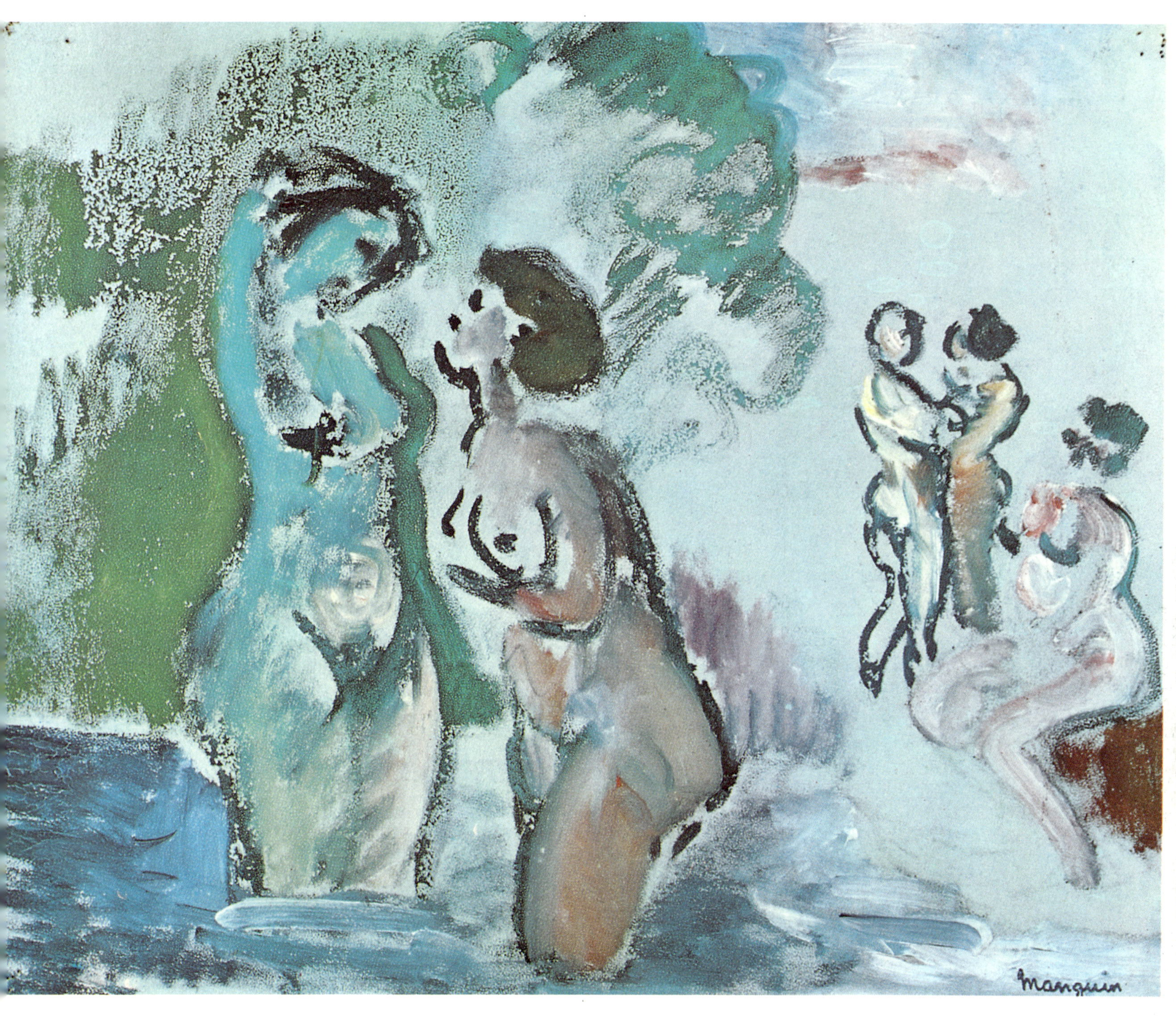

Henri Manguin
Bathers
(Sketch)
1906
Oil on canvas, 13 x 17¼ in (33 x 44 cm)
Private collection

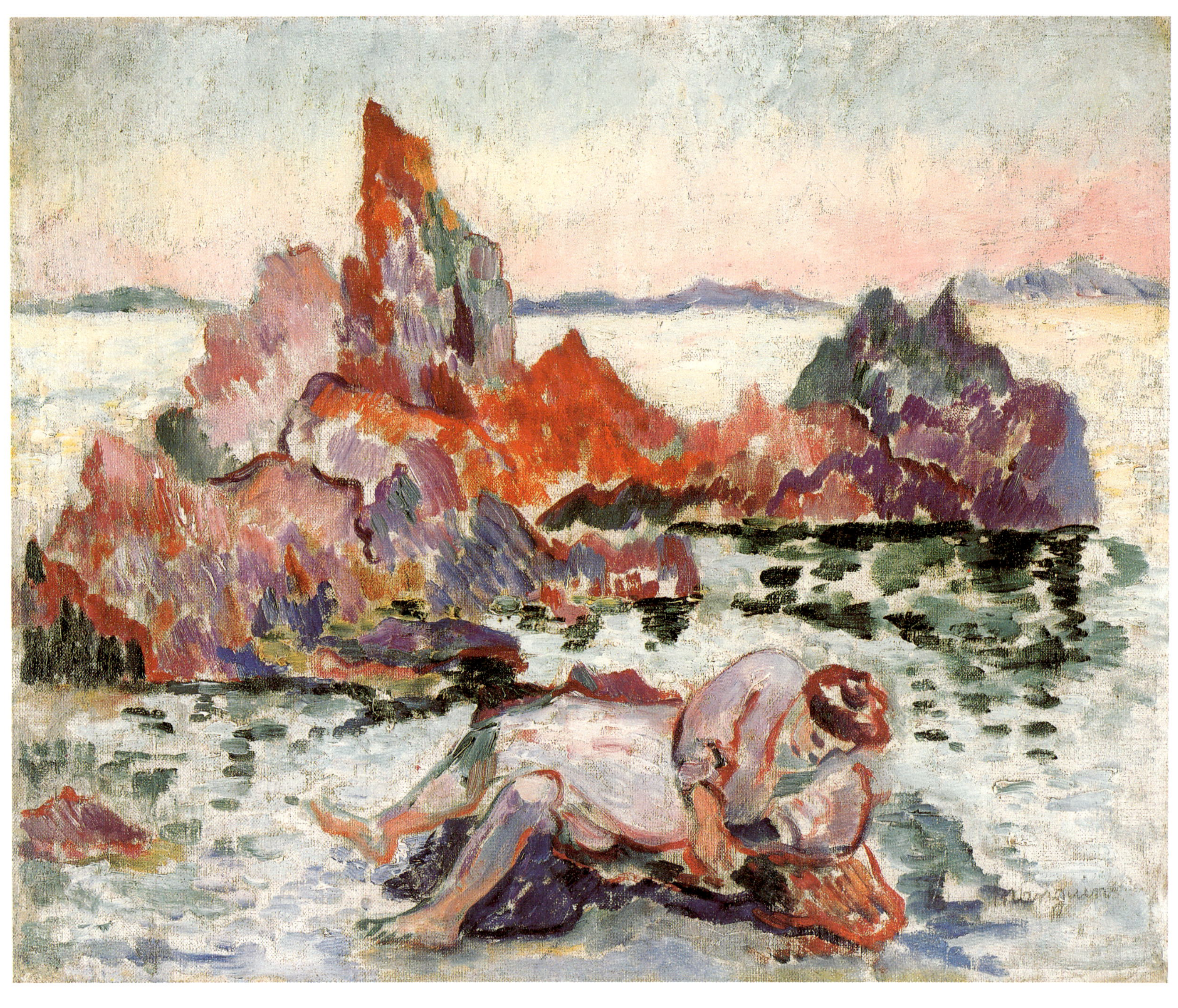

HENRI MANGUIN
Study for a Naïad
1906
Oil on canvas, 14½ x 19 in (37 x 48 cm)
Private collection

charming village in the Canton of Neuchâtel. The "vivid dark greens" of the Swiss landscape made most French artists of Manguin's generation uneasy. Cézanne, dragged by his wife on a trip to the Jura Mountains in Switzerland in 1891, had not been able to paint at all because of the intensity of the light. Manguin, on the contrary, found the strong light of Lake Leman and the Greifensee entirely to his liking.

Arthur Hahnloser's son Hans, who had known Manguin well, recalls his passion for color and tells how the artist would borrow bright Indian blankets, patterned Bukhara rugs and ceramics with striking motifs from the family home in Winterthur. Hans wrote: "Each of Manguin's painting was the result of a primal impulse, quickly transferred to paper in a decisive gesture.... My father, who was a physician, followed his career for many years and noticed that while painting, the artist was truly in a feverish state. The common expression *"artiste fébrile"* is not just a simple image, but in fact a real condition."

There are several fine works from this period such as *The Gugelhopf* (1914). Hans Hahnloser still remembers the appetizing cake, freshly baked from his grandmother's oven and hardly missing a slice when Manguin carried it off to his studio so that it wouldn't be destroyed any further–much to the children's dismay.

In the prime of life having reached forty, the artist was no longer as creative. Inasmuch as Derain was preoccupied with culture, and Vlaminck with his instincts, perhaps Manguin did not take enough time with theory. His production began to degenerate into academic, Cézannian-style nudes, and bouquets of flowers fit only to decorate bourgeois living rooms.

His success, however, never waned. Upon returning to France, he shared his time between Saint-Tropez and Paris until 1940, the year in which he moved to Avignon to escape from the German Occupation. He died nine years later after a brief illness in September, 1949 at the age of seventy-five leaving an unfinished still life on his easel.

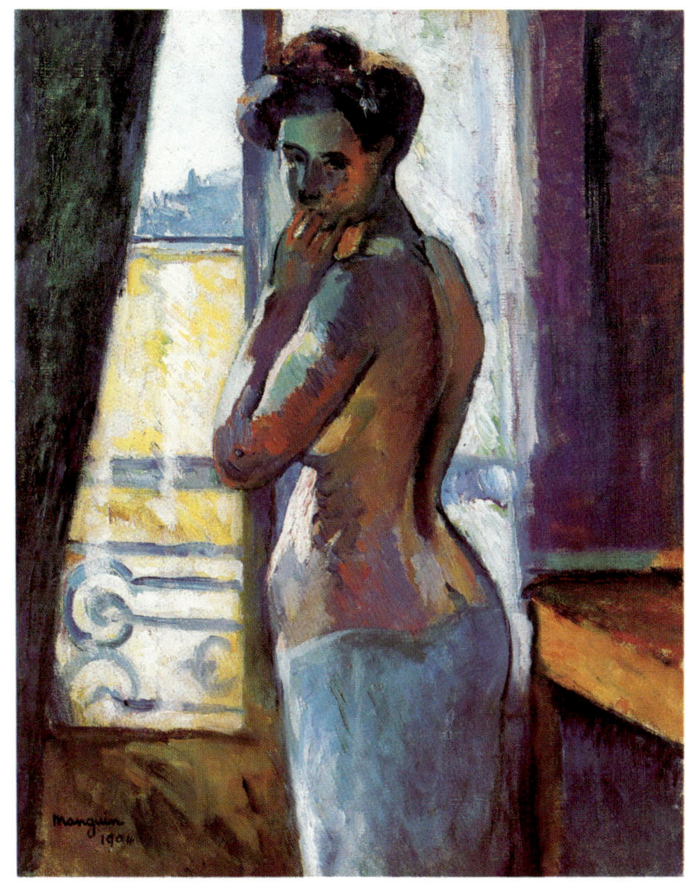

HENRI MANGUIN
Woman at the Window
1904
Oil on canvas, 24 x 19¾ in (61 x 50 cm)
Private collection

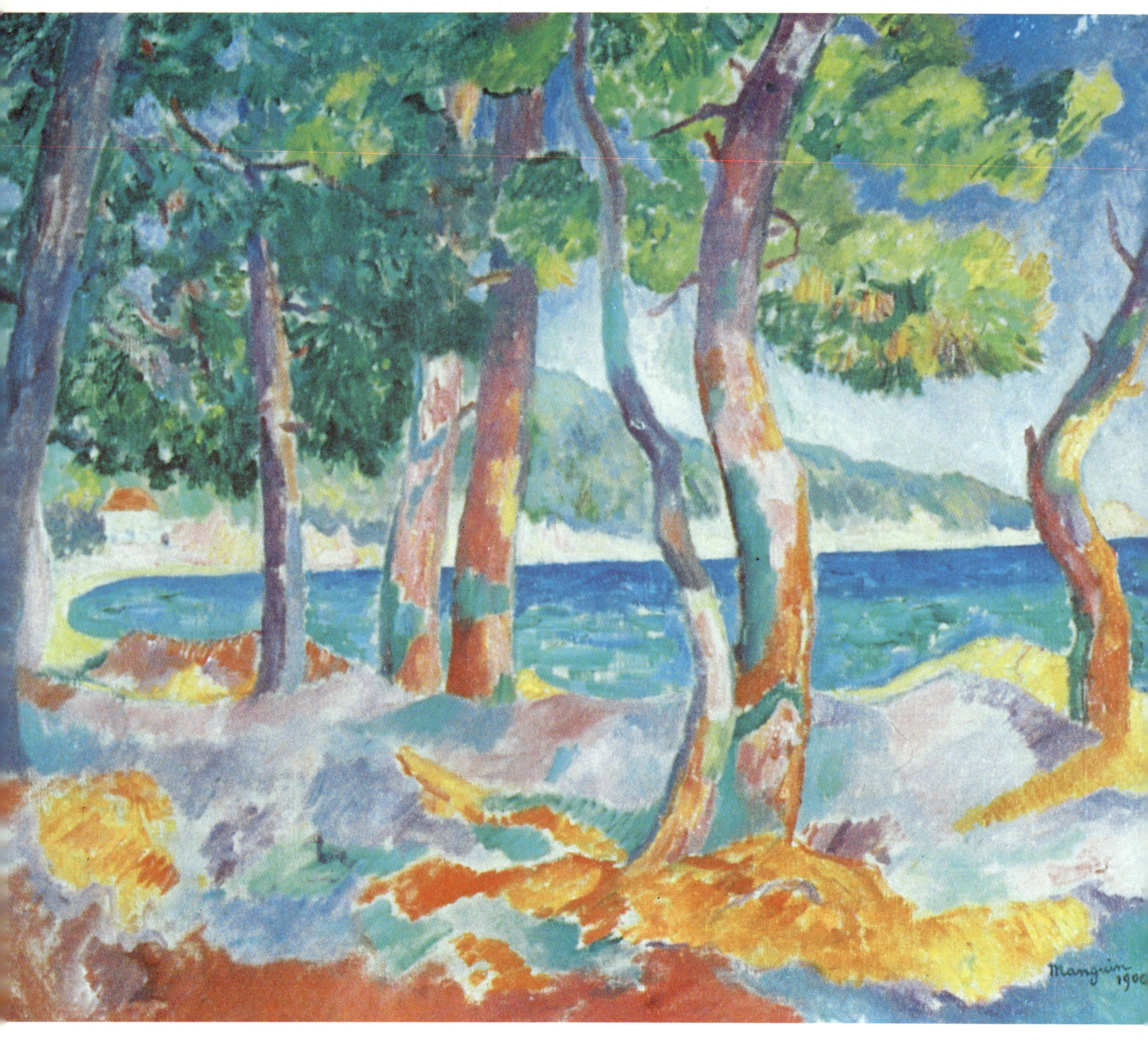

Henri Manguin
Pines at Cavalière
1906
Oil on canvas, 25½ x 32 in (65 x 81 cm)
Avignon, private collection

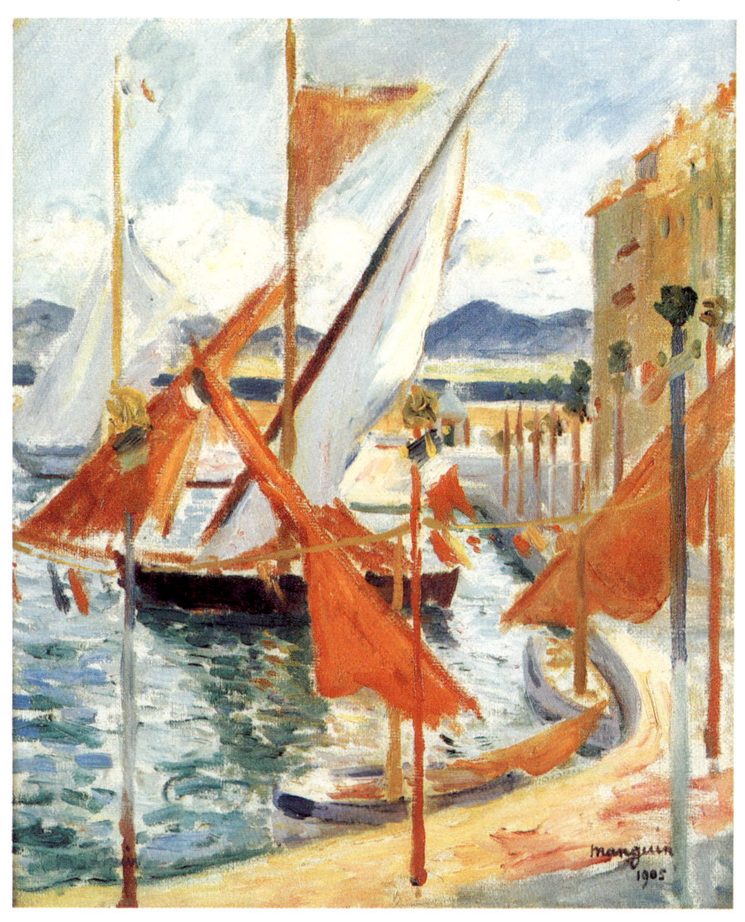

Henri Manguin
On the 14th of July at Saint-Tropez
(Left side)
1905
Oil on canvas, 24 x 19¾ in (61 x 50 cm)
Avignon, private collection

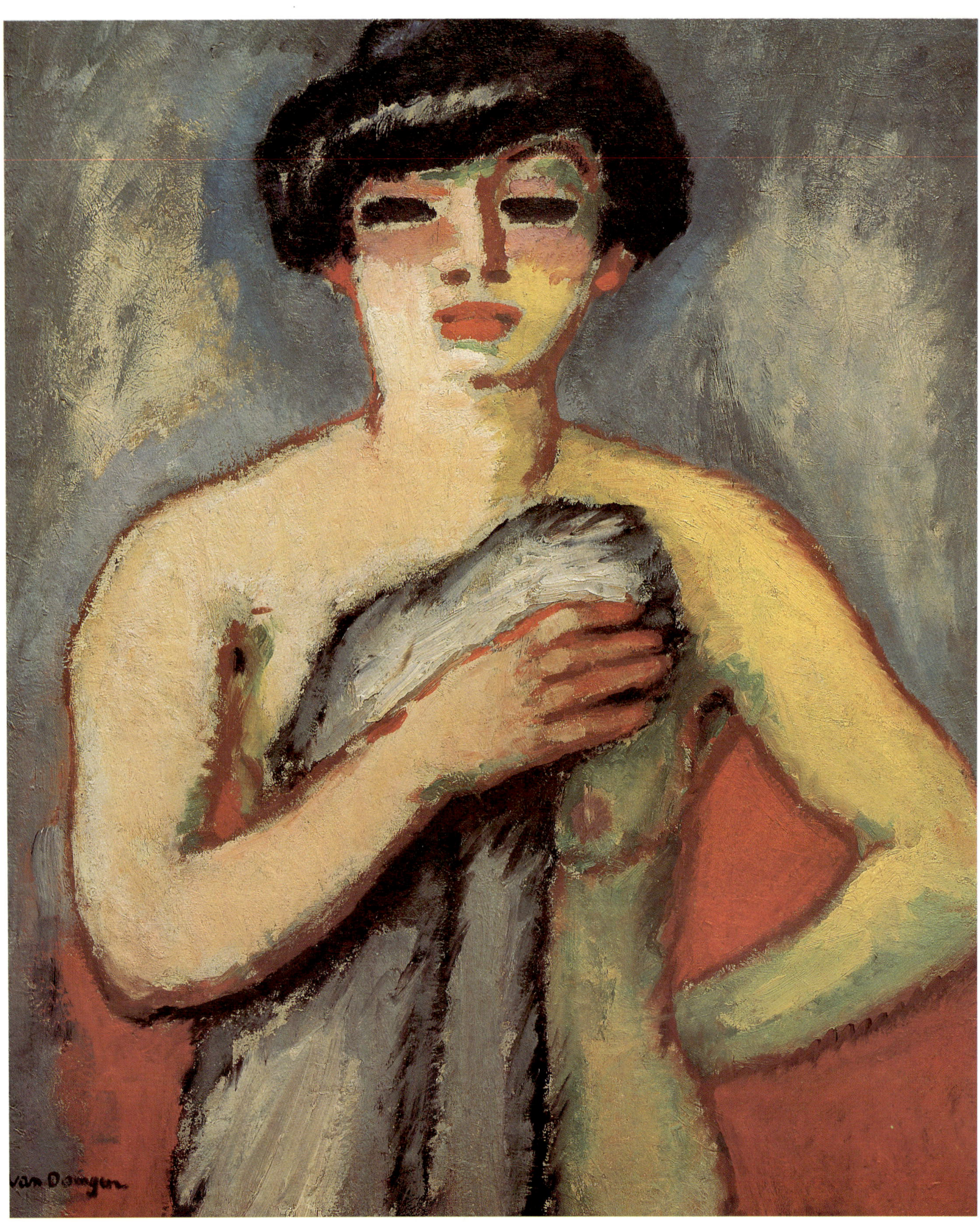
van Dongen

Eroticism in Painting:

Van Dongen

An Artist in Overalls

Was it really in 1895 that Kees Van Dongen painted the piebald horse–called *Chimera*–in the attic of his family's malt factory, or did he antedated it? This is a legitimate question if we compare this work to his others of the same period, all of which conformed to the Dutch tradition, or to his first canvases painted in Paris around 1900 when he leaned toward Impressionism. In 1895 however, no other painting had come this far and if the date of his *Chimère* is correct, its innovative treatment makes Van Dongen one of the major precursors of 20th-century art.

The enigma remains, but the story goes that Cornelius Theodorus Marie, nicknamed Kees, born on January 26, 1877, in the small town of Delfshaven in southern Holland, left primary school at the age of twelve, then worked as an apprentice in his father's malt business before entering the Academy of Fine Arts in Rotterdam at the age of eighteen. In 1897, he traveled to Paris for the first time, then he settled there permanently two years later. To make ends meet, he fought in wrestling contests, set up stands at fairgrounds, made quick sketches for a few francs at the terraces of cafés, drew caricatures for satirical newspapers such as *Le Rire*, *Gil Blas*, and *L'Assiette au beurre* before meeting Félix Fénéon, who found him a job at *La Revue Blanche*. In 1901, he married Augusta Preitinger–nicknamed Guus–who bore him a daughter named Dolly in 1905.

The novelist Roland Dorgelès, who watched Van Dongen move into a studio at the Bateau-Lavoir in 1906, opposite from the one Picasso shared with Fernande Olivier, described him in these terms: "A man in blue overalls, barefoot in his sandals, with a red beard, a

Kees Van Dongen
Portrait of Fernande Olivier
1905
Oil on canvas, 39¼ x 32 in (100 x 81 cm)
Paris, Samir Traboulsi collection

KEES VAN DONGEN
The "Parisienne" from Montmartre
1911
Oil on canvas, 25½ x 21¾ in (65 x 54 cm)
Le Havre, musée des Beaux-Arts André Malraux

pipe and a smile." Van Dongen, recalling his years of hard times with emotion, told how he, Picasso and several other painters tried to sell for "*cent sous*" canvases that they lined up along the sidewalk near the Médrano Circus not far from Pigalle. He would also steal bread and milk in the early morning from doorways where the milkman and baker had just delivered their goods.

Having integrated himself into the artistic milieu of Montmartre, he took part in various exhibitions and was able to show two of his works–*Torso* and *Shirt*–in the famous "wild-beast cage" at the Salon d'Automne in 1905. Although he had been assimilated with the Fauves, Van Dongen was more interested in painting figures–especially women's faces and bodies–than scenes on the banks of the Seine or landscapes at Collioure. His *Torso*, in fact, was not very "Fauve" in comparison to Matisse's *Woman with the Hat*, exhibited in the same room, and it is easy to understand what opposed the two artists. Xavier Gérard, who has recently written on Van Dongen, remarks that the artist created a new type of nude in the tradition of Rembrandt, Degas and Gauguin. He explains that there was not much Fauvism there in spite of the vibrant red highlights, but rather an effort to return to a type of modeling that Divisionism had abandoned. He notes that the most novel aspect of Van Dongen's technique was the treatment of outlines and goes on to explain how the artist roughly sketched out solid shapes, often in a dark tone, then heavily overpainted them but left the verges of the underpainted shapes uncovered, thus delimiting figures and objects and accentuating contours to strengthen the composition.

The Painter of Sensuality

Van Dongen's very distinctive way of painting is demonstrated in *Fernande Olivier* and *Woman with the Large Hat* painted in 1906. Fernande Olivier and Picasso met at the Bateau-Lavoir one stormy day in 1904. On his way back home, the Spanish artist had rescued a stray kitten from the rain and offered it to the young woman who was busy drawing water from the one-and-only tap installed on a landing of the old building where they lived. She was so elegant and alluring that he could not get her out of his mind. Picasso was proud of having a mistress who excited attention whenever they went out to their favorite bohemian restaurants: Azon's rue Ravignan and Vernin's, in the rue Cavalotti. The beautiful Fernande, who incarnated health and youth, provided a welcome change from the promiscuous fly-by-night models that the Montmartre artists passed back and forth to each other, not to mention the prostitutes that he no longer cared to frequent. Picasso gave vent to his passion in several drawings and sketches of the young woman proudly showing off her breasts, carrying herself with majesty and wearing an immense feather hat; but none of these matched Van Dongen's emotional demonstrations.

Van Dongen's portrait of *Fernande Olivier*, with all its seductiveness, is still a far cry from Picasso's *Demoiselles d'Avignon*; these ghoulish figures exhibiting oversize breasts and feet seemed so aggressive that they made Braque shriek the first time he saw them. With the exception, perhaps of his late *Nudes*, Picasso's cruel relationship with the female body drove him to create a kind of erotic castoff, an object to be used and thrown away according to his desire. As a Spaniard, Picasso liked to tear and lacerate. Van Dongen, being Dutch, liked to caress his

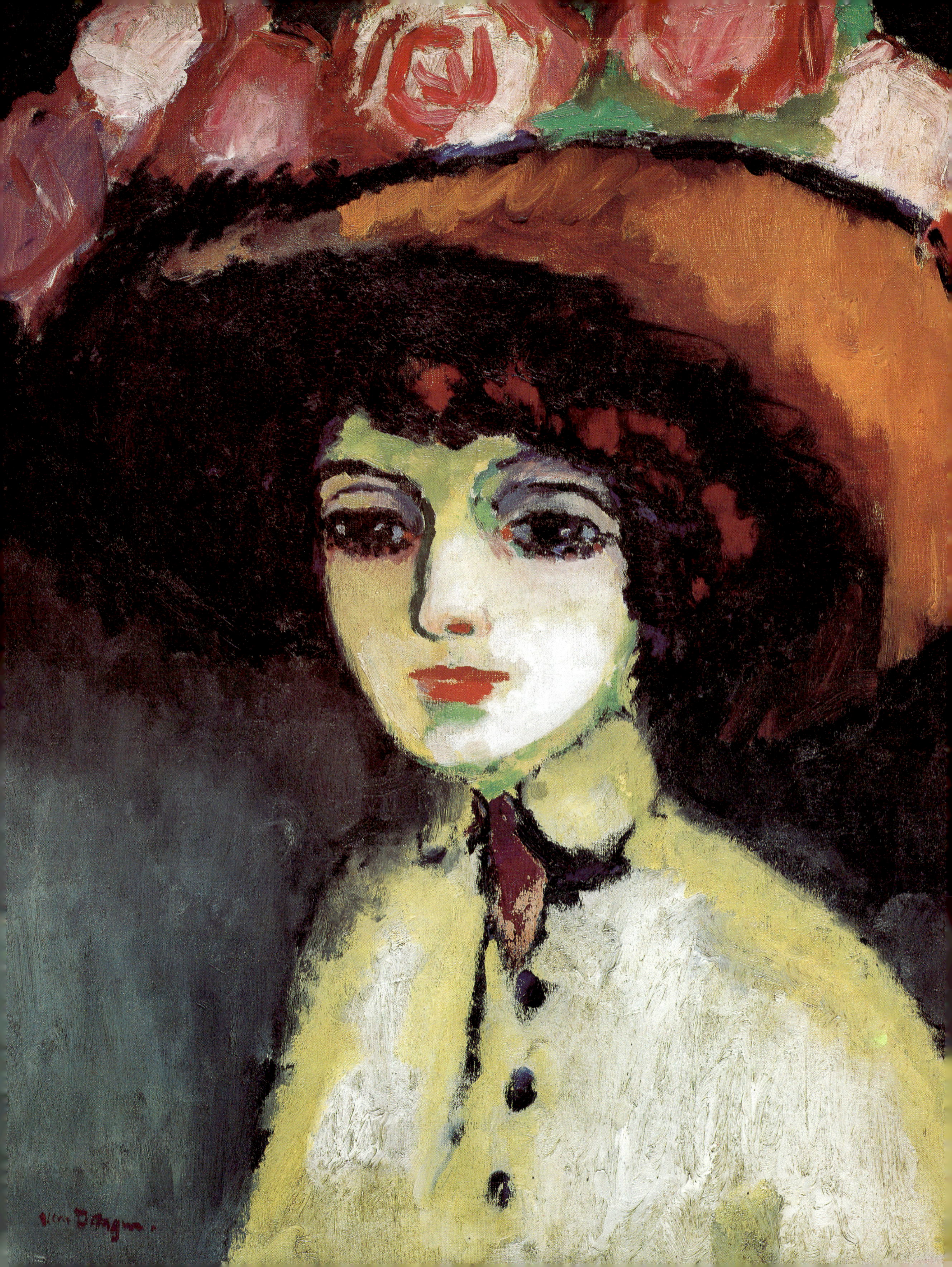

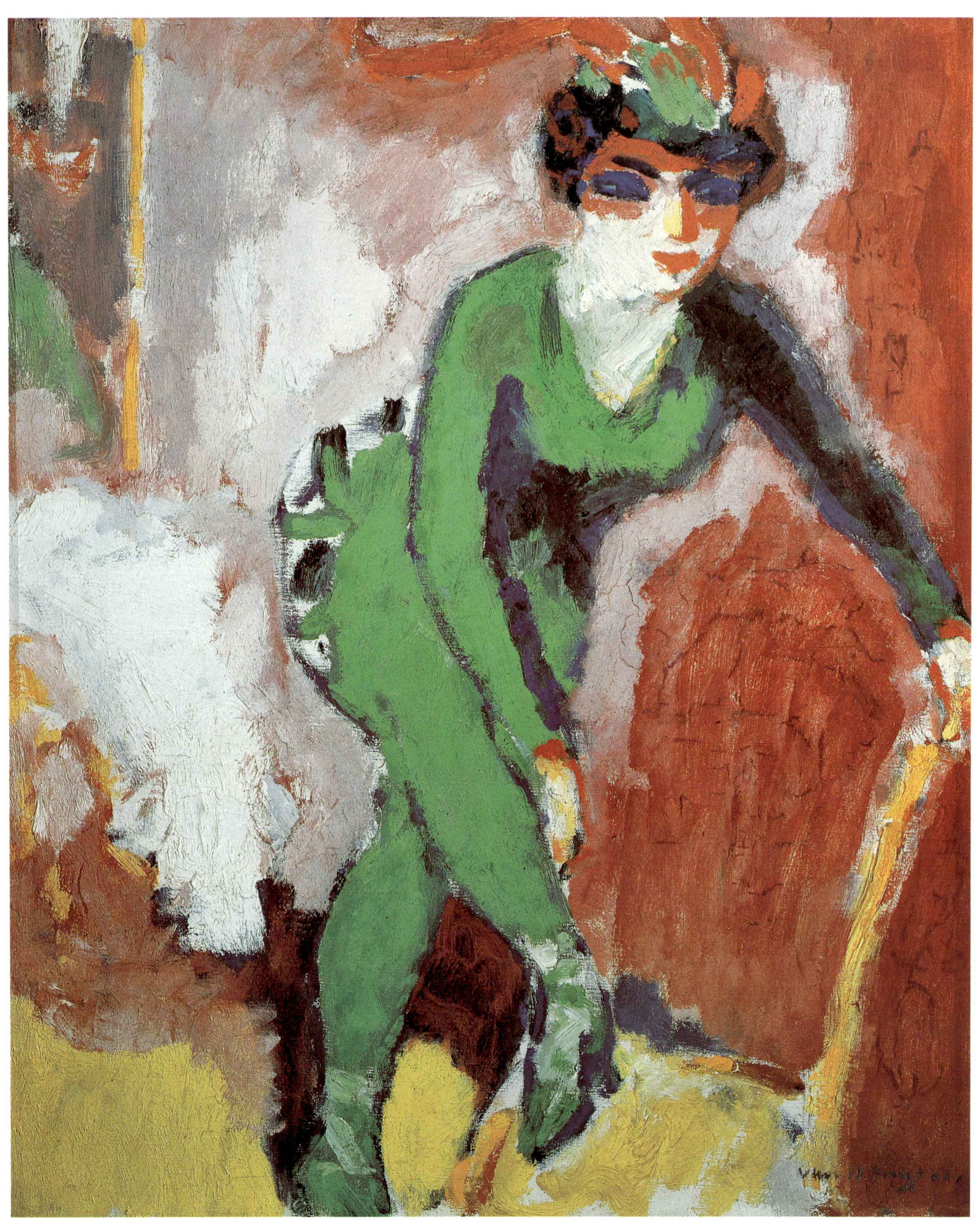

canvases; it was not the lascivious postures, nor the amorous attitudes of female figures that make his paintings so voluptuous but the brushwork itself. The sinuous lines and rich tones all exude sensual delight. It is difficult to understand therefore, why, in 1913 the police were called in to remove his *Tableau* from an exhibition, a nude for which Guus had posed. This work and Stravinsky's *Rite of Spring* were to be the major scandals in Paris that year.

There are very few examples in art that can be compared to this pictorial flame; it may be necessary to go back as far as Rembrandt's *Bathsheba* to find an equal passion. A passion so strong that it is blatant not only in Van Dongen's nudes but in all his paintings of women, such as *Woman in Green Tights*, also from 1905, with its contrasting almond green, orange, gray, white and purplish-red, or *Woman with Black Gloves* (1908), superbly suggestive with its browns, whites and grays. The treatment of these women's eyes, necks, breasts and legs bring Toulouse-Lautrec to mind. At the end of his life, the latter sat in the same first-row seat at the Théâtre des Variétés for twenty successive performances of *Chilpéric*, a mediocre comic operetta starring Marcelle Lender, for no reason than it allowed him to observe the diva's body.

Van Dongen was the quintessential painter of women in the sense that: "Woman represents the earth and all that is real, the fire of life; the wife as well as the mistress; the epitome of sensuality." This explains why he became the master of female portraiture even after reaching fame and fortune when he put his art at the service of High Society. Although his later portraits–*The Sphinx* (or *Woman with Chrysanthemums*) from 1925, and *Mme T*, painted in 1929–had to conform to the bourgeois taste of his clients, he lost nothing of his perceptive judgment nor talent as a portraitist

Like Lautrec, Van Dongen also knew how to be scathing. In *Modjesko, Soprano Singer*, his palette was harsher, enveloping the luminous yellow flesh in a flaming red halo; the colored contrasts were more brutal and the surfaces more agitated than in most of his female figures. In *Nini, the Prostitute* (both portraits are from 1907), the color-scheme had darkened and the spirited brushstrokes of the dress and bust had become less sensual and more deliberately vulgar. This was the world of honky-tonk, sideshows and brothels that had inspired his predecessor, Toulouse-Lautrec. The passage of several years had not changed the motley crowd of dancers, street-walkers and onlookers that haunted the Grands Boulevards down the hill from Montmartre where he lived.

Contrary to the other Fauves, Van Dongen was hardly a landscapist. It seems that he was bored by trees and flowers (*Spring*, 1908); he found no pleasure in them and did not make any effort to paint them. When he did, his vigorous impasto petered out into a thin glaze and quite clearly his heart was not in it. When he tried his hand at portraying the rich polychrome façades of houses of Amsterdam, lining the canals, the result was even more disastrous. His horse pictures (*Chimera* 1894 and *Horses*, 1904) are not so bad, particularly those he integrated into a circus setting and that display feminine qualities.

But nature as a whole did not offer him anything truly interesting. Because his subject-matter was chiefly the human being, we might conclude that Van Dongen was associated rather with Expressionism. Yet on closer look, there was never the slightest dissonance nor the slightest lapse into uncontrolled colors in his work; it was entirely consistent in technique from start to finish, until his decline in the twenties.

KEES VAN DONGEN
Woman in Green Tights
1905
Oil on canvas, 21¾ x 18 in (55 x 46 cm)
Paris, private collection

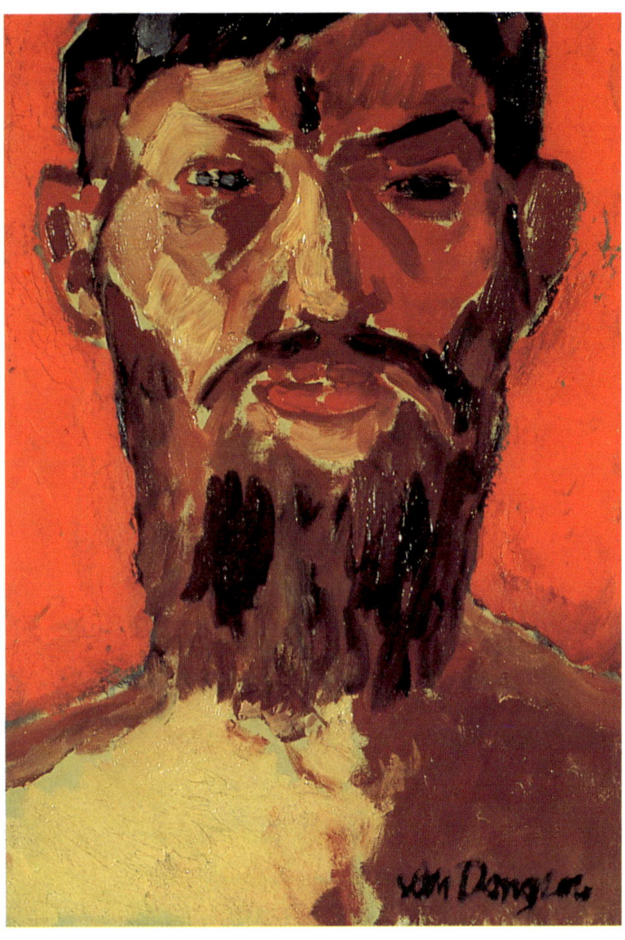

KEES VAN DONGEN
Self-portrait
1905-1906
Oil on canvas, 21¾ x 18¼ in (55 x 48 cm)
Private collection

Opposite:

KEES VAN DONGEN
Nini, the Prostitute
1907
Oil on canvas, 51¼ x 38¼ in (130 x 97 cm)
Paris, musée national d'Art moderne

The Archangel's Tango

In 1913, Van Dongen was already fairly well known, but the uproar in the press during the *Tableau* scandal turned him into a celebrity overnight. Then, the costume balls that he gave the next few years in his vast studio at 33, rue Denfert-Rochereau made him the talk of the town.

Van Dongen captivated his guests with the extravagance of his soirees. The critic André Warnod noted that they were attended by the *"Tout-Paris."* The painter would greet his friends bare-chested, wearing loose pastel-colored trousers, his hair and beard decorated with tiny pink ribbons." The couturier Paul Poiret came disguised as a Roman emperor. Later on when Van Dongen was no longer with Guus, he lived with Jasmy Jacob, alternately known as *"Jasmy la Divine"* or *"Jasmy la Terrible."* The grandiose reception-exhibition that he organized every Monday evening in his magnificent house on rue Lambert during the spring season were the height of fashion: "There is nothing smarter, more Parisian, more chic than the party for the vernissage." Each guest rushed off to find his own picture; portraits of fashionable women hung next to those of nude dancers, important politicians, clients of Maxim's restaurant and the smart set that vacationed in Deauville: from the opera star, Mademoiselle Vix to the socialite Countess Cassati and the cabinet minister Joseph Caillaux.

The quality of his work ranged from the best to the worst. *The Archangel's Tango* (1930) that portrays a woman clothed only in stockings and high-heeled shoes dancing in the tender embrace of an "archangel" dressed in black pants and a tail coat is, with its ambiguity, one of the artist's most disturbing pictures. On the other hand, his slapdash self-portrait as Neptune with a trident in his hand and several strands of beads hanging over his naked chest, is absolutely ridiculous.

The man in blue overalls, if he really possessed "a truly authentic talent," according to his friend Francis Jourdain, went from hard times to fame, and without making a large fortune, had the satisfaction of earning a good living. All this was a total break with his past as a bohemian anarchist. He was now a member of the elite, whatever that was.

At the beginning of the Occupation he was, for some reason, unable to resist the temptation to cater to the Nazi authorities in charge of culture and accepted an official invitation to travel to Germany. The purpose of the visit was to become acquainted with the artistic endeavors of the IIIrd Reich, to conform to the spirit of collaboration approved by Hitler and Pétain during a meeting in Montoire, and to make fraternal ties between French and German artists in preparation of what was to be called for a time the "New Europe."

In September-October 1941, a group of writers were sent to a literary symposium in Weimar. In November, at the incentive of Arno Brecker, the Fuhrer's favorite artist, painters and sculptors followed suit. With a sense of foreboding, Maurice Denis, Matisse, and Bonnard refused. Was Van Dongen simply flattered at being invited, or did it make him feel that he was returning to the fore of the artistic scene, now that his work was no longer in fashion? Vlaminck and Derain, both members of the former Fauve group, accepted the invitation as well. The excursion took them through the art centers of Nazi Germany.

Van Dongen's reputation was damaged by this episode. In 1942, the Charpentier Gallery in Paris held the artist's most

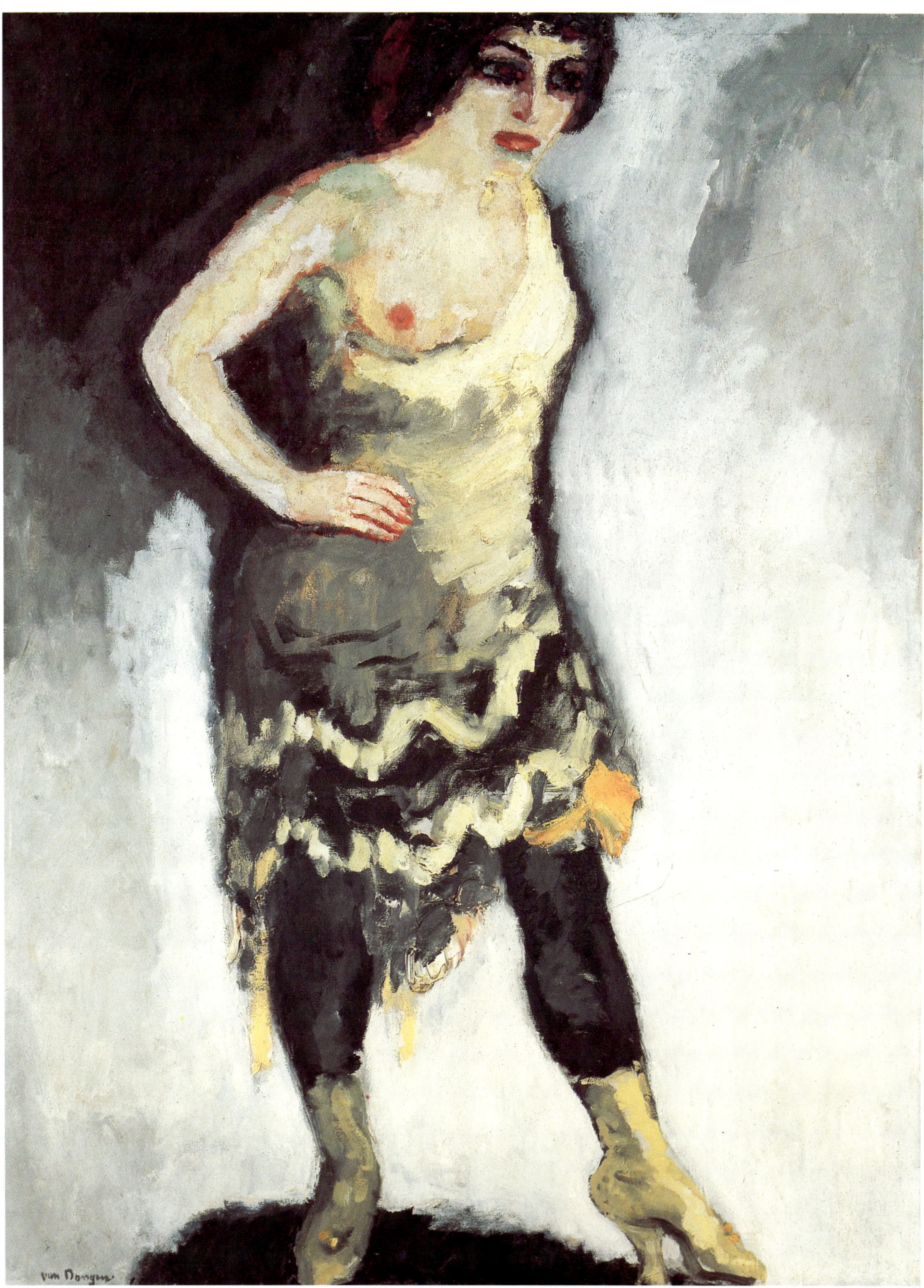
van Dongen

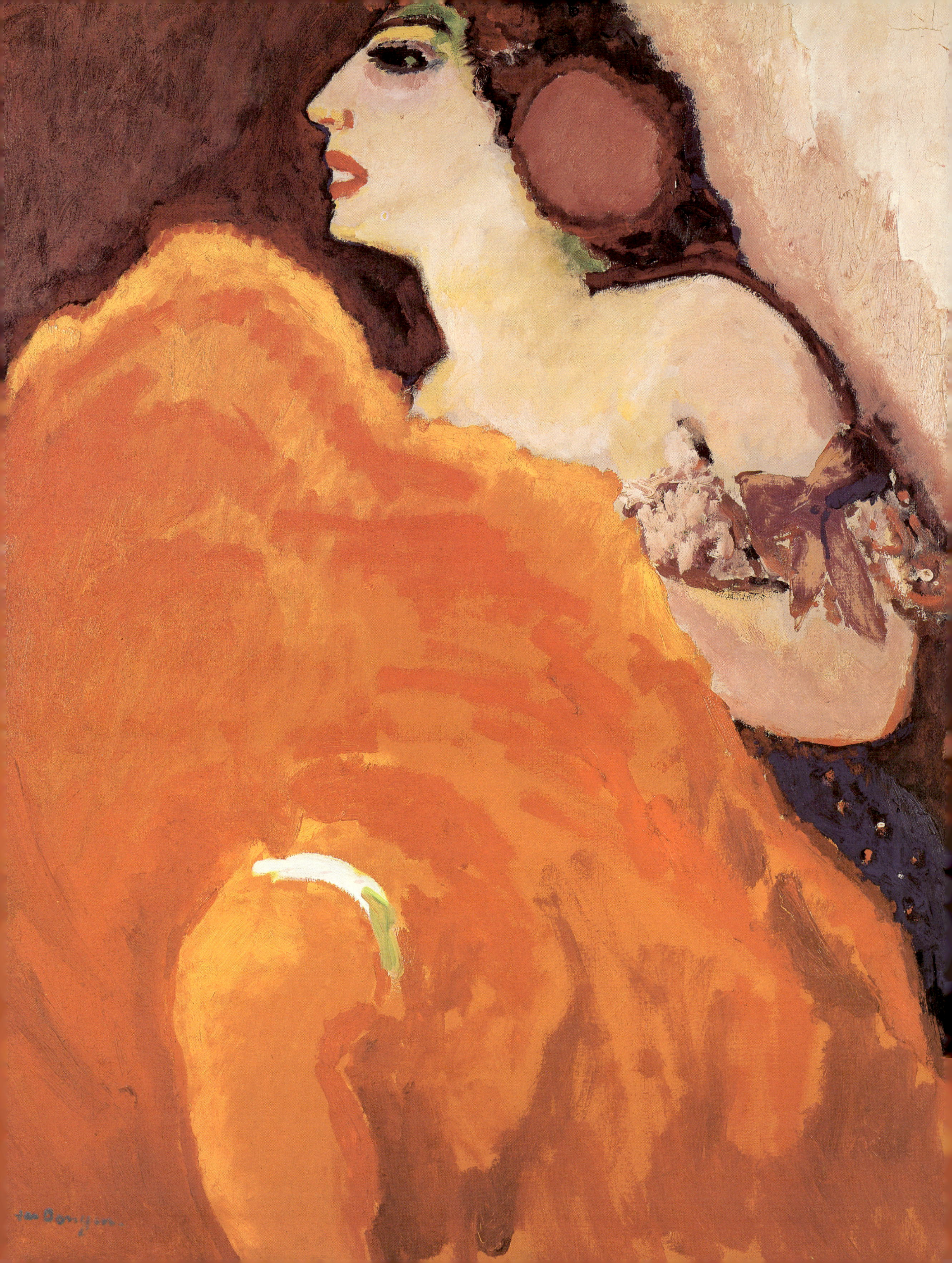

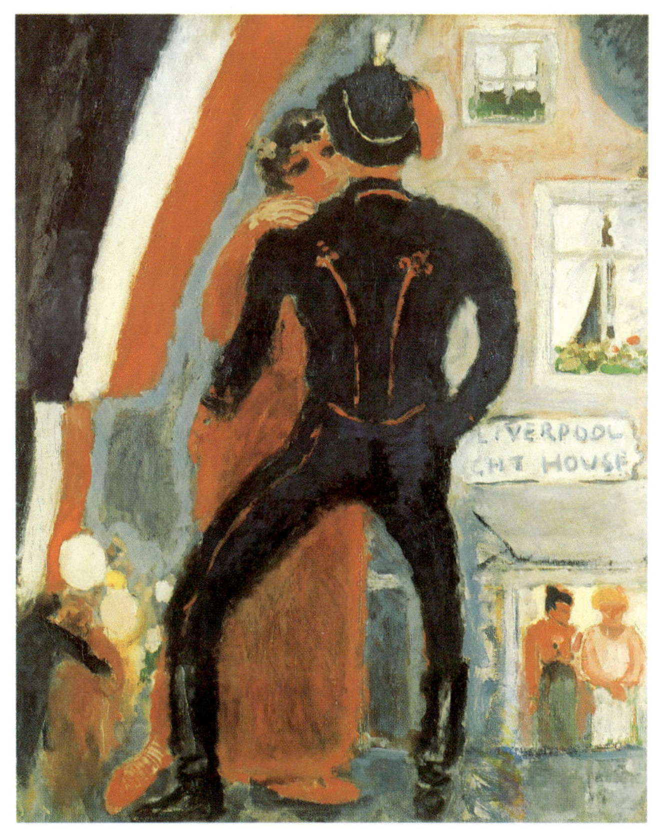

KEES VAN DONGEN
"Liverpool Light House" in Rotterdam
1907
Oil on canvas, 39¼ x 32 in (100 x 81 cm)
London, Fridart Foundation

Opposite:

KEES VAN DONGEN
The Red Dancer
1907
Oil on canvas, 39 x 31½ in (99 x 80 cm)
St. Petersburg, Hermitage Museum

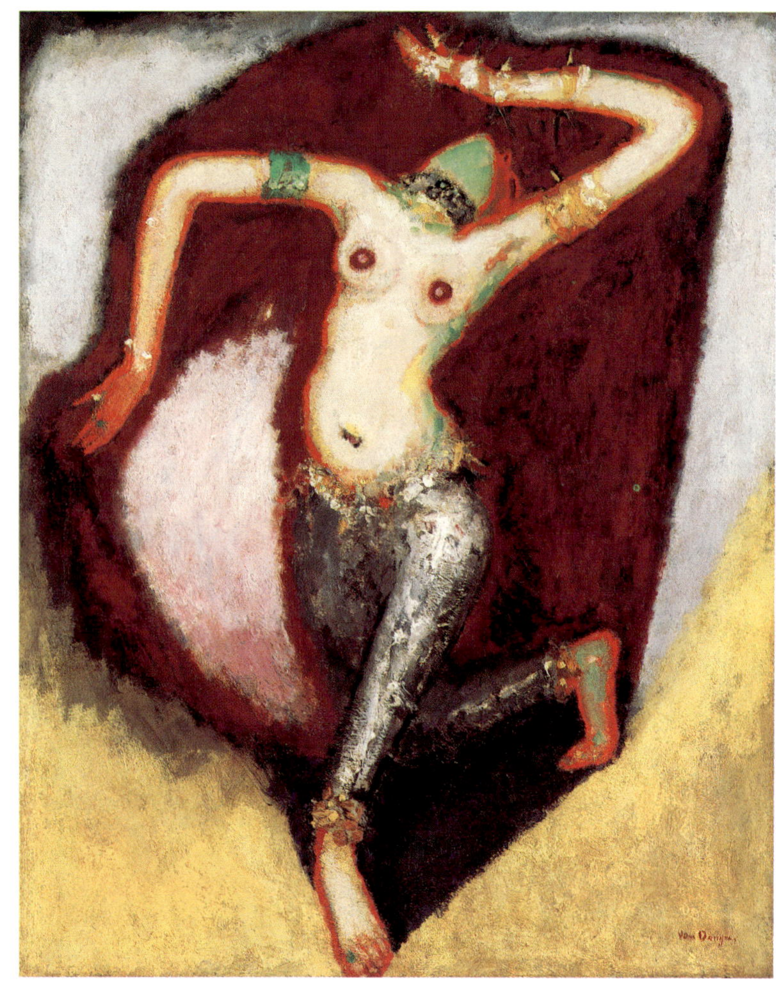

Kees Van Dongen
The Indian Dance
1907
Oil on canvas, 39½ x 17¾ in
(100 x 81 cm)
Private collection
(courtesy of Ellen Melas Kyriazi)

Opposite:

Kees Van Dongen
The Gypsy
1910-1911
Oil on canvas, 21¼ x 17¾ in (54 x 45 cm)
Saint-Tropez, musée de l'Annonciade

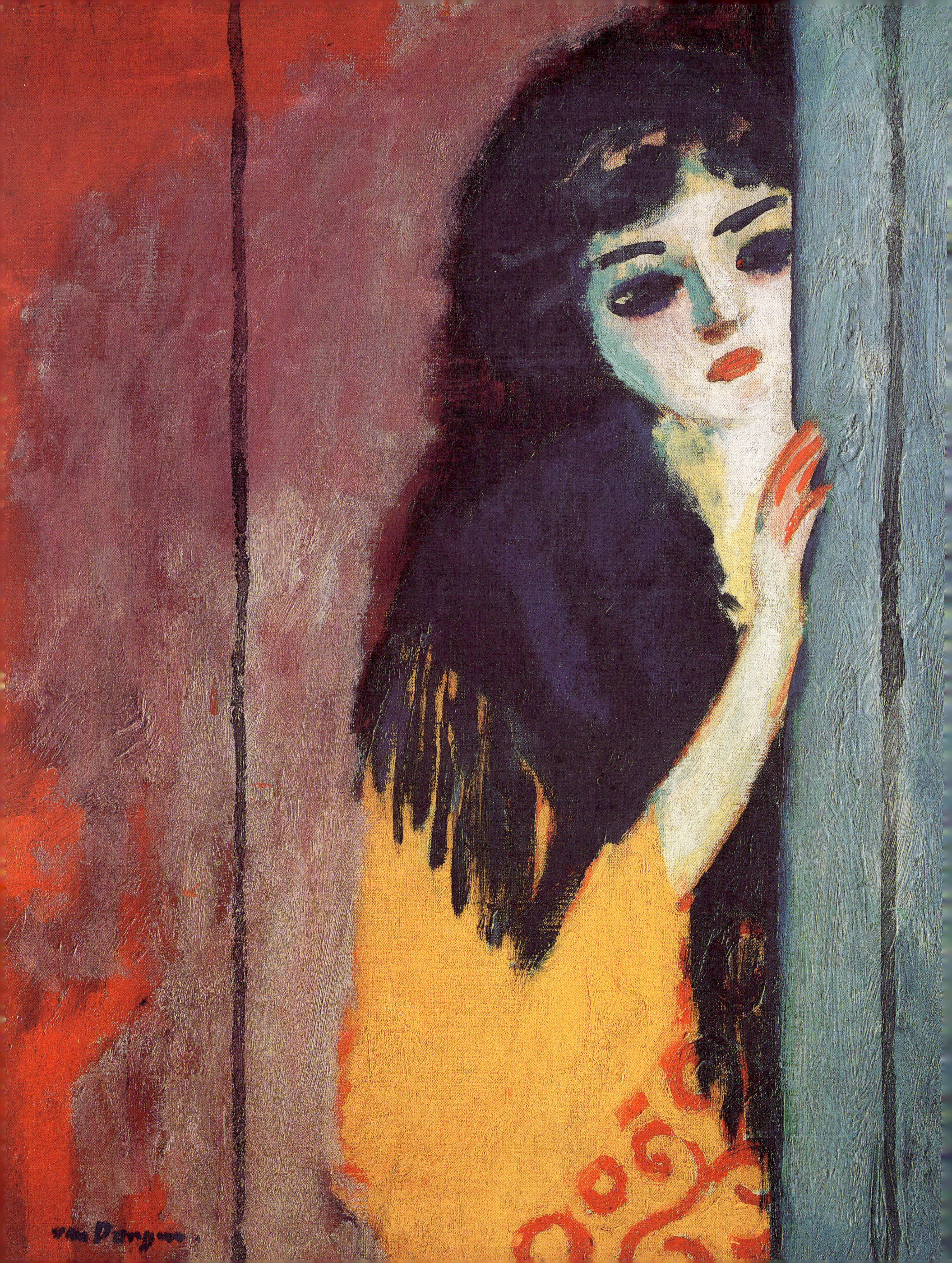
van Dongen

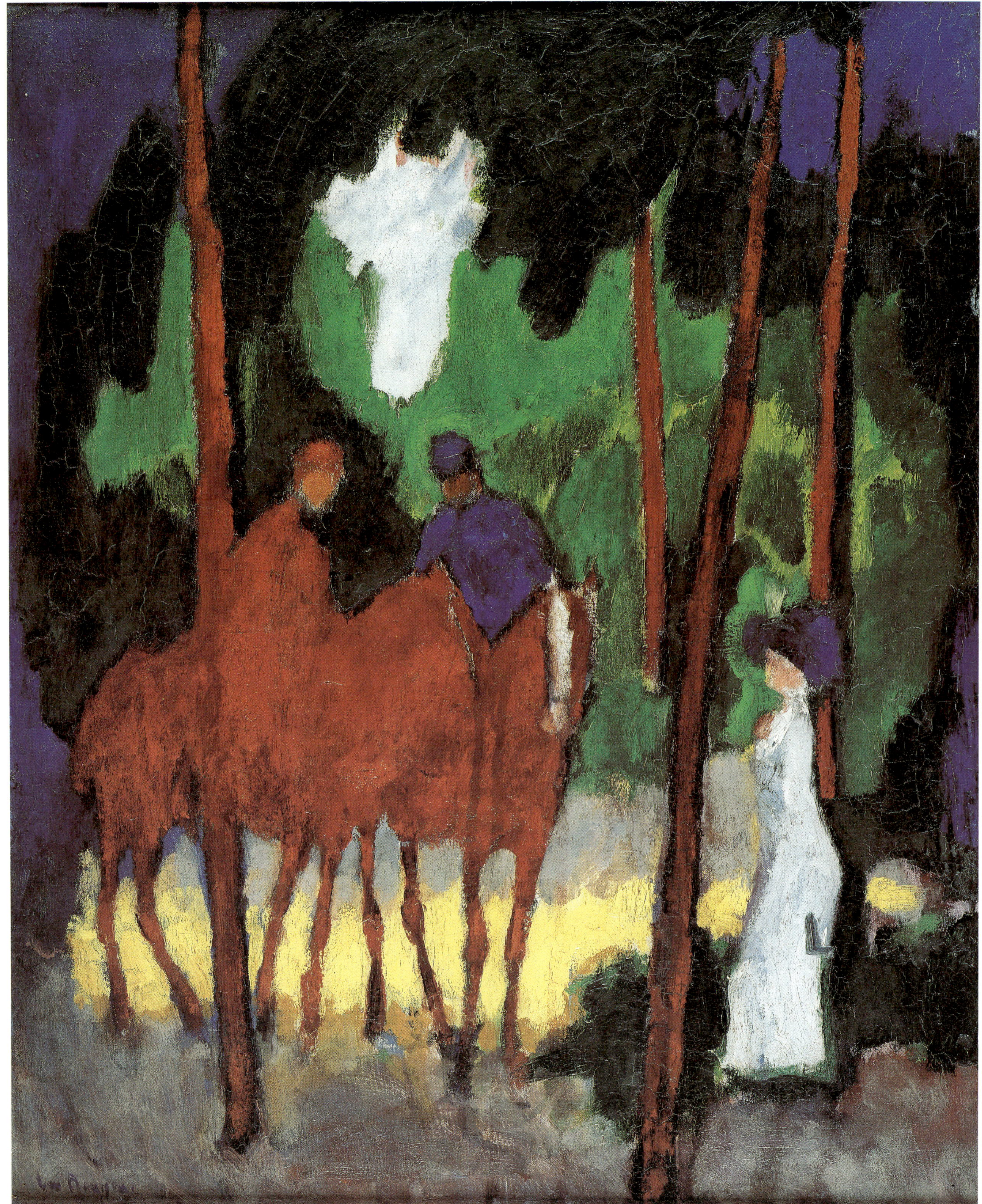

important retrospective exhibition: two hundred and fifty-eight works to honor his "Fifty Years of Painting." But the show turned out to be far less successful than anticipated, for Van Dongen had been ostracized because of his German junket.

After the war he decided to settle on the Riviera and made an attempt to re-establish his standing as a major artist of the century, but when he died on May 28, 1968 in Monte-Carlo at the age of ninety-one, he had ceased to exist as a creator for more than a half a century.

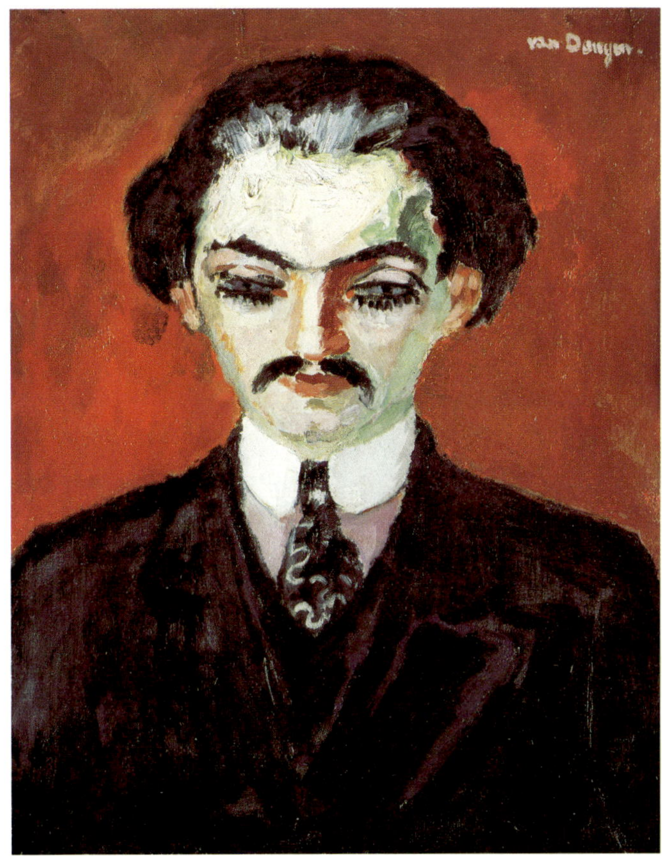

KEES VAN DONGEN
Portrait of Daniel Henry Kahnweiler
1907
Oil on canvas, 25½ x 21¼ in (65 x 54 cm)
Geneva, musée du Petit Palais

Opposite:

KEES VAN DONGEN
Riders in the Bois de Boulogne
1906
Oil on canvas, 36¼ x 23½ in (92 x 60 cm)
Le Havre, musée des Beaux-Arts André Malraux

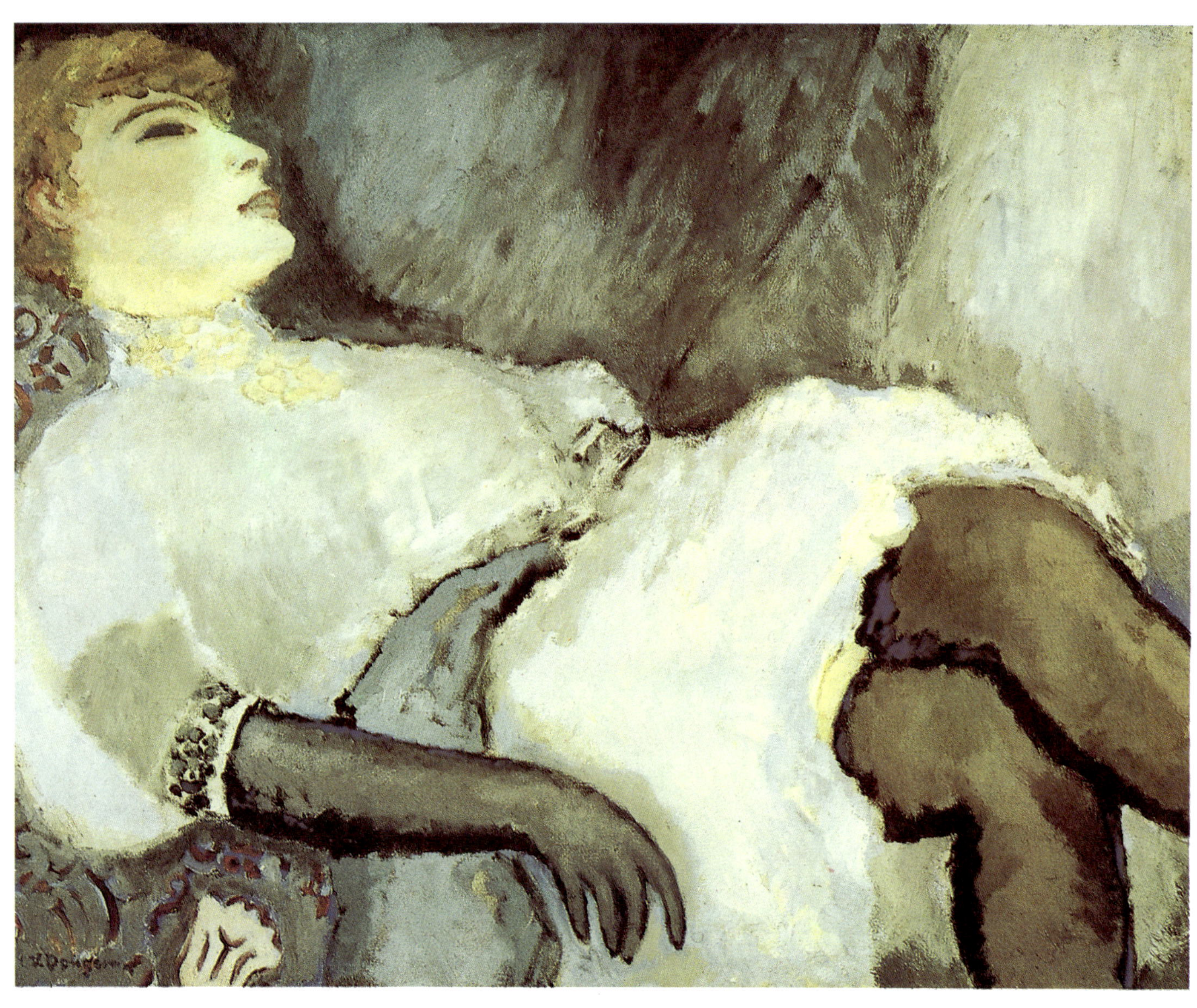

Kees Van Dongen
Woman with Black Gloves
1908
Oil on canvas, 28¾ x 35¾ in (73 x 91 cm)
Moscow, Pushkin Museum

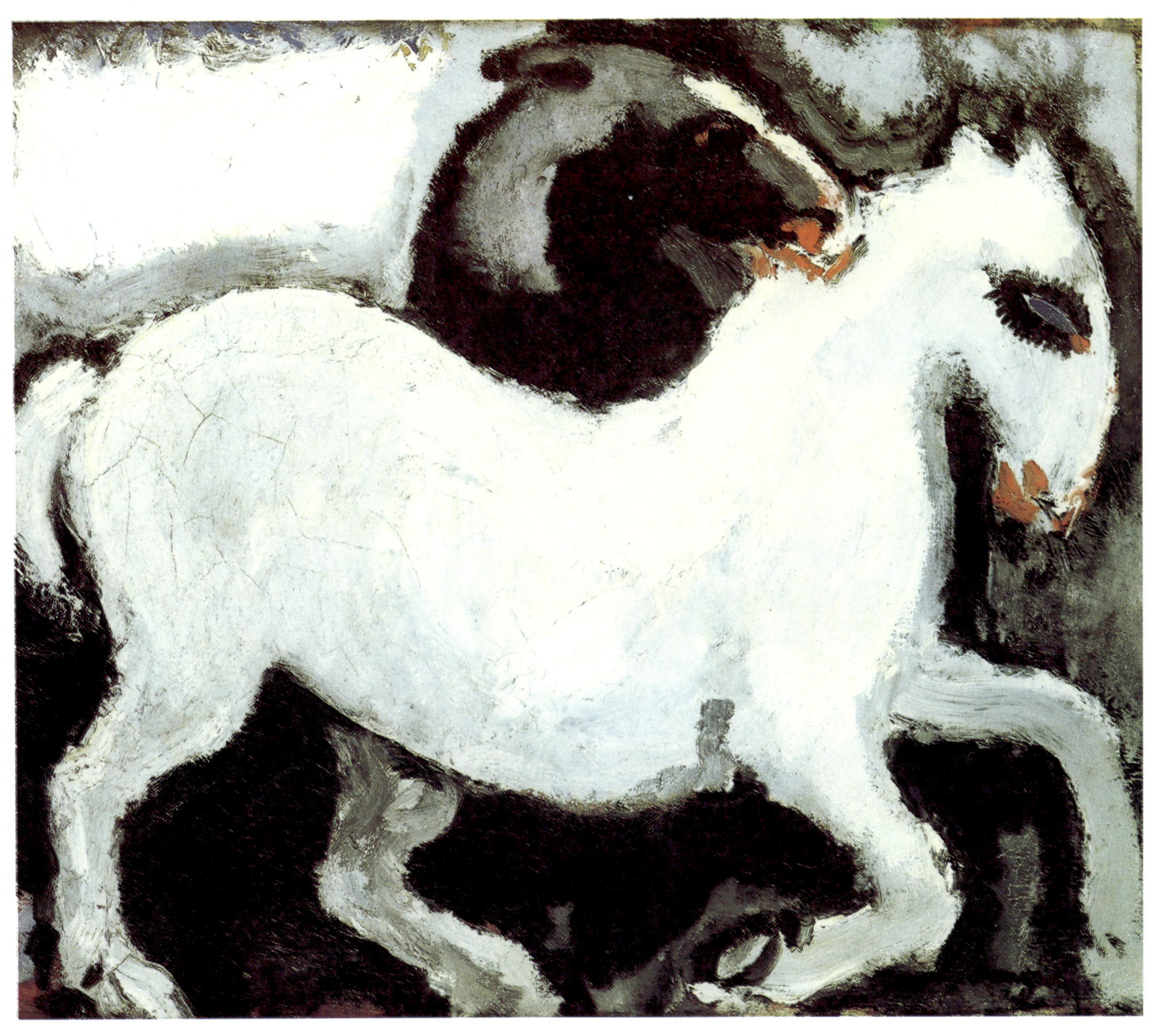

Kees Van Dongen
Horses
1904
Oil on canvas, 18 x 21¾ in (46 x 55 cm)
Private collection
(courtesy of Ellen Melas Kyriazi)

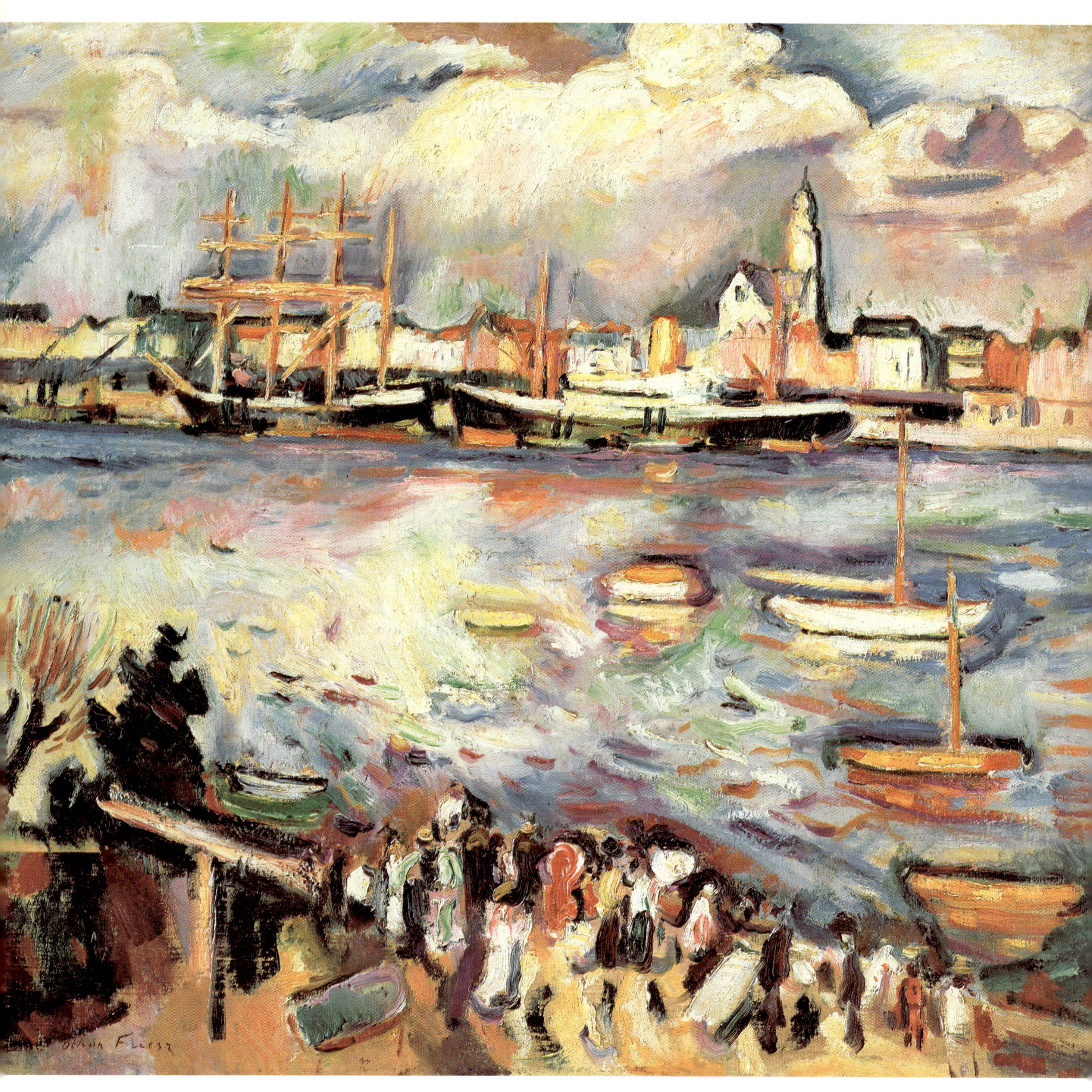

Colored Orchestrations:

Friesz

Othon Friesz was born in Le Havre on February 6, 1879 bearing a Christian name associated with Emperors and a surname heavy with consonants. His towering and severe father was an ocean-going captain often away on the high seas who left the education of his only child in the hands of his wife, an excellent musician. She began giving her son music lessons when he was only five years old. Othon, however, was more drawn to the lively activities of the port. When he was twelve he expressed a keen appetite for drawing and painting, and from 1897 on he decided to devote all his time to it. He entered the local art academy in his native city and studied under Charles Lhuillier, an able artist and remarkable teacher who not only recognized Friesz's talent but also discovered Braque and Dufy. The next year Othon was awarded a scholarship of 1,200 francs a year to permit him to study, first at the Beaux-Arts in Paris in Bonnat's class, and then with Gustave Moreau, where he joined the group of future Fauves.

From the start, Friesz decided not to work with raw sienna or the delightful crimson-brown tones of bituminous oil colors. Bitumen was especially popular among painters of the 19th century because of the "museum-look" it produced; but this practice was very detrimental in the long run, causing extensive damage to the paint, forming craquelures, hard speckles, and bleeding into neighboring colors. Instead, Friesz adopted yellow and red ochers, emerald greens, vermilions and cadmiums, all safe and permanent pigments. His palette was reminiscent of the paintings at Pompei. He then felt the need to lighten up his palette and chose tints closer to the saturated colors of the spectrum. This evolution culminated in the *Pont-Neuf* series (1903-1904)

OTHON FRIESZ
The Port of Antwerp
1906
Oil on canvas, 27¼ x 31½ in
(69,5 x 80 cm)
Saint-Tropez, musée de l'Annonciade

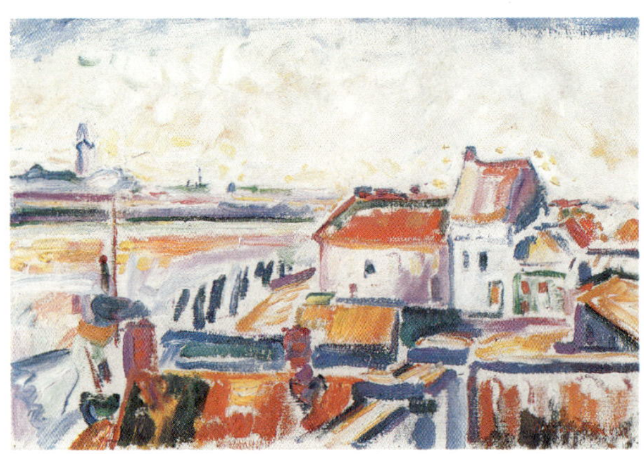

OTHON FRIESZ
The Port of Antwerp
1906
Oil on canvas, 11¾ x 17¾ in (30 x 45 cm)
Grenoble, musée de Peinture
et de Sculpture

Opposite:

OTHON FRIESZ
Portrait of Fernand Fleuret
1907
Oil on canvas, 29½ x 23½ in (75 x 60 cm)
Paris, musée national d'Art moderne

that ended his period of apprenticeship. He then became closer to Matisse, Derain and Vlaminck and adopted their manner of expression through the interplay of complementary or contrasting colors.

From 1905 until 1907, Friesz was just one Fauve among the others, preoccupied essentially with the arrangement of colored masses, with a predilection for large landscapes, grandiose motifs and ample rhythms. He painted series of landscapes in Antwerp with Braque, then in the South of France with Matisse, and in Normandy. Some of his works took on a rather baroque twist: works from this periods such as *Cruiser Dressed in Flags* and *Terrace over the Scheldt River* (1906) are an excellent example of the use of curves that, in the eyes of the artist, expressed a great emotional impact as opposed to angular shapes which he felt manifested agitation and impatience.

Because Friesz was well aware of the risk of poorly-controlled color, he later remarked: "We were the creators of Fauvism, but we were also the first to slay it." In 1908, while painting a hillside at La Ciotat, he felt the need to return to drawing and this step led him progressively toward a more sedate and classical mode of expression. Commenting on this new orientation in the preface of the 1908 exhibition catalogue of the Cercle de l'art moderne du Havre, of which Friesz was a founder, Apollinaire referred to what he called "The Three Pictorial Virtues"–Purity, Truth and Unity–which "pinned nature to the ground."

Indeed, Friesz had always admired Cézanne, like all his fellow-artists, but he was able to understand the teachings of the old master. His Cézannism derived not from abstractions or theory, but from direct contact with the Provencal landscape. Friesz wrote: "It was in Provence that Matisse, Derain, and I rediscovered an idea forgotten by the Impressionists, that a painting from nature must be reworked in the studio in order to acquire what Mallarmé called 'authenticity.' This classical conception of painting came to us through the Provence countryside and through Cézanne, of course."

Friesz had the strange idea that the human form, standing or reclining, would integrate spontaneously into the "arid and intellectual" landscape of Provence, where plant-life consists mainly of fir and cypress trees, while man's presence "seemed superfluous in a meadow in Normandy or on a riverbank in Brittany, where nature alone suffices." Such considerations as these marked the end of Fauvism in Friesz's art and resulted in works such as *Bathers* or *L'Estaque* (1907). The best example is found in one of his major pictures, *Autumn Labors*, where the artist went beyond a simple orchestration of color and developed a clever treatment of arabesques and volumes, producing a synthesis that made a great impression on his fellow painters at the 1908 Salon des Indépendants.

During the next few years, Friesz' work sparked an enthusiasm that is hard to explain today. In the twenties, Jean-Louis Vaudoyer wrote: "The pathos of this uncompromising art has something cruel in it like a strong wind blowing against you on a mountain top." And Pierre Courthion noted: "There is something of Delacroix in this artist." Most of Friesz's paintings from this second period however present a feigned rigor and give an ambiguous impression of "orderly chaos," an impression confirmed by the monumental decoration for the Palais de Chaillot, *River Seine* (1937).

Othon Friesz died without warning on January 9, 1949, at the age of seventy, having completed and signed the drawing of a nude the day before.

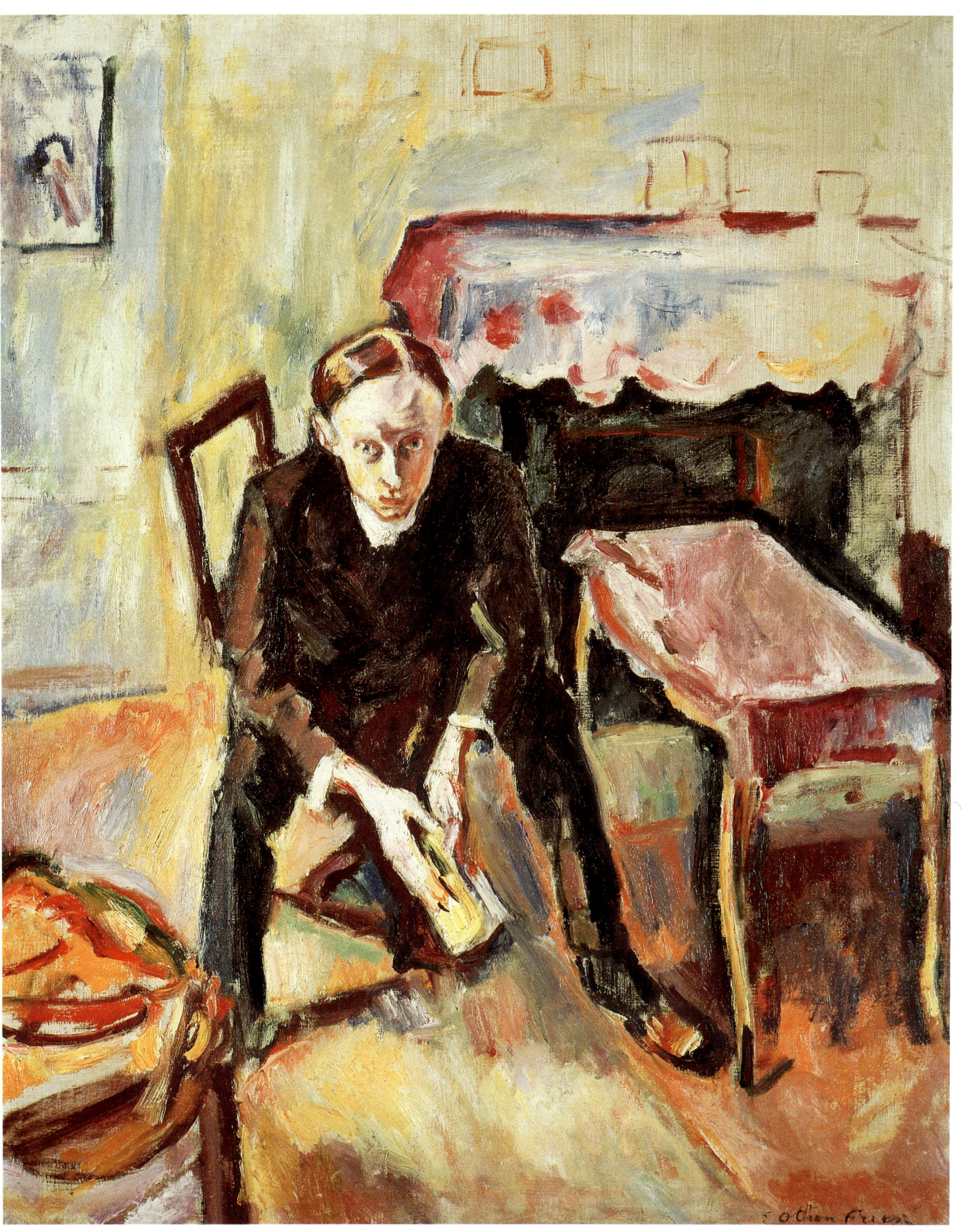
E Othon Friesz

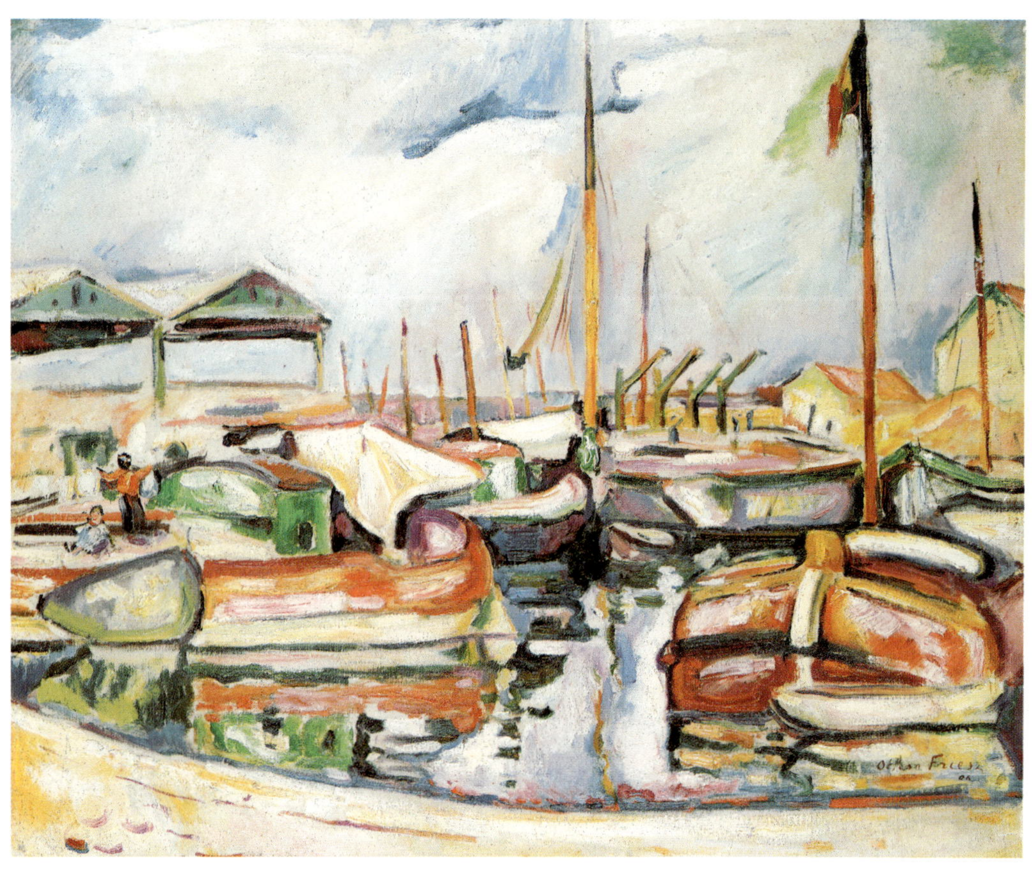

OTHON FRIESZ
Barges at Antwerp
1906
Oil on canvas, 23½ x 28¾ in (60 x 73 cm)
Paris, Daniel Malingue Gallery

Opposite:

OTHON FRIESZ
Port of Antwerp
1906
Oil on canvas, 21¼ x 25½ in (54 x 65 cm)
Liège, musée d'Art moderne

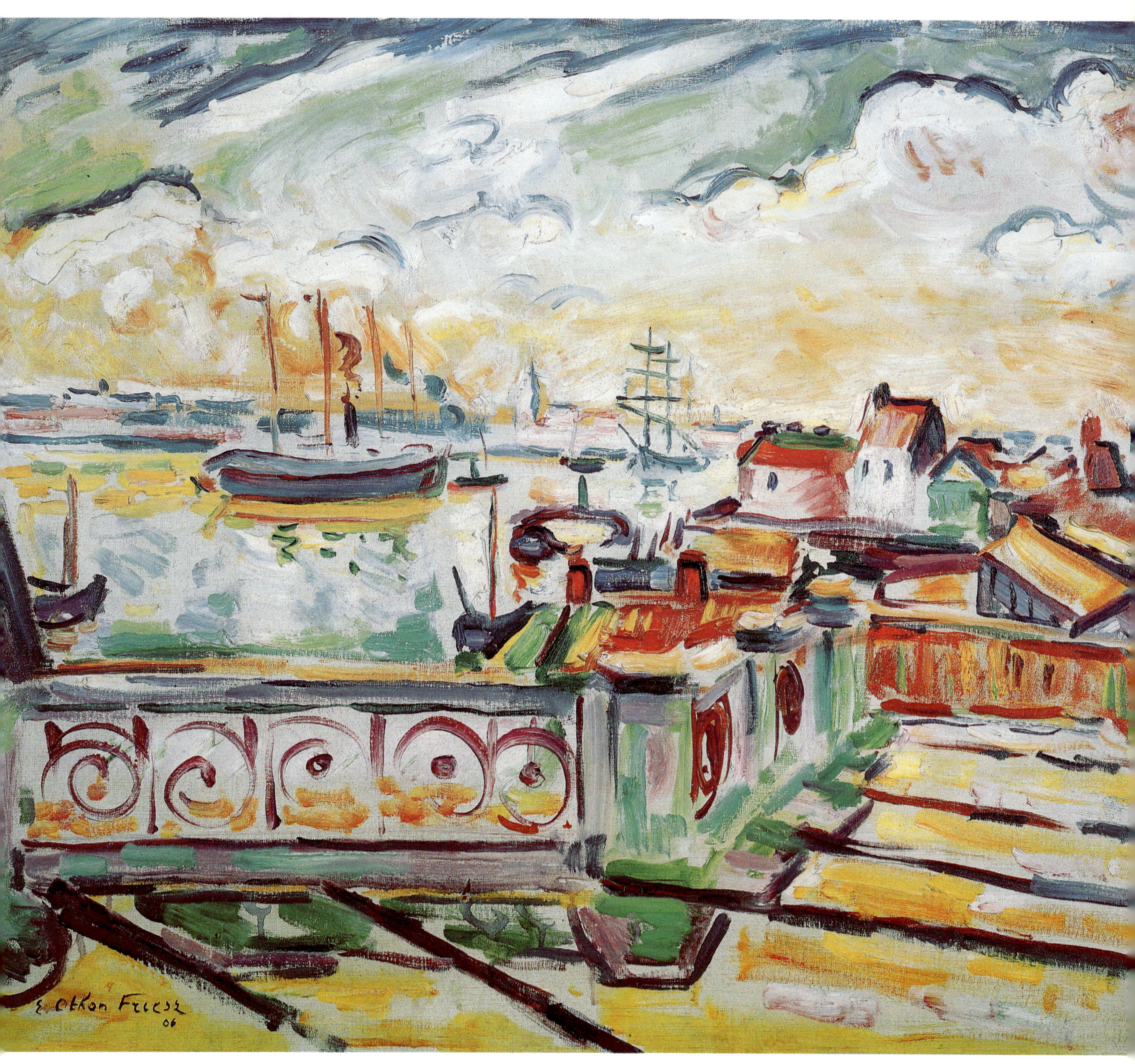
E. Othon Friesz
06

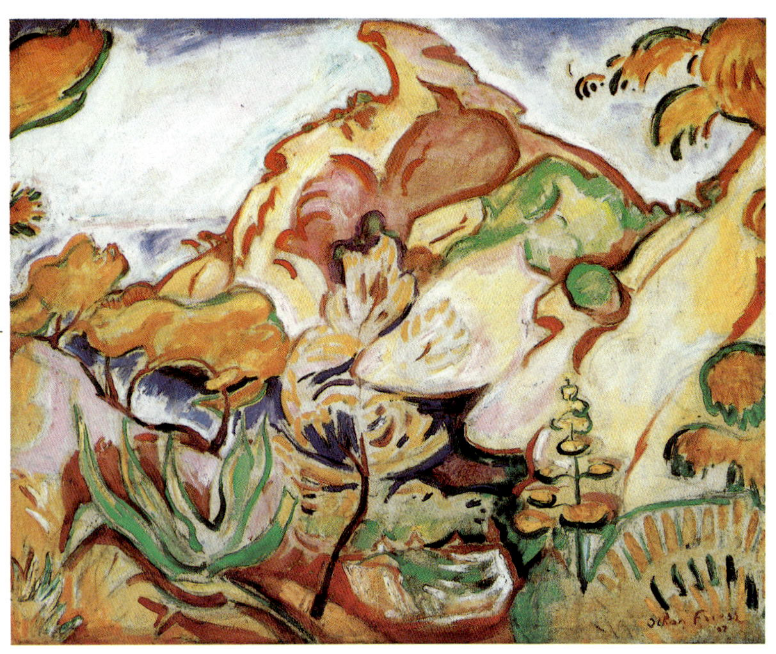

OTHON FRIESZ
Landscape at La Ciotat
(Le Bec de l'Aigle)
1907
Oil on canvas, 25½ x 32 in (65 x 81 cm)
Troyes, musée d'Art moderne

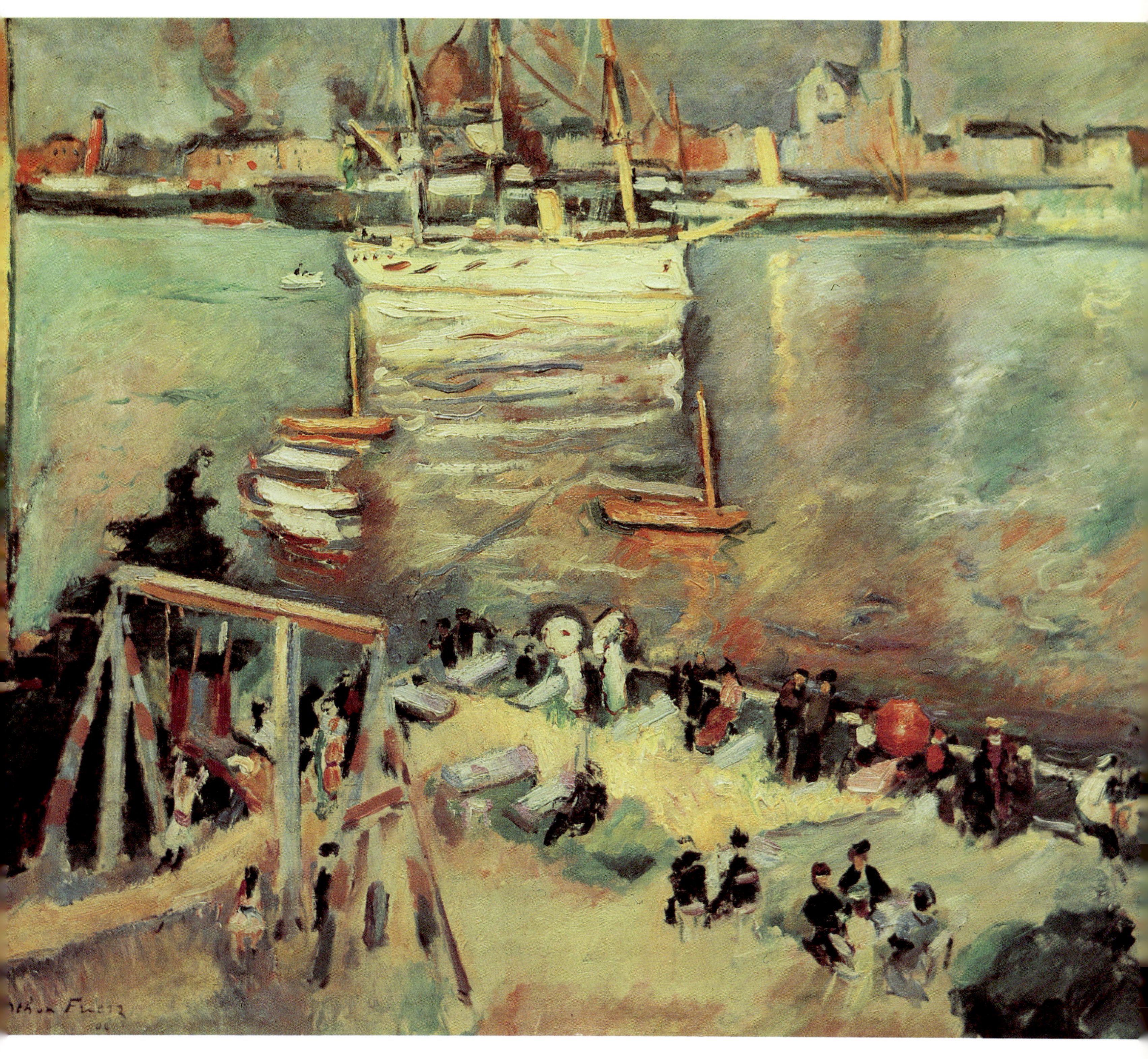

OTHON FRIESZ
Corvette Entering the Port of Antwerp
1906
Oil on canvas, 23½ x 29¼ in (60 x 74 cm)
Geneva, musée du Petit Palais

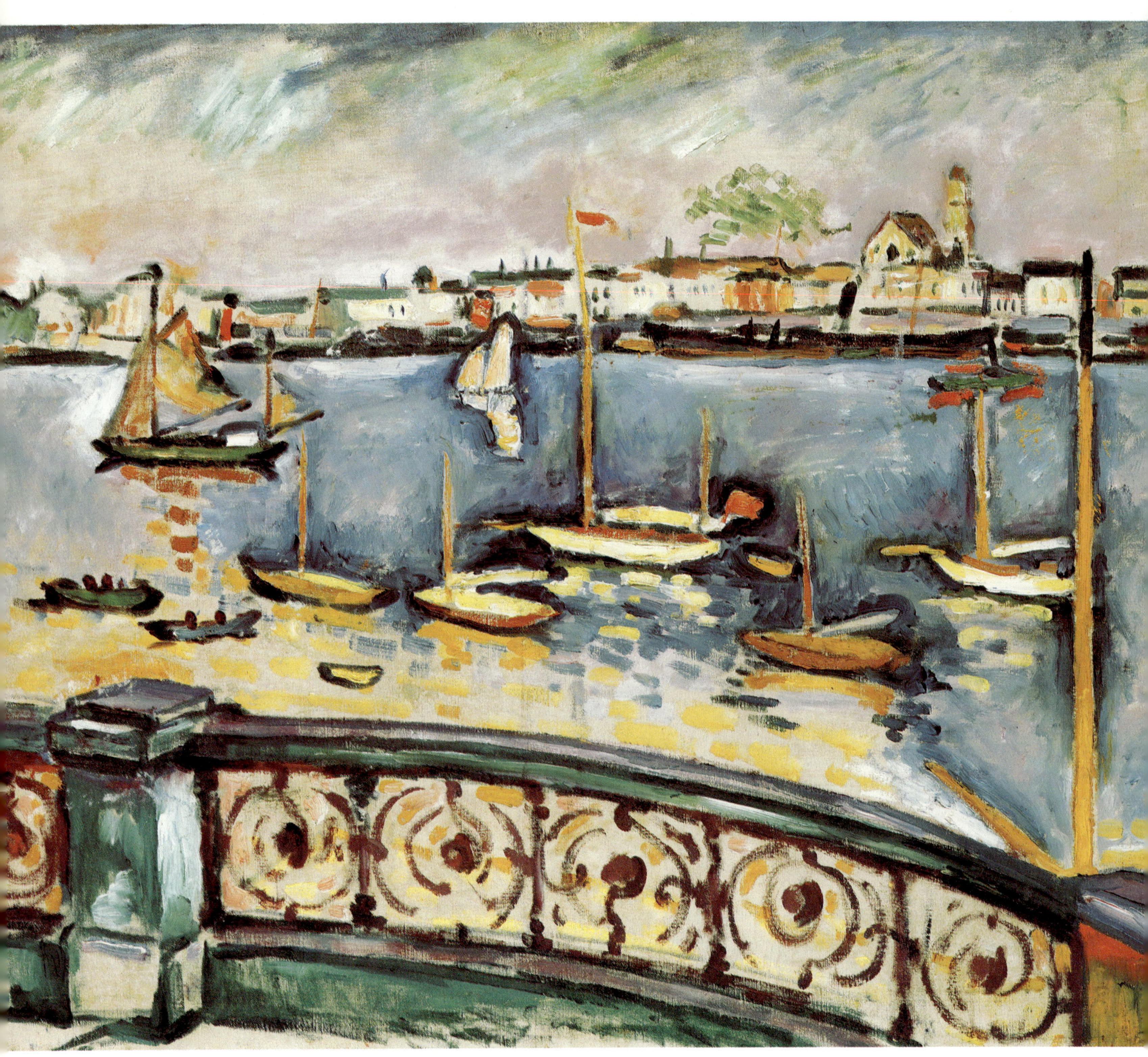

The Renegade:

Braque

From Boxing to Fauvism

Georges Braque is universally known as the co-inventor, with Picasso, of Cubism in 1908. Before radically changing his style the artist belonged to the Fauve Movement for three years, and his few works from this period lack neither in talent nor personality.

Born on May 13, 1882 in Argenteuil he spent a happy childhood in a loving family. His grandfather and father ran a house-painting business, and as Sunday painters, would make landscapes of the surrounding countryside. Toward 1890, Braque's family moved to Le Havre at a period when the busy port was expanding rapidly and needed master craftsmen to build new lodgings and portuary installations. Braque therefore was living in Normandy, Monet's country and the cradle of Impressionism. Finding it hard to buckle down to the rigors of the classroom, he took up sports: swimming, rowing, hiking, bicycling, activities which gave him the body of an athlete. On Sundays, in his father's company, he would ride to the country in a horse-drawn carriage to paint from life. He then discovered Corot's and Boudin's work at the fine arts museum in Le Havre. At the age of seventeen he left school to learn the family trade, while taking evening classes at the Ecole des Beaux-Arts.

In the fall of 1900, his parents sent him to Paris to complete his apprenticeship with one of their former employees and obtain a house-painter and decorator certificate. During his Parisian stay, he lived on rue des Trois-Frères in Montmartre and studied drawing at a public school in the Batignolles neighborhood; yet no one then could have predicted his far-reaching future. He presented himself as a solid, healthy boy, proficient at boxing and playing the accordion, and could

GEORGES BRAQUE
The Port of Antwerp
1906
Oil on canvas, 19½ x 24 in
(49.8 x 61.2 cm)
Ottawa, National Gallery of Art

also sing and dance better than anyone else. Toward the end of 1902 after his military service, he was able to undertake an artistic career thanks to an allowance from his father, by then a man of some means.

After a brief stint at the Beaux-Arts in Paris in 1903 under Bonnat, whose uncompromising disposition he could not stand, he spent two years at the Académie Humbert where a less conformist spirit prevailed. During his vacations he painted landscapes in Normandy and Brittany, destroying most of them afterwards. One of his earliest paintings to survive, *Boat in the Port of Le Havre*, was painted in 1905, the same year that the "wild-beast-cage" scandal blew up at the Salon d'Automne. The colorful sailboat, whose rigging makes up the strong composition, shows solid painterly qualities. When fifty years later someone asked Braque why he had joined the Fauves he answered: "Fauve painting had a newness that appealed to me"; he was twenty-three years old at the time and just starting out.

It was not until the following year, however, that his painting became entirely emancipated. He spent the summer of 1906 in Antwerp with Othon Friesz–also from Le Havre–who was an ardent advocate of "colored orchestrations." The two colleagues rented a studio on the banks of the Scheldt River, where cliffs offered them a plunging view of the port. In one of his initial attempts, he emphasized the elegant scrolls of the ironwork balustrade in the foreground, but his treatment was still hesitant. Another of his canvases on the same theme, *The Port of Antwerp* (1906), which shows a merchant ship in the background with an impressive hull composed of two horizontal overlayed flat-color areas of mauve and red dominating a green sea, demonstrates a better control of the color effects and a consummate mastery of composition.

Braque appreciated the "physical" side of Fauvism even more than its flamboyance. But because of his family origins and education, his art always leaned toward conscientious craftsmanship and a respect for "métier." At the time, he was able to effectively tolerate this aspect of Fauvism.

The personal biases that set him apart from the Fauve group would become more evident during his different trips to L'Estaque, the first of which took place in the fall of 1906. Cézanne, who had painted the site in a number of exceptionally forceful works, had just died. It is certainly not a coincidence that Braque also went there to paint; this pilgrimage was to honor the memory of the great master from Aix as well as an opportunity to measure himself up to him. Surrounded by hills, the bay of L'Estaque, to the west of Marseilles, abounded in superb motifs. Braque began working in the same fiery color-scheme that he had just adopted in La Ciotat, in his view of *La Ciotat Harbor* (1907). But his lines and volumes became progressively more distinct; the trees, houses, and rock formations were organized into simplified planes overlapping each another from near to far, creating depth; curves and circles were traced in yellow, orange and violet and outlined with reds and blues.

Nonetheless, the most revealing paintings in this new direction are those depicting the railway viaduct along the bay, dividing it horizontally as in *The Viaduct at L'Estaque* (1907). Like Marquet and Dufy in 1906, who were fascinated by the flashy billboards on the shorefront in Trouville and turned their backs to the ocean in order to illustrate them, Braque also turned away from the sea to paint these landscapes, into which he introduced geometrical elements like masonry arches and pillars, taking Fauvism to its limits.

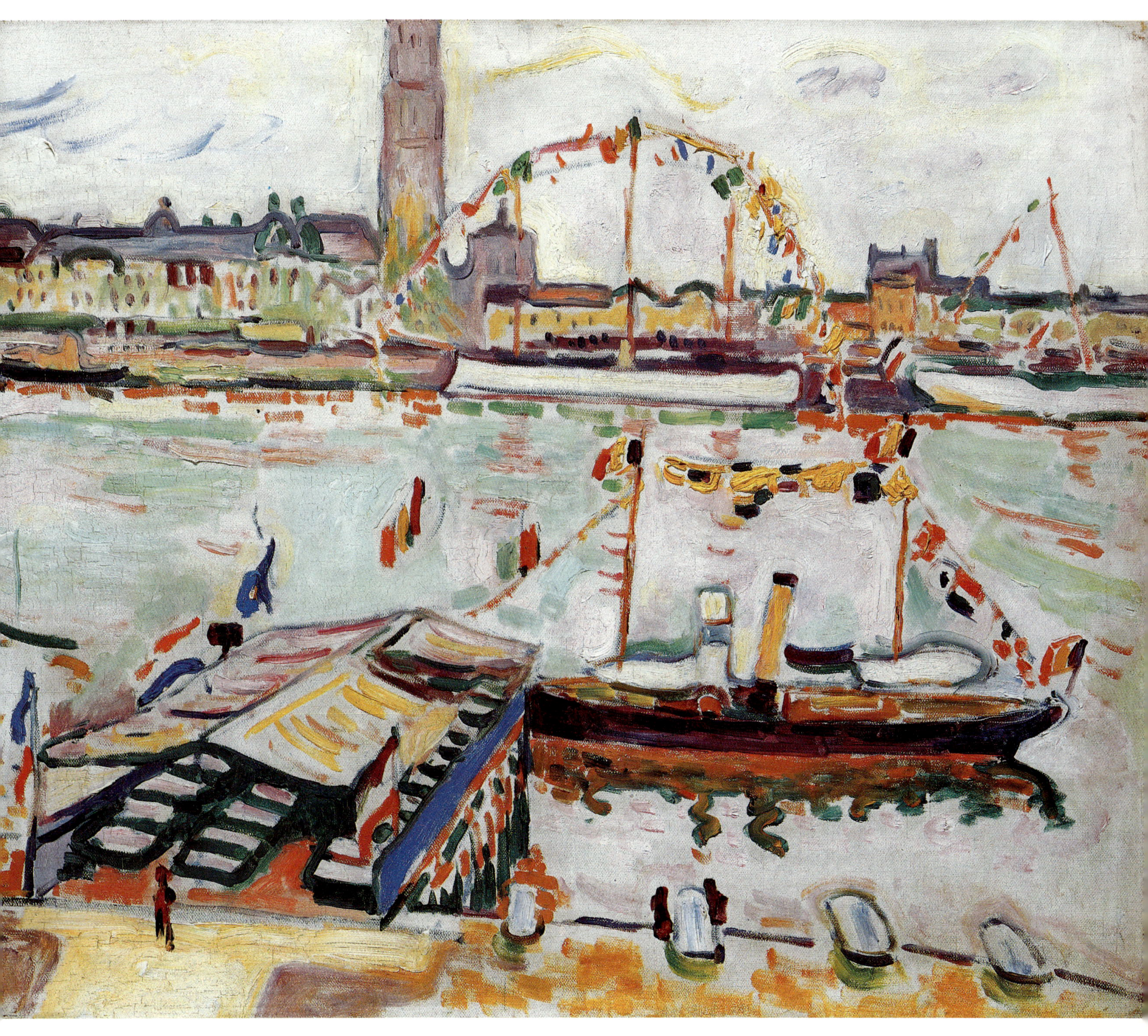

Georges Braque
The Port of Antwerp
1906
Oil on canvas, 20 x 24¼ in (50.5 x 61.5 cm)
Basel, Museum of Fine Arts

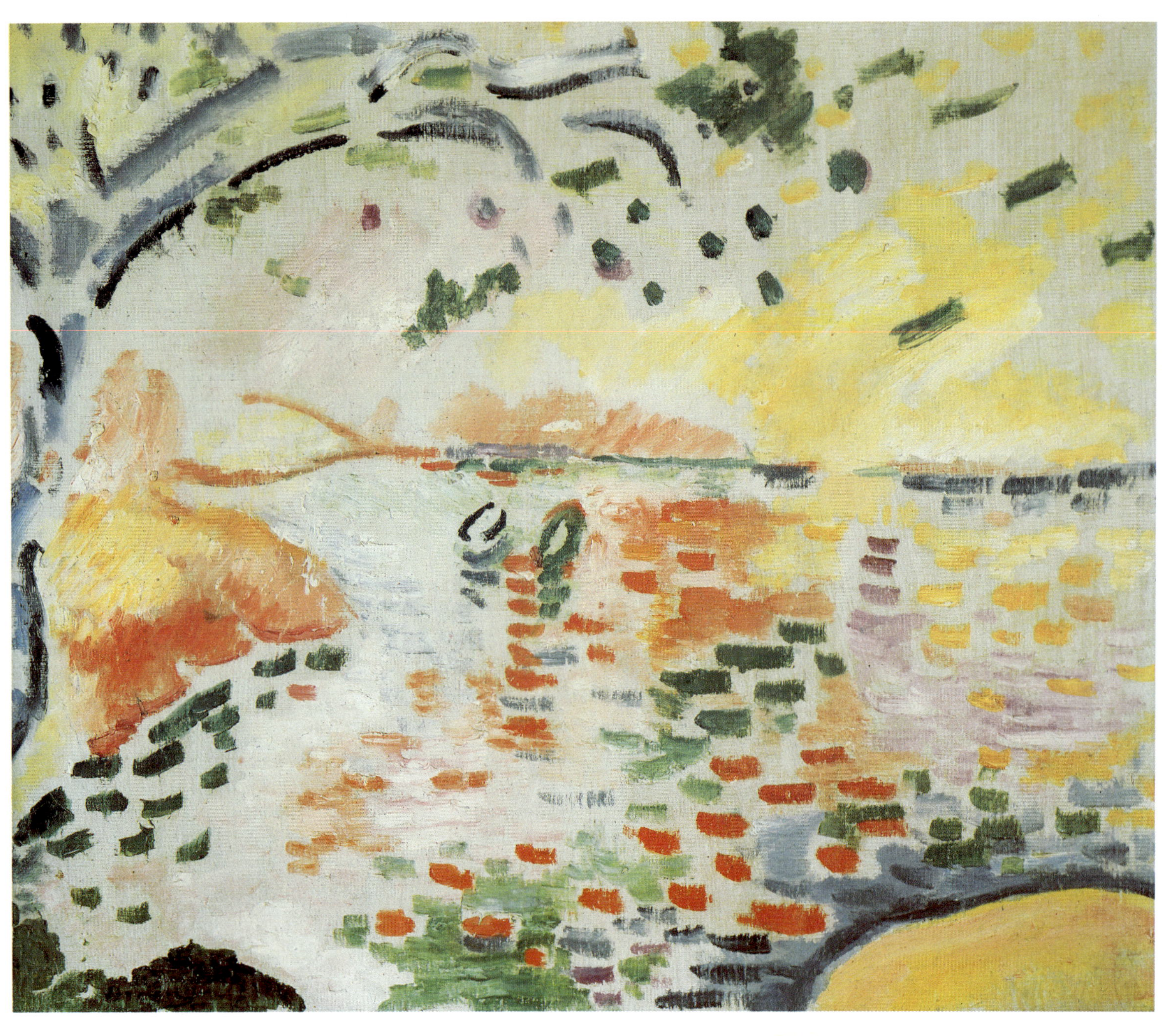

GEORGES BRAQUE
Small Bay at La Ciotat
1907
Oil on canvas, 14¼ x 19 in (36 x 48 cm)
Paris, musée national d'Art moderne

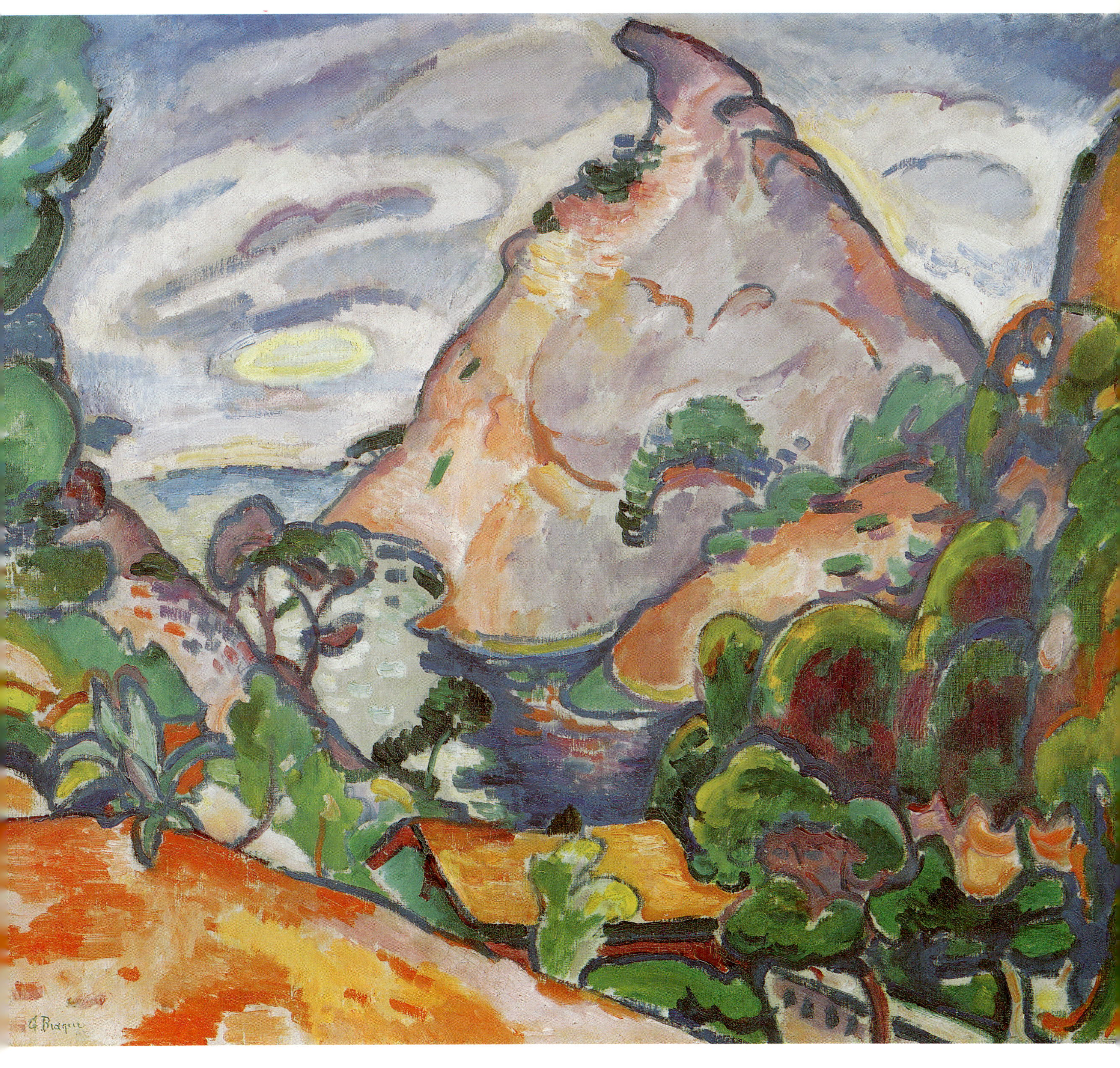

GEORGES BRAQUE
"La Calenque," Overcast
1907
Oil on canvas, 23½ x 28¾ in (60 x 73 cm)
Munich, Neue Staatsgemäldegalerie

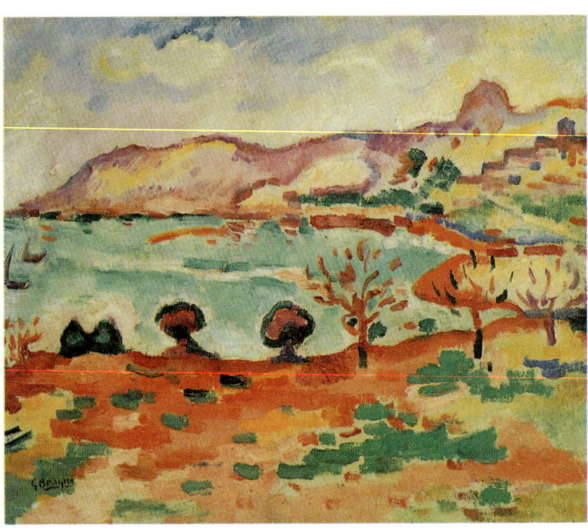

Georges Braque
Landscape at L'Estaque
1907
Oil on canvas, 14½ x 18 in (37 x 46 cm)
Troyes, musée d'Art moderne

Demoiselles not to be Associated With

In October 1907, right after his return to Paris, Braque visited Picasso's studio at the Bateau-Lavoir in Montmartre accompanied by Apollinaire. We know from eye witnesses that when Braque first found himself face to face with *Les demoiselles d'Avignon*, he had a terrific shock. It is unlikely that Braque's break with Fauvism was due to just this one episode as it has often been claimed, for the radical changes in his style were due as much, if not more, to Cézanne. At the same time, the retrospective taking place at the Salon d'Automne gave young painters the opportunity to study the work of the controversial genius, in exhaustive detail.

Picasso's painting, inspired by African masks and Spanish statuary, is a savage caricature of flesh, a biting reply to Cézanne's *Bathers* and Ingres' *Turkish Bath*. The young Spaniard steered an opposite course. An unimaginable barbarity, utterly foreign to Western art–ancient or modern–emerges from these women with their shrunken expressions and outlandish breasts which seem to have been hewn out with an ax. Unbearable! Cutting short any explanations that might have been advanced by their creator, Braque complained: "Listen, Pablo! It is as though we were supposed to exchange our usual diet for one of wicks and kerosene!" This comment, probably an allusion to the fire-eaters who performed in the Paris streets and squares, was destined to be inscribed in the annals of art history.

But Braque was no less shaken in his own artistic activity. When he returned to L'Estaque in 1908, accompanied by Dufy, he continued along the lines that he had already shown in *Houses at L'Estaque*. This work and those refused by the Salon d'Automne were exhibited at the Kahnweiller Gallery, and inspired the critic Louis Vauxcelles–the nominal father of Fauvism–to make the following remark. "M. Braque is a very daring young man. Picasso's and Derain's example have toughened him up. He reduces everything–places, figures and houses–to geometric diagrams in fact, to cubes."

A page had been turned in the artist's life. Cubism became the adventure of two men who, until the outbreak of the First World War, worked even more closely together than Derain and Vlaminck had during the hey-day of the Ecole de Chatou.

When Braque died on August 31, 1963, leaving an immense work to posterity, he was given the honors of a national funeral. In front of the bier set up in state in the Cour Carrée of the Louve, André Malraux, the Minister of Culture at the time, emphatically proclaimed: "He is as much at home in the Louvre as the Angel is on the Cathedral of Rheims," a belated, if official, gesture to express an acceptance of 20th-century art.

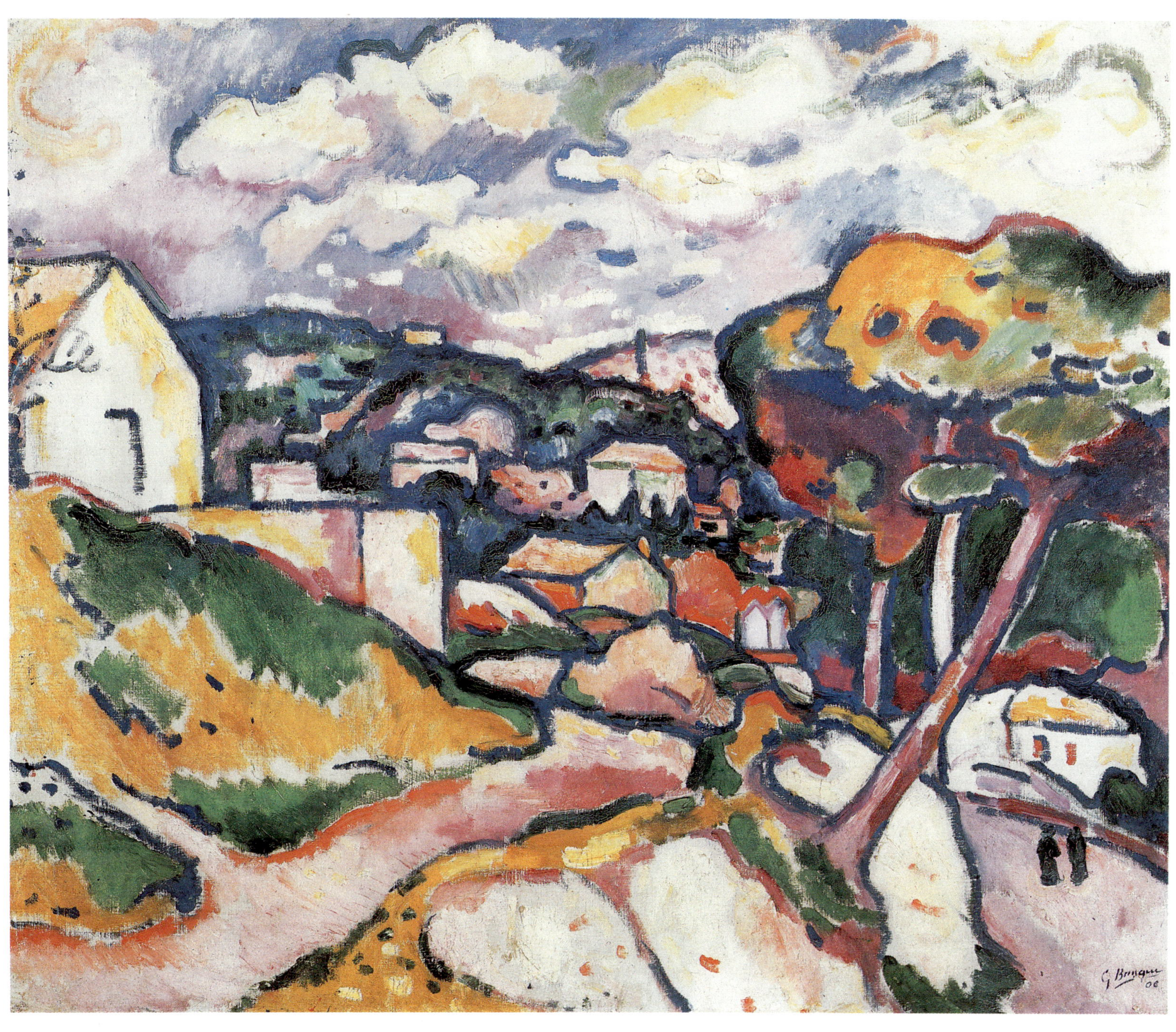

GEORGES BRAQUE
Landscape at L'Estaque
1906
Oil on canvas, 23½ x 28¾ in (60x 73,2 cm)
Saint-Tropez, musée de l'Annonciade

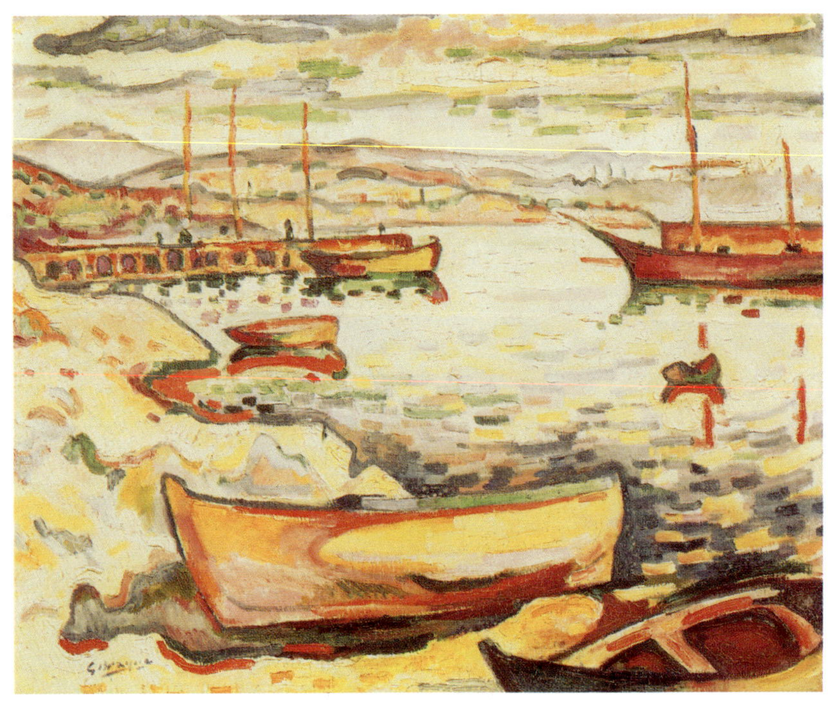

Georges Braque
L'Estaque Harbor
1906
Oil on canvas, 19¾ x 24 in (50 x 61 cm)
London, Fridart Foundation

Opposite:

Georges Braque
L'Estaque
1906
Oil on canvas, 23½ x 29 in (60 x 73,5 cm)
Paris, musée national d'Art moderne

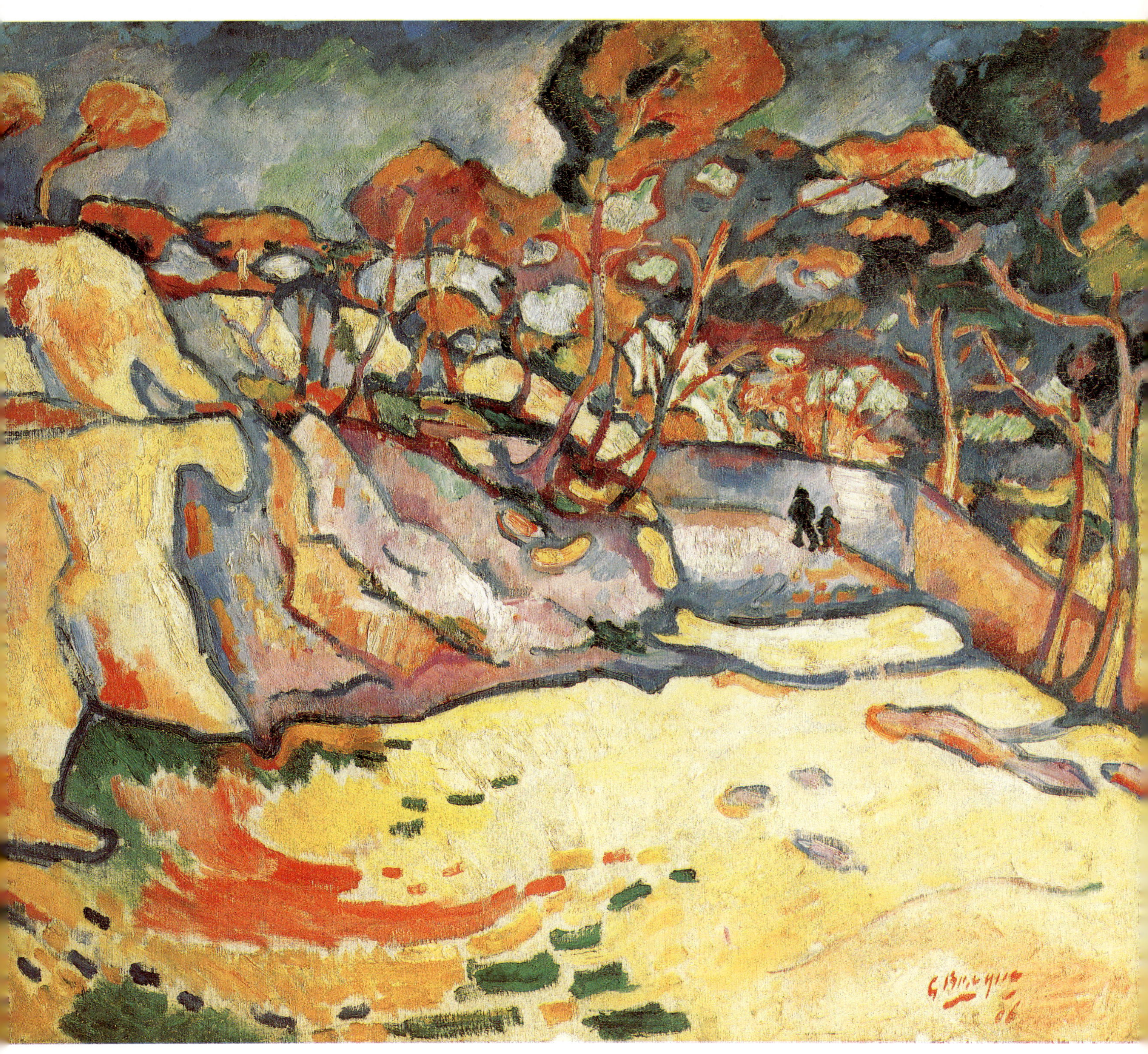

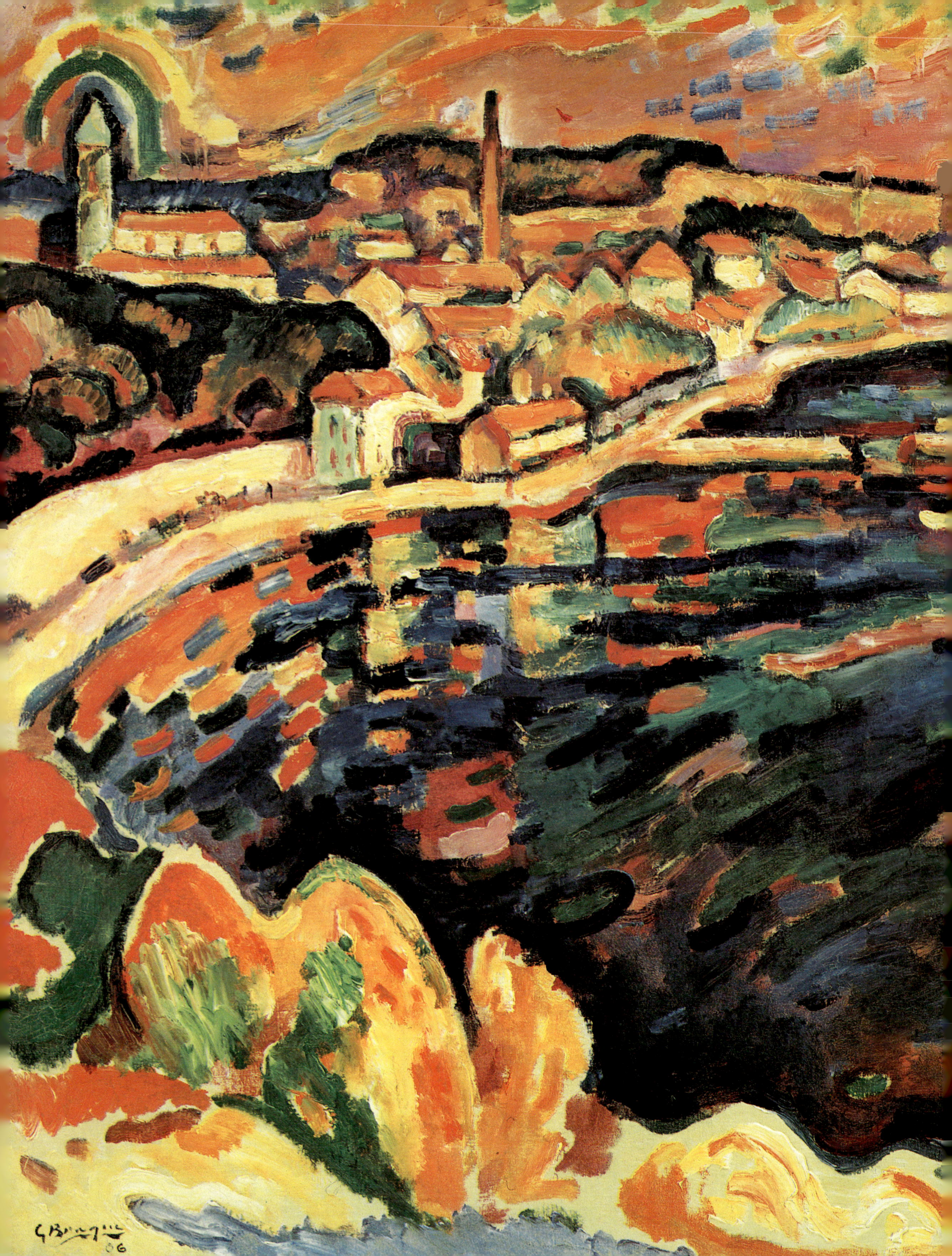

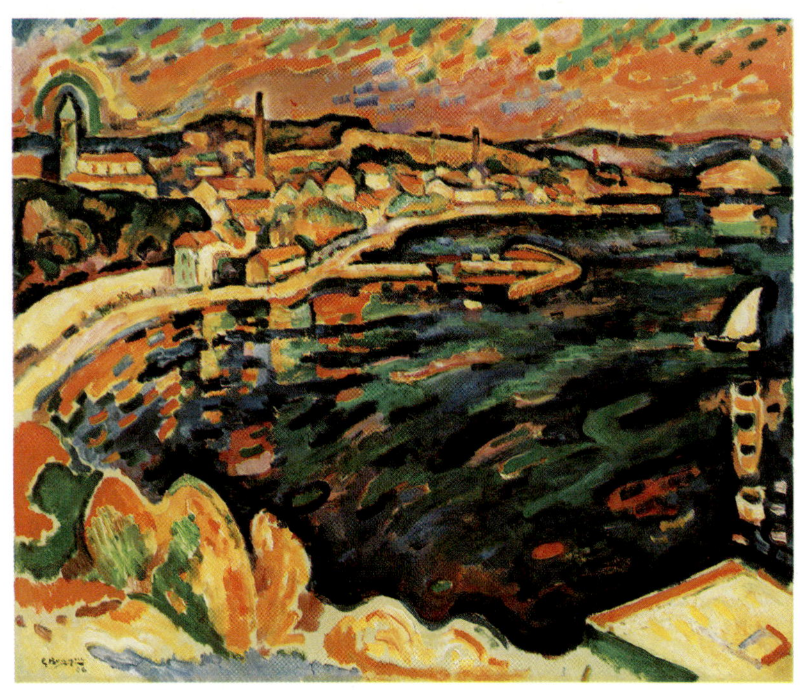

Opposite (detail) and above:

Georges Braque
L'Estaque Harbor
1906
Oil on canvas, 23¾ x 28¾ in
(60,5 x 73 cm)
Copenhagen, Statens Museum for Kunst

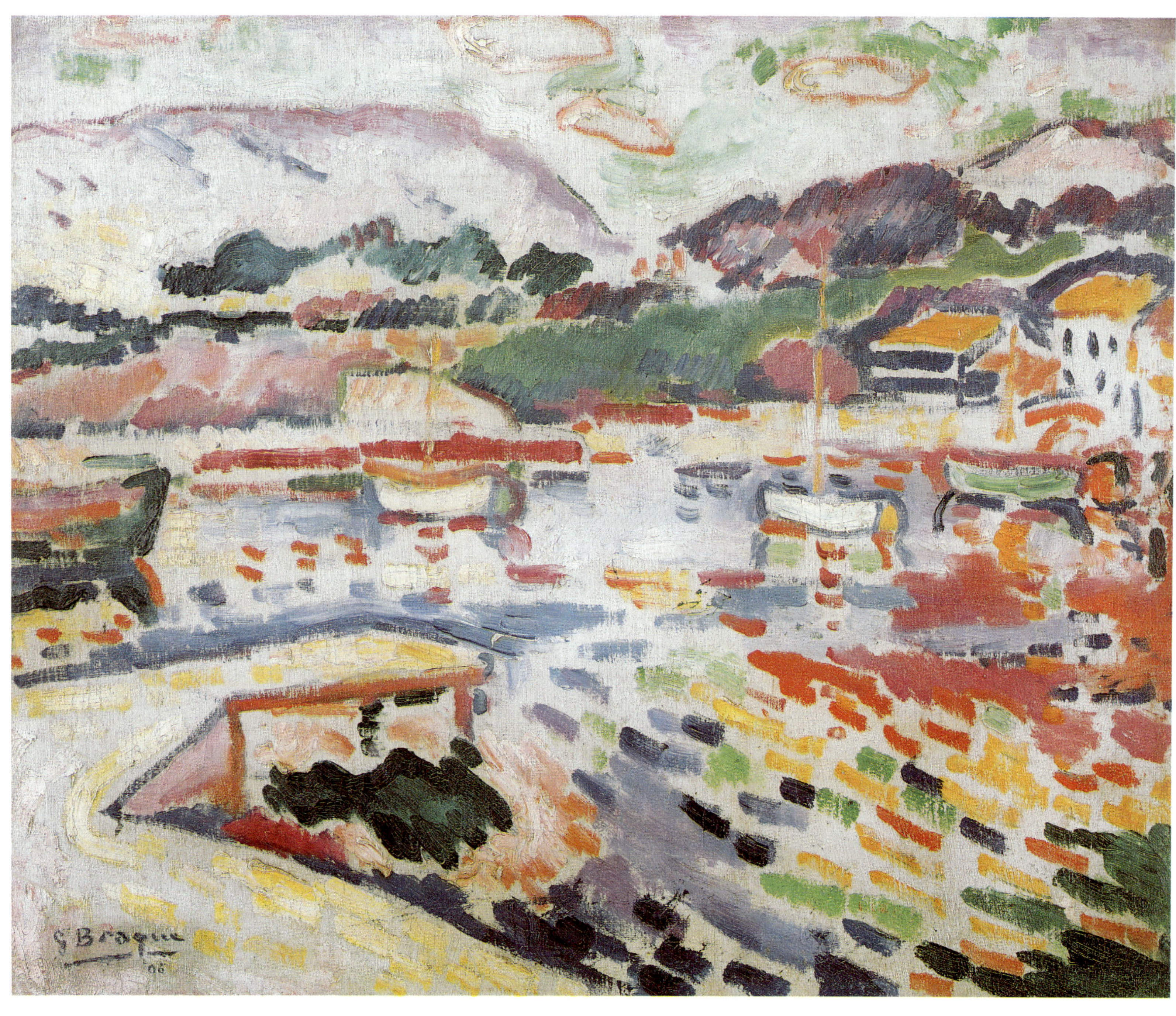

Georges Braque
L'Estaque, the Pier
1906
Oil on canvas, 15¼ x 18 in (38,5 x 46 cm)
Paris, musée national d'Art moderne

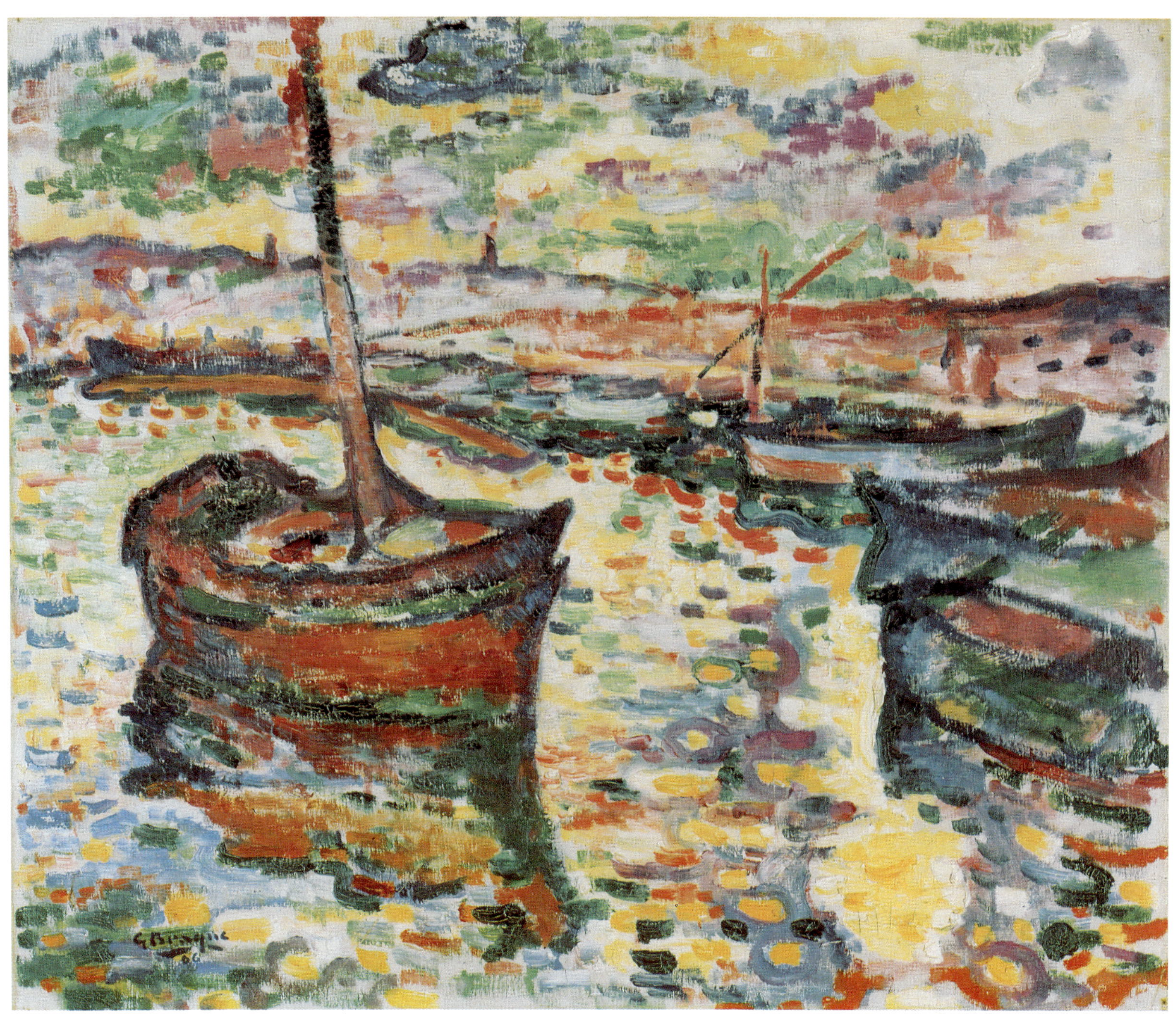

GEORGES BRAQUE
Barques at Collioure
1906
Oil on canvas, 18 x 21¾ in (46 x 55 cm)
London, Fridart Foundation

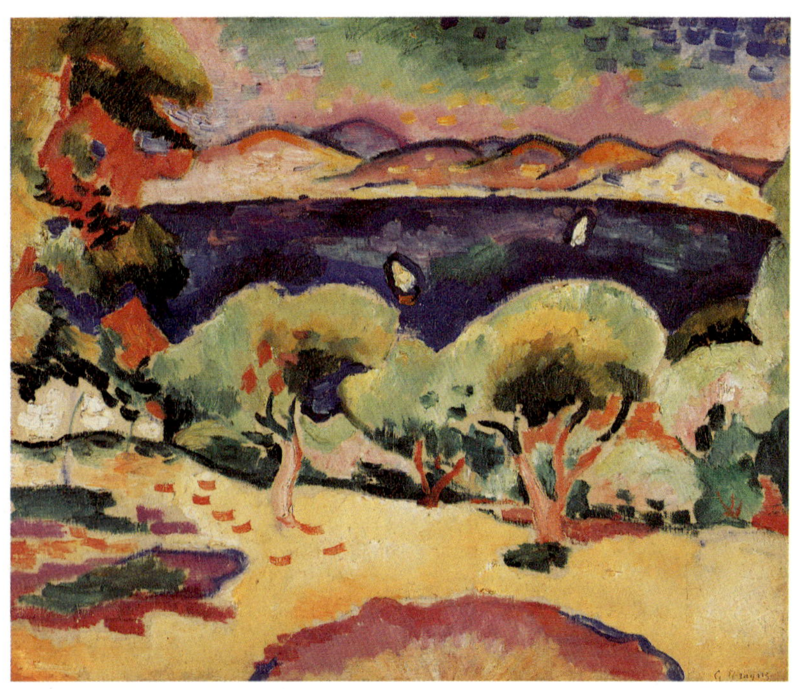

Georges Braque
The Gulf at Les Lecques
1906
Oil on canvas, 15 x 18 in (38 x 46 cm)
Paris, musée national d'Art moderne

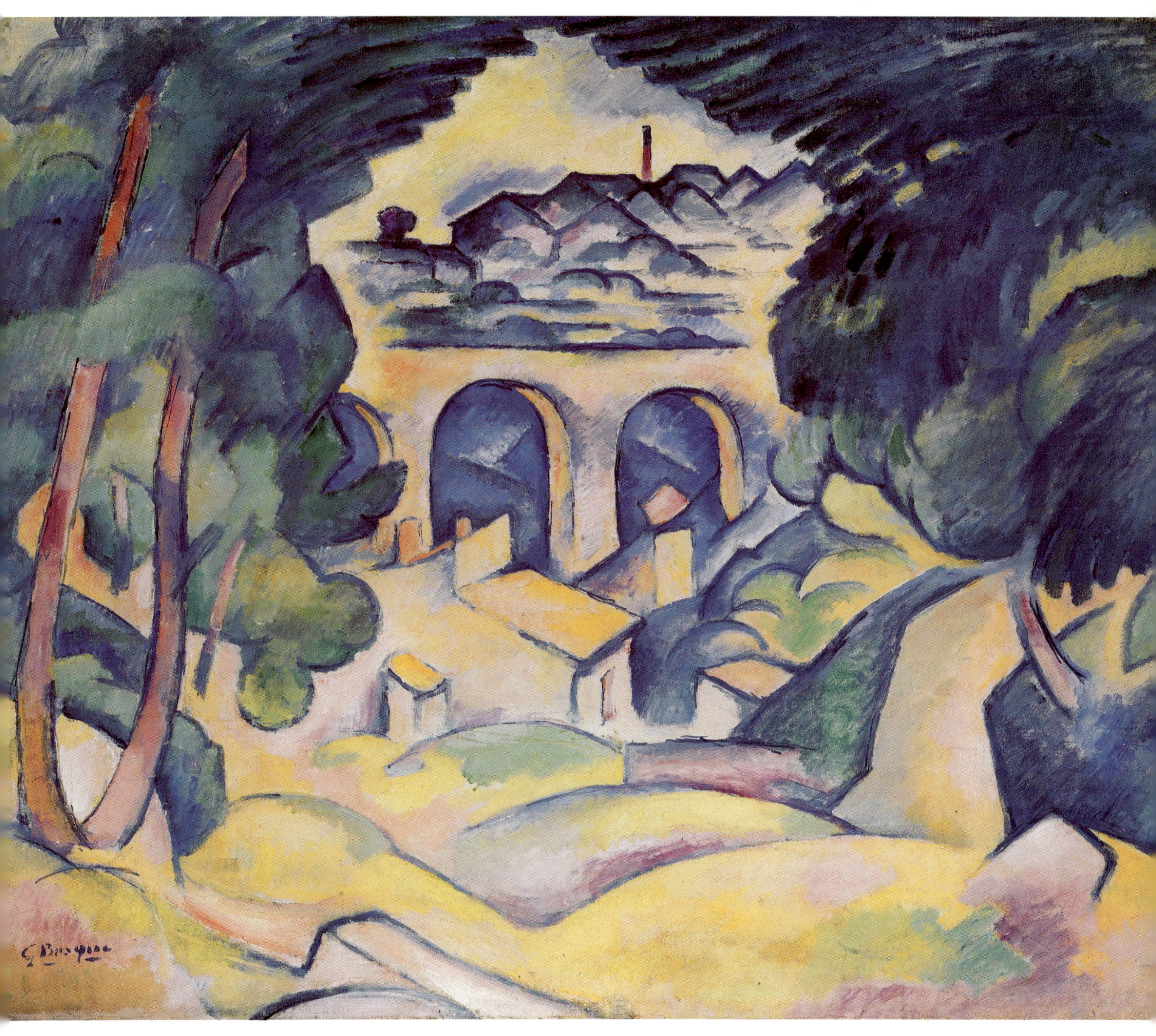

GEORGES BRAQUE
The Viaduct at L'Estaque
1906
Oil on canvas, 25¾ x 22 in (65,1 x 81 cm)
Minneapolis, Institute of Modern Art
(acquisition by John R. Van Derlip Fund,
Fiduciary Fund, Mr. and Mrs. Patrick
Butler and others)

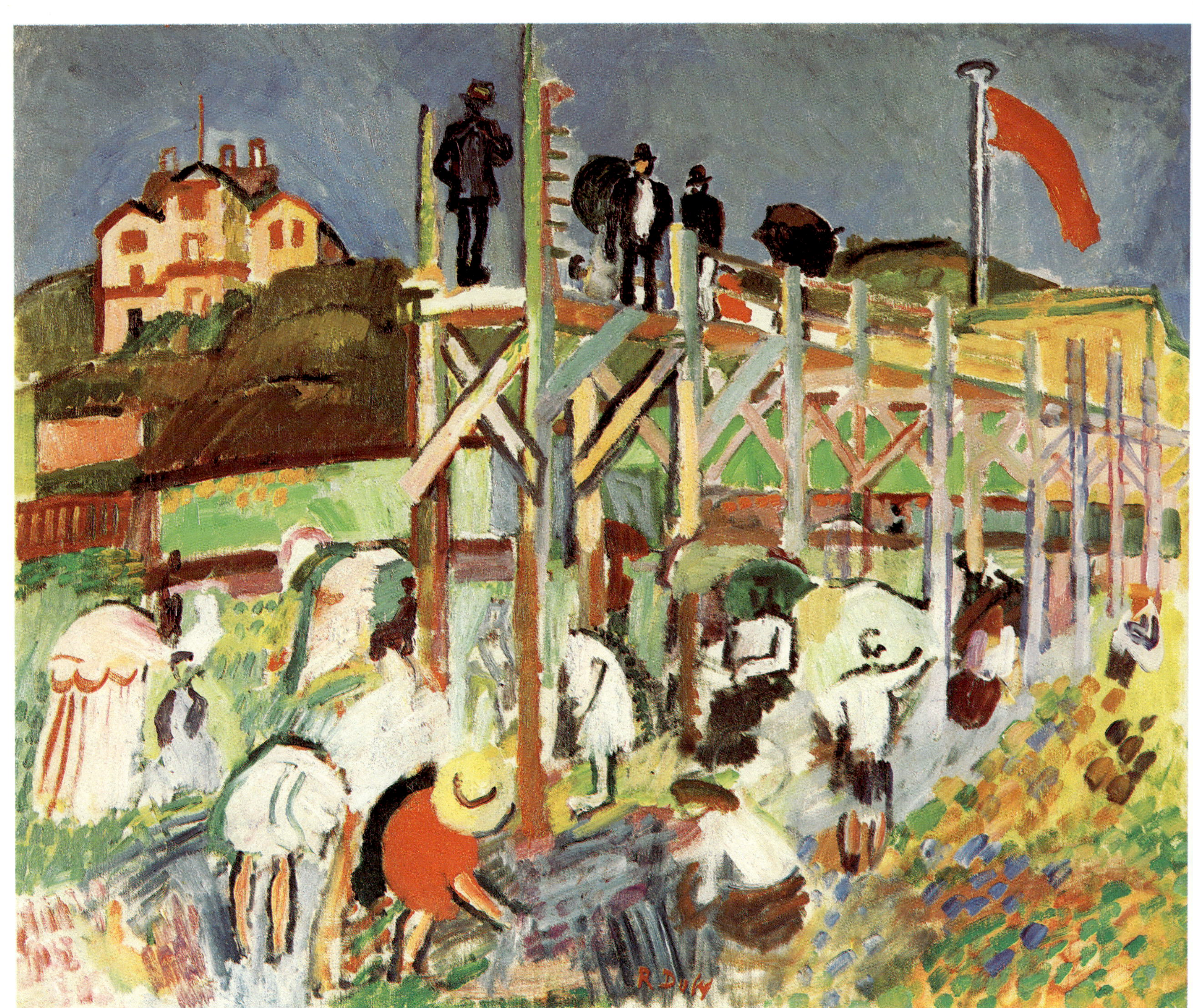

A Rhapsody of Color:

Dufy

The Smell of Coffee

Raoul Dufy was a young man with a "fair complexion, turned-up nose, blond curly hair, prominent pale-blue eyes and an absent-minded look." He was also "spirited, gallant and a bit giddy," according to one of his childhood friends.

He was born in Le Havre on June 3, 1877 into a large family. His father, who worked as an accountant in a metal factory and played the organ in his moments of leisure, transmitted a love of music to his children. One of his four brothers, Léon, became an organist, and another, Gaston, a flutist and director of a review called *Courrier Musical*. When Raoul left home to study painting in Paris in 1900, having been granted a monthly scholarship of one hundred francs by his native city, he was too poor to haunt the cabarets in Montmartre like the other daubers of the period. He preferred to give up a meal than miss a concert in the Colonne series.

Dufy was attracted to drawing and painting at a very early age, but since his parents could not support him they convinced him to learn a trade; he told himself that if he could not make his dream come true he would become a wealthy merchant and have a collection of paintings. In order to reach this goal he began working at the age of fourteen in a Brazilian coffee import-export business. His job consisted of controlling the outgoing and incoming merchandize and toiling on the decks of steamers to supervise the loading of the burlap bags for shipment to Belgian and Dutch ports. "From the smell, I knew if the boat had come from Texas, India or the Azores and this fired my imagination," he remarked later on.

RAOUL DUFY
The Jetty at Sainte-Adresse
1906
Oil on canvas, 25¾ x 31½ in
(65.1 x 80 cm)
Milwaukee, Art Museum
(gift of Mrs. Harry Lynde Bradley)

RAOUL DUFY
Promenade along the Jetty
1906
Oil on canvas, 25½ x 32 in (64,5 x 81 cm)
Paris, Daniel Malingue Gallery

At the age of fifteen he took night courses taught by Charles Lhuillier, a student of Cabanel and admirer of Ingres, at the fine-arts academy in Le Havre. This teacher, who had also been Braque's and Friesz's master, was a great awakener of talent. Dufy immediately showed a great amount of skill; to increase the challenge, he took up drawing with his left hand, though continuing to write with his very deft right hand.

Living on his small scholarship in Paris, he signed up for Bonnat's class at the Ecole des Beaux-Arts. He lived on rue Cortot in modest lodgings that he shared with Friesz. On the way to school, he would take the rue Laffite to inspect the paintings at the Durand-Ruel Gallery, which did not convince him to follow academic training too closely. One day while a pretty, vivacious red-headed model was sitting for the class and Dufy was happy enough with what he had put down on his canvas, his professor came over and asked him if he was really aware of which colors he was using. Dufy understood then that he had nothing to learn at the famous school on the quai Malaquais, yet he continued for four more years. He was to remark later on: "The Beaux-Arts was very practical for me; there was a studio, free models; and for the not-so-rich, it wasn't something to sniff at."

His real apprenticeship took place elsewhere, thanks to his commitment to contemporary art. Not far from Durand-Ruel's gallery Ambroise Vollard exhibited works of Cézanne and Gauguin while Clovis Sagot, a small but enthusiastic dealer, showed Degas. In 1901 the famous Bernheim-Jeune gallery exhibited the Van Goghs that had made such an impression on Vlaminck. Dufy was especially interested in Jongkind, Pissarro, and Monet's renditions of beaches and cliffs. In 1902 Dufy made the acquaintance of Berthe Weil who owned a small boutique on rue Victor Massé, crammed with bric-à-brac of all kinds, as well as works by Matisse, Marquet and Van Dongen. In 1905, he visited the Salon des Indépendants and was dumbstruck when he discovered Matisse's *Luxe, calme et volupté*, which made him understand "the miracle of imagination contained in drawing and color." Although an admirer of the great Fauve's impressive métier, he felt closer to Marquet, who became his favorite companion on his return trips to Normandy.

The Sea and Music

Baths of Casino Marie-Christine at Sainte-Adresse, among Dufy's first works, is part of a series that he painted between 1902 and 1904 depicting a characteristic boat landing. It is a typical beach scene teeming with bathers and parasols in changing light under a sky full of billowing clouds. On his canvas, Dufy displayed a technique still influenced by Impressionism, creating atmospheric effects with an easy fluency in a manner closely related to Boudin, the old master for whom he felt a particular affinity. Eugène Boudin (1824-1898), another native of Le Havre, had painted the same kind of seascapes while sojourning at the Saint-Siméon Inn near Honfleur, causing Courbet to exclaim enthusiastically in 1859: "My God! you're a Seraph; you know about skies!" However, by the time that Dufy took up the theme two years later, in a work called *Bathing*, everything had changed. The sea was rendered with a thin wash of green, the bathers had become red, brown and black dots. Along with the pure Fauve tones were also touches of pinks, whites and blues that prefigured the harmonious subtlety of his later work.

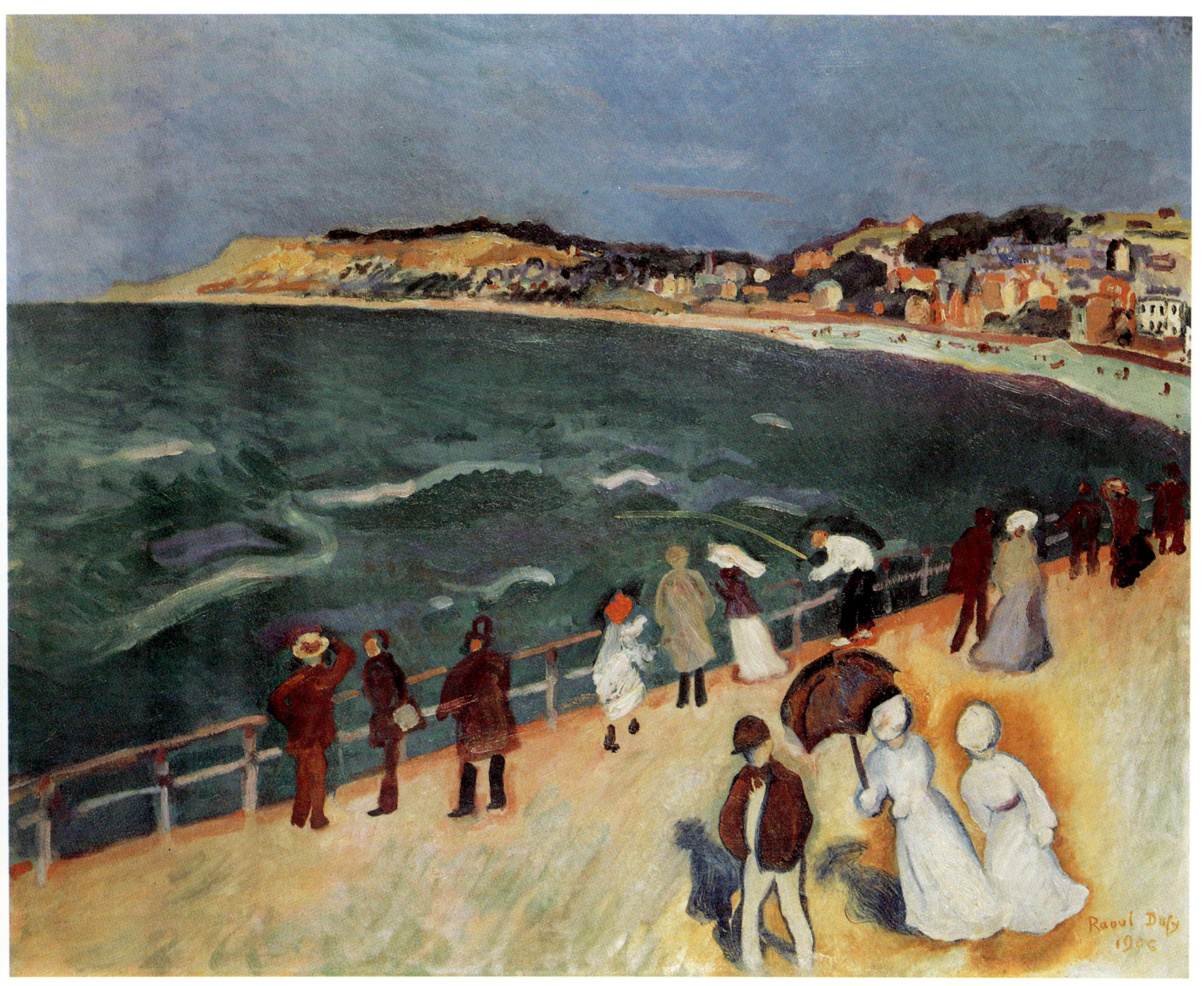
Raoul Dufy

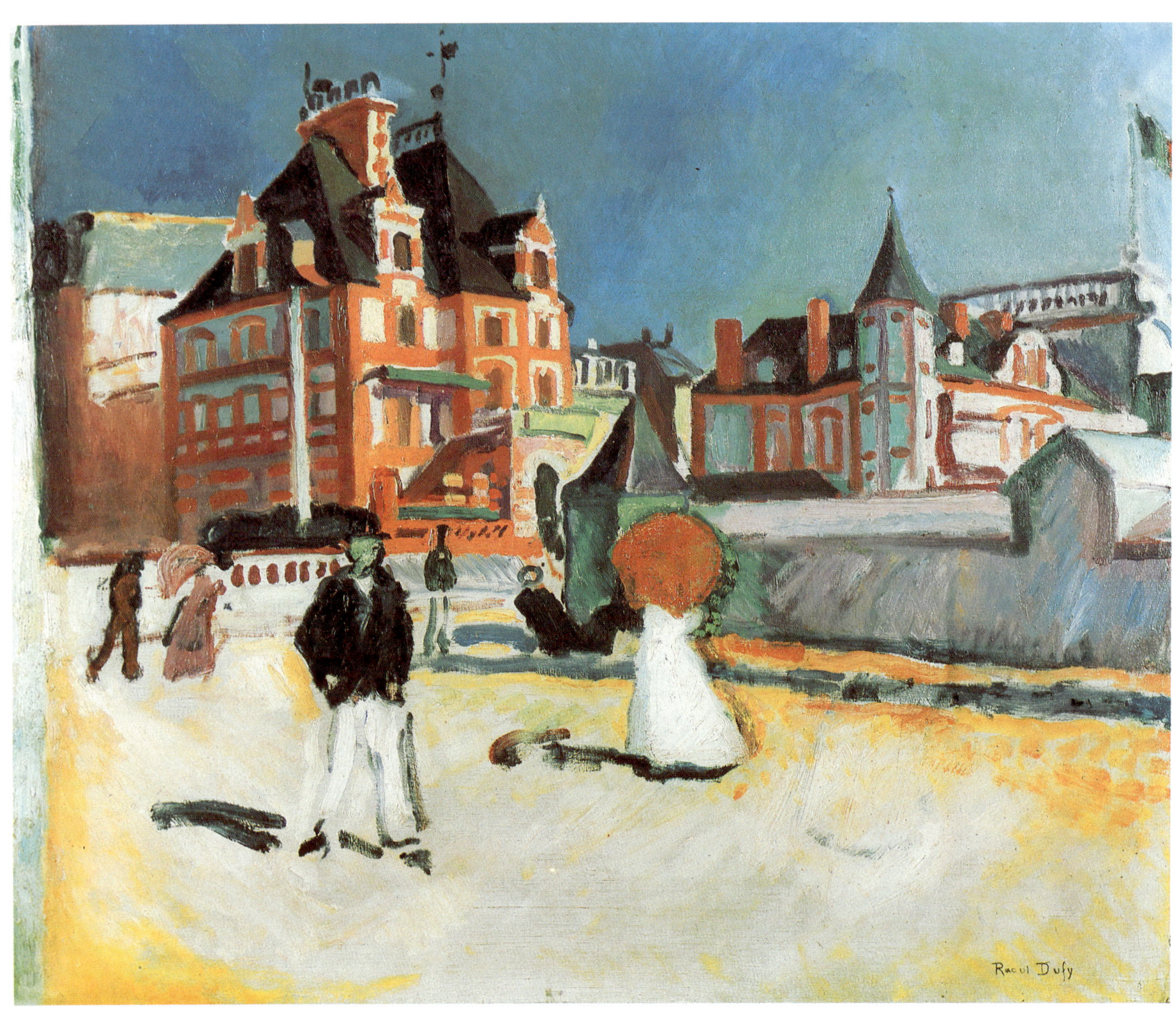

RAOUL DUFY
Trouville
1907
Oil on canvas, 21½ x 25¾ in
(54.3 x 65.3 cm)
London, Fridart Foundation

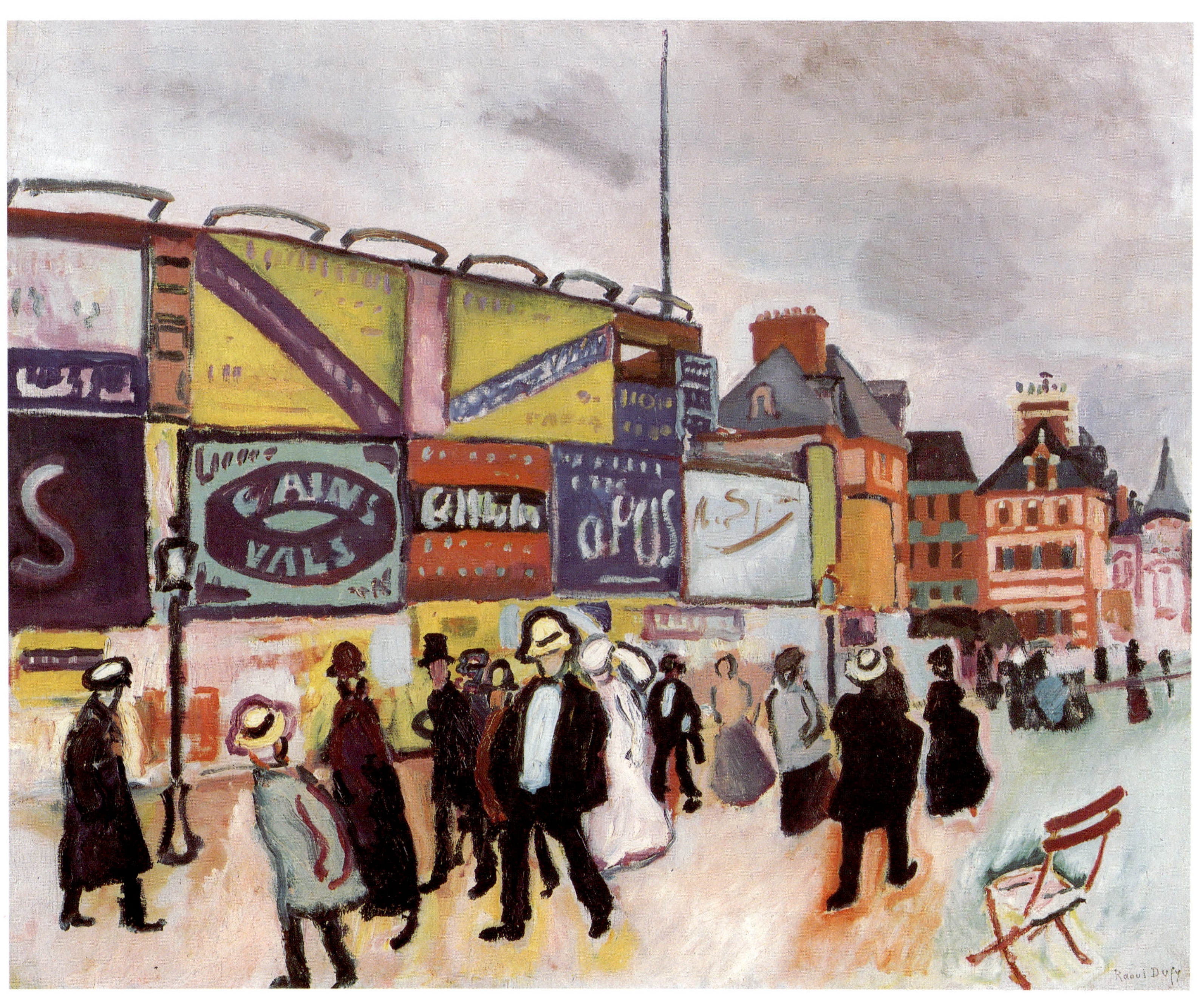

RAOUL DUFY
Billboards at Trouville
1906
Oil on canvas, 25½ x 32 in (65 x 81 cm)
Paris, musée national d'Art moderne

Some years after, when Dufy began his famous orchestra series, his aim was to render the timbre of the instruments rather than their color: "If you want to bring out the distinct sound of flutes," he jotted down on the back of a watercolor, "light up the two or three instrumentalists with sparks and thunderbolts using a dash of white and Veronese green. For the oboe and the clarinet, the effet is achieved with round shapes (in brown with blue or red highlights, for example). For violons, draw a simple sinuous line on top; for trombones or trumpets, use stars; for timbals, a clover shape; for the violas, make cloud-like forms." Dufy had reached such subtle perfection that his friend, the cellist Pablo Casals, exclaimed in front of one of the orchestra series: "I cannot say which piece your orchestra is playing, but I can recognize what key it is in."

RAOUL DUFY
Barques at Martigues
1907
Oil on canvas, 21¼ x 25¼ in
(54 x 64.1 cm)
London, Fridart Foundation

But during his Fauve years Dufy had not yet reached this stage. His works from this period–*Yacht Dressed with Flags* (1904), *Billboards at Trouville* (1906)–were striking; flat-color areas embedded in one another to produce a strong composition. Solidity and strength were the dominant features of his *Three Parasols* (1906), whose bright colors were outlined in black. He had already begun to dissociate line and color in other paintings such as *The Beach at Le Havre* (1906), with its immense shore at low tide composed of lightly-brushed pinks and pale-green patches applied independently from the scattering of tents, parasols, and bathers. This technique, very unusual for the period, actually came to symbolize Dufy's art when it reached maturity.

Although they never met and came from totally different aesthetic horizons, Dufy reminds one of Paul Klee, who was also very much a music lover: his father was choirmaster at the Staatlichen Lehrerseminar in Hofwyl, outside Bern. Klee once hesitated between the violin–which he played as an amateur all his life–or a career as a painter. A parallel may be made between some of his paintings which resemble a music score and Dufy's outlined shapes that seem to glide over previously-applied patches of color. Contrary to the effect of mass which Derain used to establish his flat-color areas, and to Matisse who, as we have already seen, attempted to create an extreme tension within objects through line, Dufy's shapes became more and more disconnected from his outlines, as if the freely-executed arabesques had gained autonomy from the colors on the surface of the canvas.

This technique, latent from the start, led the artist to paint *Black Cargo* (1952) just one year before his death. In this incomparable masterpiece he depicted an immense jetty in the port of Le Havre and the hillsides of Sainte-Adresse; a blue scumble in the center of an unbounded flat black area represents a vessel. Having lived around boats since childhood, Dufy was evidently fascinated by them and their multicolored flags, as we can see in *Yacht Dressed with Flags* (1904) and *Boat Dressed with Flags* (1905). His last painting, however, was concerned with entirely different considerations, for the large flat area of black simultaneously represented the smoke and the grease-and tar-covered hull of the cargo vessel in all its sluggish force, as it slowly entered the channel to the docks. Dufy's picture emits a muted sound, something with the timbre of a voice or a musical instrument.

Surprisingly, the freedom which Dufy achieved toward the end of his career seems unrelated to the formalism he indulged in during the fall of 1907. At that time the careful imbrication of shapes in *Barques at Martiques* were leading him to the doorstep of Cubism; he was definitely moving away from Fauvism.

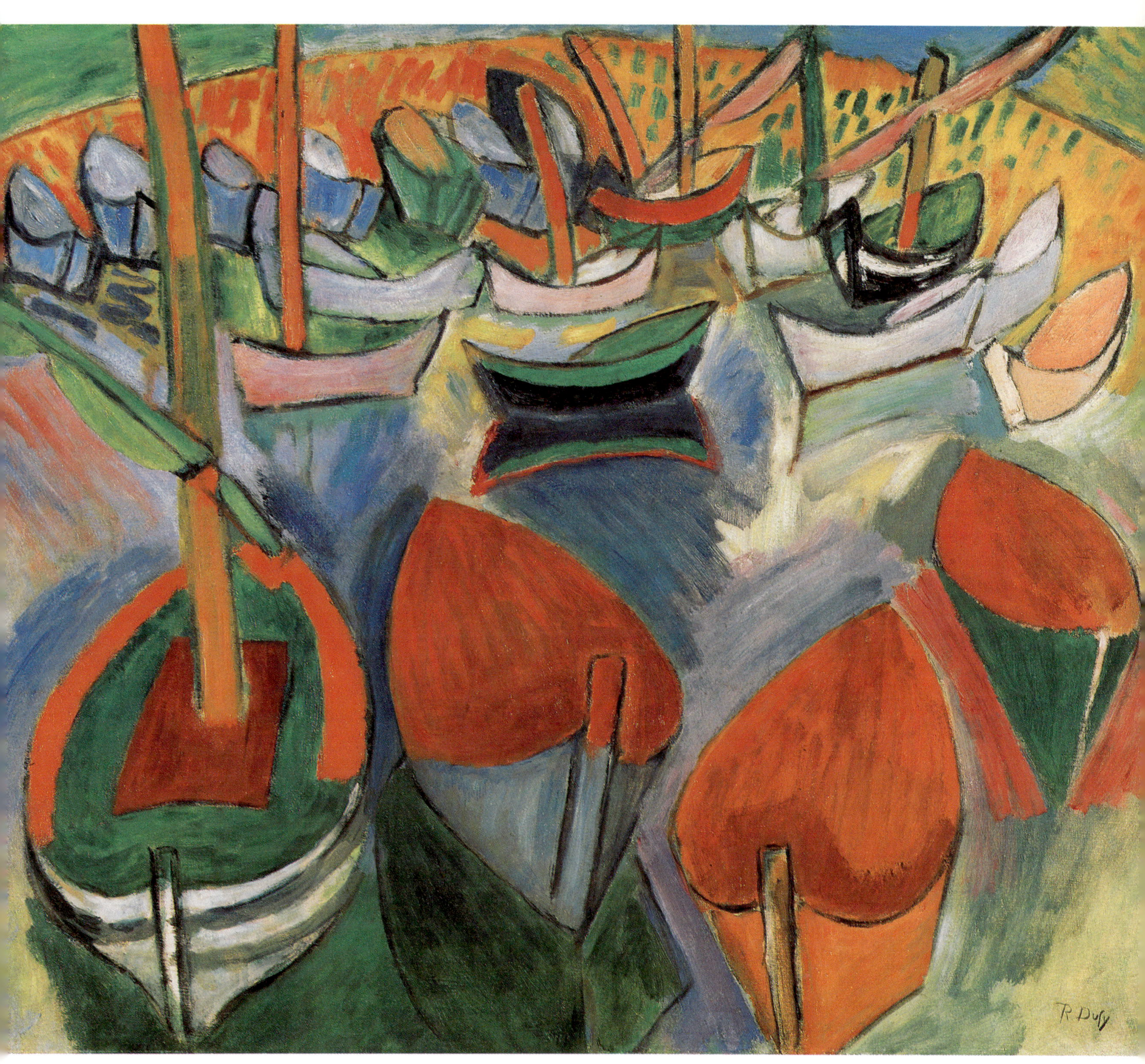
R Dufy

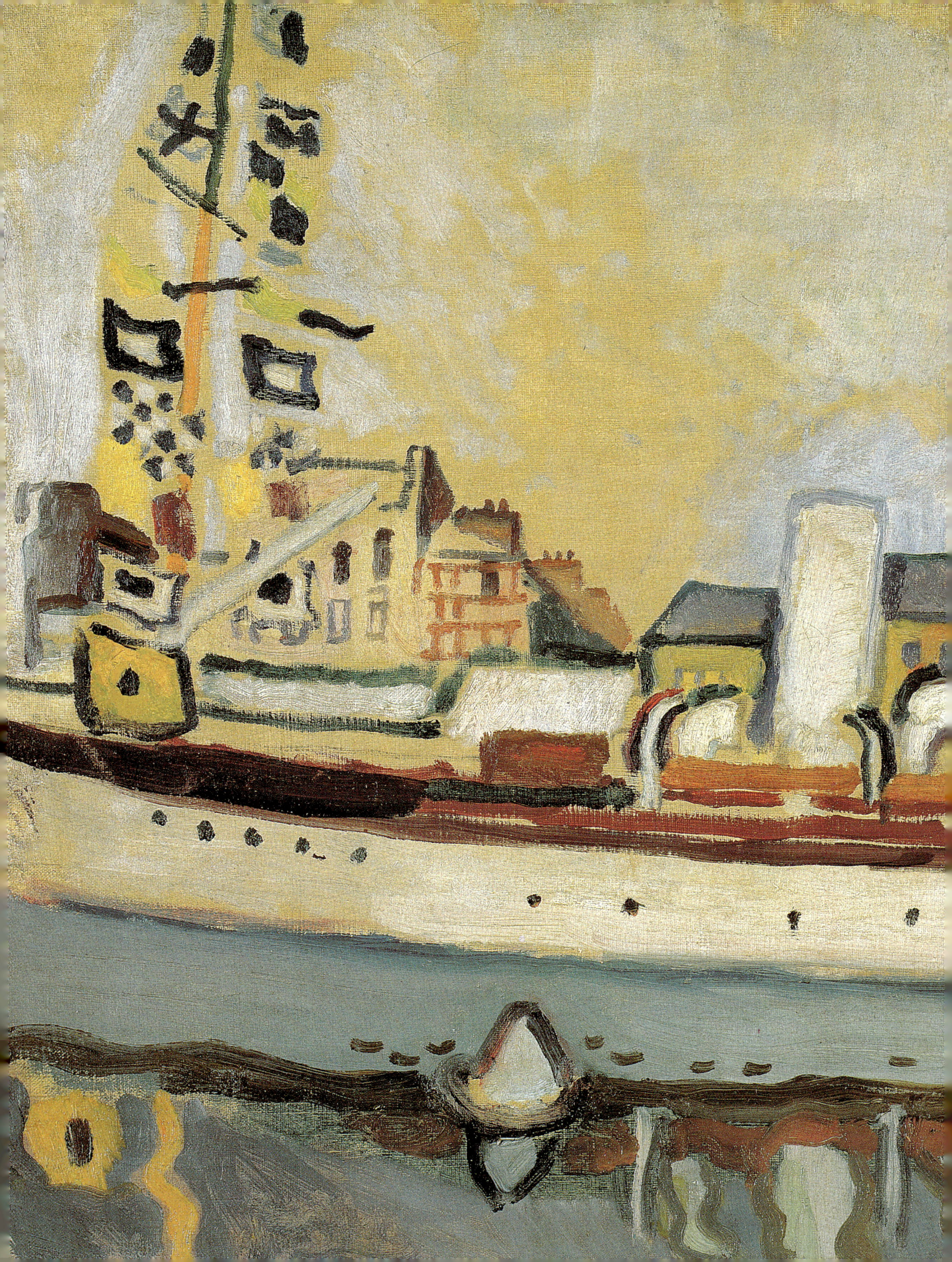

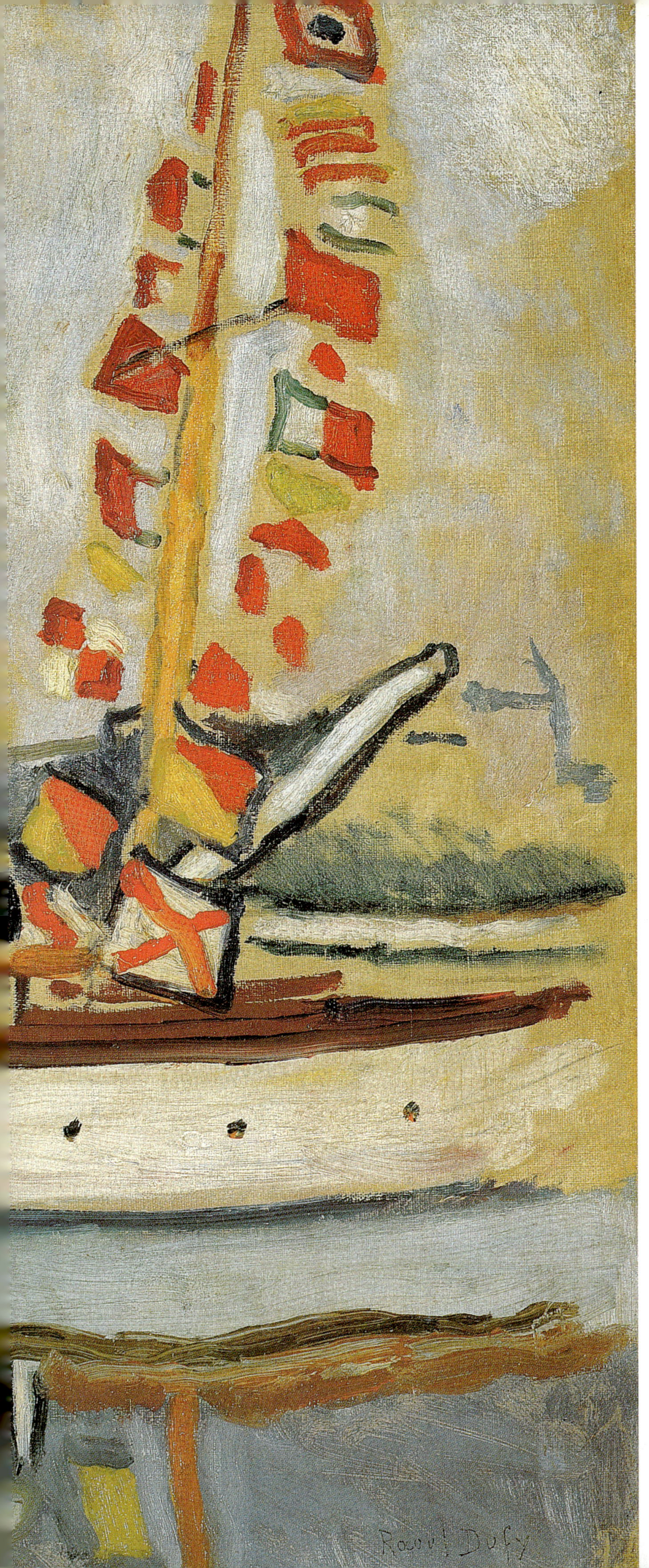

Raoul Dufy
Boat Dressed with Flags
1905
Oil on canvas, 21¼ x 25½ in (54 x 65 cm)
Lyon, musée des Beaux-Arts

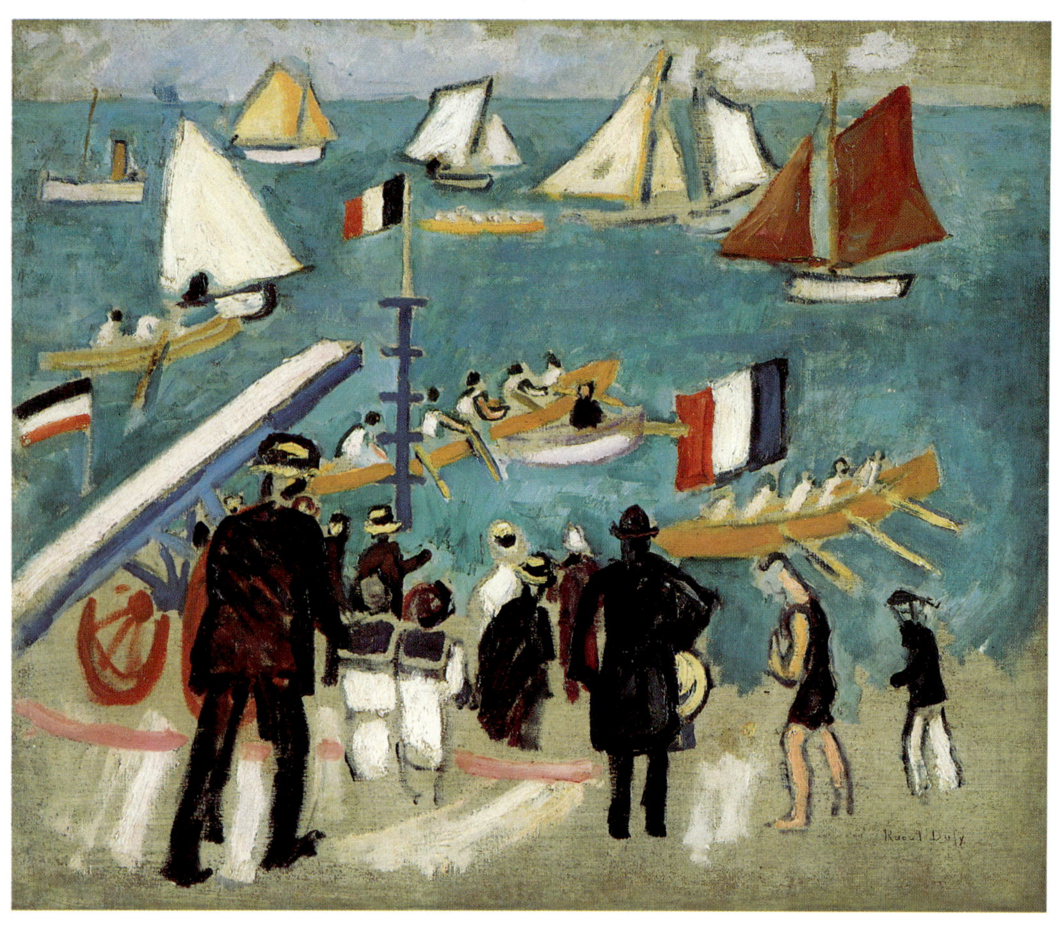

Raoul Dufy
Regatta
1908-1909
Oil on canvas, 21¼ x 25½ in (54 x 65 cm)
Paris, musée d'Art moderne de la ville de Paris

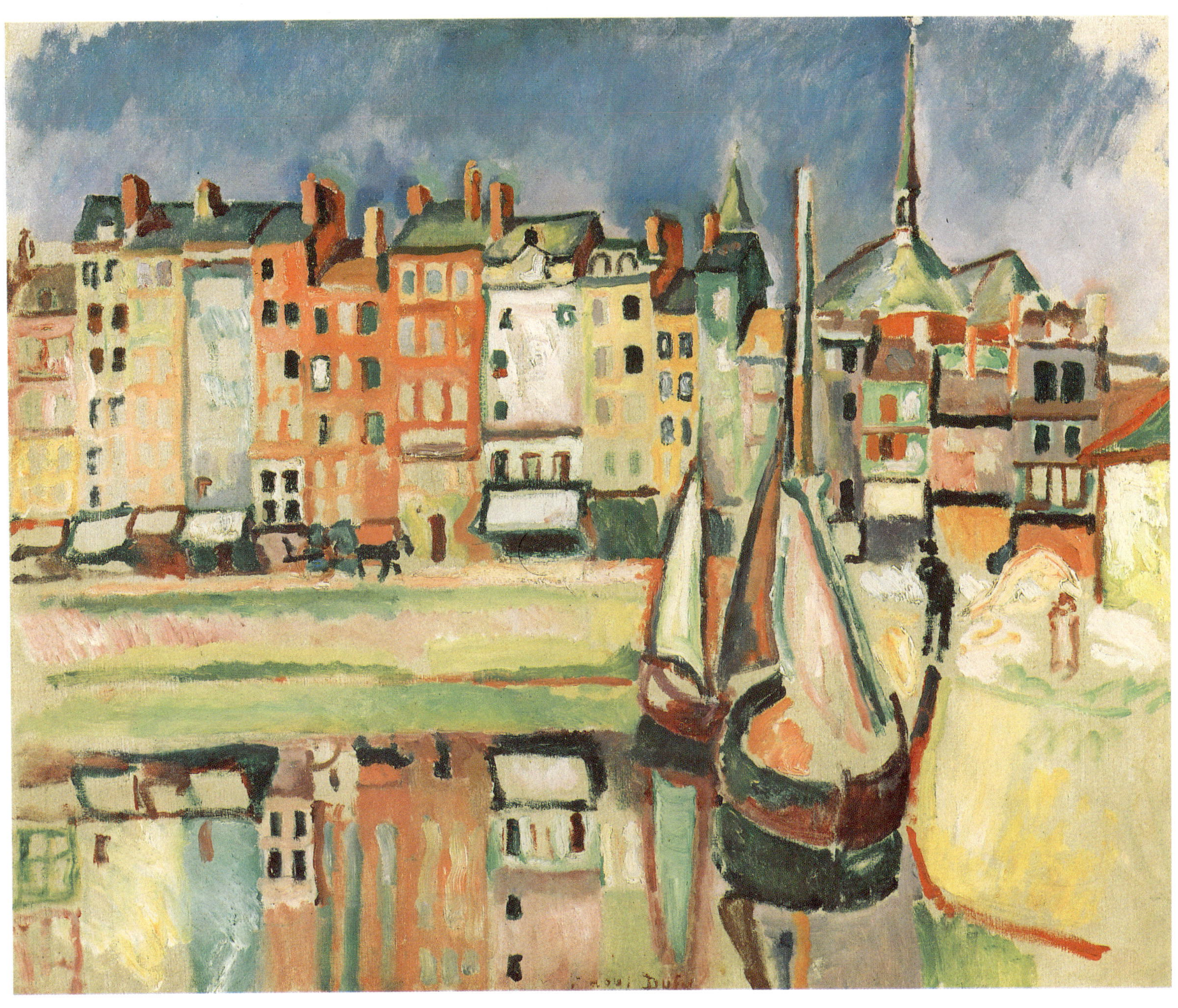

RAOUL DUFY
Old Houses in Honfleur Harbor
1905-1906
Oil on canvas, 23½ x 28¾ in (60 x 73 cm)
London, Fridart Foundation

RAOUL DUFY
Saint-Henri Tilery
1908
Oil on canvas, 12½ x 15¾ in (32 x 40 cm)
Marseille, musée Cantini

His trip to L'Estaque, a Cézannian pilgrimage which he made with Braque the following year, marks the turning-point in his style. There, he painted *Green Trees L'Estaque* inspired by two of his companion's works, *Trees* and *Houses at L'Estaque*, judging by their great similarity. The composition consisted of overlapping planes tightly framed by tree trunks and foliage bent to form an arch; the parallel brushstrokes were treated diagonally and the color-scheme restricted to greens and ochers. Here, everything contradicted Dufy's recent works; after an orgy of color, he now set himself strict limits. Was it the sign of an artistic adventure coming to a close? Not entirely, for Dufy always referred to this period as a necessary parenthesis for research and renewal.

This was in no way a renunciation of the values of Fauvism, as his later works tend to prove. With its cleverly-constructed houses painted on a green and blue ground, *Landscape at Sainte-Adresse* (1930) represented one of his favorite themes; in it, he merely exploited what he had been building up to in the first decade of the century and gave it a definite Fauve touch.

With the execution of *La fée Electricité* for the 1937 World's Fair, a mural that now hangs in the musée d'Art moderne de la ville de Paris, Dufy became the only artist who, along with Matisse and his two versions of *La Danse* commissioned in 1932-1933 by Dr. Albert C. Barnes of Philadelphia, contributed a monumental composition to the glory of Fauvism.

The Biggest Painting in the World

La feé Electricité, composed of two hundred and fifty panels covering an area of six hundred square meters inside the Palais de la Lumière designed by the architect Robert Mallet-Stevens, was the highlight of the exposition. Sixty meters long and ten meters high, it occupied a concave wall lit by a row of projectors that gave it a crude lighting because of the total darkness of the room in which it was housed. Various pieces of machinery were on permanent exhibition in front of the immense painting such as a gigantic five-hundred-thousand-volt electric circuit-breaker, a feat of engineering at the time. Steam and hydraulic turbines were designed to complete this grandiose demonstration of the importance of electricity in modern civilisation.

The mural itself consisted of one hundred and ten figures from all epochs who had contributed in the discovery of electric energy. Represented standing in the midst of waterfalls or in front of electric plants and transformers are the ancient philospher Lucretius, Archimedes, Leonardo da Vinci, and Otto von Guericke, inventor of the first friction engine; Zénobe Gramme, a brilliant tinkerer who invented the dynamo, as well as Bernouilli, Watt, Edison, etc.. In order to portray them, Dufy gathered a complete documentation on the question and brought in actors from the Comédie-Française to pose for him, one after the other in a studio rented for the occasion in Saint-Ouen. The project was completely successful. The eager public jostled each other in front of the biggest painting in the world, delighted to contemplate the heros of technology in somewhat the same manner as during the Middle Ages when the faithful came to admire the saints represented in stained-glass windows.

This titantic project was not the invention of any eccentric demiurge grappling with destiny. Roland Dorgelès, who had

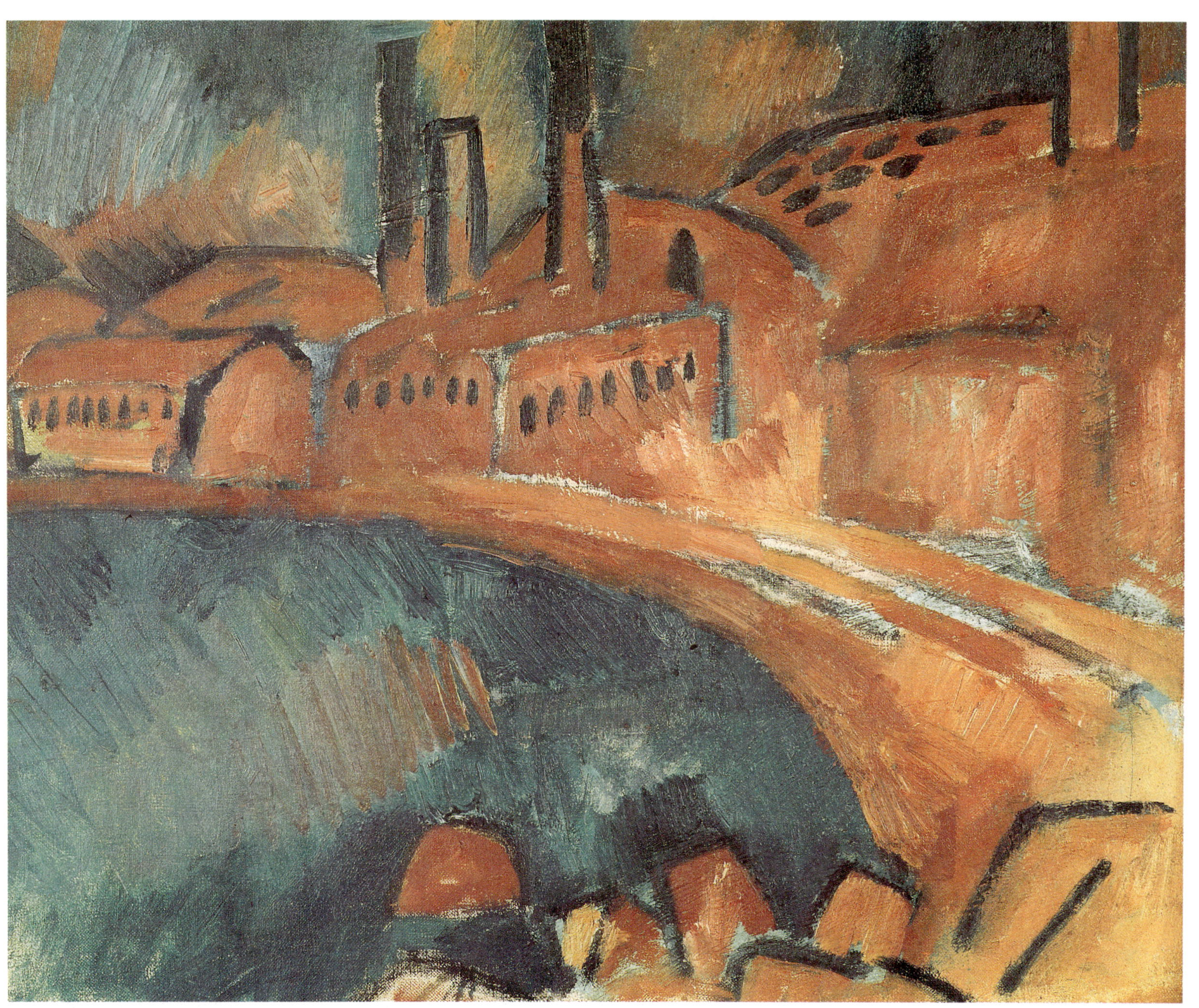

met Dufy in 1900, had been impressed with the artist's sensible point of view: "Even in Montmartre at the time, no one could lead a fancy life with only one hundred francs a month. Yet, Raoul Dufy somehow made ends meet.... Never did he appear unkempt, collarless or shuffling around in espadrilles like so many of his colleagues. Bohemian life horrified him. His shirt was always clean, his shoes properly shined, and he carried his pennilessness proudly." Once famous, he lost none of his rigor or modesty. What a contrast with someone like Adolf Hitler, both unsuccessful painter and false genius, who thought that he could put an end to modern art. On July 18, 1937 in Munich, the Nazi Führer inaugurated in grand pomp the first exhibition of "Degenerate Art," which consisted entirely of works confiscated from the German museums and destined to be destroyed. Not a Fauve or any of the sons of Fauvism had been left out, as well as Cézanne, Gauguin, Seurat. The story ended otherwise, as we know: Art finally had the last word.

Opposite:

RAOUL DUFY
On the 14th of July at Le Havre
1906
Oil on canvas, 18¼ x 15 in (46.5 x 38 cm)
London, Fridart Foundation

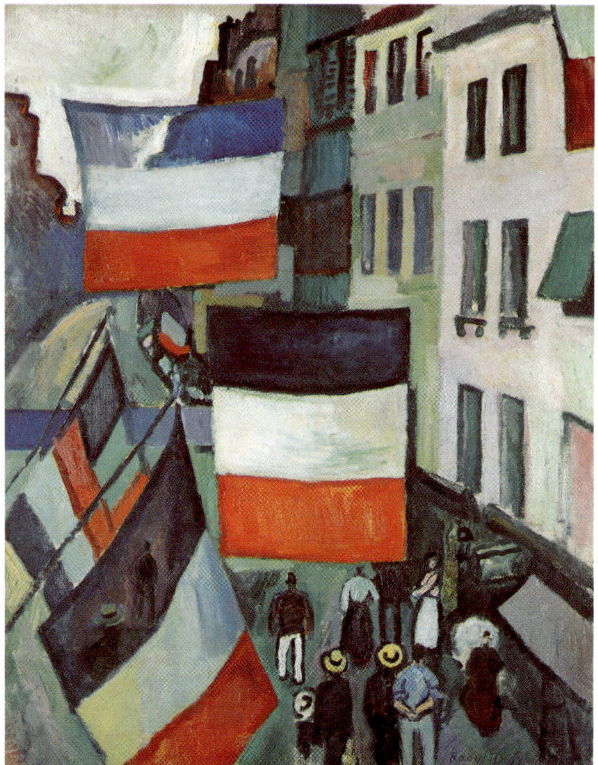

RAOUL DUFY
Street Decked with Flags
1906
Oil on canvas, 25½ x 32 in (65 x 81 cm)
Paris, musée national d'Art moderne

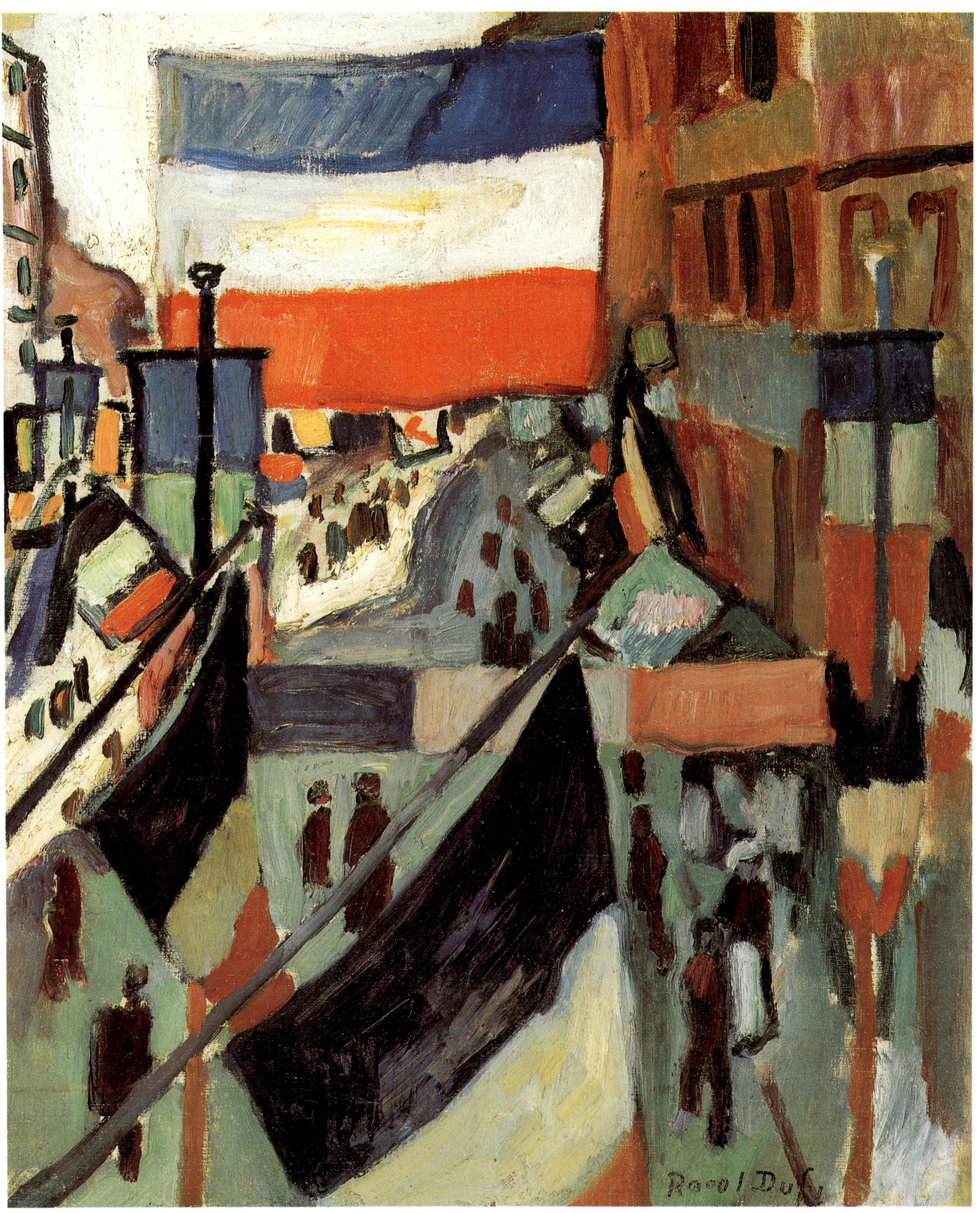

Raoul Dufy
Jeanne with Flowers
1907
Oil on canvas, 35½ x 30¾ in (90 x 78 cm)
Le Havre, musée des Beaux-Arts André Malraux

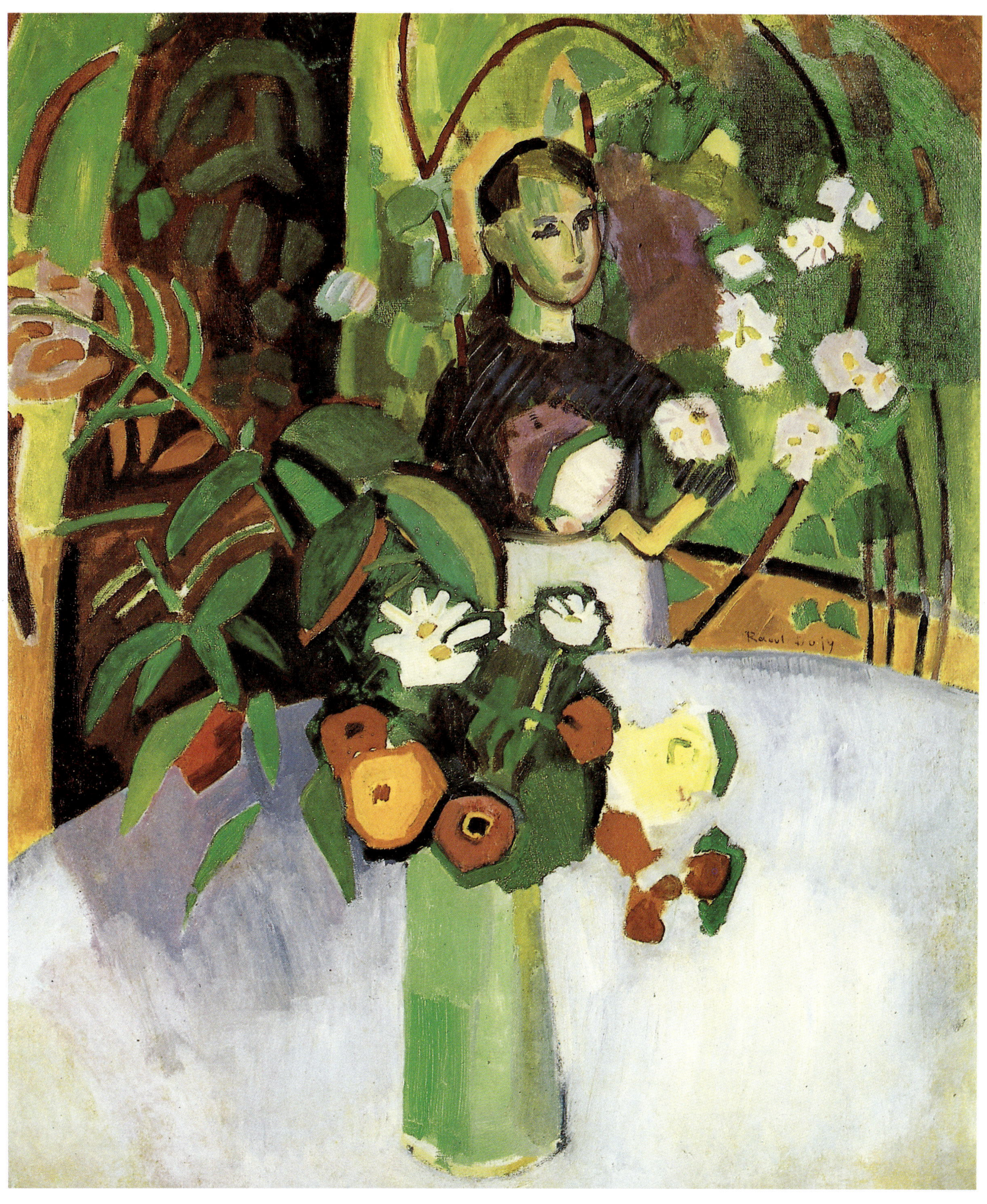
Raoul Dufy

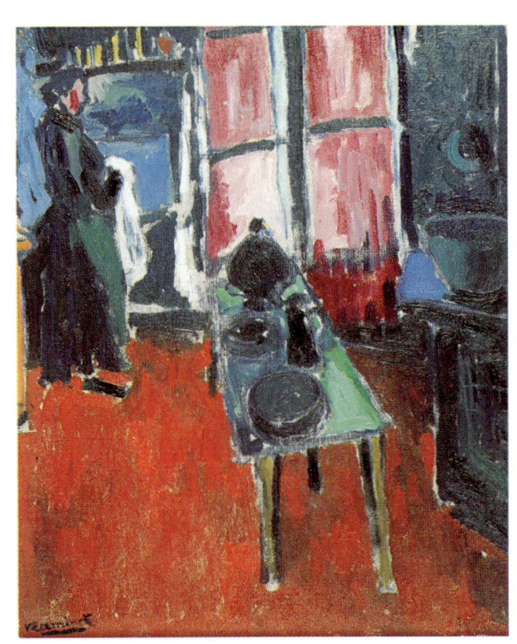

Conclusion

Fauvism Today

For the last fifteen years or so the avant-garde has not been what it used to be. The most blatantly outlandish works such as bicycle wheels or heaps of coal, have ceased to produce any kind of scandal when they make their appearance in national museums. Added to this fact is the idea that we have reached "the end of ideologies," a feeling intensified by the fall of the erstwhile credo of Marxism, which died a natural death even before entering the 21st century. No matter what artists attempt to do, art has ceased to be anti-establishment or revolutionary; everything seems to have already been done.

This is why Fauvism has come back into fashion. Content merely with color and light, the Fauves did not presume that art could change society which they accepted with all its qualities and faults. They did not think it necessary to destroy painting like Marcel Duchamp or the Dada Movement, but strove instead to further it. From the greatest to the least of the Fauves, all gave forceful expression to a simple attitude which this book has tried to present–the joy of painting. This is what makes them important to us today.

MAURICE DE VLAMINCK
Inside the Kitchen
1904
Oil on canvas, 21¾ x 15¾ in (55 x 40 cm)
Paris, musée national d'Art moderne

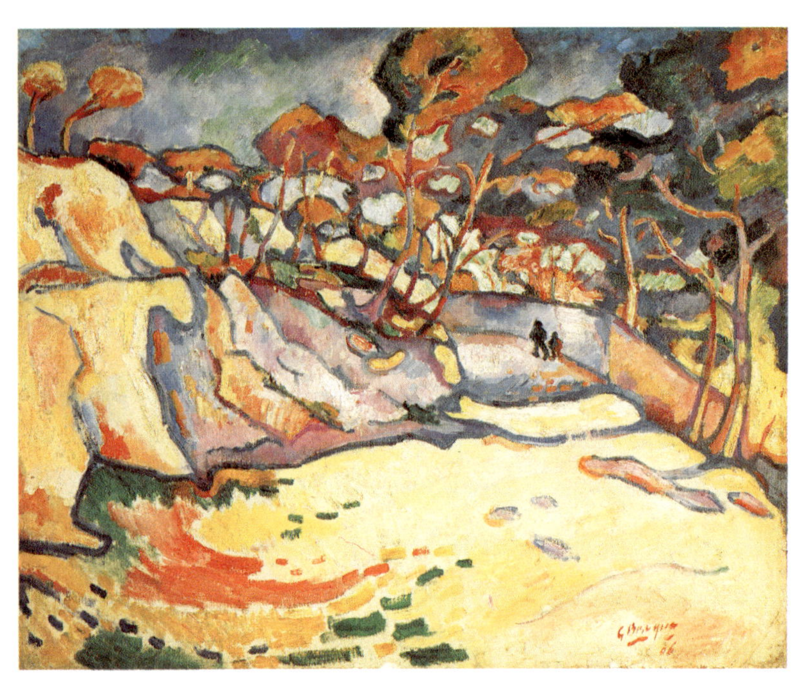

Biographical Notes

Georges BRAQUE

Braque was born in Argenteuil, France in 1882 and died in Paris in 1963. After starting out as a house-painter, he took courses at the Academie Humbert. He leaned toward Fauvism, and in 1906 rented a studio in Antwerp with Friesz. In spite of his success at the Salon des Indépendants in 1907, his art quickly took other directions: geometrical compositions and a rejection of violent colors (*Houses at L'Estaque*, 1908). His first one-man show at the Kahnweiler Gallery in 1908 and his meeting with Picasso, with whom he would work in close collaboration, marked the beginning of a great artistic adventure in modern art: Cubism (1908-1914). In 1912, he invented the technique of *papier collé*. Drafted in 1914, he was discharged in 1917 after suffering a serious head wound. From 1943 on, he took up sculpting and painted monumental canvases: *The Salon*, *Billiards* (1944). From 1949 until 1956 he made a series of studio scenes, *Ateliers*. In *Atelier III* (1949) he introduced the motif of a bird into the composition that would become a symbol in his further work. The bird became the central theme on the ceiling of the Etruscan Room which he executed in 1953 at the Louvre. Although Braque's career was somewhat uneventful, he was awarded the Grand Prix at the 1948 Venice Biennale. He also designed many ballet sets for Diaghilev and illustrated a host books and periodicals.

SELECTED MUSEUMS

Musée national d'Art moderne, centre Georges Pompidou, Paris
Museum of Modern Art, New York
Kunstmuseum, Basel

GEORGES BRAQUE
L'Estaque
1906
Oil on canvas, 23½ x 29 in (60 x 73,5 cm)
Paris, musée national d'Art moderne

Charles CAMOIN

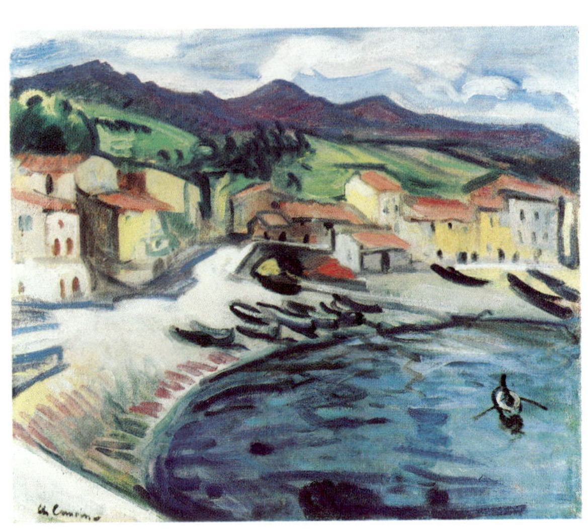

CHARLES CAMOIN
Village by the Sea
1905
Oil on canvas, 21¼ x 25½ in (54 x 65 cm)
Geneva, musée du Petit Palais

Camoin was born in Marseilles in 1879 and died in Paris in 1965. Encouraged by a father who worked in the decorating business, he left for Paris in 1896 to study in Gustave Moreau's class where he became friends with Marquet. On the lookout for subject-matter, he haunted the music-halls and *café-concerts*. In 1902 he made the acquaintance of Cézanne and carried on a regular correspondence with him. Many of his works, such as the *Portrait of Albert Marquet* (1904-1905), were influenced by this great master's art. Camoin was not a fervent Fauve, but his participation in the group allowed him to benefit from the aid of Berthe Weill in whose gallery he exhibited each year between 1904 and 1907. In 1905 he took part in the Salon d'Automne. Contrary to his colleagues, Camoin proceeded less by exaltation of color than by the suggestive interpretation of tone: *Le Moulin rouge*, (1904). He never participated in any avant-garde movement. During a leave from the army in 1918 he visited Renoir in Cagnes. This meeting was followed by immediate repercussions in his style which mellowed (*The Blue Cup*, 1930). From 1940 until 1943 he lived in the South of France. The sales of his nudes, his interiors, and Mediterranean landscapes with their pearly tones brought him wealth and made his life pleasant in both Saint-Tropez and Paris. In 1958 a retrospective of his work was given at the Bernheim Gallery. In 1962 he was the only survivor of Moreau's studio at the Beaux-Arts to attend the inauguration of the exhibition dedicated to "*Gustave Moreau and his students.*"

SELECTED MUSEUMS

Musée des Beaux-Arts, Menton
Musée national d'Art moderne, centre Georges Pompidou, Paris
Musée des Beaux-Arts, Marseilles

André Derain

Derain was born in Chatou in 1880 and died in Chambourcy in 1954. Expected by his father to enter the elite Ecole Polytechnique, he instead chose painting as a career in 1898 and became a friend of Matisse. In 1900, he met Vlaminck and shared a studio with him in Chatou. After a period spent painting landscapes at Le Pecq, Saint-Germain-en-Laye, etc., he worked in the South of France in the company of Matisse (*Collioure*, 1905). His works, highly colored but without brutality, were exhibited at the Salon d'Automne in the same year he painted *The Bridge at Collioure* (1905). At the suggestion of the art dealer Ambroise Vollard he left for London and painted views of its most famous sites. In 1907 while living in Montmartre, where he frequently visited Picasso, he thickened his palette and began to produce more geometrical shapes. He was among the first to "discover" African and folk art. Although his move toward Cubism was deflected, his works became more and more structured (*Bathers*, 1908). After the war, he settled in the South of France and returned to a traditional concept of perspective and modeling in a series of *Tables garnies*, (1921-1923). In 1930 he had a very successful show thanks to the art dealer Paul Guillaume and at the same time designed many theater sets. He also made color woodblock prints to illustrate a superb edition of Rabelais' *Pantagruel*, published by Albert Skira in 1945.

Selected Museums

Musée national d'Art moderne, centre Georges Pompidou, Paris
Musée de Peinture et de Sculpture, Grenoble
Pierre Lévy collection, Troyes
National Gallery of Art, Washington
Tate Gallery, London

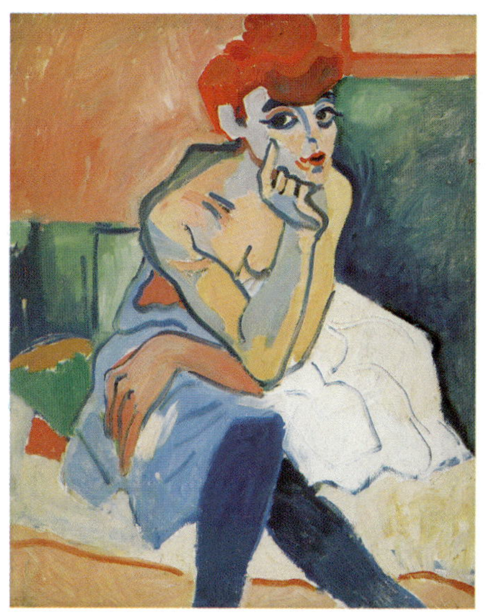

André Derain
Woman with a Blouse
1906
Oil on canvas, 39¼ x 32 in (100 x 81 cm)
Copenhagen, Statens Museum for Kunst

RAOUL DUFY
Promenade along the Jetty
1906
Oil on canvas, 25½ x 32 in (64,5 x 81 cm)
Paris, Daniel Malingue Gallery

Raoul DUFY

Dufy was born in Le Havre in 1877 and died at Forcalquier in 1953. After work, he took courses at Le Havre municipal school of fine arts in the company of Friesz. In 1900 thanks to a scholarship from his home town, he left for Paris to study in Bonnat's class at the Ecole des Beaux-Arts and became interested in Neo-Impressionism. In 1905, after discovering Matisse's *Luxe, calme and volupté,* he turned toward more simplified and colorful forms. He worked alongside Friesz and Marquet, and in 1906 took part in the Salon d'Automne for the first time (*Street Decked with Flags,* 1906). A trip with Braque to L'Estaque converted him to a more Cézannian-type treatment. He then took up engraving and illustrating (Apollinaire's *Bestiary*). In 1911 he designed fabrics for the couturier Paul Poiret and started a decorating business printing his own designs on textiles (*Marine, Autumn*). After the war and several peregrinations through the South of France, he gained a more vivid color scale and liberated his style (*Landscape at Vence,* 1920). In 1937 for the World's Fair in Paris, he executed the biggest mural in the world on a six-hundred square meter wall. It represented the history of *La fée Electricité.* In 1952 Geneva's Art and History museum organized a major exhibition of his work.

SELECTED MUSEUMS

Musée national d'Art moderne, centre Georges Pompidou, Paris
Musée d'Art moderne de la Ville de Paris

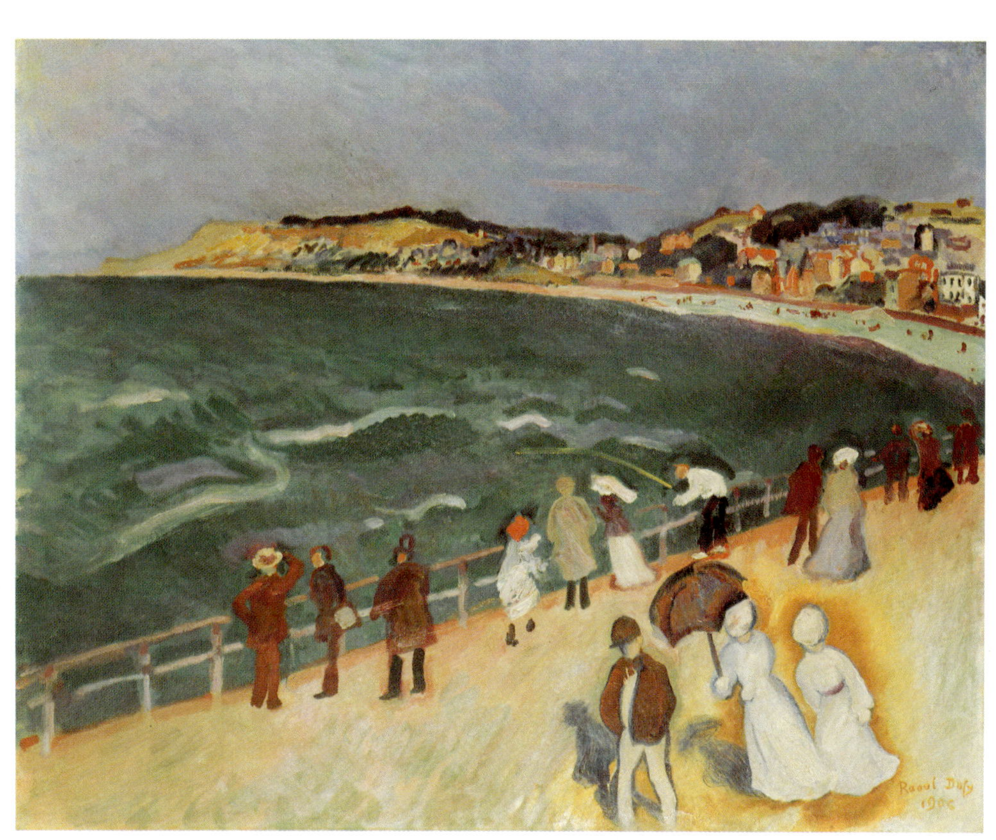
Raoul Dufy

Othon Friesz

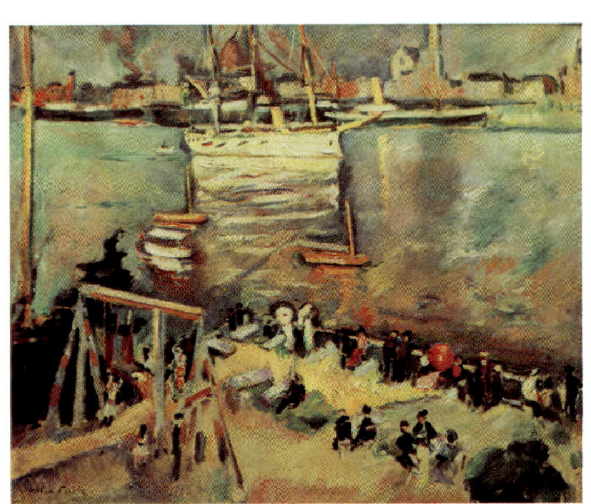

Othon Friesz
Corvette Entering the Port of Antwerp
1906
Oil on canvas, 23½ x 29¼ in (60 x 74 cm)
Geneva, musée du Petit Palais

Freisz was born in Le Havre in 1879 and died in Paris in 1949. He took courses with Raoul Dufy from the local master, Charles Lhuillier. Arriving in Paris in 1898, he spent more time in the Louvre than in class at Bonnat's studio. He exhibited at the Salon des Indépendants as early as 1903. In 1905 he took part with his friends in the Salon d'Automne. His brand of Fauvism was close to that of Matisse but with more exuberance (*La Ciotat*, 1905). In 1906, he spent some time in Antwerp with Braque. From 1907 until 1912 his landscapes with figures had a more Cézannian air but with darker tones, which demonstrated a certain distance from Fauvism (*Bathers*, 1907). Friesz soon limited himself to contrasts of pale ocher and austere tones. He gave his portraits a very original turn (*Portrait of Fernande Fleuret*, 1907). In 1912 he started an art class in his studio and took up teaching once again in 1921 at the Scandinavian Academy. His art moved toward a baroque and tormented realism in muted harmonies (*Portrait of Madame Friesz*, 1923). Faithful to the traditional genres of landscapes, nudes and portraits, he settled into an official career and executed a State commissioned decoration of the Palais de Chaillot in collaboration with his friend Dufy, for the 1937 World's Fair.

Selected Museums

Musée de Peinture et de Sculpture, Grenoble
Musée national d'Art moderne, centre Georges Pompidou, Paris
Musée Pushkin, Moscow
Musée du Petit Palais, Geneva

Henri Manguin

Manguin was born in Paris in 1875 and died in Saint-Tropez in 1949. At the age of fifteen he left school to take up painting. In 1894, he was admitted into Gustave Moreau's class where he met Marquet and Matisse. The Cézanne (1901) and Van Gogh (1905) retrospectives were a revelation to him and he decided to work with pure color. In 1902 he participated for the first time at the Salon des Indépendants. During the summer of 1905 he discovered the exceptional light of the South of France (*On the 14th of July at Saint-Tropez*, 1905). At the Salon d'Automne of the same year, his five paintings hung in the Fauve "wild-beast cage," alive with color and done in an unrestrained and impressive treatment (*Nude in an Interior*, 1905). The following year the art dealer Vollard bought some hundred and fifty works of his while Druet organized a one-man show in 1907. In 1908 he left for Italy accompanied by his friend Marquet. When the two were not traveling together they painted from life in Brittany or Normandy. Manguin was a discrete Fauve; his landscapes, still lifes and nudes are a hymn to life (*Anemones*, 1934). He also painted several watercolors whose aerial transparency contrasts with the exuberance of his oils.

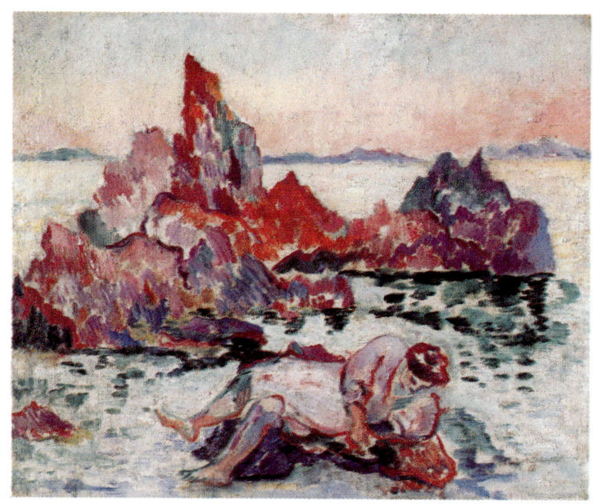

Henri Manguin
Study for a Naïad
1906
Oil on canvas, 14½ x 19 in (37 x 48 cm)
Private collection

Selected Museums

Hermitage Museum, St. Petersburg
Musée national d'Art moderne, centre Georges Pompidou, Paris
Musée du Petit Palais, Geneva

Albert Marquet

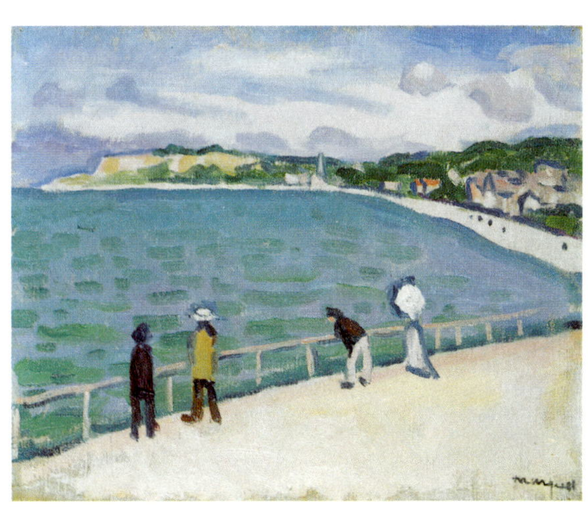

ALBERT MARQUET
On the Jetty at Sainte-Adresse
1905-1906
Oil on canvas, 13 x 16¼ in (33 x 41 cm)
Paris, Daniel Malingue Gallery

Marquet was born in Bordeaux in 1875 and died in Paris in 1947. In 1897 he studied with Matisse in Gustave Moreau's class at the Ecole des Beaux-Arts in Paris. A Fauve before the fact, he had difficult beginnings but in 1901 was able to exhibit for the first time at the Salon des Indépendants. The influence of Van Gogh and Cézanne is easily recognizable in his treatment of landscapes with schematic compositions and calm handling of muted tones applied in large flat colors. The year before participating in the Salon d'Automne of 1905, he often worked in the company of Matisse on the banks of the Seine. Nicknamed "our Hokusai" by Matisse, Marquet also made small ink-drawings of people in the street. He was the Fauve who cared the most for composition, paying great attention to atmospheric effect in his landscapes (*The Beach at Fécamp* and *On the 14th of July at Le Havre*, 1906). His favorite theme remained views of the Seine River as seen from above; these were painted from his apartments quai Saint-Michel and afterwards quai Conti (*Pont-Neuf at Night*, 1935). His success was assured in 1910 and allowed him to gratify his passion for travel; he visited Egypt, Norway, etc. He lived in Algiers from 1940 until 1945 and brought back from these peregrinations many seascapes and port scenes alive with color, and several views of gardens in bloom.

SELECTED MUSEUMS

Musée national d'Art moderne, centre Georges Pompidou, Paris
Musée des Beaux-Arts, Besançon
Musée des Beaux-Arts, Bordeaux

Henri Matisse

Matisse was born in the North of France at Le Cateau-Cambrésis in 1869 and died in Nice in 1954. In 1892, he abandoned a law career to become a student of Gustave Moreau at the Ecole des Beaux-Arts in Paris. When his master died in 1898, he joined Carrière's studio where he was trained in drawing the human figure. After applying Neo-Impressionist theories (*Luxe, calme et volupté*, 1904) he adopted a palette of pure colors and a generous technique (*Woman with a Hat*, 1905). At the Salon d'Automne of 1905, his works along with those of his colleagues, Derain, Vlaminck, Marquet, etc. caused a scandal. Matisse was given the title "Chief of the Fauve group" by the critics (1905-1908). From 1908 until 1917 he made many trips to Germany, Algeria and Morocco searching for a more linear style with a more colorful expression of space (*Harmony in Red, La desserte rouge*, 1908). In 1917 he settled in the South of France; his painting became more decorative and was composed of large distinct flat-color areas as we can see in the two versions of *La danse*, executed in 1933 for the Barnes Collection near Philadelphia. Exhibitions of his works followed each other from 1944 until 1947, particularly in London and Paris. At the end of his life he achieved his long sought-after union of line and color in an abundant series of gouache cutouts. In 1951, his life's work culminated in the Chapel of the Rosary for the Dominican nuns at Vence, for which he accepted to design the whole program (stained glass, furniture, architectural decor...). One year later, museums devoted to Matisse's work opened their doors in Le Cateau and in Cimiez.

Selected Museums

Musée national d'Art moderne, centre Georges Pompidou, Paris
Musée Matisse, Nice
Musée Pushkin, Moscow
Hermitage Museum, St. Petersburg
Museum of Modern Art, New York

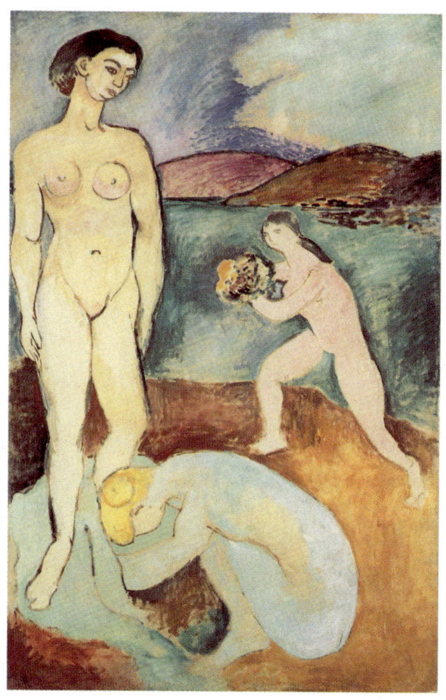

Henri Matisse
Le luxe I
Collioure, summer 1907
Oil on canvas, 6 ft 10⅝ x 54⅜ in
(210 x 138 cm)
Paris, musée national d'Art moderne

JEAN PUY
Noble Landscape
1904
Oil on canvas, 37 x 28¾ in (94 x 73 cm)
Rouen, musée des Beaux-Arts

Jean PUY

Jean Puy was born in 1876 and died in 1960 in Roanne. After studying architecture at the Ecole des Beaux-Arts in Lyons, he attended the Académie Julian in Paris in 1898. In 1899 he was admitted to the Académie Carrière, where "one could paint according to one's own desire and temperament." He became friends with Derain and Matisse. The latter imparted to him a great admiration for Cézanne. In 1900 Puy took part in the Salon des Indépendants and in 1903 exhibited in the first Salon d'Automne. He began as an Impressionist before joining the Fauve Movement in 1905 (*Woman Reading*, 1902). However, unlike his colleagues he preferred the fullness of forms and highly luminous and exuberant tones. (*The Painter and his Model at Belle-Ile*, 1905). Puy continued to paint his pale landscapes whether he was in Brittany, Savoie, or in his native Massif Central (*Fishermen's Village*, 1908). Fleeing the German occupation of Paris, he returned to Roanne for good. Vollard, the art dealer, handled his work for seventeen years and was relayed by Blot, Druet and Bernheim. It was not until the Salon d'Automne of 1959, a few months before his death, that the work of this "tame Fauve" would really be noticed. Very attached to traditional painting, Puy became famous for his rendering of *chiaroscuro* and for his seascapes. Ever precise in his nudes, he had only one aim: "to put life into his paintings."

SELECTED MUSEUMS

Musée national d'Art moderne, centre Georges Pompidou, Paris
Musée Joseph Déchelette, Roanne
Oscar Ghez Foundation, Geneva

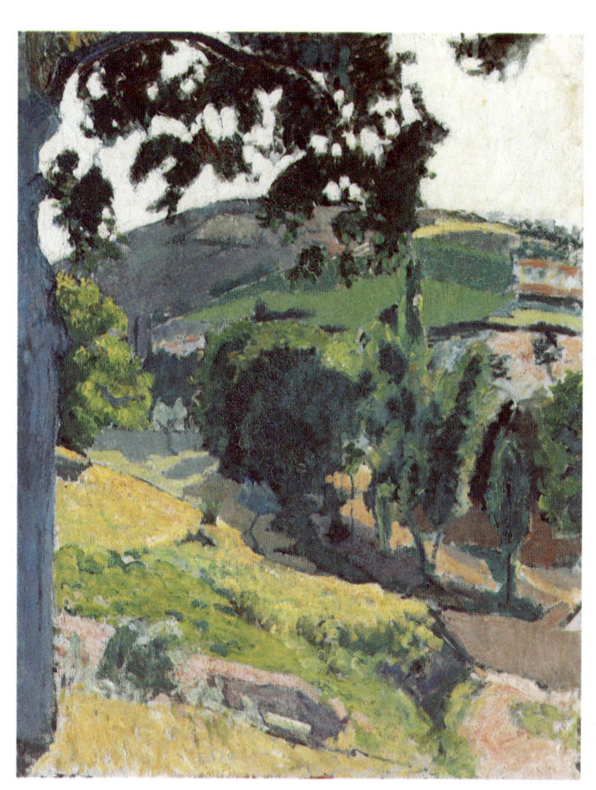

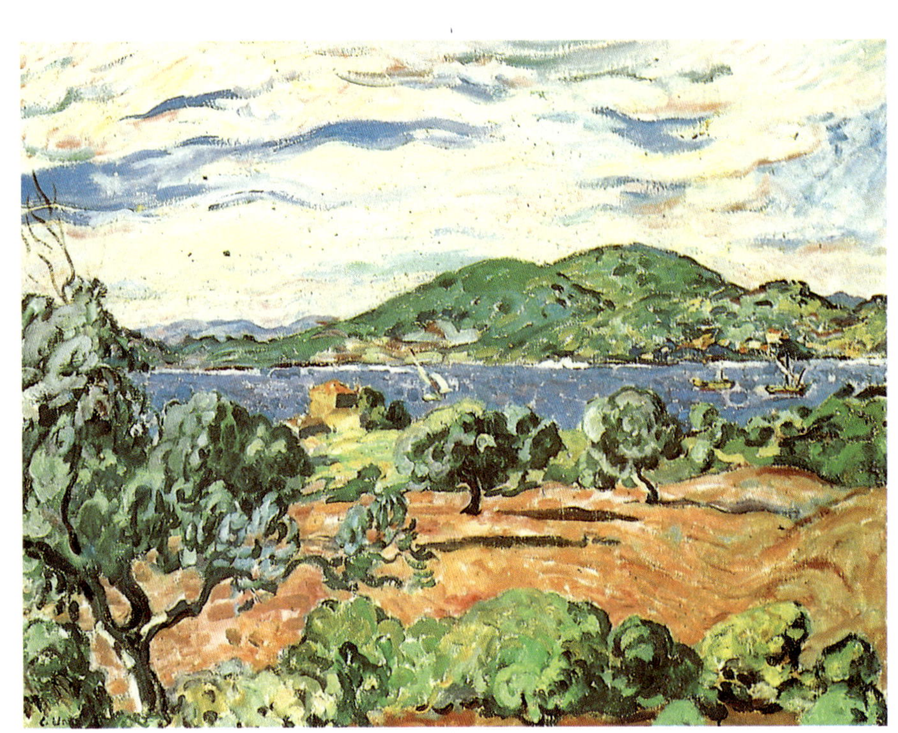

Louis Valtat

Louis Valtat was born in Dieppe in 1869 and died in Paris in 1952. In 1888 he entered the Académie Julian in Paris where he learned Gauguin's principles of pure color from Paul Sérusier and assumed the duties of student in charge of the studio *(massier)*. The next year he was for a brief time in Gustave Moreau's class. In 1894, with Toulouse-Lautrec, he executed the sets of the play *Chariot de terre cuite* for the Théâtre de l'Œuvre. The painting he exhibited at the 1903 Salon d'Automne, with its generous technique and pure color sometimes underscored by black lines here and there, announced that Fauvism was in the air. At the 1905 Salon d'Automne, though Valtat's style was no more shocking than his works of previous years, his paintings caused a scandal comparable to the one which his friends had occasioned in "the wild-beast cage" (*Fauve Landscape*, 1905). Valtat cultivated his taste for vibrant tones and an innate sense of movement (*Algiers*, 1906). In 1914 he left the South of France and settled permanently in Paris. But from 1924 on, he spent half of his time in the vallée de Chevreuse where he had bought property. Devoted to family life, his wife and son often modeled for him (*Jean Valtat on a Balcony*, 1915). The contract that he signed with Vollard in 1900 lasting from 1900 to 1912 was instrumental in introducing his work to great collectors such as the Russian Morozov. In 1948 when he lost his sight, Valtat was forced to abandon painting.

Selected Museums

Musée du Petit Palais, Geneva
Oscar Ghez Foundation, Geneva

Louis Valtat
The Gulf of Antheor
1907
Oil on canvas, 29¼ x 36½ in (74 x 93 cm)
St. Petersburg, Hermitage Museum

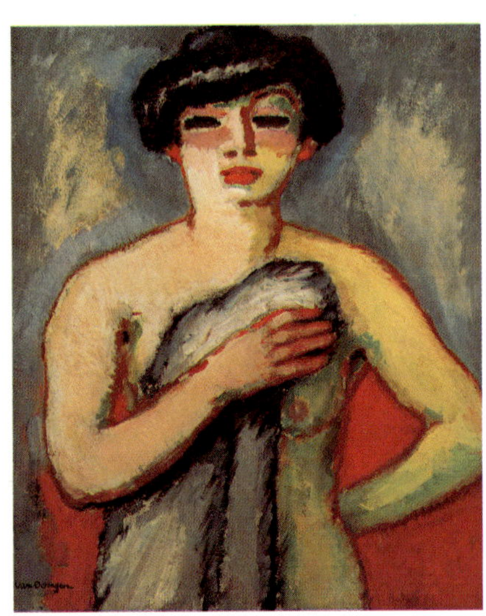

KEES VAN DONGEN
Portrait of Fernande Olivier
1905
Oil on canvas, 39¼ x 32 in (100 x 81 cm)
Paris, Samir Traboulsi collection

Kees VAN DONGEN

Kees Van Dongen, a French artist of Dutch origin, was born in Delfshaven near Rotterdam in 1877 and died in Monte-Carlo in 1968. He began as a student at the fine-arts Academy of Rotterdam but abandoned the school because he found the teaching too academic. He preferred to make sketches of sailors and street-walkers along the docks. In 1897 when he arrived in Paris, he made several drawings for satirical reviews such as the *Revue Blanche* and exhibited at the Druet gallery and at Vollard's (1904). In 1905 he participated in the Salon d'Automne. Two years later he moved into the Bateau-Lavoir in Montmartre where he joined Picasso's retinue (*Portrait of Kahnweiller*, 1907). He then moved to Montparnasse where he gave the first of the many costume balls and soirées which he organized until the end of his life. In 1913, his love affairs with Countess Cassati and Jasmy Jacob led him to a more mundane type of artistic production: colorful portraits of members of high society and of the *demi-monde* (Mademoiselle Vix, the diva), not to mention the minister Joseph Caillaux. In spite of his insolent and sometimes cruel disposition, these works made him a celebrity. Although Van Dongen remained faithful to the cult of women, freely portraying them with lively colors (*The Archangel's Tango*, 1930), he painted some landscapes during short visits to the country.

SELECTED MUSEUMS

Musée national d'Art moderne, centre Georges Pompidou, Paris
Musée de Peinture et de Sculpture, Grenoble
Museum of Modern Art, New York

Maurice de VLAMINCK

Vlaminck, of Flemish background, was born in Paris in 1876 and died in Rueil-la-Gadelière in 1958. He had no formal training and discovered painting with the naive artist Henri Regal. At the age of nineteen he divided his time between bicycle racing and giving violin lessons in order to make ends meet. In July 1900 he met Derain in Chatou and decided to devote his life to painting. He frequented the Azon café, favorite haunt of Max Jacob, Van Dongen, Picasso and Apollinaire. Influenced by Van Gogh, he exhibited for the first time at the 1905 Salon d'Automne in the famous "wild-beast cage." His works were impelled by a great chromatic violence that excluded and replaced line (*Landscape with Red Trees*, 1906). In 1908, however, during the Cézanne retrospective (he died in 1906), Vlaminck opted for softer colors and more robust shapes (*River Banks*, 1909). His work is based for the most part on the theme of the Seine and the Ile-de-France region. At the end of the First World War he settled in the country and continued to paint the same landscapes with dense brushstrokes producing a thick impasto (*House with a Canopy*, 1920). He also left his memoir in the form of novels such as *Tournant dangereux* and *Haute folie.*

SELECTED MUSEUMS

Musée national d'Art moderne, centre Georges Pompidou, Paris

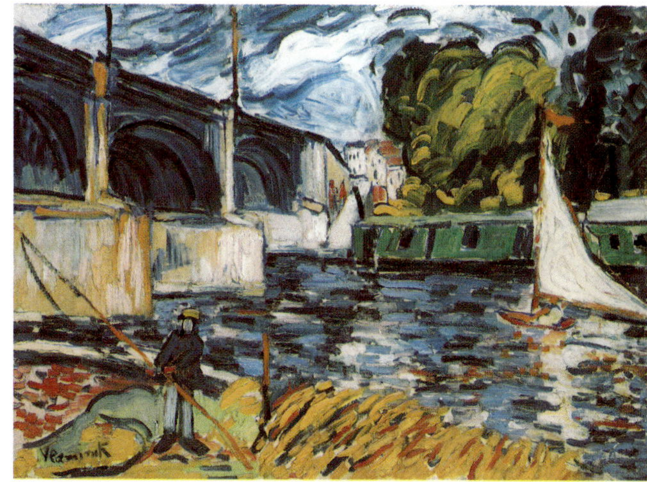

MAURICE DE VLAMINCK
The Bridge at Chatou
1907
Oil on canvas, 26¾ x 37¾ in
(68 x 96 cm)
Berlin, Staatliche Museen Preussischer Kulturbesitz Nationalgalerie

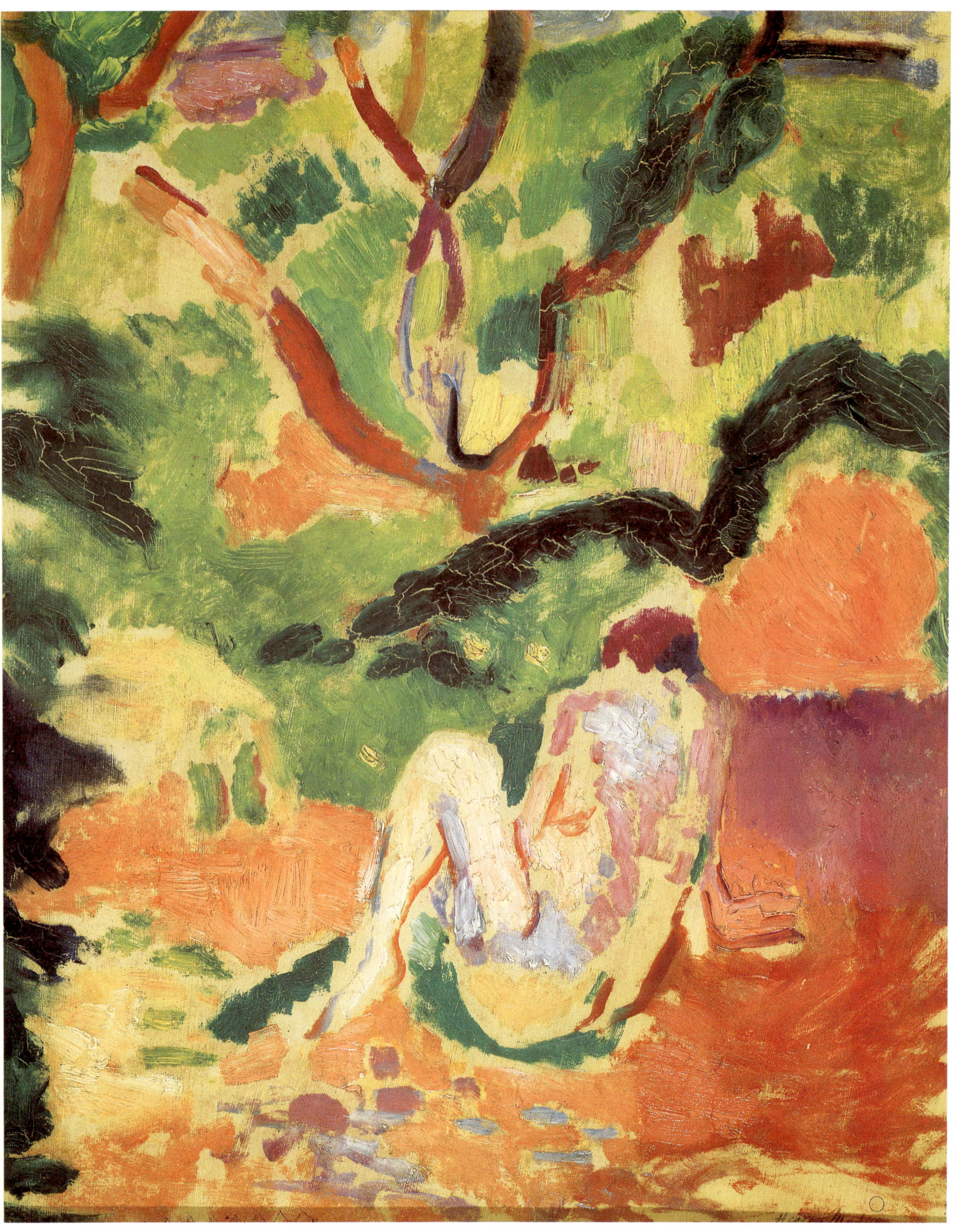

Selective Bibliography

GENERAL

CHASSÉ, Charles, *Les Fauves et leur temps*. Lausanne & Paris: Bibliothèque des Arts, 1963.

CRESPELLE, Jean-Paul, *Les Fauves*. Neuchâtel: Ides et Calendes, 1962.

DIEHL, Gaston, *Les Fauves*. Paris: Editions du Chêne, 1943; rpt., 1948.

DUTHUIT, Georges, *Les Fauves*. Geneva: Editions des Trois collines, 1949.

FREEMAN, Judi, ed. *The Fauve Landscape*. Los Angeles & New York: Editions Abeville, 1991.

GIRY, Marcel, *Fauvism: Origins and Development*. Trans. Helga Harrisson. New York: 1982.

HERBERT, James D., *Fauve Painting, the Making of Cultural Politics*. New Haven & London: Yale University Press, 1992.

LEYMARIE, Jean, *Le fauvisme*. Geneva: Skira, 1959; rpt., 1987.

TEXTS AND MONOGRAPHIES

BRAQUE

LEYMARIE, Jean, *Braque*. Geneva: Skira, 1961.

PAULHAN, Jean, *Braque le patron*. Paris: Gallimard, 1952.

CAMOIN

GIRAUDY, Danièle, *Camoin, sa vie, son œuvre*. Marseilles: La Savoyenne, 1972.

DERAIN

CABANNE, Pierre, *André Derain*. Paris: Somogy, 1990.

DERAIN, André, *Lettres à Vlaminck*. Paris: Flammarion, 1955.

DUFY

LASSAIGNE, Jacques, *Dufy*. Geneva: Skira, 1954.

PEREZ-TIBI, Dora, *Dufy*. Paris: Flammarion, 1989.

FRIESZ

GAUTHIER, Maximilien, *Othon Friesz*. Geneva: Pierre Cailler, 1957.

MANGUIN

CABANNE, Pierre, *Manguin*. Neuchâtel: Ides et Calendes, 1964.

DELAFOND, Marianne, *Henri Manguin*. Paris: Musée Marmottan, 1989.

HENRI MATISSE
Nu dans la forêt
1905
Oil on canvas, 16 x 12¾ in
(40.6 x 32.8 cm)
New York, The Brooklyn Museum

MARQUET

JOURDAIN, Francis, *Marquet*. Paris: Editions Cercle d'Art, 1959.

MARQUET, Marcelle, *Marquet*. Paris: Laffont, 1951.

MATISSE

FLAMM, Jack D., *Matisse: The Man and His Art, 1869-1918*. Ithaca & London: Cornell University Press, 1986.

MATISSE, Henri, *Ecrits et propos sur l'art*. Texts, notes and index edited by Dominique Fourcade, Paris: Hermann, 1972. Eng. trans. *Matisse on Art*. Ed. Jack D. Flamm, New York: Phaidon, 1973; reprint., New York: Dutton, 1978.

SCHNEIDER, Pierre, *Matisse*. Paris: Flammarion, 1984; Eng. ed., New York: Rizzoli, 1984.

VAN DONGEN

DIEHL, Gaston, *Van Dongen*. Paris: Flammarion, 1952.

MUSÉE D'ART MODERNE DE LA VILLE DE PARIS, *Kees Van Dongen*. Paris: 1990.

VLAMINCK

SELZ, Jean, *Vlaminck*. Paris: Flammarion, 1975.

VLAMINCK, Maurice de, *Tournant dangereux*. Paris: Stock, 1929.

VLAMINCK, Maurice de, *Portrait avant décès*. Paris: Flammarion, 1943.

Photo Credits

Allschwill, Colorphoto Hinz: p. 25, 171
Amsterdam, Stedelijk Museum: p. 100
Bagnols-sur-Cèze, musée municipal/Photo Daspet: p. 111
Basel, Beyeler Gallery: p. 98, 106
Berlin, Bildarchiv Preussischer Kulturbesitz: p. 96, 219
Bordeaux, musée des Beaux-Arts: p. 109, 117, 121
Buffalo, Albright-Knox Art Gallery: p. 83
Chartres, musée des Beaux-Arts: p. 62
Chicago, The Art Institute of Chicago: p. 88
Copenhagen, Statens Museum for Kunst: p. 28, 30, 33, 46, 53, 55, 86, 178, 207
Dallas, Dallas Museum of Art: p. 15
Draguignan, musée des Beaux-Arts: p. 129
Düsseldorf, Kunstsammlung Nordrheim-Westfalen: p. 35, 77
Essen, musée Folwang: p. 18, 105
Florence, Scala: p. 34, 44, 47, 70
Geneva, musée du Petit Palais: p. 124, 125, 157, 167, 206, 210
Grenoble, musée de Peinture et de Sculpture: p. 45, 52, 118, 162
New Orleans, New Orleans Museum of Art: p. 84
Liège, musée d'Art moderne: p. 165
London, Ellen Melas Kyriazi: p. 21, 154, 159, 166
London, Fridart Foundation: p. 95, 103, 128, 153, 176, 181, 188, 191, 195, 199
London, Tate Gallery: p. 54, 61
Lyons, musée des Beaux-Arts/Studio Basset: p. 192
Marseilles, musée Cantini: p. 197
Milwaukee, Milwaukee Art Museum: p. 184
Minneapolis, Institute of Modern Art: p. 2, 51, 75, 183
Munich, Artothek: p. 173
New York, The Brooklyn Museum: p. 220
New York, The Metropolitan Museum of Art: p. 68, 81, 102
Nice, musée Matisse: p. 37
Ottawa, National Gallery of Canada: p. 99, 168
Paris, Artephot: p. 152, 155
Paris, private collection: p. 148
Paris, Samir Traboulsi collection: p. 144, 218
Paris, Dagli Orti: p. 122, 123
Paris, Daniel Malingue Gallery: p. 114, 164, 187, 209, 212
Paris, Giraudon: cover, p. 6, 16, 80, 91, 97, 115, 147, 156, 215
Paris, Matisse heirs: p. 39, 43 (above & below), 56
Paris, musée national d'Art moderne, centre Georges Pompidou: p. 10, 31, 36, 48, 64, 65, 74, 78, 90, 94, 108, 113, 116, 120, 127, 151, 163, 172, 177, 180, 182, 189, 198, 202, 204, 213
Paris, Photothèque des musées de la ville de Paris: p. 49, 76, 87, 104, 194
Paris, Réunion des musées nationaux: p. 27, 73, 93, 101, 116
Philadelphia, Philadelphia Museum of Art: p. 24
Rotterdam, Boymans-van-Beuningen Museum: p. 119
Saint Louis, Saint Louis Art Museum: p. 50
Saint-Tropez, musée de l'Annonciade: p. 5, 8, 69, 71, 160, 175
Henri Manguin estate: p. 130, 132, 133, 134, 135, 136, 138, 139, 140, 141, 142, 143, 211
Toronto, Art Gallery of Ontario: p. 58
Troyes, musée d'Art moderne: p. 72, 85, 166, 174
Washington, National Gallery of Art: p. 66, 174
Zurich, private collection: p. 40, 67, 79
Rights reserved: p. 12, 63, 112, 150, 158, 201, 216

Printed in Italy
La Zincografica Fiorentina